One of the world's greatest Bible teachers of this century, W. Graham Scroggie wrote in a way that both laymen and clergy could enjoy. *Scroggie's Bible Handbook* is a testimony to that fact.

Formerly a part of his *Know Your Bible* set, this book is an in-depth study, examining each book of the Bible. As he probes each book, Scroggie points out words and themes that provide enriching by-paths for further study.

In each book of the Bible, the author helps you to achieve an accurate understanding by presenting:

- An outline and analysis
- A brief discussion of the author of each book
- The purpose of the book
- The value of the book

Take time to know your Bible. Let *Scroggie's Bible Handbook* be the start of your quest for more knowledge of God's wonderful Word.

W. Graham Scroggie (1877–1958) was born in Great Malvern, England, the son of an evangelist. He attended Spurgeon's College in London to train for the ministry and later served as pastor for 17 years at the Charlotte Baptist Chapel in Edinburgh. His scholarship and ministry in that city earned him an honorary D.D. from the University. He served seven years as pastor of Spurgeon's Tabernacle in London during World War II. His retirement years were spent in Bible teaching and writing. Among his works in use today are *Psalms* and *A Guide to the Gospels*.

Scroggie's Bible Handbook

W. Graham Scroggie

Fleming H. Revell Company
Old Tappan, New Jersey

ISBN 8007-5313-5

Published by the Fleming H. Revell Company
Old Tappan, New Jersey 07675
Printed in the United States of America

Contents

THE WISDOM WRITINGS

THE PROPHETICAL WRITINGS

THE NEW TESTAMENT

THE EVANGELICAL WRITINGS

THE APOSTOLICAL WRITINGS

THE PAULINE EPISTLES

First Group

Second Group

Third Group

Fourth Group

THE CATHOLIC EPISTLES

THE JACOBEAN EPISTLES

THE PETRINE EPISTLES

THE JOHANNINE EPISTLES

Foreword

This volume is intended to lay the foundation for future study, and must not be considered in itself as adequate for a satisfying knowledge of the Scriptures. Foundations are valueless by themselves, but they are indispensable to superstructures. It is the house, not the foundation, in which the tenant lives.

The supreme values of Holy Scripture are ethical, devotional, spiritual and practical, but these rest on and rise from other values, historical, geographical, chronological and literary; and these latter are the means to the former ends. Faith must have a historical foundation, for divine revelation has been made in living human terms, and the eternal has found experssion in time. "The Word became flesh and tabernacled among us."

Two tendencies must, therefore, be guarded against; on the one hand the tendency to pursue the spiritual and practical, regardless and even contemptuous of the historical and literary; and, on the other hand, the tendency to pursue these latter as ends in themselves, instead of recognizing them to be what they are, means to an end. There is no easy way to knowledge, and he who would know the Scriptures must bring to them not only a hungry heart, but also an attentive mind. The method in this volume is to provide a brief introduction to each of the books of the Bible, and also to the various groups of books together with a detailed analysis of each.

The approach throughout is practical, and not critical, and so, much is assumed which might be argued.

Questions of chronology and authorship must always be of secondary importance, and until we can speak on these subjects with more assurance than is possible at present, we shall here follow conservative views on both these subjects, without emphasis or dogmatism, and with a mind open to all new light that may be given. An event is always of more importance than the time of it, and the Writings, such as the Epistle to the Hebrews, have a value which is independent of the question of authorship.

A word must be said about the arrangement of the Books. The order in our Bibles is not chronological, but is on a grouping plan. In the Old Testament the Historical Writings are all together first, then, the Poetical and Wisdom Writings, and finally, the Prophetical Writings. In like manner, in the New Testament, the Historical come first, then the Doctrinal, and finally the Prophetical. A strictly chronological arrangement would entirely break with this classification, and might confuse the general reader, so I have ventured upon a compromise, namely, chronological order within the groups. Thus, the Old Testament Prophets are kept together, but are in their supposed chronological order; the Gospels are kept together, but MARK comes first; and Paul's Letters are kept together, but are in the order in which they were written. Of the Epistles, JAMES is believed to be the earliest, but it is kept in the Catholic group. This amended order will help us to discern how our Bible grew to its completion.

All these Writings are divided into two main groups, which are called the Old and New Testaments, or Covenants. These are vitally related to one another, and reveal the progress of the Divine revelation. The Old Covenant is of Law, and the New is of Grace, and the one led to the other (Gal. iii. 17–25). The New is in the Old contained, and the Old is in the New explained. The Old commences what the New completes. The Old gathers round Sinai, and the New round Calvary. The Old is associated with Moses, and the New with Christ (John i. 17). Without the New Covenant the Old is a start that has no finish; and without the Old the New is a finish that has no start.

These Covenants are related to one another as were the Cherubim on the Mercy Seat, facing and answering to one another.

In the Old Testament are thirty-nine Writings, and in the New are twenty-seven Writings, and these sixty-six constitute our Bible.

THE OLD TESTAMENT

Introduction

IT has become fashionable in quarters to exalt
the New Testament at the expense of the
Old, and, except for its literary value in places, to
regard it as having only an antiquarian interest.
This, however, is as far from the truth as anything
could be.

The literary value of some of these thirty-nine
Writings is very great, but their cumulative ethical
and religious value is incalculable. Here the
foundations of religion are laid in the revelation
of the one and only true God. Here the sin-
blight in its origin and development is disclosed,
the curse which separates men from God. Here
is clearly taught the utter inability of the law to
bring to man the salvation he needs. Here is
anticipated the saving purpose and plan of God,
in prophecies and types. Here the Saviour Himself is promised, the Son, the Servant, the Prophet,
the Priest, and the King. Here we find men
at grips with great moral problems, such as of sin,

and of suffering. Here is made evident the immanence of God in history, and the fact that a principle of righteousness underlies universal government. Here all the chords of the human heart are swept in immortal songs. And here we learn of the rise and progress of that People to whom God was pleased to reveal His purpose, and by whom He is fulfilling it through Jesus Christ.

Although these Books were written at different times, and by different persons, across a period of some sixteen hundred years, yet there is discernible in them progress both historical and doctrinal.

Historically, there is progress from a nomadic state to national life, and from precarious leadership to the order of a Kingdom. And doctrinally there is a steady movement forward from the Law of Sinai to the Sermon on the Mount : from outward observance of the law of God to inward conformity to it ; and from domestic and tribal to individual responsibility. The Family of Genesis expands into a Nation from the Exodus and onward, and contracts into a Church from the Exile and forward.

The Writings of the Old Testament are divisible broadly into three classes, history, literature, and legislative and genealogical material. The Bible reader will have no difficulty in differentiating these. To history belong Genesis, Exodus, Numbers, Joshua to Esther, and parts of Daniel; to literature belong Job, parts of Deuteronomy, Psalms, Proverbs, Ecclesiastes, The Song, and all the Prophetical Books; and to the third division belong Leviticus, parts of Deuteronomy, parts of 1 Chronicles, and parts of Ezra and Nehemiah.

Through these millenniums we may trace the development of the redemptive purpose through the Ante-diluvian and Post-diluvian periods; the Patriarchal period; the period of Egyptian Enslavement and of Wilderness Wandering; the period of Joshua and the Judges; the period of the Kingdom United, Divided, and Single; the period of Babylonian Captivity; and the Post-Exilic period to the end of Old Testament history in NEHEMIAH. Of the remaining 400 years, until the Messiah's advent, we have no canonical records, but most valuable history and literature are to be found in the Apocryphal Books.

Through all these ages "one increasing purpose runs," a way is being prepared for the feet of the Redeemer. The revelation is organic and progressive, and it is consummated in Christ.

These Writings raise endless critical questions, but such should never be allowed to obscure from our vision, nor dull our appreciation of, the ethical and spiritual value and authority of these Books. They are an integral part of the "Word of God, which liveth and abideth for ever."

NOTE 1

Old Testament Morality.

ONE of the difficulties felt by many readers of the Old Testament relates to its morality. Many are stumbled at such things as the summary mode of dealing with human life, the sacrifice of Isaac, the visitation of parents' sins upon their children, exterminational wars, the law of retaliation, and the imprecatory Psalms, and the morality of the New Testament is pointed to as in complete opposition to all this. The matter, however, is not quite as simple as that. Under-lying all the things objected to are great ethical principles which persist in every age; and then there is the fact that revelation is progressive. The Jewish dispensation did not promulgate at once what was absolutely true in religion or morals but prepared people for it. The pace, so to speak, of the revelation was to some extent determined by man's power to apprehend. This is equally evident in the New Testament, for Christ said to His disciples: "I have many things to say unto you, but ye cannot bear them now." In our study of the Old Testament we should suspend judgment on many matters until we have a better grasp of the facts.

THE PENTATEUCHAL WRITINGS

INTRODUCTION

GENESIS
EXODUS
LEVITICUS
NUMBERS
DEUTERONOMY

NOTE 2

Progressive Revelation in the Pentateuch.

IN approaching the books of the Pentateuch it will be well to view the collection as a whole. The Pentateuch is the foundation of the entire Divine Library, the seed plot of the whole after harvest; here are the origins of all issues, the beginnings of all ends. The historical, geographical, chronological, religious, and ethical values of these Books are very great. In essence and summary, explicitly or implicitly, all religious truth is here revealed, and it is not mere fancy to see in the present order of the Books the progress of revelation.

The greatest subjects which the human mind can contemplate relate to God's eternal inscrutable counsels, His historical manifestation, the conditions of man's approach to Him, His guiding activity in the life of man, and His Self-revelation as Love. These, let it be said, are the themes of the Pentateuch Writings.

Genesis treats of the first, *Exodus* of the second, *Leviticus* of the third, *Numbers* of the fourth, and *Deuteronomy* of the fifth. Divine *election* takes us behind all history; *redemption* is the expression in time of a timeless purpose; religious and ethical conditions open the way for man's *communion* with God; but man is a pilgrim and needs guidance, and God is pledged to give him *direction*; and all this leads to the profound *instruction* that the God of righteousness loves us.

THE PENTATEUCH
Introduction

THE Hebrew Bible is divided into three main
parts which, in LUKE xxiv. 44, are called the
Law, the Prophets, and the Psalms, the third part
being called the Psalms because the Psalter is first
in that group of Books. The Law, or Torah,
comprises the first five Books of the Old Testament,
as the word Pentateuch indicates. Why there are
only five books in this group we cannot say, but
it is interesting to observe that the Psalter is in
five parts, and that another group of Hebrew
Writings, the "Megilloth," or Rolls, also comprises
five books, RUTH, ESTHER, SONG OF SONGS, ECCLESI-
ASTES, and LAMENTATIONS.

It is regrettable that the Pentateuch has been
viewed much more from the critical than from the
spiritual standpoint. Libraries have been written
on questions of authenticity, genuineness, authors,
editors, documents, style, date, and so on, and the
consideration of these matters may easily blind
one to other great facts and values. There is a
wide land between the position that Moses had
little to do with the Pentateuch, and that he wrote
the whole of it, including the account of his own

death. Criticism is allowable and is inevitable, but results must be based on something more substantial than hypotheses and theories.

The Mosaic authorship of these Books does not exclude the employment of existing documents. Every historian has his sources and authorities. Nor does the Mosaic authorship rule out the ideas of additions and editorial care in succeeding ages (*e.g.*, Gen. xiii. 7 ; xxxvi. 31 ; Exod. xvi. 35 ; Deut. xxxiv). We may assume, therefore, that in the Pentateuch are pre-Mosaic and post-Mosaic elements, but that the dominating element is Mosaic. Here are the Writings, and they constitute a unity, giving the Hebrew cosmogony, the origin of the people of Israel, and the foundation of their national constitution.

It is most probable that the Book of the Law, which was found in the Temple in the days of Josiah (2 Chron. xxxiv.) was the Pentateuch, and there is no reason to doubt that it was the Pentateuch which Ezra read to the people in 445 B.C. (Neh. viii).

The historical, literary, biographical, ethical, legislative, prophetical and spiritual values of these Writings are beyond estimate. These are their true values, and can little be affected by purely critical considerations.

GENESIS

THE title GENESIS, which is Greek, means "Origin," and the first word in the Hebrew means "Beginning," words which indicate both the scope and the limits of the Book.

As to scope, GENESIS tells us of the beginning of everything, except God. The beginning of the universe, of life, of man, of the sabbath, of covenants, of nomenclature, of marriage, of sin, of redemption, of death, of family life, of sacrifices, of nations, of government, of music, of literature, of art, of agriculture, of mechanics, of cities, and of languages ; indeed, of every thing that we know. As to its limits, it is only the beginning ; there is here no finality. It is a kind of daybreak book, a wondrous dawn, an hour of revelation and vision. It is the seed basket out of which the harvest of all after revelation comes ; it is the fountain-head from whence flows "the river of God which is full of water" ; it is the mighty root from which has spread throughout the world the Tree "whose leaves are for the healing of the nations" ; it is the small window through which may be seen, beyond the dark valley, the Land of Delights; it is the foundation on which the whole superstructure of Divine revelation rests.

GENESIS should be studied historically, prophetically, dispensationally, typically and spiritually. Its outstanding characters are Abel, Noah, Abraham, Jacob, and Joseph. Its outstanding events are the Creation, the Fall, the Deluge, the Call of Abraham, and the Descent into Egypt. Its outstanding prophecy is chapter iii. 15.

Divine electing grace dominates the book of GENESIS. Of Adam's sons, Cain drops out, and Seth is taken; of Noah's sons, Ham and Japheth drop out, and Shem is taken; of Terah's sons, Nahor and Haran drop out, and Abram is taken; of Abram's sons, Ishmael drops out, and Isaac is taken; of Isaac's sons, Esau drops out, and Jacob is taken; and of Jacob's sons, Judah is elected to be the line of the Messiah (chapter xlix. 10). Beneath and behind the historic redemption is the eternal election (Eph. i. 4).

NOTE 3
Divine Sovereignty and Human Free Will.

DIVINE election is none the less a fact because it is a mystery. To us human free will and Divine sovereignty seem to contradict one another, but they cannot really do so; somewhere beyond our ken they must meet and harmonise. It may then be seen that our free will was always in the embrace of God's sovereignty; but the action of God foreknew and reckoned with the action of man.

Analysis of Genesis

I. PRIMEVAL HISTORY (i. 1-xi. 9).

1. From the Creation to the Fall (i.-iii.).

(i.)	The Creation, and God's Week of Work,	i. 1-ii. 3.
(ii.)	The Garden, and the Probation of Man,	ii. 4-25.
(iii.)	The Serpent, and the Fall of Eve and Adam, ...	iii.

2. From the Fall to the Flood (iv. 1-viii. 14).

(i.)	Cain and Abel, and their Offerings, ..	iv. 1-16.
(ii.)	The Genealogies of Cain and Seth, ..	iv. 17-v. 32.
(iii.)	The Great Apostasy, and Divine Judgment, ...	vi. 1-viii. 14.

3. From the Flood to Babel (viii. 15-xi. 9).

(i.)	The New Covenant of God with Man, ..	viii. 15-ix.
(ii.)	The Posterity of Noah's Three Sons, ..	x.
(iii.)	The Confederacy and Confusion at Babel,	xi. 1-9.

II. PATRIARCHAL HISTORY (xi. 10-l.).

1. The Story of Abraham (xi. 10-xxv. 18).

(i.)	THE AWAKENING OF FAITH. From the Call in Chaldea to the Settlement in Canaan, ...	xi. 10-xiii.
(ii.)	THE DISCIPLINING OF FAITH. From the Settlement in Canaan to the Birth of Isaac, ...	xiv-xxi. 21.
(iii.)	THE PERFECTING OF FAITH. From the Birth of Isaac to the Death of Abraham, ...	xxi. 22-xxv. 18.

2. The Story of Isaac (xxi.-xxxvi.).

> (i.) THE SUBMISSIVE SON. From his Birth to his Marriage with Rebekah, .. **xxi.-xxiv.**
>
> (ii.) THE FAITHFUL HUSBAND. From his Marriage to his Settlement at Beersheba .. .. **xxv.-xxvi.**
>
> (iii.) THE INDULGENT FATHER. From his Settlement at Beersheba to his Death, **xxvii.-xxxvi.**

3. The Story of Jacob (xxv. 19-l. 13).

> (i.) THE SUPPLANTER. From his Birth to his Departure from Home, ... **xxv. 19-xxviii. 9**
>
> (ii.) THE SERVANT. From his Departure from Home to his Covenant in Gilead, ... **xxviii. 10-xxxi.**
>
> (iii.) THE SAINT. From his Covenant in Gilead to his Descent into Egypt. .. **xxxii.-xlv.**
>
> (iv.) THE SEER. From his Descent into Egypt to his Burial at Mamre, .. **xlvi.-l. 13.**

4. The Story of Joseph (xxx. 22.-l.).

> (i.) THE PERIOD OF HIS TRAINING. THE SON. From his Birth at Haran to his Arrival in Egypt, ... **xxx. 22-xxxviii.**
>
> (ii.) THE PERIOD OF HIS TESTING. THE SUFFERER. From his Arrival in Egypt to his Promotion to Power, .. **xxxix.-xli. 36.**
>
> (iii.) THE PERIOD OF HIS TRIUMPH. THE SOVEREIGN. From his Promotion to Power to the End of his Life, .. **xli. 37-l. 26.**

EXODUS

THE title EXODUS, which is Greek, means "Way Out," or departure, and the book tells of the deliverance of the Israelites from Egyptian bondage. From the departure, recorded in chapter xii, to the end of the book, chapter xl, is a period of about one year. The sons of Jacob have become the people Israel, a family has become a nation. First, we see them crushed, and hear them crying; next, we see them freed, led and fed; then, we see them taught and established. Chapters i-xviii are historical; and chapters xix-xl are legislative.

The book should be studied geographically, biographically, and institutionally. Its outstanding character is Moses. Its outstanding events are the Training of Moses, the Ten Plagues, which were judgments against the gods of Egypt, the Institution of the Passover, the Exodus, the Giving of the Law, the Prescription of a Ritual, the Appointment of a Priesthood, and the Construction of the Tabernacle.

Following on Election in GENESIS is Redemption

in Exodus. The need of it is seen in the people's condition and consciousness (chapters i-ii); the way of it is by blood (chapter xii), and power (chapter xiv.); the law of it is the Divine will, set forth in the Decalogue, and the Book of the Covenant, and the medium of it is set forth in the Tabernacle and its institutions.

The connection between GENESIS and EXODUS is intimate. In the one the Divine purpose is revealed, and in the other the Divine performance is exhibited. In the one are human effort and failure, and in the other are Divine power and triumph. In the one is a word of promise, and in the other is a work of fulfilment. In the one is a People chosen, and in the other is a People called. In the one is God's electing mercy, and in the other is God's electing manner. In the one is the revelation of nationality, and in the other is the realisation of nationality.

NOTE 4
The Way Out.

IT is interesting to observe that on the Mount of Transfiguration Jesus spake of "His *exodus* which He would accomplish at Jerusalem" (Luke ix. 31); and that long after this, recalling the event on the Mount, Peter spoke of his own approaching *exodus* (2 Peter i. 15). This use of the word must be connected with the Book of which it is the title. Redemption is the only *way out* of bondage into freedom; only by *exodus* can there be *eisodus*, and so, we read, "He brought us *out*—that He might bring us *in*" (Deut. vi. 23).

Analysis of Exodus

I. SUBJECTION.

ISRAEL IN EGYPT (i.-xii. 36).

1. **The Persecution of the People** (i.).
   - (i.) National Expansion, ...   1-7.
   - (ii.) Cruel Exaction, ...   8-14.
   - (iii.) Purposed Extinction, ...   15-22.

2. **The Preparation of a Saviour** (ii.-iv. 28).
   - (i.) Moses the Prince in Egypt, ...   ii. 1-15a.
   - (ii.) Moses the Shepherd in Midian, ...   ii. 15b-iv.28

3. **The Plan and Progress of Redemption** (iv. 29-xii. 36).
   - (i.) The First Movement-Exploratory,   ..   iv. 29-vii. 13.
   - (ii.) The Second Movement-Evidential,   ..   vii. 14-x. 29.
   - (iii.) The Third Movement-Executive,   ..   xi-xii. 36.

II. EMANCIPATION.

ISRAEL FROM EGYPT TO SINAI (xii. 37-xviii. 27).

1. **To the Red Sea** (xii. 37-xiv. 14).
2. **Through the Red Sea** (xiv. 15-xv. 21).
3. **From the Red Sea** (xv. 22-xix. 2).

III. REVELATION.

ISRAEL AT SINAI (xix. 3-xl).

1. **The Will of God Disclosed** (xix.-xxxi.).
   - (i.) The Law, ...   xix.-xxiv.
   - (ii.) The Tabernacle, ...   xxv.-xxvii.
   - (iii.) The Priesthood, ...   xxviii-xxix.
   - (iv.) The Service, ...   xxx.-xxxi.

NOTE 5

The Tabernacle.

THE importance of the Tabernacle in Divine revelation may be estimated by observing what space is given to it in the book of Exodus. Omitting the two chapters on the Priesthood (xxviii., xxix.), eleven chapters are devoted to instructions about the Tabernacle (xxv.-xxvii., xxx., xxxi., xxxv.-xl), that is, more than a quarter of the whole Book.

These instructions fall into seven sections:

1. Directions concerning the structure of a Tabernacle.
    xxiv. 9-xxvii., xxix. 42-xxxi. 11.

2. Catalogue of materials needed for the Tabernacle.
    xxxv. 4-19.

3. Contributions of this material for the Tabernacle.
    xxxv. 20-xxxvi. 7.

4. Making of the Tabernacle and its Furniture.
    xxxvi. 8-xxxviii. 31.

5. Bringing of the Tabernacle materials to Moses.
    xxxix. 32-43.

6. Setting up of the Tabernacle.
    xl. 1-11.

7. Completion of the Tabernacle, and the Consecrating Glory.
    xl. 17-38.

LEVITICUS

Keyword—COMMUNION.   CHAPTERS: 27.

THE title LEVITICUS is from Levi, the priestly
tribe, and the book is one of ritual and not of
history. It does not advance the story of EXODUS.
but elaborates the ritual which is there ordained.
The book is ethical in character ; its value is moral
and spiritual. The dominating notes are oblation,
mediation, separation, sanctification.

There are five main Offerings ; the Burnt, the
Meal, the Peace, the Sin, and the Trespass. These
are enfolded in the Passover, and the Passover is
unfolded in these. There are eight great Feasts ;
the Sabbath, Passover, Pentecost, Trumpets, Atonement, Tabernacles, the Sabbatic year, and Jubilee.
Here is a Sabbatic system : seventh day, seventh
week, seventh month, seventh year, and a heptade
of years.

The outstanding character is Aaron, and the
outstanding chapter is the sixteenth, which tells of
the Day of Atonement. It is important to observe
where priesthood is introduced as an office ; it is
for a people already redeemed. Christ is the High
Priest only of believers. As Aaron and his suc-

cessors acted only on the behalf of the people of Israel, who had been behind Passover blood, so Christ is the fulfilment of that type only on the behalf of the Christian Church. There is no priesthood on the behalf of the world. Mark the connection between EXODUS and LEVITICUS. In the one the people are brought nigh to God, and in the other they are kept nigh. In the one is the fact of atonement, and in the other is the doctrine of it. EXODUS begins with sinners, but LEVITICUS begins with saints, that is, as to their standing, though not necessarily so as to their state. In EXODUS we read of God's approach to us, but in LEVITICUS, of our approach to God. In the one book Christ is the Saviour, and in the other He is the Sanctifier. In EXODUS our guilt is prominent, but in LEVITICUS, our defilement. EXODUS reveals God as Love, and LEVITICUS reveals Him as Light. In the one, we are brought into union with Him, and in the other we are brought into communion. EXODUS offers us pardon but LEVITICUS calls us to purity. In the one book we are delivered from Satan, and in the other we are dedicated to God. In EXODUS God speaks out of the Mount, but in LEVITICUS He speaks out of the Tabernacle.

Analysis of Leviticus

I. THE WAY TO GOD BY SACRIFICE.
PRIVILEGE (i.-x.).

The Work of the Son for us.
Judicial. Objective.
What He is and Does.

1. Oblation. The Law of the Offerings (i.-vii.).

   (i.) THE CHARACTER OF THE OFFERINGS,   ...   i. 1-vi. 7.

     (a) Complete Consecration. (1) Burnt Offering : Ch. i. Perfect in Death—Godward. (2) Meal Offering : Ch. ii. Perfect in Life—Manward.

     (b) Cloudless Communion. (3) Peace Offering : ch. iii. Fellowship with the Father. Fellowship with the Saints.

     (c) Continued Cleansing. (4) Sin Offering : ch. iv. Iniquity. Sin. Godward. (5) Trespass Offering : ch. v. Injury. Sins. Manward.

   (ii.) THE OFFERING OF THE OFFERINGS,   ...   vi. 8-vii. 38.
     (a) The Burnt Offering (vi. 8-13).
     (b) The Meal Offering (vi. 14-23).
     (c) The Sin Offering (vi. 24-30).
     (d) The Trespass Offering (vii. 1-10).
     (e) The Peace Offering (vii. 11-34).

2. Mediation. The Law of the Priesthood. (viii.-x.).
   (i.) CONSECRATION, ...   viii.
     The Place of the Priesthood in the Economy of Redemption.

(ii.) INAUGURATION, ... ix.
> The Service of the Priesthood in Type
> and Antitype.

(iii.) TRANSGRESSION, ... x.
> The Exercise of the Priesthood
> according to the Law.

II. THE WALK WITH GOD BY SANCTIFICATION
PRACTICE (xi.-xxv.).
> The Work of the Spirit in us.
> Experimental.　Subjective.
> What we are to Become and Do.

1. Separation.　The Law of Purity (xi.-xvi.).

(i.) THE REQUIREMENT, ... xi.-xv.
(a) The Law of Food: xi.
(b) The Law of Issues : xi.-xii.
(c) The Law of Leprosy : xiii.-xiv.

> (1) In a Person, xiii. 1-46 ; xiv. 1-32.
> (2) In a Garment, xiii. 47-59.
> (3) In a House, xiv. 33-57.

(ii.) THE PROVISION, ... xvi.
> The Great Day of Atonement.

2. Sanctification.　The Law of Holiness.
(xvii.-xxv.).

(i.) THE REQUIREMENT, ... xvii.-xxiv.
(a) Our Daily Meals : xvii.
(b) Our Social Conduct : xviii.-xx.
(c) Our Priestly Relation : xxi.-xxii.
(d) Our Public Worship : xxiii.
(e) Our Entire Life : xxiv.

(ii.) THE PROVISION, ... xxv.
> The Sabbatic Year and the Jubilee.

(a) Conclusion : Concerning the Covenant, xxvi.
(b) Appendix : Concerning Vows, xxvii.

NUMBERS

THE title NUMBERS, which is from the Greek, is given to this book because of the double numbering or census of the people (chapters i.-iv., and xxvi). It gives the history of the journeyings of the Israelites from their departure from Sinai until they arrived in the Plains of Moab. The book covers a period of about thirty-eight years, and of the twenty-seven chapters (x-xxxvi) which tell of events after the people left Sinai, seventeen are occupied with the history of the last year (xx-xxxvi). Chapters xv-xix represent a period of about thirty-seven years, the time of the *wanderings*, as distinguished from the *journeyings*, and here no itinerary is given. The movements of God's people out of His will are not on His calendar.

Outstanding characters in this narrative are Joshua and Caleb, the only two to enter Canaan, of the older generation which left Egypt. The outstanding chapters are the thirteenth and fourteenth, which tell of the great rebellion at Kadesh.

Between the Nation's Egyptian and Babylonian
captivities there were three great rebellions : this
one in 1490 B.C. ; the one in the time of Samuel,
in 1095 B.C., when they demanded a king ; and
the one in 975 B.C. when the Kingdom broke
into two after the death of Solomon.

This book is remarkable for the number of
fragments of ancient poetry preserved in it, showing,
incidentally, the use in the Pentateuch of other
writings (cf. vi. 24-26 ; x. 35, 36 ; xxi. 14, 15, 17,
18, 27-30). Moses, Aaron, and Miriam all died
before the people entered into the Land ; Law,
Priesthood, and Prophecy bring us to the borders of
our inheritance, but only our Divine Joshua can
bring us into it.

As Exodus is connected with Genesis, and
Leviticus with Exodus, so is Numbers with
Leviticus. In Leviticus the subject is the believer's worship, but in Numbers it is the believer's
walk. The one treats of purity, and the other of
pilgrimage. The one speaks of our spiritual
position, and the other, of our spiritual progress.
The one is concerned with our condition within,
and the other, with our conduct without. Leviticus
is ceremonial, and Numbers is historical. In the
one the Sanctuary is prominent, and in the other,
the Wilderness. The one emphasises privileges,

and the other, responsibilities. The one calls to fellowship with God, and the other, to faithfulness to God. LEVITICUS speaks of the priests, and access to God, and NUMBERS, of the Levites, and service for men.

NOTE 6

The Encampment of Israel.

BECAUSE of the importance of the Encampment instructions, the following Chart should be carefully studied:

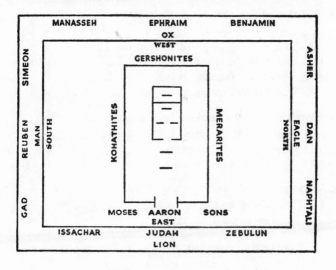

Analysis of Numbers

I. ARRAY. PREPARATION FOR THE JOURNEY (i. 1-x. 10).
THE ENCAMPMENT AT SINAI.

1. Organization of the Camp (i.-iv.).

2. Legislation for the People (v.-vi.).

3. Provision for the Service (vii.-ix. 14).

4. Anticipation of the March (ix. 15-x. 10).

II. ADVANCE. DISAFFECTION ON THE JOURNEY.
(x. 11-xiv. 45).
FROM SINAI TO KADESH.

1. The Departure from Sinai (x. 11-36).
2. The Complaint at Taberah (xi. 1-3).

3. **The Lusting at Kibroth-Hattaavah** (xi. 4-35).
4. **The Sedition at Hazeroth** (xii.).
5. **The Apostasy at Kadesh Barnea** (xiii.-xiv.).

    (i.) The Search of the Land, ... xiii. 1-25.
    (ii.) The Advice of the Spies, ... xiii. 26-33.
    (iii.) The Rebellion of the People, ... xiv.

        (*a*) The Choice of Israel (1-12).
        (*b*) The Intercession of Moses (13-19).
        (*c*) The Sentence of the Lord (20-38).
        (*d*) The Victory of the Enemy (39-45).

III. RETREAT. INTERRUPTION OF THE JOURNEY.
(xv.-xix.).

FROM THE FIRST TO THE SECOND VISIT TO KADESH

1. **Legislation for the Future** (xv.).
2. **Insurrection of the Princes** (xvi.).
3. **Vindication of the Priesthood** (xvii).
4. **Direction of the Priests and Levites** (xviii).
5. **Provision against Pollution** (xix).

IV. RETURN. CONTINUATION OF THE JOURNEY.
(xx.-xxxvi.).

FROM KADESH TO THE PLAINS OF MOAB.

1. **The Return to Kadesh** (xx. 1-21).
2. **The Sojourn at Mount Hor** (xx. 22-xxi. 3).
3. **The March through the Arabah** (xxi. 4-9).
4. **In the Coasts of the East** (xxi. 10-35).
5. **The Encampment at Shittim** (xxii.-xxxvi.).

    (i.) THE WIDE PROSPECT BEFORE THE NATION,   xxii.-xxv
        (*a*) The Call of Balaam (xxii. 1-20).
        (*b*) Balaam meets Balak (xxii. 21-41).

    (c) Balaam's Prophecies (xxiii.-xxiv.).

        First,   xxiii. 1-12.
        Second, xxiii. 13-26.
        Third, xxiii. 27-xxiv. 9.
        Fourth, xxiv. 10-25.

    (d) Balaam's Sinful Counsel and the Result (xxv.).

(ii.) THE RICH PROMISES TO THE NATION (xxvi.-xxxvi.).

    (a) *Numberings* (xxvi.).
        (1) The Warriors (1-36).
        (2) The Levites (37-65).

    (b) *Laws* (xxvii.-xxx.; xxxvi.).
        (1) Law of Inheritance (xxvii. 1-11 ; xxxvi.).
        (2) Appointment of Moses' Successor (xxvii. 12-23).
        (3) Law of the Offerings (xxviii. 1-15).
        (4) Law of the Feasts (xxviii. 16-xxix.).

            Passover,   ...   xxviii. 16-25.
            Pentecost,   ...   xxviii. 26-31.
            Trumpets,   ...   xxix.

        (5) Law of Vows (xxx.).

    (c) *Instructions* (xxxi.-xxxv.).
        (1) Concerning the Midianites (xxxi.).
        (2) Concerning the Inheritance of the Two Tribe and a Half (xxxii.).
        (3) Record of Israel's Journeyings (xxxiii. 1-49).
        (4) Concerning the Inhabitants of the Land (xxxiii. 50-56).
        (5) Concerning Possessing the Land (xxxiv.-xxxv.).

DEUTERONOMY

THE title DEUTERONOMY, which is from the Greek, and means "The Second Law," is suggested by the statement in chapter xvii. 18, that the coming king shall "write him a *copy* of this *law* in a book"; for DEUTERONOMY is just the words *copy* and *law* together. It belongs to the period during which the Israelites were in the Plains of Moab.

The book stands in relation to the four preceding books much as John's Gospel does to the Synoptic Records, in that each gives the spiritual significance of the afore-related historical facts. The dominating notes of the preceding Books are all here; the *choice* of GENESIS, the *deliverance* of EXODUS, the *holiness* of LEVITICUS, and the *guidance* of NUMBERS.

Two of the keywords of the Book are *remember* and *obey*, the one pointing back to the Wilderness, and the other pointing on to the Land.

The three Feasts emphasised are Passover, Pentecost, and Tabernacles, referring to the past, the present, and the future.

The first part of DEUTERONOMY is Historical; the second part is Legislative; and the third part is Prophetical. Moses, at the close of his life, looked upon a new generation, a new land, a new life, new duties, and a new leader, and so there was the need for this new revelation of the Divine "love," nowhere mentioned until now, though much illustrated. In chapters i-iv, we learn of God's love in the past; in chapters v.-xxvi., of His love in the present; and in chapters xxvii.-xxxiv., of His love in the future. No critical questions can lessen the moral and spiritual value of this great Book, the Orations of Moses in the Plains of Moab. It is a significant example of what De Quincey calls "the literature of power," as distinct from "the literature of knowledge." It is probably true that DEUTERONOMY is the most spiritual Book in the Old Testament.

NOTE 7
The Date of Deuteronomy.

THE popular theory among scholars that the Book of Deuteronomy originated in the time of Josiah (2 Kings xxii), and was in fact a pious fraud, is not worthy of scholarship, though it is the view taken by Reuss, Graf, Kuenen, Wellhausen, Stade, Cornill, Cheyne, and many others. But men of equal scholarly equipment are entirely opposed to such a theory. Dr. James Orr says, "If anything is clear . . . it surely is that this finding of the book of the law in the temple was regarded by everybody concerned as the *genuine discovery of an old lost book*, and *that* the 'book of the law' of Moses" (the italics are Dr. Orr's).

Even Dr. Driver says that, "If the critical view of Deuteronomy be correct, the book is a 'forgery.'

Analysis of Deuteronomy

I. A REVIEW OF ISRAEL'S WANDERINGS AND GOD'S LONGSUFFERINGS (chs. i. 1-iv. 43).
PREFACE, i. 1-5.

41

II. A REPETITION AND EXPOSITION OF THE LAW.
(chs. iv. 44-xxvi.).
PREFACE, iv. 44-49.
PART A—THE SINAITIC LAW (v.-xi.).

1. **Recital of the Decalogue** (v. 1-21).

2. **Discourse on the Decalogue** (v. 22-xi. 32).

> (i.) Moses Appointed to Mediate between Israel and Jehovah, ... v. 22-33.

> (ii.) Exhortation and Warning, ... vi.-viii.
> The Ground of Approach to God, vi. 1-9. The Sin of Forgetting God, vi. 10-vii. 11. The Blessings of Obeying God, vii. 12-26. The Past Goodness of God, viii.

> (iii). Rehearsal of Israel's Rebellions, ... ix. 1-x. 11.

> (iv.) Exhortation and Warning, ... x. 12-xi. 32.

PART B—SPECIAL LAWS (xii.-xxvi. 19).

1. **Laws Concerning Religion** (xii. 1-xvi. 17).

> (i.) The Central Sanctuary, ... xii. 1-28.
> (ii.) The Peril of Idolatry, ... xii. 29-xiii. 18.
> (iii.) The Matters of Food, ... xiv. 1-21.
> (iv.) The Tithe of the Increase, ... xiv. 22-29.
> (v.) The Year of Release, ... xv. 1-18.
> (vi.) The Firstling of the Flock, ... xv. 19-23.
> (vii.) The Annual Feasts, ... xvi. 1-17.

2. **Laws Concerning Government** (xvi. 18-xx. 20).

> (i.) Authority and Functions.
> > (a) Of the Judge, ... xvi. 18-xvii. 7.
> > (b) Of the Priest, ... xvii. 8-13.
> > (c) Of the King, ... xvii. 14-20.

NOTE 8

Deuteronomy in Other Scriptures.

THE importance of the Book of Deuteronomy may be gathered from the references which it makes, and by the references made to it in other books of the Bible.

Dr. Girdlestone finds in Deuteronomy not fewer than 259 references to the preceding books: 30 to Genesis, 94 to Exodus, 61 to Leviticus, and 74 to Numbers. As to references in other Scriptures to Deuteronomy, Dr. Girdlestone finds not fewer than 356 in Old Testament books, and 52 in New Testament books. The latter, however, is a considerable underestimate, for Westcott and Hort find no fewer than 96 quotations or allusions in the New Testament, and these, in Matthew, Mark, Luke, Acts, Romans, 1 Corinthians, 2 Corinthians, Galatians, Ephesians, Philippians, 2 Thessalonians, 1 Timothy, Titus, Hebrews, James, Jude, and the Revelation, that is, in 17 of the 27 books of the New Testament.

It is worthy of special notice that the three quotations of our Lord in the Temptation are taken from Deuteronomy. Like David, He had five pebbles when He encountered Goliath, the Pentateuch, and like David, He brought the enemy down with one, Deuteronomy, and had four to spare.

THE HISTORICAL WRITINGS

INTRODUCTION

JOSHUA

JUDGES

RUTH

1 SAMUEL

2 SAMUEL

1 KINGS

2 KINGS

1 CHRONICLES

2 CHRONICLES

EZRA

ESTHER

NEHEMIAH

Study Outline of a Thousand Years of Hebrew History.

I. THE ISRAELITISH NATION. Exodus-2 Kings xxiii. 30.

  1. THE THEOCRACY. Moses to Samuel.

    (i) Israel in Egypt.
- (*a*) Persecution of the People.
- (*b*) Preparation of a Saviour.
- (*c*) Plan and Progress of Redemption.

    (ii) Israel in the Wilderness.
- (*a*) From Egypt to Sinai.
- (*b*) Encampment at Sinai.
- (*c*) From Sinai to Shittim.

    (iii) Israel in the Land.
- (*a*) Under Joshua.
- (*b*) Under Judges.

  2. THE MONARCHY. Saul to Zedekiah.

    (i) The United Kingdom.
- (*a*) Under Saul.
- (*b*) Under David.
- (*c*) Under Solomon.

    (ii) The Divided Kingdom.
- (*a*) First Antagonism between North and South.
- (*b*) Fateful Alliance between North and South.
- (*c*) Final Antagonism between North and South.

    (iii) The Single Kingdom.
- (*a*) Judah's First Reformation and following Decline.
- (*b*) Judah's Last Reformation and Final Decline.

II. THE JEWISH CHURCH. 2 Kings xxiii. 31-Malachi.

  1. THE SUBJECTION OF JUDAH.
- (i) Reign of Jehoiakim.
- (ii) Reign of Jehoiachin.
- (iii) Reign of Zedekiah.

  2. THE CORRECTION OF JUDAH.
- (i) The Remnant in the Land.
- (ii) The Remnant in Egypt.
- (iii) The Exiles in the East.

  3. THE RESTORATION OF JUDAH.
- (i) Return and Work under Zerubbabel.
- (ii) Return and Work under Ezra.
- (iii) Return and Work under Nehemiah.

THE HISTORICAL WRITINGS

Introduction

THIS classification is general, and for the sake of convenience, and it must be remembered that large parts of the Pentateuch, and parts of the later Prophets are also historical.

The period covered by these Books reaches from the death of Moses in 1451 B.C., to the end of Old Testament history, about 396 B.C. (?), that is, approximately 1055 years, a long time in the history of a people.

This long period falls into three main parts, namely, first, from the death of Moses to the accession of Saul, 1451-1096 B.C., that is, 355 years : second, from the accession of Saul to the overthrow of Judah, 1096-586 B.C., that is, 510 years : and third, from the overthrow of Judah to the end of Old Testament history, 586-396 B.C., that is, 190 years. By getting that perspective it will be easier to follow the unfolding story. These periods represent three forms of government, relative to the Chosen Nation, first, the Theocracy, or rule of God ; second, the Monarchy, or rule of kings of their own ; and third, the Dependency, or rule of alien kings.

It must be remembered that the Old Testament story is history with a religious purpose, and selection and omission are determined by this fact. That millennium was the period of great civilisations, great characters, great cities, and great conflicts of Babylonia, Egypt, Assyria, Phoenicia, Syria, Greece, and Persia ; yet, all this fascinating story has no place in the Bible record except in so far as these powers and persons came into contact with this chosen People. And not only so, but in the history of Israel itself, much is passed over briefly which we would consider of great historical importance, while events of seeming minor importance are recorded at length. The reason for this is that the purpose of Old Testament history is moral and spiritual, and not annalistic ; it is the history of God's Self-revelation for the redemption of men. All omissions and digressions must be received in this light.

Herodotus is commonly regarded as the Father of History, but the Hebrews wrote history a thousand years before Herodotus was born. "That in these Writings other documents are named, as the depositories of ampler information, and that some of the Books were written or collected long after the events they describe, are facts which create no difficulty, and are in accordance with what we know of the general method of revelation. They account, moreover, for the occasional blending of matter evidently contemporaneous with the events described with others of clearly later origin."

Although these Books were written by different persons, at different times, and in different places, they yet present a coherent and constructive account of a thousand years of history. This can be accounted for only by assuming a Divine providence and superintendence, a Divine inspiration.

The dates attached to the following Books are given without dogmatism.

NOTE 10
The Two Kingdoms.

IN studying the history of the Divided Kingdom, 1 Kings xii. 2 to 2 Kings xviii. 12; 2 Chronicles x. to xxviii; it is important to bear the following facts in mind:

The Southern Kingdom had its centre at Jerusalem; had two of the twelve tribes (1 Kings xii. 21); was ruled over by 19 kings and one queen, all of the same dynasty. These tribes were taken captive by Nebuchadnezzar into Babylonia, and ultimately returned in large numbers.

The Northern Kingdom had its centre first at Shechem, and then at Samaria; had ten of the twelve tribes (1 Kings xi. 31); was ruled over by 19 kings, who were of nine dynasties. These tribes were taken captive by Shalmaneser into Assyria, and did not return.

The terms ten and two, applied to the tribes, is only general, and cannot be pressed, as not only were Judah and Benjamin in the South, but also the tribe of Levi, and, probably, members of all the tribes (1 Kings xi. 13, 32, 34; xii. 20, 21; Ezra iii. 8-13; vi. 16-18).

JOSHUA

Keyword—POSSESSION.   CHAPTERS : 24.

DATE : 1451-1425 B.C. ; 25 Years.

THIS Book bears the name of Joshua because
he is the hero of it, although, no doubt,
Jewish tradition is right in assuming that he also
supplied the materials of the story, which were
supplemented and edited by some later scribes.
This book goes on from where DEUTERONOMY
leaves off; Joshua completes what Moses commenced. The great event in Moses' life was the
passage through the Red Sea, and the great event
in Joshua's life was the passage through the Jordan.
The one tells of deliverance from bondage, and the
other of entrance into blessing. Moses' symbol
was the rod, but Joshua's was the spear. The
connection between DEUTERONOMY and JOSHUA is
instructive. In the one is a prospect, but in the
other, an experience. In the one is the vision of
faith, and in the other, the venture of faith. In
the one is Israel's inheritance, and in the other,
Israel's possession. In the one is the call to
conflict, and in the other is the clash of conflict.

In the one is faith in principle, and in the other, faith in action. In the one is the ideal to become actual, and in the other the ideal becomes actual. In the one is possibility, and in the other realisation. The New Testament counterparts of this Book are the ACTS and EPHESIANS.

NOTE 11

Miracles in the Book of Joshua.

OBJECTION has been taken to the miraculous element in the Book of Joshua, and it is said this is inconsistent with the known laws of nature as revealed by science. With reference to the objection Dr. Plummer has well said: "It is easy for those who have laid down for themselves as an axiom, that a miracle is an impossibility, to set aside the Book of Joshua as unhistorical, because of the large amount of miraculous details contained in it. Even if the miracles of the Book of Joshua stood alone, we might fairly protest against so summary a mode of dealing with what bears all the impress of historic reality. But the miracles which attended the conquest of Canaan stand or fall with all those which have marked God's dealings with His Chosen People, whether under the Law, or under the Gospel; and to a fair mind these are simply a question of evidence. The simple truthfulness of the author of the Book of Joshua, and the worthiness of the object for which the miracles which he records are wrought, may rightly be allowed to tell for, rather than against, the truth of miracles as a whole."

Analysis of Joshua

I. ENTERING THE LAND (i. 1-v. 12).

1. Preparation of the People (i. 1-iii. 13).

   (i.) INWARD PREPARATION. *The Law*, ...   i. 1-18.
     (a) The Lord to Joshua (1-9).
     (b) Joshua to the People (10-15).
     (c) The People to Joshua (16-18).

   (ii.) OUTWARD PREPARATION. *The Spies*,   ...   ii. 1-24.
     (a) The Mission of the Spies (1-7).
     (b) The Covenant of the Spies (8-21).
     (c) The Report of the Spies (22-24).

   (iii.) ONWARD PREPARATION. *The Ark*, ...   iii. 1-13.

2. Passage of the People (iii. 14-iv. 24).

   (i.) The Crossing of Jordan, ...   iii. 14-17.
   (ii.) The Memorial in Jordan, ...   iv. 1-18.
   (iii.) The Encampment over Jordan, ...   iv. 19-24.

3. Purification of the People (v. 1-12).

   (i.) The Consternation of the Enemy, ...   1.
   (ii.) The Circumcision of the Sons, ...   2-9.
   (iii.) The Cessation of the Manna, ...   10-12.

II. CONQUERING THE LAND (v. 13-xii. 24).

1. The Revelation of Victory (v. 13-15).

The Realization of Victory (vi.-xi.).

   (i.) The Central Campaign, ...   vi. 1-ix. 27.
     Jericho and *Ai*.

   (ii.) The Southern Campaign, ...   x.
     Gibeon and *Beth-Horon*.

   (iii.) The Northern Campaign, ...   xi.
     Merom.

NOTE 12

Moses and Joshua.

IT is written, "He brought us out from thence, that He might bring us in" (Deut. vi. 23); that is, out of Egypt, into the Land. Under God, Moses did the one work, and Joshua did the other, and the whole history has a typical value. Moses, which means "drawn out," was also a drawer out, and he typifies Christ in that aspect of His work which relates to our deliverance *from* the kingdom of Satan. Joshua, which means "Saviour" (the same as Jehoshua, Oshea, Jesus), typifies Christ in that aspect of His work which relates to what He has delivered us *to*. In the one case the Red Sea was an *exit*, and in the other, the Jordan was an *entrance*; the one experience points to the truth of regeneration, and the other to the truth of dedication.

JUDGES

Keyword—DECLENSION.   CHAPTERS : 21.

DATE : 1425-1095 B.C. ; 330 Years.

THIS Book takes its name from a characteristic of the period between the death of Joshua and the accession of Saul, namely, the rule of Judges, or saviours, whom God raised up to deliver His oppressed people. Of these there were fifteen, Othniel, Ehud, Shamgar, Deborah-Barak, Gideon, Abimelech, Tola, Jair, Jephthah, Ibzan, Elon, Abdon, Samson. Eli and Samuel. There were three leading types, the Warrior-Judge, as Gideon and Samson ; the Priest-Judge, as Eli; and the Prophet-Judge, as Samuel. The chief of these Judges were Deborah, Gideon, Samson, and Samuel.

The period of the Judges cannot be determined with any precision ; calculations have a varying margin of more than a century. We cannot conclude that all these Judgeships were consecutive ; indeed, it is almost certain that some of them were contemporaneous ; but we may reckon about 330 years for this period.

Nothing is known as to the authorship of the

Book, though tradition ascribes it to Samuel. Clearly it is a compilation, and may not have taken its present form until several centuries after the events which it records.

The main narrative is in iii. 7-xvi. 31, and 1 Sam. i.-vii.; and chapters xvii.-xxv., with RUTH, are undated episodes of the early days of the Judges, inserted between the histories of Samson and Samuel.

JUDGES is one of the saddest books in the Bible, telling, as it does, of repeated apostasy, chastisement, and mercy. Rebellion, retribution, repentance, and rest, are the dominating notes in this minor music. JOSHUA treats of the heavenlies, but JUDGES of the earthlies ; the one is of the Spirit, and the other is of the flesh. In the one is a song of joy, and in the other a sob of sorrow. In the one is victory, and in the other, defeat. In the one is progress, and in the other, decline : in the one, faith, and in the other, unbelief : in the one freedom, and in the other bondage. JUDGES teaches us, on the one hand, not to presume, and on the other hand, not to despair.

RUTH

THIS is one of the only two books of the Bible
which bear the name of a woman, and in many
respects they present remarkable contrasts.   The
one is of a Gentile woman, Ruth, who was brought
into the midst of Jews, among whom she hence-
forth lives her life ; and the other is of a Jewish
woman, Esther, who is taken into the midst of
Gentiles, where, with equal fidelity and grace, she
plays the part ordained for her by God.   RUTH is
a lovely pastoral idyll, the tale of a friendship
between two women, and the grand climax up to
which all is working is the birth of a baby.   After
reading JUDGES xvii.-xxi., RUTH is like a lovely lily
in a stagnant pool.   Here, instead of unfaithfulness,
is loyalty, and instead of immorality, is purity.
Here, instead of battlefields are harvest fields, and
instead of the warrior's shout is the harvester's
song.

Ruth's protestation of love for Naomi is as
eloquent a passage as can be found in the whole
range of world literature (chapter i. 16, 17).

The story has a typical significance, which may

be discerned in the meanings of the names which
occur: Bethlehem, House of Bread; Elimelech,
My God is King; Naomi, Sweet (?); Mahlon,
Song; Chilion, Perfection; Ruth, Satisfied; Orpah,
Skull (?); Boaz, Strength. These three women
represent—a saint backsliding, Naomi; a sinner
rejecting blessing, Orpah; and a sinner believing
and blessed, Ruth. Boaz may be regarded as a
type of Christ, as Lord of harvest (ii. 3), Dispenser
of bread (iii. 15), Kinsman-Redeemer (ii. 20),
Giver of rest (iii. 1), Man of wealth (ii. 1), and our
Strength.

This Book is one of the Megilloth or Festal
Rolls, one of which was publicly read at each
festival, RUTH being read at the Feast of Pentecost.
One of the designs of the Book is to trace the descent
of David, and to show that the Gentiles are not
outside the scope of redeeming love.

The analysis of RUTH is included in that of
JUDGES.

NOTE 13

RUTH.

OBSERVE that Ruth is one of five women who appear in
Matthew's genealogy of our Lord. Three of the five had
bad records—Tamar, Rahab, and Bathsheba; and two of the
five were Gentiles—Rahab and Ruth.

Analysis of Judges and Ruth

I. INTRODUCTION (i.-iii. 6).

1. **Retrospective** (i. 1-ii. 10).
   - (i.) The Failure of Israel, ... i.
   - (ii.) The Rebuke of the Angel, ... ii. 1-5.
   - (iii.) The Death of Joshua Recalled, ... ii. 6-10.

2. **Prospective** (ii. 11-iii. 6).
   - (i.) A Summary of the Period, ... ii. 11-23.
     - (*a*) Rebellion.
     - (*b*) Retribution.
     - (*c*) Repentance.
     - (*d*) Rest.
   - (ii.) A Summary of the Enemies, ... iii. 1-6.

II. THE HISTORY (iii. 7-xvi. 31).

1. **First Cycle,** ... ... iii. 7-11.

Enemy,...	*Mesopotamia.*
Subjection,	8 Years.
Deliverer,	*Othniel.*
Peace, ...	40 Years.

2. **Second Cycle,** ... ... iii. 12-31.

Enemy,	*Moabites, Ammonites, Amalekites.*
Subjection,	18 Years.
Deliverer,	*Ehud.*
Peace, ...	80 Years.

   (iii. 31, Shamgar delivers from the Philistines).

3. **Third Cycle,** ... ... iv. 1-v. 31.

Enemy,	*Canaanites.*
Subjection,	20 Years.
Deliverer,	*Deborah* and *Barak.*
Peace, ...	40 Years.

4. **Fourth Cycle**, ... vi. 1-viii. 32.
   Enemy,   *Midianites.*
   Subjection,   7 Years.
   Deliverer,   *Gideon.*
   Peace, ..   40 Years.

5. **Fifth Cycle**, ... viii. 33-x. 5.
   Usurpation of *Abimelech*,   3 Years.
   Judgeships of Tola and Jair,   45 Years.

6. **Sixth Cycle**, ... x. 6-xii. 15.
   Enemy,   *Ammonites.*
   Subjection,   18 Years.
   Deliverer,   *Jephthah.*
   Peace, ..   31 Years.

7. **Seventh Cycle**, ... xiii.-xvi.
   Enemy,   *Philistines.*
   Subjection,   40 Years.
   Deliverer,   *Samson.*
   Peace, ..   20 Years.

III. APPENDICES (xvii.-xxi.) Ruth.

1. **A Story of Apostasy—Micah and the Danites** (xvii.-xviii.).
   Infidelity.
   (i). Micah and his Gods, ... xvii.
   (ii.) The Danite Migration, ... xviii.

2. **A Story of Revenge—A Levite and the Benjamites** (xix.-xxi.).
   Immorality.
   (i.) The Outrage at Gibeah, ... xix.
   (ii.) The War with Benjamin, ... xx, xxi.

3. **A Story of Devotion—Ruth the Moabitess.**
   Piety and Purity.
   (i.) The Migration to Moab of the Elimelech
        Family, ... i. 1-5.
   (ii.) The Return to Judah of Naomi with
         Ruth, ... i. 6-22.
   (iii.) The Portentous Meeting of Boaz and
          Ruth, ... ii.-iii.
   (iv.) The Redemption by Boaz of Elimelech's
         Inheritance, ... iv.

1 SAMUEL

Keyword—KINGDOM.   CHAPTERS : 31.

DATE : 1150 (?) -1055 B.C. ; 95 Years.

IN this record ends what Prof. R. Moulton calls incidental history, and commences what he calls regular history. The long period of the Judges, with its unsettled Government, terminates with the judgeship of Samuel, and five centuries of Monarchy start (1095-586 B.C.). The Book may be divided into three unequal parts by a grouping of its chief characters, Eli, Samuel, Saul, and David, but it should be discerned that these parts overlap. In all likelihood chapters i-xxiv were written by Samuel, and xxv-xxxi by Nathan and Gad (x. 25 ; 1 Chron. xxix. 29).

The Warrior-Judges have passed, and a Priest-Judge has come, Eli, to be followed by a Prophet-Judge, Samuel, and with him the period of the Judges ends, and the Order of the Prophets begins (Acts xiii. 20 ; iii. 24). Until now the priest had been prominent, and from now the prophet is distinguished. By the former, the people drew nigh to God, and by the latter God drew nigh to the people. Christ is both Prophet and Priest, the former, when here on earth, and the latter, now in Heaven. This Book is rich in character studies.

ELI was probably contemporary with Samson, and he ministered from the Sanctuary in Shiloh for forty years. When Samuel was born Eli was physically old and spiritually weak, and his sons "were sons of Belial; they knew not the Lord" (chapter ii. 12).

SAMUEL is one of the greatest of the Hebrew worthies, whose influence lay not in military exploits, nor in diplomatic skill, nor in political shrewdness, but in unswerving integrity and splendid loyalty to God (chapter xii. 1-3). He is the third of the great leaders whom God raised up for Israel—Abraham, Moses, Samuel, and he is the first of three great transition-period leaders. He saw the outgoing of the Theocracy and the incoming of the Monarchy. Jeremiah saw the outgoing of the Monarchy and the incoming of the Dependency, and Paul saw the outgoing of Judaism and the incoming of Christianity.

SAUL is a strange character, exciting in us both admiration and pity; a man whom Samuel sternly rebuked (chapter xv. 20-23), and whom David lavishly praised (2 Sam. i. 19-27); a man whose morning was bright, but soon became overcast, and whose sun set in blackest clouds. Follow carefully his rise, his reign, and his ruin. Read Browning's "Saul."

DAVID is one of the greatest characters of all time, having regard to his influence upon history, national and spiritual. In this Book we see him as shepherd lad, minstrel, armour-bearer, captain, king's son-in-law, king designate, psalmist, and fugitive. He was thrice anointed, and was the founder of the royal line of which the King of kings came.

JONATHAN is a choice soul, the two chief features of whose story are, his self-suppression, and his love for David (chapters xviii, xx ; 2 Sam. i. 26). Other noteworthy features of this Book are the founding of prophetic schools, the commencement of the Monarchy, the defeat of the Philistines by the slaying of Goliath, the Song of Hannah, the first occurrence of "Messiah" (chapter ii. 10 Heb.), the campaigns against the Ammonites, Amalekites, and Philistines, and the battle at Mount Gilboa, with which the historical part of Chronicles begins (chapter x).

Analysis of 1 Samuel

I. ELI AND SAMUEL (i.-vii).

1. Contrasted Family Life in Shiloh (i.-iii.).

(i.) ELKANAH AND HIS SON.   Righteous.

(a) The Birth of Samuel, ...	...	(i. 1-ii. 11).
(b) The Ministry of Samuel,	...	(ii. 18-21, 26).
(c) The Call of Samuel, ...	...	(iii. 1-21).

(ii.) ELI AND HIS SONS.   Wicked.

(a) Their Sin, ...	...	...	(ii. 12-17 ; 22-25).
(b) Their Sentence, ...	...	...	(ii. 27-36).

2. The Philistines and the Ark of God (iv.-vii).

(i.) THE PHILISTINES VICTORIOUS, ... iv.-vii. 1.

(a) The Ark Taken ...	...	...	iv.
(b) The Ark Held, ...	...	...	v.
(c) The Ark Returned	...	...	vi. 1-vii. 1.

(ii.) THE PHILISTINES DEFEATED, ... vii. 2-17.

(a) The Dedication at Mizpeh	...	2-6.
(b) The Victory of Israel ...	...	7-12.
(c) The Judgeship of Samuel	...	13-17.

II. SAMUEL AND SAUL (viii.-xv.).

1. Saul's Election to the Throne (viii-xii.).

(i.) Israel's Demand for a King,	...	viii.
(ii.) Israel's Request Granted, ...	...	ix.-xi.
(a) Saul Selected ...	...	...	ix.
(b) Saul Appointed	...	...	x.
(c) Saul Confirmed	...	...	xi.
(iii.) Israel Addressed by Samuel,	...	xii.

2. Saul's Rejection by the Lord (xiii.-xv.).

(i.) His Sinful Impatience,	...	...	xiii.
(ii.) His Insensate Zeal, ...	...	...	xiv.
(iii.) His Miserable Hypocrisy, ...	...	xv.

III. SAUL AND DAVID (xvi.-xxxi.).

1. **David as a Shepherd** (xvi.-xvii.)
   (i.) David and Samuel, ...   xvi. 1-13.
   (ii.) David and Saul, ...   xvi. 14-23.
   (iii.) David and Goliath, ...   xvii.

2. **David as a Courtier** (xviii.-xix.).
   (i.) The Friendship of Jonathan, ...   xviii. 1-9.
   (ii.) The Devotion of Israel, ...   xviii. 10-16.
   (iii.) The Love of Michal, ...   xviii. 17-30.
   (iv.) The Jealousy of Saul, ...   xix. 1-24.

3. **David as a Fugitive** (xx.-xxxi.).
   (i.) Jonathan's Faithfulness to David,   ...   xx.
   (ii.) David's Wanderings, ...   xxi.-xxiv.
   (iii.) David and Nabal, ...   xxv.
   (iv.) David's Wanderings, ...   xxvi.-xxvii.
   (v.) Saul and the Witch of Endor, ...   xxviii.
   (vi.) David and the Philistines and Amalekites, ...   xxix.-xxx.
   (vii.) Death of Saul and Jonathan, ...   xxxi.

NOTE 14

Samuel and his Schools.

SAMUEL "laid the foundation and fostered the rapid growth of a grand system of national education. At Ramah he trained men to be Israel's teachers; but he did not confine himself to this. Most of the great ornaments of David's court were his disciples, and it is probable that large numbers of the wealthy and more promising youth of the kingdom went to his schools simply to learn something of these wonderful arts of reading and writing, which opened so new a world to the youth of a race always distinguished for its intellectual aptitudes. And through them Samuel raised the whole people mentally and morally. Trained men henceforward were never wanting for high service both at court and throughout the land.

It was Samuel who laid the broad foundations of that culture which, carried on first by prophets and then by scribes, made the Jews capable of writing the Bible, of translating the Old Testament into Greek, of teaching its principles in most of the cities of Greece, and finally of going forth as missionaries, carrying with them the Gospel of our Lord Jesus Christ."

2 SAMUEL

Keyword—CONSOLIDATION.   CHAPTERS : 24.

DATE : 1055-1015 B.C.   40 Years.

PARALLEL HISTORY : 1 Chronicles xi.-xxix.

THIS is a record of greatest importance, and of
thrilling interest.   In these historical Books,
1-2 SAMUEL, 1-2 KINGS, is discernible a dramatic
development ; Samuel supersedes Eli, Saul super-
cedes Samuel, David supersedes Saul, and David's
sons supersede their father.   The Hebrew Monarchy proper began with David, and in his reign
it reached its highest development.   He unified the
nation, obtained for it a royal capital, subdued its
enemies, and extended the kingdom from the
Red Sea to the river Orontes, and from the Mediterranean to the Euphrates.   He created a national
consciousness, and brought prosperity by extend-
ing trade.   It has been well said that "four streams
of influence have come to us from his times.
First, by establishing the City of David he set in
motion all that Jerusalem has meant in war and in
song.   Secondly, he founded a dynasty, and the
sanctity, the authority, the splendour of the House
of David have moulded the hopes of Israel and

3   65

the forms of Christian faith through all subsequent
generations.   Thirdly, his reign was marked by
a signal development of poetry and music ; he is
credited with the orchestration of wind, stringed,
and percussion instruments ; and with nobler
music the psalms of worship became more numerous and significant.   Fourthly, about this time
public records were kept with systematic care ;
Samuel left written documents (1 Sam. x. 25),
David appointed court recorders and scribes.
Nathan the prophet wrote history (1 Chron.
xxix. 29).   Under David the harassed tribes
became a conquering, self-conscious nation, and
music, song, history, and prophetic dreams sprang
to life" (C. A. Dinsmore).   The narrative is full
of graphic and convincing detail, and is written
in the best style of classical Hebrew.   It begins
with one of the most perfect elegies in any language,
David's lament over Saul called "The Song of the
Bow," and let us remember it was written over
three thousand years ago, by a young man just
turned thirty.

In the Hebrew Bible First and Second SAMUEL
are one book, as are First and Second KINGS ; and,
indeed, the four tell one story, the Story of the
Monarchy from its Rise to its Fall.   David's history
begins in 1 SAMUEL and ends in 1 KINGS, and is

divisible into four parts : his Education (1 Sam. xvi-xxxi) ; his Election (2 Sam. i-x) ; his Ejection (2 Sam. xi-xviii), and his Exaltation (2 Sam xix-1 Kings ii. 11) ; or, his Testings, Triumphs, Troubles, and Testimonies. David came to the throne, conquered from the throne, fled from the throne, and was established on the throne, stages which tell of preparation, subjugation, retribution, and restoration. As a king, David's Home Policy was the centralisation of power and worship, in which he succeeded by taking Jerusalem and bringing the Ark to it ; and his Foreign Policy was the subjugation of all enemies, and in this also he succeeded (chapter viii). Solemn indeed is the story of his fall and its consequences, whereby he has made "the enemies of the Lord to blaspheme" for three thousand years. But profound was his repentance, and out of that "eater" has come the "meat" of Psalms xxxii and li. The great shepherd became a great soldier, and the great sinner became a great saint.

Analysis of 2 Samuel

I. DAVID KING OVER JUDAH, IN HEBRON.
7½ Years. Chs. i.-iv.

1. David and the Dead (Ch. i.).
   (i.) A False Account of Saul's Death, ... i. 1-16.
   (ii.) David's Lamentation for Saul and
      Jonathan, ... i. 17-27.

2. Two Kings Crowned (Ch. ii. 1-11).
   (i.) David over Judah, ... ii. 1-7.
   (ii.) Ish-bosheth over Israel, ... ii. 8-11.

3. War Between Judah and Israel.
      (Chs. ii. 12-iv. 12).
   (i.) Joab and Abner, ... ii. 12-32.
   (ii.) Abner and David, ... iii. 1-21.
   (iii.) Joab, David and Abner, ... iii. 22-39.
   (iv.) Ish-bosheth and his Murderers, ... iv. 1-12.

II. DAVID, KING OVER ALL ISRAEL, IN JERUSALEM.
33 Years. Chs. v.-1 Kings ii. 11.

1. The Triumphs of the King (Chs. v.-x.).

   (i.) ESTABLISHMENT OF THE THRONE, ... v.-vii.
      (*a*) The New Capital and First Con-
         quests (v.).
      (*b*) The Establishment of Worship in
         Jerusalem (vi.).
      (*c*) God's Covenant with David (vii.).
   (ii.) EXTENSION OF THE KINGDOM, ... viii.-x.
      (*a*) David's Foreign Conquests (viii.).
      (*b*) David and Mephibosheth (ix.).
      (*c*) Defeat of the Syrians and Ammon-
         ites (x.).

NOTE 15

War.

"THE Second Book of Samuel gives us the history of the founding of Israel's empire. War is a dreadful thing, and involves a terrible amount of material loss and injury; but it is at once God's penalty upon national debasement, and His remedy against national meanness and selfishness. Nations rise to moral greatness through war, and when they have been sinking through social corruption and private immorality, it is generally war which reveals the gangrene in their midst, and either forces them by repeated disaster to humble themselves for it, or displaces them in order that a worthier people may fill their room."

1 KINGS i-xi

Keyword—GLORY.   CHAPTERS . 11.

DATE : 1015-975 B.C.   40 Years.

PARALLEL HISTORY :   2 Chronicles i.-ix.

THE United Kingdom lasted for one hundred and twenty years, having three kings who each reigned for forty years (1095-975 B.C.). Of these, the first was of the tribe of Benjamin, and the other two of the tribe of Judah, so that the predicted Messianic line began with David (Gen. xlix. 10). The record of his closing days is in 1 Kings i-ii. 11, where we read of Adonijah's attempt to seize the throne, of the coronation of Solomon, and of David's charge to his son and successor.

Then follows the record of Solomon's reign (1015-975 B.C.), in chapters i-xi, and 2 Chron. i.-ix. These few chapters contain events of great historical and spiritual significance.

Solomon was a strange character, and he may be regarded in various ways, personally, officially, and typically. Viewed personally, he was characterised by wisdom and wickedness : greatly gifted intellectually, he was very weak ethically. His mind and his morals were not on the same level. Viewed officially, his great work was twofold, the material development of the Kingdom, and the erection of the Temple. The Solomonic Temple was one of the most magnificent structures of the ancient world, and it has been computed that the value of the materials used in the building of it would not be less than £100,000,000. Viewed typically, it is not difficult to see an anticipation of Christ's Millennial Kingdom, when, after the extirpation of all His foes, there will be peace. Psalm lxxii., which is attributed to Solomon, reflects this view. Solomon's wisdom, and work, and waywardness unite to make him an outstanding character, whose reign and his father's constitute the golden period of the Jewish State.

NOTE 16

Solomon.

IT is only in a very limited way that any Old Testament character can typify Christ. Moses, and Aaron, and Samson, and David, and others, give a momentary flash of Messianic anticipation, and that is all. It is so also in the case of Solomon. He anticipates Christ as the Temple Builder, and as the King of Peace, but in his personal character he is low even by the standards of his fellows. How high he rose! How deep he fell! He who prayed the wonderful prayer of 1 Kings viii, kept a vast harem; and he who chose the blessing of wisdom, fell into the completest folly.

Analysis of 1 Kings i.-xi, and 2 Chron. i.-ix

I. APPOINTMENT OF SOLOMON TO THE THRONE
(Chs. i.-ii. 11).

1. Usurpation of Adonijah : i. 1-31.
2. Ordination of Solomon : i. 32-53.
3. Instruction of Solomon : ii. 1-11.

II. ESTABLISHMENT OF SOLOMON ON THE THRONE.
(Ch. ii. 12-46).

4. Execution of his Foes : ii. 12-46.

III. THE WISDOM AND WEALTH OF SOLOMON.
(Chs. iii.-iv.)

5. Revelation to Solomon : iii. 2 Chron. i. 7-13.
6. Reputation of Solomon : iv.

IV. THE TEMPLE AND HOUSE OF SOLOMON.
(Chs. v.-x.)

7. Preparation for the Temple : v.   2 Chron. ii.
8. Construction of the Temple : vi., vii. 2 Chron iii.-v. 1.
9. Dedication of the Temple : viii. 1-21. 2 Chron. v. 2-14.
10. Supplication of the King : viii. 22-53. 2 Chron. vi. 12-42.
11. Benediction of the King : viii. 54-61. 2 Chron. vi. 1-11.
12. Jubilation of the King and People : viii. 62-66. 2 Chron. vii. 1-10.
13. Consecration of the Temple : ix. 1-9. 2 Chron. vii. 11-22.
14. Possessions of the King : ix. 10-28. 2 Chron. viii.
15. Inspection by the Queen of Sheba : x. 2 Chron. ix.

V. THE SIN AND FALL OF SOLOMON.
(Ch. xi.)

16. Declension of the King : xi. 1-13.
17. Division of the Kingdom : xi. 14-43.

1 KINGS xii.-2 Kings xviii. 12

Keyword—DISRUPTION.   CHAPTERS : 28.

DATE : 975-722 B.C.   253 Years.

PARALLEL HISTORY : 2 Chronicles x.-xxviii.

THE United Kingdom record ends at 1 Kings xi, with the death of Solomon, and the Divided Kingdom record is in 1 Kings xii. 1-2 Kings xviii. 12, together with the parallel chapters in 2 Chronicles. This part of the history of the Monarchy should be kept distinct from what preceded and what follows it, that is, from the United Kingdom on the one hand, and the Single Kingdom on the other hand. The story covers over two and a half centuries, during which time the kingdom was divided into two parts, which are spoken of as Judah, the Southern Kingdom, with its capital at Jerusalem ; and Israel, the Northern Kingdom, with its capital, first at Shechem, and then at Samaria. The Tribes of Judah, Benjamin, and Levi remained loyal to the Davidic House, and the others seceded, and established a new kingdom, a new centre and object of worship, a new order of priests, a new altar of sacrifice, and a new festal month.

The way in which this part of the history is arranged makes analysis difficult, so I have felt it best to tabulate the seven salient facts, the name of each king, when he began to reign, the length of his reign, the kingdom to which he belonged, his character, and the parallel references, relating also to the history and the prophets of the period. In this way the alternating records are given with distinctiveness.

The division of the kingdom which was predicted (1 Kings xi. 26-40), was due to the idolatrous disloyalty of the Nation, and for this sin both parts of the kingdom were sent ultimately into captivity; Israel to Assyria, in 722 B.C.; and Judah to Babylonia, in 586 B.C.

During the two and a half centuries of their parallel history, three periods are to be distinguished by the relation of the kingdoms to one another. From Rehoboam to Asa in the South, and from Jeroboam to Omri in the North, a period of sixty-one years (975-914 B.C., 1 Kings xii. 1-xvi. 28), they were antagonistic to one another.   Then, by the marriage of Jehoshaphat's son (South) with Ahab's daughter (North), the kingdoms were allied to one another for seventy-five years (914-839 B.C.; 1 Kings xvi. 29-2 Kings xiii. 9).   And finally, from Amaziah to Hezekiah in the South,

and from Joash to Hoshea in the North, a period
of one hundred and seventeen years, they were
again antagonistic to one another (839-722 B.C. ;
2 Kings xiii. 10-xviii. 12).

When reading the record of this history certain
facts should be borne in mind. In the Southern
kingdom there was but one dynasty, the Davidic,
but in the Northern kingdom there were nine
dynasties. In the South were nineteen kings and
one queen ; in the North were nineteen kings.
In the South some of the rulers were good, some
unstable, and some bad ; but in the North, all
were bad. In the South were three religious
revivals, in the reigns of Jehoshaphat, Hezekiah,
and Josiah ; but in the North there were no revivals. The tribes in the South were taken into
Babylonian captivity by Nebuchadnezzar ; and
the Tribes in the North, into Assyrian captivity
by Shalmaneser.

The Foreign Powers that came into touch with
the South or the North in this period were Assyria,
Egypt, Babylonia, and Syria.

The best kings of Judah were Asa, Jehoshaphat,
Hezekiah, and Josiah, and the worst were Ahaz
and Manasseh. It should be observed that each
of the best kings made a serious mistake ; Asa,
by his alliance with Syria against Israel ; Jehosha-

phat, by his alliance with the House of Ahab; Hezekiah, by his friendliness to the Babylonian messengers from Merodach-Baladan; and Josiah, by his march against Pharaoh Necho, of Egypt.

This Divided Kingdom period was distinguished by prophetic ministry; oral, by Elijah and Elisha, and by minor prophets, Ahijah, Iddo, Shemiah, Jehu, Hanani, Azariah, Jahaziel, and Eliezer: and oral or (and) written ministry by Joel, Jonah, Amos, Hosea, Isaiah and Micah. It was distinguished also by miracles, of which there were seven in the days of Elijah, and eleven in the days of Elisha.

The northern Kingdom did not advance the Messianic purpose, but the Southern Kingdom did. The Davidic succession was maintained, and by the prophets, a true witness was kept alive. Jehovah was patient with His people, albeit He visited them in judgment for their sins.

NOTE 17

Chronological Relations.

THE Old Testament Books fall into a threefold classification: History, Poetry and Wisdom, and Prophecy, but if we would understand these Writings we must read them in their chronological relations. By the Chart on page 150, read the prophecies where they belong in the history.

Analysis of 1 Kings xii.-2 Kings xviii. 12 and 2 Chron. x.-xxviii.

REHOBOAM AND JEROBOAM (1 Kings xii. 1-19; 2 Chron. x.)

King.	Date	Years.	Kingdom.	Character.	Record.
Rehoboam,	975	17	South	Bad	1 Kg. xii. 20-24; xiv. 21-31; 2 Chr. xi.-xii.
Jeroboam,	975	22	North	Bad	1 Kg. xii. 25-xiv. 20.
Abijam, ..	958	3	South	Bad	1 Kg. xv. 1-8; 2 Chron. xiii.-xiv. 1a.
Asa, ..	955	41	South	Good	1 Kg. xv. 9-24; 2 Chr. xiv. 1b.-xvi.
Nadab, ..	954	2	North	Bad	1 Kg. xv. 25-31.
Baasha, ..	953	24	North	Bad	1 Kg. xv. 32-xvi. 7.
Elah, ..	930	2	North	Bad	1 Kg. xvi. 8-10a.
Zimri, ..	929	7 days	North	Bad	1 Kg. xvi. 10b-20.
Omri, ..	929	12	North	Bad	1 Kg. xvi. 21-28.
Ahab, ..	918	22	North	Bad	1 Kg. xvi. 29-xxii. 40.

MINISTRY OF ELIJAH (1 Kings xvii-2 Kings ii.).

Jehoshaphat,	914	25	South	Good	1 Kg. xxii. 2-33, 41-50. 2 Chron. xvii.-xxi. 3.
Ahaziah, ..	897	2	North	Bad	1 Kg. xxii. 51-2 Kg. ii. 25.

MINISTRY OF ELISHA (2 Kings ii.-xiii.).

Joram, ..	896	12	North	Bad	2 Kg. iii.-viii. 15.
Jehoram, ..	889	8	South	Bad	2 Kg. viii. 16-24. 2 Chron. xxi. 4-20.
Ahaziah, ..	885	1	South	Bad	2 Kg. viii. 25-29; 2 Chron. xxii. 1-9.
Jehu ..	884	28	North	Bad	2 Kg. ix.-x. 36.
Athaliah, ..	884	6	South	Bad	2 Kg. xi.; 2 Chron. xxii. 10-xxiii.
Jehoash, ..	878	40	South	Good	2 Kg. xii.; 2 Chr. xxiv.

MINISTRY OF JOEL
(2 Kings xii.-xvii 7; 2 Chron. xxiv.-xxvi.).

King.	Date	Years.	Kingdom.	Character.	Record.
Jehoahaz, ..	856	17	North	Bad	2 Kg. xiii. 1-9.
Joash ..	839	16	North	Bad	2 Kg. xiii. 10-25.

MINISTRY OF JONAH (2 Kings xiii., xiv.).

Amaziah, ..	839	29	South	Good	2 Kg. xiv. 1-20; 2 Chron. xxv.
Jeroboam II.,	825	41	North	Bad	2 Kg. xiv. 23-29.

INTERREGNUM OF 11-12 YEARS.

MINISTRY OF AMOS (2 Kings xiv. 21-xv. 7).

Azariah, ..	810	52	South	Good	2 Kg. xiv. 21, 22; xv. 1-7; 2 Chron. xxvi.
Zachariah,	773	1/2	North	Bad	2 Kg. xv. 8-12.
Shallum, ..	772	1/12	North	Bad	2 Kg. xv. 13-16.
Menahem,	772	10	North	Bad	2 Kg. xv. 17-22.

MINISTRY OF HOSEA (2 Kings xiv. 23-xvii.).

Pekehiah, ..	761	2	North	Bad	2 Kg. xv. 23-26.
Pekah, ..	759	20	North	Bad	2 Kg. xv. 27-31.
Jotham, ..	758	16	South	Good	2 Kg. xv. 32-38; 2 Chron. xxvii.

MINISTRY OF ISAIAH.
(2 Kings xv.-xx.; 2 Chron. xxvi.-xxxii.).

Ahaz, ..	742	16	South	Bad	2 Kg. xvi.; 2 Chron. xxviii.; Isa. vii-xii

INTERREGNUM OF ABOUT 9 YEARS.

Hoshea, ..	730	9	North	Bad	2 Kings xvii.

MINISTRY OF MICAH
(2 Kings xv. 32-xx.; 2 Chron. xxvii.-xxxii.).

2 KINGS xviii.-xxv.

Keyword—DOWNFALL   CHAPTERS: 8.

DATE : 722-586 B.C.   135 Years.

PARALLEL HISTORY : 2 Chronicles xxix. 1-xxxvi. 21.

THIS important period of the Monarchy's history falls into two unequal parts. First, from Judah's first reformation, under Hezekiah, to the close of Amon's reign ; 722-640 B.C., eighty-one years : and second, from Judah's final reformation, under Josiah, to the overthrow of the kingdom and end of the Monarchy ; 640-586 B.C., fifty-four years. That is to say, after the people of Israel had been removed to Assyria, the kingdom of Judah continued for one hundred and thirty-five years, during which time two great efforts were made to turn the people from idolatry. These efforts seemed for a while to be successful, but repentance was not deep, and so, in spite of the ministry of the prophets, the kingdom ran on to its doom.

Hezekiah, who reigned for twenty-nine years, is more unreservedly commended than any other king of Judah, and the history and literature of his reign occupy 77 chapters of the Bible. It was his lot to be placed between a wicked father and a

wicked son. The three great events of his reign
were : Judah's deliverance from the Assyrian
invasion, his own sickness and recovery, and the
religious reformation which he led.

His son, Manasseh, and grandson, Amon, were
both bad ; the former reigned longer than any other
king. Fifty-seven years after Hezekiah's death
his great-grandson, Josiah, made another and final
effort to bring the nation back to God, but in vain.
The outstanding event in his reign was the discovery in the Temple of the Book of the Law, and
the transient revival in this reign was the result
of that discovery.

Isaiah was the great prophet in Hezekiah's time,
and Jeremiah, the great prophet from Josiah's time.
Other prophets of the Single Kingdom period were
Micah, Nahum, Zephaniah, and Habakkuk.

The great foreign figures of this period were
Shalmaneser, Sennacherib, Merodach-Baladan,
Esarhaddon, Pharaoh-Necho, and Nebuchad-
nezzar, records of whom are to be found in the
British Museum.

The outstanding battle was at Carchemish in
605 B.C., in which the Babylonians conquered the
Egyptians.

The Monarchy and the Dependency periods
overlap for twenty years (606-586 B.C.), that is to

say, though the last three kings were Jews, they had their throne by the will of foreign Powers, first Egypt, and then Babylon. And it is important to see that in this score of years three prophesied events commenced: the SERVITUDE, 70 years, 606-536 B.C. (Jer. xxix. 10); the EXILE, 50 years, 586-536 B.C. ; and the DESOLATION, 70 years, 586-516 B.C. (Jer. xxv. 1-11). Twenty years of what is commonly regarded as the captivity, were, in fact, not in the period of the exile, but of the servitude.

It was when Nebuchadnezzar first attacked Jerusalem, in the reign of Jehoiakim, 606 B.C., that Daniel and the other three Hebrews were removed to Babylon; and when he made the second attack, in the reign of Jehoaichin (598 B.C.), Ezekiel and Mordecai were taken.

NOTE 18

The Monarchy and the Dependency.

THE overlapping of the Monarchy and the Dependency, or the beginning of the period of the Jewish Church, is made clear in the analysis on page 46. The Monarchy, strictly speaking, did not end until Zedekiah fell, yet, twenty years before, the kings of Judah lost their independence, and occupied the throne only by the will of their foreign master. What Judah lost in 605 B.C. has never been recovered. The twenty years B.C. 606-586 was a transition period; independent monarchy lay behind, and the Jewish Church lay before.

Analysis of 2 Kings xviii-xxv.

Kings.	Date.	Years.	Kingdom	Character.	Record
Hezekiah, ...	727	29	South	Good	2 Kings xviii.-xx ; 2 Chron. xxix.-xxxii.; Isaiah xxxvi.-xxxix.
Manasseh, ...	698	55	South	Bad	2 Kings. xxi. 1-18 ; 2 Chron. xxxiii. 1-20.

MINISTRY OF NAHUM
(2 Kings xxi.-xxiv. 7; 2 Chron. xxxiii.-xxxvi. 8.)

| Amon, ... | 643 | 2 | South | Bad | 2 Kgs. xxi. 19-26. 2 Chron. xxxiii. 21-25 |
| Josiah, ... | 641 | 31 | South | Good | 2 Kgs. xxii.-xxiii. 30; 2 Chron. xxxiv. xxxv. |

MINISTRY OF ZEPHANIAH.
(2 Kings xxii.-xxiv. 7; 2 Chron. xxxiv.-xxxvi. 8.)

MINISTRY OF JEREMIAH.
(2 Kings xxii.-xxv. ; 2 Chron. xxxiv.-xxxvi. 21.)

| Jehoahaz, ... | 609 | ¼ | South | Bad | 2 Kgs. xxiii. 31-34. 2 Chron. xxxvi. 1-4. |
| Jehoiakim, ... | 609 | 11 | South | Bad | 2 Kgs.xxiii. 35-xxiv.7. 2 Chron. xxxvi. 5-8. |

MINISTRY OF HABAKKUK.
(2 Kings xxiii. 31-xxiv. 16 ; 2 Chron. xxxvi. 1-10.)

MINISTRY OF DANIEL.
(2 Kings xxiii. 35-xxv. 30 ; 2 Chron. xxxvi. 5-23.)

| Jehoiachin, ... | 598 | ¼ | South | Bad | 2 Kings xxiv. 8-16. 2 Chron. xxxvi. 9, 10. |
| Zedekiah, ... | 597 | 11 | South | Bad | 2 Kgs.xxiv. 17-xxv.21 2 Chron. xxxvi. 11-21 Jeremiah lii. 1-30. |

MINISTRY OF EZEKIEL.
(2 Kings xxiv. 17-xxv. 30 ; 2 Chron. xxxvi. 11, 572 B.C.)

MINISTRY OF OBADIAH (586 B.C.).
The Lamentations over the Ruins of Jerusalem.
2 Kings xxv. 22-26 ; 2 Chron. xxxvi. 17-21.
Governorship of Gedaliah. 2 Kings xxv. 22-26.
Restoration of Jehoiachin. 2 Kings xxv. 27-30 ; Jer. lii. 31-34.

B.C.	KINGS OF JUDAH.	CONTEMPORARY KINGS.		
		EGYPT.	ASSYRIA.	BABYLONIA.
722	Hezekiah, 6th year		Sargon, 722-705	Merodach-Baladan, 722-710
714	Hezekiah's illness, 14th year		Sennacherib, 705-681	
701	Hezekiah attacked by Sennacherib, 27th year. 2 Kings xviii. 13-xix. 36.	Tirhakah, 701-667		
698	Manasseh. 2 Kings xxi. 1		Esarhaddon, 681-668	Esarhaddon, 681-668
		Psamatik I, 650-610		
643	Amon. 2 Kings xxi. 19			
641	Josiah. 2 Kings xxii.1			Nabopolassar, 626-605
623	Josiah's Great Passover. 2 Kings xxiii. 23			
609	Battle of Megiddo. 2 Kings xxiii. 29 Jehoahaz, 3 months Jehoiakim. 2 Kings xxiii. 36	Necho. 610-595		
			Assyrian Empire ends, B.C. 606	
				Nebuchadnezzar, 605-562
598	Jehoiachin, 3 months 2 Kings xxiv. 8			
597	Zedekiah. 2 Kings xxiv. 18			
		Psamatik II, 595-590 Hophra, 590-565		
586	End of the Hebrew Monarchy			
				Evil-Merodach, 562-560

1-2 CHRONICLES

Keyword—WORSHIP.   CHAPTERS : 65.

UNLESS the viewpoint of these two Books is understood, there can be no true appreciation of them. Like the Books of SAMUEL and KINGS, they were originally one Book, and they appear at the end of the Hebrew Bible, in the third division which is known as the PSALMS. The Hebrew title is WORDS OF DAYS, that is, Journals ; the Septuagint title is OMISSIONS, because they were regarded as supplementing what had already been written ; and the present title, CHRONICLES, dates from the time of Jerome (4th cent. A.D.), and this last is, perhaps, the best description of these records.

That these Writings are a compilation must be evident to the most superficial reader ; nor are we left in ignorance of the sources, for no fewer than twelve are named in the text. (See 1 Chron. ix. 1 ; xxix. 29 ; 2 Chron. ix. 29 ; xii. 15 ; xx. 34 ; xxiv. 27 ; xxvi. 22 ; xxxii. 32 ; xxxiii. 19.)

This fact does not permit of our thinking of an author, but only of a compiler of the CHRONICLES. The material was collected and selected with a specific end in view, and it appears to have been done with great care. Not without good reason the compiler of these records is supposed to be Ezra (cf. 2 Chron. xxxvi. 22, 23, with Ezra i. 1, 2). The scope of the record is noteworthy. It begins with Adam (1 Chron. i. 1) and ends with the Decree of Cyrus in 536 B.C.; that is, it embraces the whole sweep of Bible history in an epitomized form, and represents a period of not less than 3500 years. This fact alone gives uniqueness to the CHRONICLES, and invests them with peculiar interest. Considering, then, the title, the form, the compiler, and the scope of these Books, we must enquire as to their object. This can be determined only by a careful comparison of them with the other historical Books representing the same period. By such a comparison with the Books of SAMUEL and KINGS, we observe that in the CHRONICLES there are (a) identical passages, (b) omissions, and (c) additions ; and when we look for an explanation of these, we find it in the essentially Levitical character of the Writings. Parallels, omissions, and additions are all in pursuance of a design, and that is to show the theocratic character of the nation's calling, to show that only as God is reverenced and obeyed can the nation prosper and fulfil her high destiny.

For this reason, after the genealogies, which give the sacred line through which the Messianic promise was transmitted for over three and a half millenniums, the annals of Judah only are given, from the time of the Disruption, because Judah was the royal tribe, of which the Christ was to come. The history of the Northern Kingdom is omitted by the chronicler.

Then, again, all that pertains to worship is here emphasised ; the Temple and its services, priests, Levites, singers, and the hatefulness of idolatry. It is shown that the troubles of the nation were due to their disregard of the claims of Jehovah, and their prosperity was due to their return to Him. The KINGS are political and royal, but the CHRON-ICLES are sacred and ecclesiastical.

There are some numerical inconsistences in these records, due, no doubt, to the imperfect state of some of the Hebrew manuscripts, but the alleged many contradictions and errors cannot be proved.

Although we show the parallel passages in KINGS and CHRONICLES in the 2 KINGS Analysis, we here present an analysis of each of the latter records.

Analysis of 1 Chronicles

I. GENEALOGICAL TABLES (i.-ix).

1. The Primeval Period, ... i. 1-23.
Adam to Abraham.

2. The Patriarchal Period, ... i. 24-ii. 2.
Abraham to Jacob.

3. The National Period, ... ii. 3-ix. 44.
Posterity of Jacob's Sons.

II. KINGS OF ISRAEL (x.-xxix.).

1. The End of Saul's Reign (x.).

2. The Whole of David's Reign (xi.-xxix. 30).

    (i.) PROMINENT EVENTS, ... xi.-xxii.
        (a) His Followers (xi.-xii.).
        (b) His Enterprises (xiii.-xvii.).
        (c) His Conflicts (xviii.-xx.).
        (d) His Failure (xxi.).
        (e) His Charges (xxii.).

    (ii.) DIVISIONS OF THE PEOPLE .... xxiii.-xxvii.
        (a) Levites (xxiii.).
        (b) Priests (xxiv.).
        (c) Singers (xxv.).
        (d) Porters (xxvi.).
        (e) Soldiers (xxvii. 1-24).
        (f) Stewards (xxvii. 25-31).
        (g) Counsellors (xxvii. 32-34).

    (iii.) FINAL HAPPENINGS, ... xxviii.-xxix.
        (a) David's Charges (xxviii. 1-xxix. 5).
            (1) To the Officers (xxviii. 1-8).
            (2) To Solomon (xxviii. 9-21).
            (3) To the People (xxix. 1-5).
        (b) The Worship of Giving (xxix. 6-25).
        (c) The End (xxix. 26-30).

3. The Beginning of Solomon's Reign (Ch. xxix. 22b-25)

Analysis of 2 Chronicles

I. THE REIGN OF SOLOMON (i.-ix.).

1. **The Beginning** (i. 1-13).
   - (i.) His Act of Worship, ... 1-6.
   - (ii.) His Choice of Wisdom, ... 7-13.

2. **The Progress** (i. 14-ix. 12).
   - (i.) The Riches of Solomon, ... i. 14-17.
   - (ii.) The Treaty with Hiram, ... ii. 1-18.
   - (iii.) The Temple and its Furniture, ... iii. 1-v. 1.
   - (iv.) The Dedication of the Temple, ... v. 2-vi. 11.
   - (v.) The Prayer of Solomon, ... vi. 12-42.
   - (vi.) The Fire of Acceptance, ... vii. 1-3.
   - (vii.) The Offerings and the Feast, ... vii. 4-10.
   - (viii.) Divine Promises and Warnings, ... vii. 11-22.
   - (ix.) Various Acts of Solomon, ... viii. 1-18.
   - (x.) The Queen of Sheba, ... ix. 1-12.

3. **The End** (ix. 13-31).
   - (i.) His Wealth and Power, ... 13-28.
   - (ii.) His Death and Burial, ... 29-31.

II. THE KINGS OF JUDAH (x.-xxxvi. 21).

Name.	Reference.	Parallel.
1. REHOBOAM,	x.-xii.	1 Kings xii. 1-24; xiv. 21-31
2. ABIJAH, ...	xiii.	1 Kings xv. 1-8.
3. ASA, ...	xiv.-xvi. ...	1 Kings xv. 9-24.
4. JEHOSHAPHAT,	xvii. 1-xxi. 3. ...	1 Kings xxii. 2-30.
5. JEHORAM, ...	xxi. 4-20. ...	2 Kings viii. 16-24.
6. AHAZIAH, ...	xxii. 1-9. ...	2 Kings viii. 25-ix. 29.
7. ATHALIAH, ...	xxii. 10-xxiii. ...	2 Kings xi.
8. JEHOASH, ...	xxiv.	2 Kings xii.
9. AMAZIAH, ...	xxv.	2 Kings xiv. 1-20.

Name.	Reference.	Parallel.
10. UZZIAH, ...	xxvi. ...	... 2 Kings xv. 1-7.
11. JOTHAM, ...	xxvii. ...	... 2 Kings xv. 32-38.
12. AHAZ, ..	xxviii. ..	.. 2 Kings xvi.; Isa. vii.-xii.
13. HEZEKIAH, ..	xxix-xxxii.	.. 2 Kings xviii.-xx; Isa. xxxvi.-xxxix.
14. MANASSEH, ...	xxxiii. 1-20.	... 2 Kings xxi. 1-18.
15. AMON, ...	xxxiii. 21-25,	... 2 Kings xxi. 19-26.
16. JOSIAH, ...	xxxiv.-xxxv.	... 2 Kings xxii.-xxiii. 30.
17. JEHOAHAZ, ...	xxxvi. 1-4,	... 2 Kings xxiii. 31-34.
18. JEHOIAKIM, ...	xxxvi. 5-8,	... 2 Kings xxiii. 35-xxiv. 7.
19. JEHOIACHIN,	xxxvi. 9-10,	... 2 Kings xxiv. 8-16.
20. ZEDEKIAH, ...	xxxvi. 11-21,	... 2 Kings xxiv. 17-xxv. 21.

The Decree of Cyrus, xxxvi. 22-23,   Ezra i. 1-4.

NOTE 20
The Books of Chronicles.

IN the Hebrew manuscripts the two Books of Chronicles were one, and remained so even to the time of Jerome (340-420 A.D.).

The date of these Writings cannot be determined exactly, but internal evidence leads to the conclusion that the compilation must be placed between a limit some several years subsequent to the Return and the year B.C. 410, or thereabout.

It cannot be said definitely who the author was of the Chronicles, but the style of diction exhibits many points of similarity with that of Ezra, Nehemiah, and Esther, and there is not a little to favour the view that the compiler was Ezra the Scribe.

There are many references in the Writings to the sources which were employed by the compiler. The following passages should be examined: 1 Chron. ix. 1; xxvii. 24; xxix. 29; 2 Chron. ix. 29; xii. 15; xiii. 22; xvi. 11; xx. 34; xxiv. 27; xxv. 26; xxvi. 22; xxvii. 7; xxviii. 26; xxxii. 32; xxxiii. 19; xxxv. 27; xxxvi. 8.

Passages in Chronicles but not in Samuel or Kings: 1 Chron., chaps. xii; xxii; xxiii-xxvi; xxvii; xxviii; xxix. 2 Chron. xi. 5-23; xiii. 2-23; xiv. 8-14; xv. 1-15; xvi. 7-10; xvii.; xix.; xx. 1-30; xxi. 2-4, 11-19; xxiv. 15-22; xxv. 5-10, 14-16; xxvi. 6-16; xxvii. 5, 6; xxx. 1-27; xxxi. 2-21; xxxiii. 11-13.

Passages found in Samuel or Kings but not in Chronicles: 2 Sam. i.-iv.; vi. 20-23; ix.; xi. 2-xii. 25; xiii.-xx.; xxi. 1-14, 15-17; xxii.; xxiii.; 1 Kings i.; ii. 1-9, 26-46; iii. 1, 16-28; iv.; vii. 1-12, 13-39; viii. 56-61; xi. 1-13, 14-40; 2 Kings xii. 17, 18; xvi. 5-18; xviii. 4-8.

EZRA

Keyword—RECONSTRUCTION.   CHAPTERS : 10.

DATE : 536-458.   78 Years.

THE closing verses of 2 CHRONICLES are also the opening verses of this Book, and there are other evidences of the same compiler. The period represented is from the close of the captivity to the reformation under Ezra in 458 B.C.

Ezra appears as the writer of chapter ix., and, in all likelihood was the compiler of the whole Book, though in parts of it he is spoken of in the third person.

It is important to observe that this Writing is a compilation, and not a single narrative, and it is interesting to see what are its component parts. Of its 880 verses, 109 are narrative, 111 are registers, 44 are letters, 3 are a proclamation, 3 are an excerpt, and 10 are a prayer. Furthermore, it should be noted that chaps. iv. 8-vi. 18 ; vii. 12-26, are in Aramaic.

The Books of CHRONICLES, EZRA, ESTHER, and NEHEMIAH are ecclesiastical history, concerned almost exclusively with the institutional religion of Judah, and, although there may have been later additions to this history, it may well have been given its present form by Ezra, who was an instructor in the Law of God.

The Babylonian Empire was succeeded by the Medo-Persian Empire in 536 B.C., whereupon Cyrus offered the Jews their liberty (i. 2-4), and the number of those who availed themselves of the privilege under the leadership of Zerubbabel and Jeshua is recorded in ch. ii. of this Book. In keeping with the religious purpose of this history, we are told that the first thing they did was to build the altar of Burnt Offering, and then the Temple (iii.). The work was hindered by opposition (iv.), but in consequence of the inspirational ministries of Haggai and Zechariah the Lord's House was completed in 516 E.C., twenty years after the return from Babylon (vi. 15). With this chapter (vi.) ends the first division of the Book, and between it and the next chapter (vii.) is a period of 58 years, 516-458 B.C., to which belongs the story of ESTHER. Also in this period occurred the battles of Marathon, Thermopylae, and Salamis ; and the deaths of Confucius and Buddha.

In the second division of the Book (chs. vii.-x.) is the personal history of Ezra's journey to Jerusalem, with commission from Artaxerxes Longimanus in 458 B.C., and his exertions for the reformation of the people.

During the period covered by chapter iv. of EZRA belong chapters x.-xii., of Daniel. The things to be specially noted in this record are: the Decree of Cyrus (i. 2-4); the erection of the altar and foundation of the Temple (iii.); Haggai and Zechariah (v. 1); the letter of Darius (vi. 6-12); Ezra's prayer (ix. 6-15); the Gentile kings, Cyrus (i.), Darius I (vi.), and Artaxerxes (vii.).

NOTE 21
Divine Providences.

AMONG the remarkable dispensations of Providence recorded in this history, we may notice especially how wonderfully God inclined the hearts of several heathen princes—Cyrus, Darius, and Artaxerxes—to favour and protect His people, and to aid them in the work of rebuilding their city and temple (chaps. i., iv., vi., vii.). We see, too, how God overruled the opposition of the Samaritans, the decree of Darius being much more favourable than that of Cyrus (Ezra i. and v. 6).

"There is also another display of God's special and discriminating providence in the fulfilment of His promises to His people. Whilst in the land of *Samaria* colonies of strangers had been planted which filled the territory of Israel with a heathen race, so as to prevent the return of the ancient inhabitants; it appears that in the land of *Judah* full room was left for the return and restoration of the Jews."

(See *Bible Handbook*, ANGUS and GREEN.)

Analysis of Ezra

I. THE RETURN FROM CAPTIVITY, UNDER ZERUBBABEL.

Chapters i.-vi. 20 Years.

1. Emancipation of the Jews (i.-ii.).

    (i.) RESTORATION. The Decree of Cyrus,   **i.**

    (ii.) REGISTRATION. The Return of the Captives, ...   **ii.**

2. Inception of the Work (iii.-iv.).

    (i.) RECONSTRUCTION. The Sacrifices Renewed and the Temple Foundation Laid,..   **iii.**

    (ii.). OPPOSITION. The Samaritans Resist, and the Work of Building Stopped,   ..   **iv.**

3. Dedication of the Temple (v.-vi.).

    (i.) INVESTIGATION. The Inquiry of Tatnai and the Decree of Darius,   ..   **v.**

    (ii.) CONSUMMATION. The Completion of the Temple and Observance of the Passover, ...   **vi.**

        ("Haggai," and "Zechariah" i.-viii. here.)

(Between Chapters vi. and vii., 58 years. Book of Esther).

II. THE RETURN FROM CAPTIVITY, UNDER EZRA.

Chapters vii.-x. 1 Year.

1. The Proclamation of Artaxerxes, ...   **vii.**
2. The Liberation of the Jews, ...   **viii.**
3. The Intercession of Ezra, ...   **ix.**
4. The Reformation of the People, ...   **x.**

ESTHER

Keyword—PROVIDENCE.   CHAPTERS : 10.

DATE : 484-465 B.C.   20 Years.

WHEN this story was written, and by whom, are unknown. Its place is between chapters six and seven of the Book of Ezra, and it represents a period of about twenty years (484-465 B.C.).

Without justification, it has been spoken of as "full of improbabilities or impossibilities," and as being "the most unchristian of Old Testament books." It and RUTH are the only books in the Bible which bear the name of a woman.

The narrative owes much, it would seem, to Persian records. Evidence of this may be seen in details, such as the names of Haman's sons, in Esther being called "the queen," and Mordecai, "the Jew," and in the particulars which are given about Ahasuerus. There are references to Persian etiquette ; many Persian customs and phrases are explained, and the Persian king is referred to over one hundred and eighty times.

It is said that the name of God does not occur in the story, a statement which both is and is not true. God is here in mystery, though not in manifestation.

The objection to the Book, that the Divine name does not occur in it, itself gives us the key to it. God's actions are manifest, but He Himself is veiled. Further, it has been shown that the incommunicable Name, or Tetragrammaton, Y.H.V.H., which stand in the Hebrew for Yahweh (Jehovah), occurs in this narrative four times in acrostic form, and at the critical points in the story (i. 20 ; v. 4, 13 ; vii. 7), a fact which cannot possibly be of chance, but of Divine design, and which demonstrates, as hardly anything else could, the outstanding truth of Divine providence.

Comparatively speaking, not many of the captive Jews returned under the Edict of Cyrus, not more than 50,000, and, perhaps, 600 when Ezra returned about seventy years later. Most of the captives were born in Babylonia, and the conditions of life and business for them there were such as to disincline them to cross the desert and begin all over again in the land of their fathers. Had they all gone back under Zerubbabel, the Book of Esther could not have been written. Several things in the story should be specially noted. (1) Ahasuerus is the Xerxes of classic fame (484-464 B.C.), who attacked the Greeks by land, and lost at Ther-

mopylae; and by sea, and lost in the battle of
Salamis. It was on his return from these defeats
that he married Esther. (2) The institution of the
Feast of Purim (ix. 26). (3) The characters of the
cousins Mordecai and Esther, and of Haman.
(4) The lessons of providence and retribution.

NOTE 22
God in the Book of Esther.

THE claim that God's name is hidden in *acrostic form* four
times in *Esther* is a fact of profound importance. Two
of the occasions form the name by *initial* and two by *final*
letters. In two cases the name is spelt *backwards*, and in two
forwards. This cannot be of chance, and the difficulty of
constructing such forms will be apparent to anyone who
attempts it. Dr. A. T. Pierson has illustrated the occurrences
of the Divine title LORD in the following four couplets:

> Due Respect Our Ladies, all
> Shall give their husbands, great and small (i. 20).

> Let Our Royal Dinner bring
> Haman, feasting with a king (v. 4).

> GranD foR nO avaiL my state,
> While this Jew sits at the gate (v. 13).

> IlL tO feaR decreeD I find,
> Toward me in the monarch's mind (vii. 7)

Well might James Russell Lowell write:
"Careless seems the great avenger : History's pages but record
One death grapple in the darkness, 'twixt old systems and the
Word.
Truth for ever on the scaffold; wrong for ever on the throne!
But that scaffold sways the future; and behind the dim
unknown
Standeth God, within the shadow, keeping watch above His
own."

Analysis of Esther

I. THE GRAVE DANGER TO THE JEWS.

Chapters i.-iv.

1. The Deposition of Vashti, ...   i.
2. The Exaltation of Esther, ...   ii. 1-20.
3. The Plot against Xerxes, ...   ii. 21-23.
4. The Malice of Haman, ...   iii.
5. The Appeal of Mordecai, ...   iv.

II. THE GREAT DELIVERANCE OF THE JEWS.

Chapters v.-x.

1. The Venture of Esther, ...   v. 1-8.
2. The Design of Haman, ...   v. 9-14.
3. The Recognition of Mordecai, ...   vi. 1-12a.
4. The Downfall of Haman, ...   vi. 12b-vii. 10.
5. The Avengement of the Jews, ...   viii.-ix. 16.
6. The Feast of Purim, ...   ix. 17-32.
7. The Greatness of Mordecai, ...   x.

NEHEMIAH

Keyword—REFORMATION.   CHAPTERS : **13**.

DATE : 445-420.   **25 Years.**

IN NEHEMIAH, as in EZRA, there are parts which
are written in the first person, and, no doubt,
Nehemiah himself was the author of these, though
there is evidence of much later addition (*e.g.*,
Jaddua, xii. 11, 22, 351-331 B.C.). With this Book
Old Testament history ends.

Zerubbabel went to Jerusalem in 536 B.C., and
effected religious reforms. Eighty years later, in
458 B.C., Ezra went to Jerusalem and effected
ethical reforms. Twelve years later, in 445 B.C.,
Nehemiah went to Jerusalem and effected civil
reforms. From Zerubbabel's return to Nehemiah's
was about ninety years. Of the twelve years
between Ezra's and Nehemiah's returns, Prof.
Sayce says : "Megabyzos the satrap of Syria, had
successfully defied the Persian king, and forced
him to agree to his own terms of peace, thus giving
the first open sign of the internal decay of the
Empire. It is possible that the disaffection of the
satrap may account for the silence in Scripture as

to the events which followed Ezra's reform. Deprived of the royal support, he would no longer be able to maintain himself as governor in face of the opposition he was certainly to experience from the Samaritans. It would also account for the condition in which we find the Jews when the Book of Nehemiah opens. The walls of the city are still unbuilt, Ezra has ceased to be governor, the people are in great affliction and reproach, the Arabs are encamping close to Jerusalem, Sanballat and his allies are all-powerful, and priests and laity alike have gone back to their heathen and foreign wives."

The story in NEHEMIAH is full of rapid movement and vigorous energy. Action and unction everywhere characterise it, because there move to and fro two men on whom in a wonderful degree rested the Spirit of God. The narrative opens in the twentieth year of the reign of Artaxerxes Longimanus, and ends in the reign of Darius II.

In this Book we have excellent autobiography. Nehemiah is a great character, courageous, resolute, and energetic ; an untiring worker, and a model organizer. Dr. A. T. Pierson has analysed his method under five points—division of labour, adaptation of work and worker, honesty and economy in administration, co-operation in labour, and concentration at any assaulted point. Nehe-

miah's personal diary in chs. i.-vii., should be
frequently read.

Outstanding passages are those which record
Nehemiah's conflict with his enemies; his great
lead as a governor (v.) the reading of the Law
(viii.); the prayer of the Levites (ix.), and the
correction of abuses (xiii.). In this enterprise
Malachi was to Nehemiah what Haggai and
Zechariah had been to Ezra.

NOTE 23

A Thousand Years of History.

WITH *Nehemiah* end the historical books of the Old
Testament. These began with *Joshua*, but it should be
remembered that large portions of the Pentateuch and parts
of the later Prophets are historical, while in the more strictly
Prophetical group of Books there are historical portions; and
in the Historical group there are prophetical portions. The
divisions, therefore, of these Books into historical and prophetical is general and for convenience.

The period covered by this history is about 1020 years
(B.C. 1451-432). During this period great changes took place
in Israel—the conquest of Canaan; the rule of the Judges for
more than four centuries; the introduction of monarchic
government; the United Kingdom under Saul, David, and
Solomon; the Divided Kingdom, from Rehoboam to Hoshea,
the Single Kingdom from Hezekiah to Zedekiah; the Captivity in Babylonia, and the Restoration under Zerubbabel,
Ezra, and Nehemiah. It was during this millennium that
the prophets spoke, the psalmists sang, and the sages uttered
their wisdom. During this period great peoples uncon-
sciously played their parts in the providential unfolding of the
redeeming purpose—Phoenicia, Syria, Egypt, Assyria, Babylonia, Media and Persia. And during this period great men
of heathen nations appeared, Hesiod, Lycurgus, Solon, Confucius, Buddha, Herodotus, Thucydides, Pericles, Xenophon,
and Plato.

Analysis of Nehemiah

I. THE REBUILDING OF THE WALL OF JERUSALEM
Chapters i.-vii.

II. THE CONSECRATION OF THE PEOPLE.
Chapters viii.-x.

III. THE CONSOLIDATION OF THE WORK.
Chapters xi.-xiii.

NOTE 24

Reading Summary of Israel's History.

I. AGE OF THE THEOCRACY. Time: B.C. 1635-1095—540 years.

> Reading.—Exodus to 1 Samuel vii. Parts of 1 Chronicles ii. 3-ix.

  1. ISRAEL IN EGYPT. Time: B.C. 1635-1491—144 years. Exodus i. 1-xii. 36.

  2. ISRAEL IN THE WILDERNESS. Time: B.C. 1491-1451—40 years. Exodus xii. 37 to Deuteronomy xxxiv. Psalms xc., xci.

  3. ISRAEL IN THE LAND. Time: B.C. 1451-1095—356 years. Joshua, Judges, Ruth, 1 Samuel i-vii.

II. AGE OF THE MONARCHY. Time: B.C. 1095-606—490 years.

  1. THE UNITED KINGDOM. Time: B.C. 1095-975—120 years.

> Reading.—1 Sam. viii. – 1 Kings xi. 1 Chron. x. – 2 Chron. ix. Solomon's Writings. Psalms.

Saul's Election to the Throne. 1 Sam. viii. - xii.

Saul's Deflection from the Course. 1 Sam. xiii. - xv.

Saul's Rejection by the Lord. 1 Sam. xvi. - xxxi. 1 Chron. x.

David's Testings. 1 Sam. xvi.-xxxi. 1 Chron. i.-x. Psalms viii., xix., xxiii., xxix., cxl., cxli., lix., xiii., xi., lvi., xxv., xxxiv., cxlii., lvii., lii., lviii., xxxv., liv., vii., xvii.

David's Triumphs. 2 Sam. i-x., 1 Chron. xi.-xix., Psalms lxxviii., xvi., ci., xxiv., xv., cx., cxxxviii., xx., xxi., lx., cviii., ix., ii., xviii., lxviii.

David's Troubles. 2 Sam. xi.-xviii. Psalms li., xxxii., vi., xxxviii., xxxix., xli., xl., lxx., v., x., xii., xiv., liii., lxii., lxiv., cxliii., lxiii., xxvii., lv., cix., lxix., xxii., xxxi., lxi., iii., iv.

David's Testimonies. 2 Sam. xix. 1 to 2 Kings ii. 11, 1 Chron. xx. 4-xxix. 30. Psalms xxxvi., xxxvii., cxxxiii., xxvi., xxviii., xxx., cxxxix., cxxxi., lxxxvi., cxlv.

Solomon's Friends and Foes. 1 Kings ii. 12-46. Psa. lxxii.

Solomon's Wisdom and Wealth. 1 Kings iii.-iv., 2 Chron. i. 2-13., Psa. xlv.

Solomon's Temple and Palace. 1 Kings v. 1-ix. 9, 2 Chron. ii.-vii., Psalms cxxxii., cxxvii., cxxviii., l., lxxxi., lxxvii., lxxxii., xlii., xliii., lxxxiv.

Solomon's Glory and Decline. I Kings ix. 10-xi. 43, 2 Chron. i. 14-17, viii., ix., Cant., Prov., Eccles., Psalms lxxxviii., xlix., lxxiii., cxi., cxii.

2. THE DIVIDED KINGDOM. Time: B.C. 975-722—253 Years.

First Antagonism between North and South. I Kings xii.-xvi. 28. 2 Chron. x.-xvii. Psa. lxxxix.

Fateful Alliance between North and South. I Kings xvi. 29 to 2 Kings xiii. 9. 2 Chron. xviii.-xxiv. Psalms xxxiii., lxxxiii., xlvi., xlvii., xlviii.

Final Antagonism between North and South. 2 Kings xiii. 10-xviii. 12. 2 Chron. xxv.-xxxi. Joel. Jonah. Amos. Hosea. Isa. i.-xii. Micah i.-ii. Psalms lxxx.

3. THE SINGLE KINGDOM. Time: B.C. 722-586—135 Years.

Judah's First Reformation and Following Decline. Under Hezekiah. 2 Kings xviii. 13-xx. 2 Chron. xxix.- xxxii. Micah iii.-vii. Isa. xiii.-lxvi. Psalms xlviii. lxv., lxvi., lxvii., lxxv., lxxvi., lxxxiv., lxxxvii., lxxxviii., xcii.-xcv., c., cxx., cxxi., cxxiii., cxxv., cxxvi., cxxix., cxxx., cxxxii., cxxxiv.
Under Manasseh. 2 Kings xxi. 1-18. 2 Chron. xxxiii. 1-20. *Under Amon.* 2 Kings. xxi. 19-26. 2 Chron. xxxiii. 21-25.

Judah's Last Reformation and Final Decline. Under Josiah. 2 Kings xxii.-xxiii. 30. 2 Chron. xxxiv., xxxv. Nahum. Zeph. Jer. i.-vi., xi., xii. *Under Jehoahaz.* 2 Kings xxiii. 31-34. 2 Chron. xxxvi. 1-4. *Under Jehoiakim.* 2 Kings xxiii. 35-xxiv. 7. 2 Chron. xxxvi. 4-8. Habakkuk. Jer. vii.-x., xxvi., xiv.-xx., xxii., xxiii., xxxv., xxxvi., xlv., xxv., xlvi.-xlix. Psa. xliv. Dan. i., ii.-iv., vii., v., viii., ix., vi. *Under Jehoiachin.* 2 Kings xxiv. 8-16. 2 Chron. xxxvi. 9, 10. Jer. xiii. *Under Zedekiah.* 2 Kings xxiv. 17-xxv. 21. 2 Chron. xxxvi. 11-21. Jer. xxiv., xxvii.-xxxiii., xxi., xxxiv., xxxvii.-xxxix., l.-lii. 30, Ezek. i.-xxxii. Lam. Obad. Psa. lxxiv.

THE POETICAL WRITINGS

INTRODUCTION

PSALMS

SONG OF SONGS

LAMENTATIONS

THE POETICAL WRITINGS

Introduction

WE have included only the PSALMS, the SONG
OF SONGS, and LAMENTATIONS in this group,
but very much of what passes for prose in the
Scriptures is in reality poetry. This is true of large
portions of the PROPHETICAL WRITINGS, and parts of
the GOSPELS and of the EPISTLES. Furthermore,
poetry is to be found scattered throughout the
prose of the Old Testament, as for example in
Gen. iv. 23, 24 ; Exod. xv. ; Num. xxi. 14, 15, 17,
18 ; 27-30 ; Judges 5 ; 2 Sam. i. 17-27. Poetic
forms are manifold, and in the Scriptures are many
of these, as, for example, the Ode, the Elegy, the
Lyric, the Idyll, the Epic, and the Drama. JOB
is dramatic, the PSALMS are lyrical, and the SONG
OF SONGS is elegiac.

English poetry depends largely for its effect
upon the recurrence of sound, but Hebrew poetry
cultivates the recurrence of thought. This is the
parallelistic method, and is of many varieties, such
as the synonymous, antithetic, synthetic, intro-
verted, iterative, responsory, alternate, and cli-

macteric, all of which forms are to be found in the Psalter. The acrostic device is also found in Hebrew poetry, in LAMENTATIONS, and some of the Psalms. Poetic form in the Scriptures is important for interpretation, and unless the structure of a passage is discerned, its meaning may easily be missed. Let us remember also that poetry must be read as poetry, and not as history, or as doctrine.

NOTE 25
Poetic Forms.

ODE.—Poem meant to be sung. Song of chorus in Greek play. Israel's National Anthems: Pss. cv., lxxviii., cvi., cxxxvi. Processional Ode: Psa. lxviii. Songs: Pss. xviii., xxix., ciii., civ., cvii., lxxxix.

LYRIC.—Expressive of reflection; the writer's thoughts and sentiments. Pss. xxii., xc., cxxi., viii., lxxxiv., v., xxvi., xvi., lxxiii., xix.

ELEGY.—Song of lamentation. Pss. cxxxvii., lxxiv., lxxx., xliv., lxxix., lxxxviii., cii.

IDYLL.—Description in verse or prose of picturesque scene or incident. The Song of Solomon: See the seven Idylls in the analysis.

EPIC.—Narrative of a poetic story; embodying a nation's conception of its past history. In secular literature the most famous epics are in verse; for example, Homer's *Iliad* and *Odyssey*; but in the Bible there is no *verse* narrative. Examples of prose epic are: Joseph and his Brethren; Moses and the Plagues of Egypt; feud between David's Sons, and Revolt of Absalom; Book of Esther.

DRAMA.—The Bible has no example of drama as acted poetry, but it has literature in dramatic form, and leavened by the dramatic spirit.
Job. Micah vi. 1-8; vi. 9-vii. Hosea xi. 1-11; xiii.-xiv. Jer. x. 17-25.

The importance of the Bible as literature is not apprehended by the Bible-reading public as it should be.

THE PSALMS

THE Psalter is the hymn book of the Hebrews, and a hymn book does not lend itself to formal analysis. Each Psalm may do so, to some extent, but the whole collection allows only of certain classifications, which, however, are of considerable value.

DIVISIONS.

The Psalter is in five parts or books, each of which, except the last, ends with a doxology of a liturgical character. These divisions are : i.-xli.; xlii.-lxxii.; lxxiii.-lxxxix.; xc.-cvi.; cvii.-cl.

AUTHORSHIP.

Of the 150 Psalms, 100 are, by their titles, related to authors. Of these 73 are assigned to David, 10 to the School of Korah, 12 to the School of Asaph, 2 to Solomon, 1 to Ethan, 1 to Heman, 1 to Moses, and 50 are anonymous. The LXX mentions Jeremiah as the author of Psa. cxxxvii., and Haggai and Zechariah as the authors of Psalms cxlvi. and cxlvii.; and it is quite likely that Ezra

wrote Psalm cxix., and that Hezekiah wrote
Psalms cxx.-cxxxiv. (Isa. xxxviii. 20). These
particulars provide a basis for investigation as to
authorship.

DATE.

It is impossible with any precision to fix dates
to most of the Psalms, but it may with confidence
be stated that the great Song period in Israel's
history was the three hundred years from David's
time to the time of Hezekiah. In the Psalter are
Songs which belong to the period before and after
this, but the majority are to be placed within those
limits.

PREFIXES.

All the Psalms have some title except the following thirty-four: i., ii., x., xxxiii., xliii., lxxi.,
xci., xciii.-xcvii., xcix., civ.-cvii., cxi.-cxix., cxxxv.-
cxxxvii., cxlvi.-cl. Of those titled, fourteen bear
the name of David, and claim to be related to
certain events in his varied career (vii., lix., lvi.,
xxxiv., lii., lvii., cxlii., liv., xviii., lx., li., iii.,
lxiii., xxx.). It should be known that though these
prefixes may be helpful, they are not authoritative.

DIVINE TITLES.

Anywhere in the Bible, Divine names or titles

represent Divine qualities, attributes, and attitudes, and their occurrence has both a chronological and a theological value. The following chart shows what Divine names or titles occur in the Psalter, and where.

Book.			I.	II.	III.	IV.	V.
ADON,	..	..	2	1	—	1	5
ADONAI,	..	..	11	18	15	1	7
JAH,	..	..	—	—	2	12	31
JEHOVAH,	..	..	277	31	43	101	226
EL, ..	..	..	15	14	21	9	10
ELOHIM,	..	..	48	188	59	19	28
ELOAH,	..	..	1	1	—	—	2
ELYON,	..	..	3	4	5	4	1
SHADDAI,	..		—	1	1	1	—
PSALMS,	..	..	1-41	42-72	73-89	90-106	107-150

The Hebrews never thought of God in an abstract way ; to them He was a Divine Being, living and active, transcendent and yet immanent. They believed also that God was One, and was from everlasting. On God's Personality, Unity, and Eternity the Bible revelation rests, and this triple truth is in the very substance of the Psalms.

CLASSIFICATIONS.

These Hebrew Songs may be classified in many ways, and such groupings are eminently suggestive and instructive. The following are a few suggested classifications :

Messianic Psalms, ... *i.e.*, 16, 22, 24, 40, 68, 69, 118.

Penitential Psalms,... ,, 6, 32, 38, 51, 102, 130, 143.

Hallelujah Psalms, ... ,, 106, 111, 112, 113, 117, 135, 146-150.

Didactic Psalms, ... ,, 1, 5, 7, 15, 17, 50, 73, 94, 101.

Pilgrim Psalms, ... ,, 120-134.

Prayer Psalms, ... ,, 17, 86, 90, 102, 142.

Royal Psalms, ... ,, 92-100.

Devotional Psalms,... ,, 3, 16, 54, 61, 86, 28, 41, 59, 70, 67, 122, 144.

Morning Psalms, ... ,, 3-5, 19, 57, 63, 108.

Evening Psalms, ... ,, 4, 8, 143.

Meditation Psalms, ,, 16, 56, 60.

Trouble Psalms, ... ,, 4, 5, 11, 28, 41, 55, 59, 64, 109, 120, 140, 143.

Prophetical Psalms, ,, 2, 16, 22, 40, 45, 68, 69, 72, 97, 110, 118.

Historical Psalms, ... ,, 78, 105, 106.

SELECTED STUDIES.

Some, if not all, of the above classifications lend themselves to profoundly instructive development, from which I select one for the purpose of illustration, the Messiah (pages 112, 113).

PROPHETICAL PSALMS.

That there is a prophetic element in the Psalter will not seriously be called into question, for indeed, as Westcott says : "A Divine counsel was wrought out in the course of the life of Israel. We are allowed to see in ' the people of God ' signs of the purpose of God for humanity. The whole history is prophetic. It is not enough to recognise that the Old Testament contains prophecies ; the Old Testament is one vast prophecy."

We may say that the three strands which make the web of Hebrew prophecy relate to the Messiah, Israel, and the Gentiles. All three are found in the Psalter, and it must be evident that they are vitally related to one another. Messiah is the hope of the world, and Israel is the medium of the Divine revelation and mission, "the instrument for accomplishing the world-wide extension of His Kingdom."

The time is predicted when all nations shall acknowledge Christ's sovereignty (xxii. 27 ; lxv. 2, 5 ; lxvi. 4 ; lxviii. 29-33 ; lxxxvi. 9 ; cii. 15, 22 ; cxxxviii. 4). Examine carefully these and kindred passages.

That this consummation is to be reached through Israel does not need to be argued. Whatever may be one's view of the Messianic Kingdom of the future, whether it be regarded as visible, or as only spiritual, no one can question that Israel, through whom Christ came, and from whom we have received the Bible, has been chosen of God for its realisation, and there is abundant evidence in the Scriptures that this race has been preserved by

God for the fulfilment of the Abrahamic covenant (lxviii.; lxxxviii.; cii. 13-16 ; xcvi.-xcviii.). This implies, of course, Israel's own restoration and felicity in the future, of which Psalm cxxvi., beyond any past fulfilment, may be regarded as a prophecy.

But behind and beneath Israelitish and Gentile prophecy is Messianic prophecy, of which the Psalter is full. We have Christ's own warrant for looking for Him in the Psalms, for He said : "All things must be fulfilled which were written in . . . the Psalms concerning Me" (Luke xxiv. 44), and on several occasions He interpreted of Himself passages in the Psalter. Compare, *e.g.*, Psalm cxviii. 22 with Matt. xxi. 42 ; and Psalm cx. 1 with Matt. xxii. 42-45 (*et al.*). Christ's Apostles also make this use of the Psalms, cf. Acts iv. 11 and 1 Peter ii. 7, with Psalm cxviii. 22 ; John ii. 17, with Psalm lxix. 9 ; and Matt. xiii. 35, with Psalm lxxviii. 2 (*et al.*).

The Messianic reference in some of the Psalms must be obvious to all who read, but far more numerous are references which are not so obvious, but which the New Testament warrants us in regarding as Messianic.

These references tell of His Manhood, viii. 4, 5 (Heb. ii. 6-8) ; His Sonship, ii. 7 (Heb. i. 5) :

cx. i. (Matt. xxii. 42-45); His Deity, xlv. 6, 11
(Heb. i. 8); His Holiness, xlv. 7; lxxxix. 18, 19
(Heb. i. 9); His Priesthood, cx. 4 (Heb. v. 6); His
Kingship, ii. 6; lxxxix. 18, 19, 27 (Acts v. 31;
Rev. xix. 16); His Conquests, cx. 5, 6 (Rev. vi.
17); His Eternity, lxi. 6, 7; xlv. 17; lxxii. 17;
cii. 25-27 (Heb. i. 10); His Universal Sovereignty,
lxxii. 8; ciii. 19 (Rev. xix. 16); His Obedience
xl. 6-8 (Heb. x. 5-7); His Zeal, lxix. 9 (John ii.
17); His Sufferings, lxix. 9 (Rev. xv. 3); His
Betrayal, xli. 9 (Luke xxii. 48); His Death,
xxii. 1-21 (Gospels); His Resurrection, ii. 7,
xvi. 10 (Acts xiii. 33-36); His Ascension, lxviii.
18 (Eph. iv. 8); and His Coming again to judge,
xcvi.-xcviii. (2 Thess. i. 7-9). These, and other
such references, may be classified in various ways,
but, in the main, the Messianic prophecies tell of
His Person, God, and Man; of His Character,
Righteous and Holy; of His Work, Death and
Resurrection; and of His Offices, Priest, Judge,
and King. A mine of instruction on this whole
subject will be found in Bishop Alexander's Bamp-
ton Lectures (1876), "The Witness of the Psalms
to Christ and Christianity."

VALUES.

In addition to the above are other values in the
Psalter which it will be most profitable to trace—

literary, imaginative, ethical, prophetical, religious, and devotional values. No part of Holy Scripture has made a more universal appeal than has the Psalter, and it is noteworthy that out of a total of 283 direct citations from the Old Testament in the New, 116 are from the Psalms. Here, as Calvin has said, "The Holy Spirit has represented to the life all the griefs, sorrows, fears, doubts, hopes, cares, anxieties, in short, all the stormy emotions by which human minds are wont to be agitated." Other parts of Divine revelation represent God as speaking to man, but here, man is represented as speaking to God. As a devotional handbook there is nothing like it, or better, in the world.

SUBJECTS.

As a guide to the reading of the Psalms, the following subject-titles may prove helpful :

1. Two Portraits.
2. God's King.
3. God My Help.
4. Before Going to Bed.
5. Talk and Walk.
6. Appeal and Answer.
7. Not Guilty.
8. Man the Viceroy of God.
9. The Righteous and the Wicked.
10. The Perils of the Pilgrim.
11. Why Flee ?
12. God's Words and Man's.
13. From Sighing to Singing.
14. The Natural Man.
15. God's Guests.
16. God-satisfied.
17. At the Throne of Grace.
18. The Hebrew *Te Deum.*
19. God Hath Spoken.
20. Before the Battle.
21. After the Battle.
22. The Sob and the Song.
23. All I Want.
24. Holy Worshippers.
25. The Simple Trust of an Uplifted Soul.
26. The Claim to Integrity.

NOTE 26

The Psalms in the New Testament.

"IT was upon the Psalms that our Lord's spiritual life was nourished. The story of the tempter's quotation of Psalm xci. lay in the fact that its words were a precious reality to Him. He sang the 'Hallel' (Pss. cxiii.-cxviii) with His disciples at the Last Supper (Matt. xxvi. 30). A Psalm was the subject of His meditation as He hung upon the Cross, and with the words of a Psalm He gave up His life. In the Psalms He and His disciples found the foreshadowing of His own experience (John xiii. 18; ii. 17), and He taught His disciples to understand how they prepared the way for His coming (Luke xxiv. 44). The first Christian hymns—the Magnificat, Benedictus, and Nunc Dimittis—are composed after the model of Psalms, and contain numerous echoes of them. Doubtless the hymns which Paul and Silas sang in the prison at Philippi (Acts xvi. 25) were Psalms."

THE SONG OF SONGS

THIS Book has always been ranked among the Canonical Writings of the Old Testament, and the universal voice of antiquity ascribes it to Solomon. In the Hebrew Canon the Song belongs to the third division, the Hagiographa, and is the first of the five Megilloth, or "Rolls," the others being RUTH, LAMENTATIONS, ECCLESIASTES, and ESTHER.

Peculiar difficulties beset the interpretation of the Writing, and we should at least be tolerant of wide differences of opinion. It is never referred to in the other Books of the Old Testament, nor in the Old Testament Apocrypha, nor in the New Testament, nor in Philo, nor in Josephus; and the name of God does not appear in it. I am only stating these facts, and not drawing any inferences from them.

Many interpretations have been assigned to this Biblical Epithalamium, which may be summarised as follows :

1. That it was written to celebrate the marriage of Solomon with Pharaoh's daughter.

2. That it is an account in song of how Solomon

wooed and won a fair maiden from the Lebanon hills, and of their mutual love.

3. That it sets forth the true devotion of a youth and a maiden in humble life, in spite of the attempt made by Solomon to turn the heart of the latter to himself.

4. That it is a collection of several independent poems (Budde distinguishes twenty-three) treating of the subject of love.

5. That it is not historical, but allegorical, depicting (i.) the history of the Jews from Abraham to the Messiah ; (ii.) the deliverance of Israel from Egypt, their wilderness wanderings, and their entrance into Canaan ; (iii.) the union of Jehovah with ancient Israel ; (iv.) the union of Christ and the Church ; and (v.) the love-life of the soul and the Lord.

Difficulties accompany each of these interpretations, and it is not possible for us to say what the design of the author was, but that need not interfere with our discerning a value or values in the Song.

Our view is that here, as in JONAH, we have allegory emerging from history. As to the *history*, we take the view, influentially held, that in the Song there are not two, but three, chief characters, Solomon, Shulamith, and a shepherd lover. The story briefly is this : A beautiful country girl from

Shulam (*i.e.*, Shunem, 5 miles north of Jezreel) was surprised by the king on one of his journeys to the north (vi. 11f), was brought to Jerusalem and placed in the royal palace (i. 4b, 5), where, as the poem opens, the ladies of the harem ("daughters of Jerusalem,") are singing the praises of Solomon. The king himself makes great efforts to win the affection of the Shulamite (i. 9, etc.); but she remains faithful to the memory of her shepherd lover (i. 7, etc.), who at last appears, and is allowed by the magnanimous monarch to return to his mountain home with his bride (viii. 5ff).

The climax of this story in viii. 6, 7, George Saintsbury has called perfect English prose.

As to the *allegory*, what is literal may well point to something spiritual, and the Song has always been read in this way by mystic saints, such as Bernard of Clairvaux, who preached eighty-six sermons on the first two chapters, and McCheyne, and Spurgeon. If we regard the king in the poem as the World, the shepherd-lover as Christ, and the Shulamite as the individual soul, we shall not fail to be helped.

In the face of all the world's allurements we are expected by our Lord, the "Lover of our souls," to be faithful to Him, and one day He will consummate His love for us in glory.

Analysis of the Song of Solomon

A.—LOVE'S FIRST ENTRANCING DAYS.
Chapters i. 2-v. 1.

PART I. The Wedding Day (i. 2-ii. 7).

PART II. The Courtship Days (ii. 8-iii. 5).

PART III. The Betrothal Day (iii. 6-v. 1).

B.—LOVE'S DEEP ABIDING JOYS.
Chapters v. 2-viii. 14.

PART IV. The Troubled Dream (v. 2-vi. 3).

NOTE 27

Interpretation of the Song of Solomon.

IT has been said that "if the Shepherd-hypothesis be true, the presence of the book in the canon is inexplicable. It represents the shame of Solomon. And yet Solomon is either its author or its hero according to the superscription. Elsewhere Solomon is represented as the inspired author of wisdom, and the Prince of Peace. That his shame should be thus depicted without a hint either of his repentance or his punishment is incredible." (Dr. J. H. Raven).

But the same kind of objection could be brought against Ecclesiastes. If his despair is depicted, why should not his shame be? Nuptial purity cannot bear any relation to a man who had "seven hundred wives, and three hundred concubines."

THE LAMENTATIONS

Keyword—DISCONSOLATE.   CHAPTERS : 5.

THIS is an Acrostic Dirge, written by Jeremiah, rhapsodic in character, and of great beauty and pathos.

The occasion of it was the destruction of Jerusalem and its Temple by Nebuchadnezzar in 586 B.C. The Writing is one of the "Rolls" (see on SONG of SONGS).

Its form is well worthy of careful examination. There are here five complete poems, represented by our chapters. In each of the first, second, fourth, and fifth are 22 verses, corresponding to the number of letters in the Hebrew alphabet, and in the third are three times twenty-two. In the first. second, and fourth poems, each verse begins with a letter of the Hebrew alphabet in order (as, *e.g.*, 1, a ; 2, b ; 3, c ; etc.), and in poem three there are three verses to each letter (as, *e.g.*, 1-3, a, a, a ; 4-6, b, b, b, etc.), and in poem five, though there are just the 22 verses, the acrostic is dropped. Further, in the first and second and third poems there are three clauses to each verse, but in the third poem there is an acrostic initial to each clause. The fourth poem has only couplets; and the fifth drops both acrostic structure and dirge rhythm (see Moulton's Modern Reader's Bible). Taken together, these poems enforce the exhortation of Heb. xii. 5, and were designed to teach the Jews neither to "despise the chastening of the Lord," nor to "faint" when "rebuked of Him" (cf. Luke xix. 41, 42).

"Jeremiah's vision of Jerusalem wasted and Babylon exulting should be compared with John's vision of Babylon destroyed and the New Jerusalem revealed in triumph and heavenly beauty (Rev. xviii., xxi., xxii.). Better to be one with Jerusalem in afflictions that issue in glory, than one with Babylon in the pride that ends in shame."

NOTE 28
Lamentations and the Prophecies of Jeremiah.

LAM.	JER.	LAM.	JER.
i. 2	xxx. 14	ii. 20 } ii. 10 {	} xix. 9 {
i. 8b, 9	xiii. 22b, 26		
i. 16a	ix. 1, 18b		
ii. 11a	xiii. 17b	ii. 22	{ vi. 25 { xx. 10
iii. 48, 49	xiv. 17	iii. 14	xx. 7
ii. 11 } iii. 48 iv. 10 {	{ vi. 14 { viii. 11,21	iii. 15	{ ix. 15 { xxiii. 15
		iii. 47	xlviii. 43
ii. 14 } iv. 13 {	{ ii. 8 { v. 31 { xiv. 13 f { xxiii. 11	iii. 52	xvi. 16b
		iv. 21b	{ xxv. 15 { xlix. 12
		v. 16	xiii. 18b

Analysis of the Lamentations

THE WISDOM WRITINGS

INTRODUCTION

JOB

PROVERBS

ECCLESIASTES

Wisdom and the Wise.

PHILOSOPHY, in the narrower sense of the word, "which confines it to human speculations in pursuit of abstract truth, to syste matised thoughts, constructed on a basis of metaphysics and ruled by strict laws of reasoning, is foreign to the Jewish habit of mind, and finds no place in the Scriptures."   (Dr. W. T. DAVISON)

The main field of Biblical Wisdom is ethical, the main stress of its counsel is practical.   "Perhaps the most obvious lesson of the Old Testament lies in the gradual construction of a Divine philosophy by fact, and not by speculation.   The method of Greece was to proceed from life to God; the method of Israel (so to speak) was to proceed from God to life.   The axioms of the one are the conclusions of the other."   (Bishop WESTCOTT)

Passages on Wisdom which should be carefully considered: 1 Kings iv. 29-34.   From Solomon's time the strain of teaching known by the specific name of "Wisdom" takes its rise and derives much of its character.   Psalms i., xxxvii., l., lxxiii., cxii.   Job xxviii.   Proverbs viii. 1 Cor. i. 18-ii. 16.   James iii. 13-18.   The two non-canonical books, *Ecclesiasticus*, written in Aramaic by Jesus, son of Sirach, in the second century before Christ, and the *Wisdom of Solomon*, written in Greek by an unknown author, perhaps as late as the beginning of the Christian era, should be studied.

The orders in Israel of old of prophets, priests, and kings is readily acknowledged, but it is clear that there was another order, that of the *Chakamim*, or wise men; these were Israel's sages or philosophers, and attention to their sayings is commanded.   See Isaiah xxix. 14. Jeremiah xviii. 18.   Proverbs xxii. 17.   Ecclesiastes xii. 11.   Daniel i. 4.

It is likely that 1 Corinthians i. 30 should be read as "Christ Jesus— of God is made unto us wisdom, *even* righteousness, sanctification, and redemption."   By this reading the three terms are an analysis of wisdom, and are not in addition to it.

THE WISDOM WRITINGS

Introduction

FOUR types of mind are recognised in the Bible, which account for four kinds of literature—the priest, the poet, the prophet, and the philosopher (cf. Jer. xviii. 18). It is the last of these we are now to consider, from whom we receive the Wisdom Literature.

"Side by side with prophets defending the theocracy, and singers taking their inspiration from the Temple service, with historians compiling annals of kings, and scribes expounding the Law, there was a class of wise men, who had habits of thought and forms of literature peculiar to themselves" (Prof. R. Moulton). This type has adorned the letters of every great people, as may be seen by reference to Ptahhotep in Egypt, Epictetus in Greece, Marcus Aurelius in Rome, Alexander Pope in England, and Benjamin Franklin in America. We need not be surprised then, to find Wisdom Literature in the Bible. It is found in brief in scattered places in the form of Riddle (Judg. xiv. 14), Fable (Judg. ix. 8. 15), Maxim

(Eccles. iv. 9-12), Epigram (Prov. xxiii. 1-3), Sonnet (Prov. iv. 10-19), Dramatic Monologue (Prov. i. 20-33), and Proverb (Prov. xxii. 1) ; and in elaborated form in JOB and ECCLESIASTES, and in the non-canonical books ECCLESIASTICUS and the WISDOM OF SOLOMON. Nor is this kind of literature confined to the pre-Christian period, for it is represented in the New Testament by parts of the Sermon on the Mount, the Parables, and the Epistle of JAMES. In all likelihood there were of old, schools of wisdom in which the ancients taught their pupils (cf. 1 Sam. xxiv. 13 ; Job xii. 12), and, it would appear, wise men sat for this purpose at the gate of the city (Prov. xxxi. 23). Pre-eminent among the wise was Solomon, who is said to have composed 1005 Songs and 3000 Proverbs (1 Kings iv. 29-34).

Prophet, priest, and philosopher approached the same subject from different angles. Of righteousness, the prophet would say, "It is just" ; the priest would say, "It is commanded" ; but the philosopher would say, "It is prudent". Of sin, the prophet would say, "It is disobedience" ; the priest would say, "It is defilement"; but the philosopher would say, "It is folly". The Wise Men were observers of life, and the Wisdom Books are the product of their analytic observations. To remember this will help us to understand why there is scarcely any reference in these Writings to Israel, or the Temple, or the Messianic Hope (cf. Prov. viii. 22-31).

The simplest form of wisdom in the Bible is in what we call the Book of PROVERBS; and the most elaborate form is in ECCLESIASTES, where reflective analysis is turned upon the sum of things, and in JOB where we have dramatised a philosophical discussion on the Problem of Suffering. JOB may equally well be classed as a poetical Writing, for it contains specimens of all the three main elements of poetry—epic, lyric, and dramatic composition.

NOTE 30

Wisdom and Goodness.

"WISDOM is never in Scripture ascribed to other than God or good men, except in an ironical sense, and with the express addition, or sub-addition of, "of this world" (1 Cor. i. 20), "of this age" (1 Cor. ii. 6), or some such words (2 Cor. i. 12); nor are any of the children of this world called 'wise,' except with this tacit or expressed irony (Luke x. 21); being never more than such as "professing themselves wise, became fools" (Rom. i. 22). For, indeed, if wisdom includes the striving after the best ends as well as the using of the best means, is mental excellence in its highest and fullest sense, there can be no wisdom disjoined from goodness. . . . Wisdom is goodness itself contemplated from one particular point of view." (ARCHBISHOP TRENCH).

JOB

THE author of this Writing is unknown, as are the time of writing and the period in which Job lived. That the hero of the poem was a real person and not the creation of imagination is evident from such references as Ezek. xiv. 14, 20 ; Jas. v. 11 ; as also from internal evidence.

The dramatic form in which the story is cast in no way invalidates its historical trustworthiness.

So little is there in the poem to indicate the age in which Job lived that opinions have varied by as much as one thousand years. Some take the view that he lived before Abraham, and would place the story between the eleventh and twelfth chapter of GENESIS ; and others would place him in the captivity or post-captivity period. This shows that the value of the Writing is quite independent of date, and is indeed, as to its great message, dateless.

The first thing that claims our attention is the form of the story. There are epic and lyric elements in the composition, but the poem is a magnificent drama, in which no element of dramatic effect is

wanting.   The analysis which follows make this
evident.

This book might well be placed with the Poetical
Writings, for, as to its form, it is a poem, but having
regard for its theme, we place it with the Wisdom
Writings, with the PROVERBS and ECCLESIASTES.
These three Books deal with the fundamental
principles of the Bible, and of all religious philosophy.   PROVERBS declares that wisdom, or
"fear of the Lord," is the true blessedness.   To
this proposition there appear to be two exceptions ;
the one is set forth in JOB, and the other in ECCLESI-
ASTES.   In JOB we see a man who "was perfect and
upright ; one that feared God, and eschewed
evil," and yet he suffered great adversity.   In
ECCLESIASTES we see a man, Solomon, who from
being the wisest of men, became the worst, who
did not fear God, and yet prospered.   Solomon's
conclusion was, "All is vanity ;" but Job's conclusion was, "The fear of the Lord, that is wisdom" (Job xxviii. 28 ; cf. Prov. i. 7 ; xv. 33).   The
mistake of Satan was in thinking that Job served
God for what he could get.   The mistake of Job's
wife was in thinking that with the loss of the visible
and human all was lost.   The mistake of Job's
friends was in thinking that Job's suffering was the
direct outcome of his sin.   The mistake of Elihu was

in thinking that he was right, and that all the others were wrong; and the mistake of Job was in thinking that God was unkind. The problem of pain is not solved in this Book, but we are shown what kind of a God God is. We are shown first His power in creation, and man's weakness; and then, His wisdom in government, and man's ignorance. At the end of the mighty Drama, Satan is routed, the friends are rebuked, and Job is rewarded. "The Eternal does not answer our insistent questions; God does not explain, but He does give to the anguished spirit such a sense of the Divine greatness that questioning ceases in the peace of submission."

Then, the Poem has manifold values. There is a philosophic value in its discussion of the under-lying meaning of life as a whole; a scientific value in its observation of nature; a prophetical value in its authoritative Divine message; a biographical value in its delineation of character; a rhetorical value in its many and marvellous speeches; a historical value in its references to places, people, and customs; a literary value in its whole conception and form; a providential value in its view that God allows His people to suffer for their good; a spiritual value in its revelation of another world and super-human beings; and a practical value in its teaching on fearing and trusting God.

The theme of the Drama is "The Mystery of Suffering," or "The Problem of Pain," and in the discussion of this are introduced God, Satan, Job, the friends, and Elihu. The prose Prologue begins with Job and God, and the prose Epilogue ends with them, and between the Prologue and the Epilogue is the Drama, describing the struggle. The Book, it has been said, is a key to the whole Bible, and to man's history from creation to completed redemption. (1) Man unfallen and tried; (2) sinning and suffering; (3) seeking human help in legality, morality, philosophy; (4) needing and receiving a revelation from God; (5) humbled, penitent, believing; and (6) restored to a better estate than at first.

The Poem teaches that suffering is not always penal and retributive, but may be, and sometimes is, disciplinary and educative.

Of Job, Thomas Carlyle has said:

"I call this Book, apart from all theories about it, one of the grandest things ever written with pen. One feels, indeed, as if it were not Hebrew; such a noble universality, different from noble patriotism or sectarianism, reigns in it. A noble Book, all men's Book! It is our first, oldest statement of the never ending problem—man's destiny and God's ways with him here in this earth. And all in such free, flowing outlines; grand in its sincerity, in its simplicity, and its epic melody, and repose of reconcilement. There is the seeing eye, the mildly understanding heart. So true every way; true insight and vision for all things; material things no less than spiritual. . . . Such living likenesses were never since drawn. Sublime sorrow, sublime reconciliation; oldest choral melody as of the heart of mankind; so soft, and great; as the summer midnight, as the world with its seas and stars! There is nothing written, I think, in the Bible or out of it, of equal literary merit."

NOTE 31

The Five Great Problems and their Solution.

THE central part of the Old Testament, comprising the Wisdom and Poetical Books, treats of the five great problems of all ages. Job, the Problem of Suffering. Psalms, the Problem of Prayer. Proverbs, the Problem of Conduct. Ecclesiastes, the Problem of the Chief Good. Song of Solomon, the Problem of Love.

The solution of all these problems is found only in Christ. He suffered, He prayed, He behaved perfectly, He revealed God, and He is Love.

Analysis of Job

THE PROLOGUE (i.-ii. PROSE).

1. Job's Circumstances Before his Trial (i. 1-5).

2. The First Assault (i. 6-22).

3. The Second Assault (ii. 1-10).

4. The Coming and Conduct of Job's Friends (ii. 11-13)

THE DRAMA (iii.-xlii. 6).

1. The Lamentation of Job (iii.).

2. The Discussion of the Friends (iv.-xxxi.).

NOTE 32
The Revelation of Jehovah in Job.

THE REVELATION OF JEHOVAH (xxxviii. 1-xlii. 6) may be detailed as follows :
   (i) *The Divine Power in Creation, and Man's Weakness* (xxxviii. 1-xl. 2).
   (ii) *Job's Confession* (xl. 3-5).
   (iii) *The Divine Wisdom in Government* (xl. 6-xli. 34).
   (iv.) *Job's Submission* (xlii. 1-6).

Under (i), mark the references to earth, sea, dayspring, origins and issues, light and darkness, snow and hail, rain and dew, ice and frost, planets, clouds, lightning; the lion, raven, wild goat, wild ass, unicorn, ostrich, horse, hawk, and eagle.   Under (iii), mark the elaborate descriptions of behemoth, the hippopotamus, leviathan, and the crocodile.

PROVERBS

IN approaching this Work we must recognise that it is different and distinct from any other Book in the Bible. It is not history, nor poetry, nor rhapsody, nor prophecy, nor law, nor ritual, nor story, nor dogma ; and although it belongs to the Wisdom Literature, it differs from the other Wisdom Books, JOB and ECCLESIASTES. It is unfortunate, to say the least, that this Work is divided into chapters and verses, for this artificial arrangement buries literary form and hinders the appreciation thereof.

AUTHORSHIP.

All that we know of this is what may be learned from PROVERBS itself, where 'are named, as responsible for the various collections : Solomon (i. 1 ; xxv. 1) ; The Wise (xxii. 17) ; Men of Hezekiah (xxv. 1) ; Agur (xxx. 1) ; and King Lemuel and his mother (xxxi. 1). Solomon we know, and among "the men of Hezekiah" were probably Isaiah and Micah (cf. 2 Chron. xxxi. 13), but of the others we have no information.

DATE.

We must distinguish between the time of the writing of these Proverbs and the time of their

being collected and edited. The reference to
Hezekiah and his wise men "copying out" proverbs
of Solomon (xxv. 1), indicates that in Hezekiah's
time wisdom lore was being collected, and it may
be that some editing was done by Ezra. In any case,
these collections are the product of the Wisdom
Schools (see Introduction on the Wisdom Writings),
and extend over a long period.

CONTENTS.

The Book of PROVERBS no more lends itself to
formal analysis than does the Psalter, because
of its diversified contents ; it must suffice therefore
to introduce it according to its character.

Like the Books of Moses, the Psalter, and the
Historical Books of the New Testament, PROVERBS
is in five main parts, with an introduction, as
follows :

INTRODUCTION (i. 1-6).
> Indicating the practical purpose the Collection is in-
> tended to serve.

PART I.   Chs. i. 7-ix. 18.   Proverbs of Solomon (i. 1).
> The value and attainment of true wisdom.

PART II.   Chs. x. 1-xxii. 16.   Proverbs of Solomon.
> On practical morality.

PART III.   Chs. xxii. 17-xxiv. 34.   Proverbs of the Wise.
> Admonitions on the study of wisdom.

PART IV.   Chs. xxv.-xxix.   Proverbs of Solomon selected
> by the men of Hezekiah.
> Ethical and Economical.

PART V.   Chs. xxx.-xxxi.   Words of Agur and of King Lemuel
> Enigmatical and Domestic.

LITERARY FORM.

The method and form of these Sayings are matched to the design, which is to state truth so briefly and vividly that it can easily be remembered. In pursuance of this, three devices are adopted : antithesis, as in xvi. 22 ; comparison, as in xvii. 10 ; and imagery, as in xxvii. 15. The Unit Proverb is employed in chs. x. 1-xxii. 16 ; and there are here 375 of these in couplet form, each quite distinct, though having a common thought-basis.

The Proverb Cluster is employed, that is, an aggregation of Unit Proverbs on a common theme, as on Fools (xxvi. 3-12).

The Epigram is employed, that is, a Unit Proverb, organically enlarged, as on the Transitoriness of Riches (xxiii. 4, 5).

The Dramatic Monologue is employed, wherein wisdom is personified, as in Wisdom's Cry of Warning (i 20-33).

And the Sonnet is employed, as in The Commandment and its Reward (iii. 1-10).

Of Part II, chs. x. 1-xxii. 16, Professor Nourse has said : "These are not mere popular sayings, but products of fine literary workmanship. . . . What we have to do with here is the choicest product of the Wisdom Schools, and presupposes long training and practice before such art could be brought to the degree of perfection we see exhibited in Proverbs."

Themes.

The topics treated in this wonderful collection are many. Wisdom, Sin, Goodness, Wealth, the Tongue, Temptation, Pride, Humility, Justice, Friendship, Human Freedom, Idleness, Poverty, Education, Forgiveness, Folly, Love, Marriage, Family Life, Pleasures, Diligence, Dishonesty, Revenge, Strife, Gluttony, Success, are all dealt with in final forms of expression, and dynamically.

There are here also wonderful cameo pictures of social types :

"The prating fool, winking with his eye ; the practical joker, as dangerous as a madman casting firebrands about ; the talebearer, and the man who ' harps upon a matter,' separating chief friends ; the whisperer whose words are like dainty morsels going down into the innermost parts of the belly ; the backbiting tongue, drawing gloomy looks all around as surely as the north wind brings rain ; the false boaster, compared to wind and clouds without rain ; the haste to be rich ; the liberal man that scattereth and yet increaseth, while others are withholding only to come to want ; the speculator holding back his corn amid the curses of the people ;

the man of wandering life, like a restless bird ; the unsocial man that separateth himself, foregoing wisdom for the sake of his own private desire ; the cheerfulness that is a continual feast."

Social problems are also to be found here, such as the relations of husband and wife, of master and servant, of parents and children, of rich and poor. Also many human experiences are reflected in these proverbs, such as care, joy, feebleness, satiety, sorrow, and so on ; and although not much is said about religion, it is clear that the morality of these sayings is based upon it. Vice is condemned and virtue commended, by appeals to the highest motives (cf. v. 21 ; xv. 11 ; xvi. 6 ; xix. 29 ; xxiii. 17-19 ; xxvi. 10).

TEACHING.

The design of these Proverbs is stated at the outset (i. 1-6). The fundamental note of wisdom is "the fear of the Lord" (i. 7, 9, 10 ; xv. 33). The teaching is positive and practical. Existing religious institutions, the Law, priests, and sacrifices are not in view, but the tone of the teaching is definitely monotheistic ; there is here no scepticism, but a sincere belief in God, and in His wise and just government of the world. If the teaching seems to be utilitarian, it is because no other than this life was in the view of the writers; they had not the New Testament outlook upon the future.

We must be careful not to assume that all these Proverbs are of unlimited and universal application; on the contrary, we can find in the Scriptures many exceptions to what is here affirmed; for example, ch. x. 27, with Gen. iv. 8, and 2 Sam. i. 23; and xvi. 7, with Acts xiv. 19. Most of the teaching of the Scriptures is relative, not absolute; and regard must always be had for whether this life only, or the next also, is in view.

NOTE 33
The Septuagint and the Book of Proverbs.

"THE Greek version of Proverbs, known as the Septuagint, contains very considerable and remarkable deviations from the Hebrew. Some of these are of the nature of glosses, or explanations of obscure passages, others seem to be attempts to complete imperfect sentences, others are emendations, whilst there are to be found in addition interpolations of some length, omissions of many detailed verses, and the transposition of entire passages. So great is the diversity between the Greek and the Hebrew, that it seems tolerably clear that in very early times—say, the second century B.C.—there were two different recensions of the Book of Proverbs, one current in Palestine, the other in Alexandria. For the most part, the Hebrew gives undoubtedly the purer text; but in places the LXX may be consulted with advantage. Some of the additions, for example, are quite as lofty in conception as the original, and may perhaps be viewed as 'fruits grown on the stock of the noble poetry of wisdom among the ancient Hebrews,' or perhaps as relics of early Solomonic wisdom which had escaped other collectors." (Dr. W. T. DAVISON).

Let it be remembered that our Lord and His Apostles generally quote, not from the Hebrew, but from the Septuagint.

ECCLESIASTES

Keyword—VANITY.   CHAPTERS : 12.

THIS Book is the most mysterious in all the
Bible.   It has been called "the sphinx of
Hebrew literature, with its unsolved riddles of
history and life."   About no Biblical Writing has
there been such diversity of opinion as to the
Book's authorship, date, motive, and place.   The
Solomonic authorship has been, and is, stoutly
defended and denied.   Dates assigned for the Book
range over nearly a thousand years.   Dogmatism
and scepticism have alike claimed the author as their
champion.   And as to plan, some regard the Book
as a formal treatise, and others regard it as a collection of unconnected thoughts and maxims, like
Pascal's "Pensées," or Hare's "Guesses at Truth."

The consideration of these matters lies outside
the scope of this publication, and I have felt it
best just to give a detailed analysis of the Work as
it appeals to me, and to leave the reader to form
his own conclusions.

Four things may safely be said of the Book :
(1) that it belongs to the Wisdom Literature ; (2)
that its theme is "The Quest for the Chief Good";

(3) that it writes "Vanity" on all things "under the sun"; and (4) that the final verdict of the Book is that to fear and obey God is the whole duty of man.

Of ECCLESIASTES, Mr. E. C. Stedman says : "Whether prose or verse, I know nothing grander in its impassioned survey of mortal pain and pleasure, its estimate of failure and success; none of more noble sadness; no poem working more indomitably for spiritual illumination. Here, as nowhere else, immortal poetry has been made out of the body's decay (xii. 1-7)."

NOTE 34

The Need for Ecclesiastes.

"THERE is no need to point at length the contrast between Ecclesiastes and Christ's Gospel. There is perhaps some need to insist on the fact that the appearance of the new Evangel has not made void or useless the Wisdom-Literature of an earlier age. It did its work in its own time, and it has work to do still. There are times in a man's history when he is not ready to sit at the feet of Jesus, and when it is better for him to go to school to Koheleth. The heart must be emptied before it can be truly filled. The modern preacher has often to enforce the lesson, not yet obsolete, nor ever to become obsolete, "Fear God and keep His commandments, for this is the whole duty of man." He must come to Christ to learn how to do this effectively, and to be taught those higher lessons for which this does but prepare the way. But Wisdom is justified of all her children, and he who follows with toil of heart and knees and hands the wise man of old time in his quest of the chief good will find it in the service of Him Who came that we might have life, and have it more abundantly."

(Dr. W. T. DAVISON).

Analysis of Ecclesiastes

TITLE : i. 1.   *Theme :* "THE CHIEF GOOD" (vi. 12).

I. THE PROBLEM STATED (i. 2-11).

The wearisome monotony of all things human and earthly.
Affirmation (2).
Interrogation (3).
Illustration (4-11).

II. THE PROBLEM STUDIED (i. 12-xii. 7).

PART I.—Inductions (i. 12-vi. 12).

(i.) THE PREACHER'S EXPERIENCES,   ...   i. 12 - ii. 26.

    (*a*) *The Quest by Wisdom and Pleasure,*   i. 12 - ii. 11.
        By Wisdom (i. 12-18).
        By Pleasure (ii. 1-11).

    (*b*) *The Wise and Foolish Compared,*   ...   ii. 12-23.
        Wisdom is better than Folly (ii. 12-13)
        The Wise and the Foolish have the
        same end (ii. 14-17).
        The Wise Man leaves his Gains to
        the Fool (ii. 18-23).

    c) *The Conclusion of the Matter* (ii. 24-26)

(ii.) THE PREACHER'S OBSERVATIONS,   ...   iii. 1 - vi. 12.

    (*a*) *The Divine Order and Human Im-
        potence* (iii. 1-15).
        The Providence of Times and Seasons
        (iii. 1-8). Four pairs of contrasts.
        The Uncomprehending Longing of
        Man (iii. 9-11).
        The Need of a Practical Philosophy
        (iii. 12-15) : Make the Best of
        the Present (iii. 12-13). Recog-
        nise Immutable Law (iii. 14, 15).

(b) *The Alternating Hope and Despair of Man* (iii. 16-22).

Hope that there will be Retributive Justice (iii. 16, 17).

Despair because of the Uncertain Future (iii. 18-21).

The Practical Conclusion (iii. 22).

(c) *Hindrances to the Attainment of the Chief Good* (iv. 1-16).

Oppression (iv. 1-3).

Envy (iv. 4-6).

Loneliness (iv. 7-12).

Vicissitudes (iv. 13-16).

(d) *Reflections on Certain Phases of Life* (v. 1-17).

On Religion (v. 1-7).

On Politics (v. 8, 9).

On Riches (v. 10-17).

(e) *Conclusions Drawn from these Reflections* (v. 18-vi. 12).

The Desirability of Moderation (v. 18-20).

Prosperity without Power to Enjoy (vi. 1-6).

The Insatiableness of Desire (vi. 7-9).

The Vanity of Life (vi. 10-12).

PART 2.—Deductions (vii. 1-xii. 7).

(i.) A RETROSPECTIVE VIEW, ...   vii. 1-ix. 18.

(a) *Some Practical Rules of Life* (vii. 1-14).

Seriousness is better than Gaiety (vii. 1-7).

Impatience is a Root Evil (vii. 8-10).

There is Wisdom in Resignation to Providence (vii. 11-14).

(b) *Exhortation to Opportunism* (vii. 15-24).

Concerning Righteousness and Wickedness (vii. 15-20).

Concerning Conduct and Censure (vii. 21, 22).

Dissatisfaction with this Advice (vii. 23, 24).

(c) *A Verdict on Women and Men* (vii. 25-29).

The Snare of Woman (vii. 25, 26).

The Perversion of Man (vii. 27-29).

(d) *A Policy of Submission Enjoined* (viii. 1-9).

To Rulers (viii. 1-5).

To Providence (viii. 6-9).

(e) *Perplexing Anomalies in God's Moral Government* (viii. 10-15).

The Godless and the Righteous (viii. 10, 11).

Faith in Justice at Last (viii. 12-14).

Meanwhile Accept things as they are (viii. 15).

(f) *The Mystery of Providence further Contemplated* (viii. 16-ix. 18).

No human wisdom can fathom Providence (viii. 16-ix. 1).

A like fate befalls all men (ix. 2-6).

Enjoy life while you may (ix. 7-12).

Wisdom is not always rewarded (ix. 13-16).

On Wisdom and Folly (ix. 17-18).

(ii.) A PROSPECTIVE VIEW, ... x. 1-xii. 7.

   (a) *Observations on Wisdom and Folly* (x. 1-20).

     A little folly mars wisdom (x. 1-3).

     Wise conduct under foolish rulers (x. 4-7).

     Proverbs commending Prudence (x. 8-10).

     Sagacity and Loquacity (x. 11-15).

     Foolish rulers and wise subjects (x. 16-20).

   (b) *How Wisely to Order One's Days* (xi. 1-xii. 7).

     Do good, and worry not about results (xi. 1-6).

     Live the present in the light of the future (xi. 7-xii. 7).

III. THE PROBLEM SOLVED (xii. 8-14).

1. The Preacher's Theme, ... xii. 8

2. The Preacher's Method, ... xii. 9-11.

3. The Preacher's Advice, ... xii. 12.

4. The Preacher's Verdict, ... xii. 13, 14.

THE PROPHETICAL WRITINGS

INTRODUCTION

JOEL	JEREMIAH
JONAH	HABAKKUK
AMOS	DANIEL
HOSEA	EZEKIEL
ISAIAH	OBADIAH
MICAH	HAGGAI
NAHUM	ZECHARIAH
ZEPHANIAH	MALACHI

Table of Reading.

PROPHECY	HISTORY.	DATE.
JOEL, ...	2 Kings xi., xii., ...	837-800(?)
JONAH, ...	2 Kings xiii., xiv., ...	825-782
AMOS, ...	2 Kings xiv. 23-xv. 7, ...	810-785
HOSEA, ...	2 Kings xv. 1-xviii. 1, ...	782-725
ISAIAH, ...	2 Kings xv-xx.; 2 Chron. xxvi.-xxxii.	758-698
MICAH, ...	2 Kings xv. 8-xx. Isaiah vii., viii.; Jer. xxvi. 17-19; 2 Chron. xxvii-xxxii., ...	740-695
NAHUM	(Jonah. Isaiah x. Zeph. ii. 13-15),	640-630
ZEPHANIAH,	2 Kings xxii. 1-xxiii. 34. 2 Chron. xxxiv. 1-xxxvi. 4,	640-610
JEREMIAH,	2 Kings xxii.-xxv. 2 Chron. xxxiv.-xxxvi. 21, ...	627-585
HABAKKUK,	2 Kings xxiii. 31-xxiv. 2 Chron. xxxvi. 1-10, ...	608-598
DANIEL, ...	2 Kings xxiii. 35-xxv. 2 Chron. xxxvi. 5-23, ...	606-534
EZEKIEL,	2 Kings xxiv. 17-xxv. 2 Chron. xxxvi. 11-21, ...	592-572
OBADIAH,	2 Kings xxv. 2 Chron. xxxvi. 11-21	586-583
HAGGAI,	EZRA i.-vi., ...	520
ZECHARIAH,	Ezra i.-vi., ...	520-518
MALACHI, .	Nehemiah viii.-xiii., ...	433-425

Some of these dates cannot be fixed with certainty, and the margin here given, *e.g.*, Hosea, 782-725, is that *within* which the prophet ministered, and does not represent the *duration* of his ministry.

The
PROPHETICAL WRITINGS

Introduction

THERE is a sense in which the whole of the
Old Testament is prophetical. Bishop Westcott
has said : "The Old Testament is one vast prophecy. The application of prophetic words in each
case has regard to the ideal indicated by them, and
is not limited by the historical fact with which they
were connected. But the history is not set aside.
The history forces the reader to look beyond."
It is most important to bear this in mind, lest, on
the one hand, we imagine that the prophets spoke
to their own generation only, or, on the other hand,
that they spoke to a future generation mainly.
Neither of these views is correct. The prophets
were first *forth-tellers*, addressing messages to their
own people, concerning themselves, or other
peoples, and then, they were *fore-tellers*, because
their day was only a moment in the progress of a
Divine plan. The prophets had both *insight* and
foresight, and foresight because of their insight.
Theirs was a manifold function, for they combined
in themselves preacher, teacher, statesman, re-

former, and herald. They appeared at times of crisis in their nation's history as the champions of righteousness ; they were essentially the moral conscience of their age. The prophets were men of their time, and for all time. "Holy men of God spake as they were moved by the Holy Spirit" (2 Peter i. 21). They were conscious of the gift of inspiration, for one of their commonest phrases is, "Thus saith the Lord," but they were also conscious that what they said had a significance beyond their apprehension (1 Peter i. 10, 11).

The historico-predictive themes of Hebrew prophecy are, Israel, the Gentile nations, and the Messiah, and in the Hebrew seers we have a unique group of men, and a unique literature. It has well been said that "nowhere is there to be found a succession of men like them in character, in vision, in eloquence. They were a composite of oracle, reformer, poet, and statesman. They uttered truth in ecstasy; the soberest judgments of a statesman was spoken with the passion of a reformer and with the lyrical cadence of poetry."

There is in the Old Testament an unmistakable development of the prophetic consciousness and message, and while the priestly factor was always present in the life of Israel, the prophetic factor became dominant.

Prophets and prophecy preceded the time of Samuel (Deut. xviii. 15-22), but with him schools of prophets began (1 Sam. x. 10). They were not a succession as were the priests (cf. Amos vii. 14), but they did become an Order. Their earliest work was oral, and is exemplified in the ministry of Moses, Samuel, Elijah, Elisha, and many minor seers ; and their latest work was literary, that is, they left written records of their preaching, and, probably, in an instance or two, the message was written only, and not preached.

In the Hebrew Bible the Prophets are in two groups. The Former Prophets are the historical Writings, JOSHUA, JUDGES, 1-2 SAMUEL, 1-2 KINGS ; and the Latter Prophets are, ISAIAH, JEREMIAH, EZEKIEL, and the twelve Minor Prophets. The Book of DANIEL is partly historical, and partly prophetical and apocalyptical, but it was never classified with the prophets, but with another group of Books called "The Latter Writings" (Dan.; Ezra ; Nehemiah ; 1-2 Chronicles). In the following pages the Prophetical Books are presented in their chronological order so far as our knowledge allows. One advantage of this is in that it enables us better to locate the prophets historically, and also better to follow the development of their teaching.

JOEL

Keyword—VISITATION.   CHAPTERS : 3.

Prophet No. 1.   *Southern Kingdom.*   *Pre-Exilic.*

Pre-Assyrian Period.   DATE : 837-800 B.C.

JOEL is the name of fourteen men mentioned in the Bible. It is compounded of two Divine names, Yahveh (Jehovah) and El, and it means "The Lord is God."

The author of this Writing ministered either early or late in relation to the writing prophets. Both views are contended for. Recent scholarship is almost unanimous in assigning a post-exilic date, the fourth century, or later ; but there are good reasons for the view that Joel was the earliest of the literary prophets, and ministered in the reign of Amaziah or Uzziah, that is, between 838-756 B.C. The point of controversy is that he does not mention the Assyrians and Babylonians, and therefore must have written either before they became formidable, or after they had ceased to be so. If we accept the early date for this Prophecy, Joel was contemporary with Jonah, Amos, and Hosea. In any case, his message is to Judah, and not to Israel.

The style is elegant, clear, and impassioned, and must be given a high place in Hebrew literature.

The Book falls into two main parts. In the first, Joel speaks, and in the second, Jehovah. The first part is historical, and the second, prophetical. The first tells of desolation, and the second of deliverance.

The interpretation of the locusts may be actual, allegorical, or apocalyptical. Without doubt it is the first, and in all likelihood the other two also, the one pointing to an invasion of the land by hordes of enemies, and the other making the locusts emblems of world forces which shall appear in the last days.

The outstanding passages are those which relate to the locust invasion (ii. 1-11), the outpouring of the Holy Spirit (ii. 28-32; cf. Acts ii. 16-21), and the final felicity of Judah (iii. 18-21)

Other things to note are, references to "the Day of the Lord"; references to Tyre, Zidon, Palestine, Grecians, Sabeans, Egypt and Edom; and ch. i. 4 with ch. ii. 25.

The use which Peter makes in Acts ii. 16-21, of Joel 28-32, is noteworthy. It is clear that Pentecost was in Joel's prophecy, but it is not clear that Pentecost exhausted that prophecy; verses 30-32 seem to point to a time yet future; a time which falls in the period of the apocalypse of Matthew xxiv. 29-31.

Analysis of Joel

I. HISTORICAL.—JOEL SPEAKS.
Chapters i. 1-ii. 17.

Key : DESOLATION.

1. The Fact of Desolation (i. 1-20).
Locusts Relentless in the Country.

(i.) THE SITUATION, ... **1-4.**
Hear (2). Tell (3). The Tale (4).

(ii.) THE EXHORTATION, ... **5-14.**
Drunkards (5-7) ; Virgin Zion (8-10) ;
Husbandmen (11, 12) ; Priests (13, 14)

(iii.) THE SUPPLICATION, ... **15-20**
A Fear (15) ; A Plea (16-18.)
A Hope (19, 20).

2. The Means of Desolation (ii. 1-17).
Locusts Resistless in the City.

(i.) THE SITUATION, ... **1-11**
The Day of the LORD (1-2a).
The Camp of the LORD (2b-10).
The Word of the LORD (11).

(ii.) THE EXHORTATION, ... **12-17a**
A Call to Penitence (12-14).
A Call to Prayer (15-17a).

(iii.) THE SUPPLICATION, ... **17b.**

II. PROPHETICAL.—JEHOVAH SPEAKS.

Chapters ii. 18-iii. 21.

Key : DELIVERANCE.

1. **The Promise of Present Blessing** (ii. 18-27).

   (i.) Reversal of Conditions, ... **18-20.**

   (ii.) Recovery of Joy, ... **21-27.**

2. **The Promise of Future Blessing**
   (ii. 28-iii. 21).

   (i.) Its Initiation, ... ii. **28-32.**
   In a mighty visitation of the Spirit.

   (ii.) Its Progression, ... iii. **1-17.**
   In the utter rout of all enemies,

   (iii.) Its Consummation, ... iii. **18-21.**
   In a restored and established nation.

NOTE 36

The Seven Stages in the Prophecy of Joel.

PROF. RICHARD MOULTON says that the seven stages into which the action of this prophecy falls advance regularly to a crisis, and then, as with the figure of an arch, turn round, the later corresponding to the earlier, until the final stage is seen as a reversal of the first.

4. Relief and Restoration, ii. 18-27.

3. Repentance at the last moment, ii. 12-17.

5. Afterward: Israel spiritualised—the Nations summoned to Judgment, ii. 28-iii. 8.

2. Judgment visibly advancing; Crisis, ii. 1-11.

6. Advance to the Valley of Decision; Crisis, iii. 9-16.

1. The Land of Israel desolate and mourning, i.

7. The Holy Mountain and eternal Peace, iii. 17-21.

JONAH

Keyword—COMMISSION.   CHAPTERS : 4.

Prophet No. 2.   *Northern Kingdom.*   *Pre-Exilic.*

Assyrian Period.   DATE : 825-782

JONAH, which means "dove," was a real person and not a creature of human fancy. The son of Amittai, of the tribe of Zebulun, he lived at Gath-hepher, in the province of Zebulun, and was a prophet of the Northern Kingdom. We learn from 2 Kings xiv. 25 that he exercised his ministry during the reign of Jeroboam II (825-782 B.C.), and, it would seem, it was at his instigation that the coast of Israel was restored, and in his time the people attained to a height of prosperity which has no parallel in the history of this kingdom. Of himself and his work we know no more than this, and what is recorded in the Book before us. His contemporaries were Joel, Amos, and Hosea.

This Book is not really a prophecy, but the history of a prophet. With the exception of chapter ii., it is straight-forward narrative, telling of Jonah's commission to Nineveh, and what he did with it.

Two opposite views are held of the historicity of the Book. On the one hand it is regarded as "an imaginative work with a moral lesson, and that the ancient prophet is chosen as its hero for his known anti-Assyrian bias." On the other hand, it is regarded as genuinely historical, and it is claimed that Jesus believed it to be so (Matt. xii. 39-41 ; xvi. 4 ; Luke xi. 29, 30). In spite of all that has been said to the contrary, we take this latter view.

The object of the Writing seems to have been to correct the extreme form of Jewish nationalism which then prevailed, and to proclaim the mercy of God for Gentiles as well as for Jews. That the Book may, and indeed, does, have an allegorical significance, we do not question. It is prophetic in outlook and catholic in spirit. Its subject is not a "whale," but Foreign Missions. The Book illustrates Faber's great lines :

> "There's a wideness in God's mercy
> Like the wideness of the sea
> There's a kindness in His justice
> Which is more than liberty."

The miraculous element in it is only such as inheres in all Israel's history, authenticating the revelation which was given to them.

In JONAH "the religious spirit of the Old Testament reaches its purest and amplest expression." Of it Charles Reade has said, "JONAH is the most beautiful story ever written in so small a compass.

It contains 48 verses and 1328 English words. . . .
There is growth of character, a distinct plot worked
out without haste or crudity. Only a great artist
could have hit on a perfect proportion between
dialogue and narrative." We agree that Jonah was
"a great artist," but do not believe that he "hit on"
the product of his genius, but rather that the Holy
Spirit employed the ability He had given to him.
Things to specially note are, the miraculous element
in the story; the characterization of the heathen
mariners (i. 5-16); Jonah's prayer (ii. 1-9), trace
its clauses in the Psalms; what is said of Nineveh
(iii.); Jonah's reason for fleeing (iv. 2); the number
of young children in Nineveh (iv. 11); the patience
and mercy of God throughout.

NOTE 37
The Education of Jonah.

"THE glorious mercy of Jehovah the prophet had conceived
as the heritage of the Hebrew people; he watches with
indignation its extension to the heathen. As in the earlier
part of the prophecy he was led to see that Divine *power* was
not confined to the land of Israel, but that the dominion of
Jehovah extended over the universe, so now he is to be taught
that the supremacy of *mercy* over judgment is an attribute of
God in which all races may feel that they have an interest."

(Prof. RICHARD MOULTON).

Analysis of Jonah

I. THE DIVINE COMMISSION.
Chapters i. 1-iii. 2.

1. The First Call, ... i. 1-2.
2. The Flight, ... i. 3.
3. The Storm, ... i. 4-14.
4. The Chastisement, ... i. 15-17.
5. The Prayer, ... ii. 1-10.
6. The Second Call, ... iii. 1-2.

II. THE NATIONAL CONSEQUENCE.
Chapter iii. 3-10.

1. The Prophet's Message,... ... ... 3, 4.
2. The Immediate Effect, ... 5, 6.
3. The Royal Edict, ... 7, 8.
4. The Heathen's Hope, ... 9.
5. The Averted Judgment, ... 10.

III. THE PROPHET'S COMPLAINT.
Chapter iv.

1. Jonah's Indictment, ... 1-3.
2. Jehovah's Remonstrance, ... 4.
3. The Miracle-Parable, ... 5-8.
4. The Divine Rebuke, ... 9-11.

6

AMOS

Keyword—THREATENED.   CHAPTERS : 9.

Prophet No. 3.   *Northern Kingdom.*   *Pre-Exilic.*

Assyrian Period.   DATE : 810-785.

A MOS means "bearer" or "borne" (by God), and he is the author of the Book which has his name (vii. 8 ; viii. 1, 2). If the date of JOEL is late, and not early, as we have supposed, then, Amos began a new era of prophecy, in that he was the first to write his messages. According to the chronology adopted here, he was contemporary with Joel, Jonah, and Hosea. He tells us that he was a herdman from the region of Teḳoa, and while pursuing his daily round of duties he was, like Elisha, called to the high dignity of the prophetic ministry. He was not of the schools of the prophets, that is, he had no professional training, neither was he in the line of the prophets (vii. 14, 15). His experience teaches us that God's agents are determined by the law of His choice, and not by any human succession or profession. His manner of life is reflected in the illustrations he employs, the bird in the nest, two men meeting in the desert, a shepherd snatching from the mouth of a lion two legs and the piece of an ear, sycamore trees, grasshoppers, a basket of summer fruit, the waggon loaded with sheaves, cattle-driving, corn-winnowing, and so on. But though Amos had no academic training, as we would say, it has been said that in vigour, vividness, and simplicity of speech he was not surpassed by any of his successors.

The Book consists of a series of Oracles (i. 3-ii. 16), a series of Sermons (iii. 1-vi. 14), and a series of Visions (vii. 1-ix. 10), with an Introduction and a Conclusion.

The style of Amos is elaborate and finished, and he is not limited to one literary form. The first part of his message is in the form of lyric prophecy (i.-ii.), and here is a free interchange of rhythm and recitative, of poetry and prose. The poetic refrains tell of ideal transgressions and doom, and the prose portions tell of actual sins and sorrows. Mark the formula (i. 3, 4) which is eight times repeated. The second part of the message (iii.-vi.) is in the form of discourse, and here there are five speeches on the sin and doom of Israel. Each ends with a "therefore," the first three beginning with "Hear ye this word," and the last two with "Woe." The third part (vii.-ix.) is in the form of dramatic vision, five visions, with narrative portions.

Amos charges Israel with avarice, injustice, uncleanness, and profanity (ii. 6-12), and they excused themselves on the ground that they were the chosen people (iii. 2). The prophet's reply is that their relation to God is an aggravation of their offence. In the midst of Israel's compromise and corruption the prophet proclaims the sovereignty of God, the God of all creation (i. 2; iv. 13; v. 8).

The threats of doom are interspersed with exhortations to "seek the Lord" (five times), and with the promise of a better day to dawn (ix. 11-15. Things to regard specially in this Book are its style, figures of speech, autobiographical material, the political and religious situation at home and abroad, the story of Amaziah's opposition, and references to places and peoples.

NOTE 38
The Mission of Amos.

"THE people of Israel were now at the summit of worldly prosperity, but were rapidly filling up the measure of their sins. The mission of Amos was, therefore, rather to threaten than to console. He rebukes, among other things, the corruption of their manners, which kept pace with their prosperity: he charges the great men with partiality as judges, and violence towards the poor; and he foretells, as a punishment from God, the captivity of the ten tribes in a foreign country—a prediction accomplished about sixty years afterwards, when Shalmaneser and Sargon, Kings of Assyria, destroyed the kingdom."

(*The Bible Handbook*: ANGUS and GREEN).

Analysis of Amos

PROLOGUE (i. 1).
The Prophet, and the Time of his Prophecy.

I. DECLARATION OF SIN AND JUDGMENT AGAINST EIGHT NATIONS (i. 2-ii. 16).

1. Damascus (3).   3. Tyre (9).   5. Ammon (13).   7. Judah (4).
2. Gaza (6).   4. Edom (11).   6. Moab (1).   8. Israel (6).

II. EXPANSION OF THE SIN AND JUDGMENT OF ISRAEL (iii.-vi.)

DISCOURSE 1.—The Prophet is appointed to predict judgment (iii.).

DISCOURSE 2.—The rejection of repeated warnings should lead them to prepare for judgment (iv.).

DISCOURSE 3.—If they had sought the Lord, the "Day of the Lord" would not have overtaken them, but now Assyria will usher in that Day (v.-vi.).

III. VISIONS OF THE SIN AND JUDGMENT OF ISRAEL (vii.-ix. 10).

1. THE DEVOURING LOCUST. Prayer and Answer (vii. 1-3).
2. THE CONSUMING FIRE. Prayer and Answer (vii. 4-6).
3. THE SEARCHING PLUMBLINE. No Prayer and Answer (vii. 7-11, 12-17). Historical Narrative.
4. THE BASKET OF SUMMER FRUIT. Judgment : Its Consummation, Cause, and Character (viii.).
5. THE LORD BESIDE THE ALTAR (ix. 1-10).

EPILOGUE (ix. 11-15).
The Ultimate Restoration of Israel.

HOSEA

Keyword—ESTRANGEMENT.   CHAPTERS : 14.

Prophet No. 4.   Northern Kingdom.   Pre-Exilic.

Assyrian Period.   DATE : 782-725 B.C.

HOSEA, Hoshea, Joshua, and Jesus are identical in derivation, and mean "Salvation" (cf. Matt. i. 21). Hosea's contemporaries were Joel, Jonah, Amos, Isaiah, and Micah. As, in the South, Uzziah, Jotham, Ahaz, and Hezekiah reigned during his ministry, it would seem that he prophesied across a period of from sixty to seventy years, a longer time, probably, than any other prophet. He, too, ministered in the prosperous and corrupt reign of Jeroboam II. He is the first, but not the last, prophet whose personal history is made a symbol to his countrymen.

Unlike those of Amos, Hosea's language and style are difficult and abrupt. "He flashes forth brilliant sentences, but writes no great chapters." Here are not the imagination, the fire, and the vivid concreteness of Amos, but in some respects he is deeper ; indeed, it has been said that his religious message is one of the most profound and spiritual in the Old Testament. The Book falls into two

main parts. The first part is personal (i.-iii.), and
the second is national (iv.-xiv.). The faithless
wife in the first division has her counterpart in the
faithless people in the second ; and the faithful
husband in the one, answers to the faithful Lord
in the other.

Hosea's *motif* is not common in literature. Much
has been written of the loyalty of a pure woman to
an unfaithful husband, but little of the loyalty of a
strong man to an unfaithful wife. A comparison
is found in Tennyson's treatment of Arthur's
forgiveness of Guinevere :

"Lo ! I forgive thee, as Eternal God
Forgives : do thou for thine own soul the rest."

In the study of this Book three things must be
kept prominent.

First, the PERSONAL NARRATIVE (i.-iii.), with
its reference to the husband, the wife, and the
children. Consider carefully the names of the
children : Jezreel, "God will scatter" ; Lo-Ruhamah, "Unpitied" ; and Lo-Ammi, "Not my
People" (cf. 1 Peter ii. 10).

Second, the NATIONAL INTERPRETATION (iv.-
xiv), with its dominating notes, Transgression,
Visitation, and Restoration. Israel was situated
midway between Egypt and Assyria, and in the
kingdom two factions existed, one favouring

alliance with the one Power, and the other, with the other Power. Special reference to this is found in chapters iv. 1-xi. 11. In Hosea are nine brief allusions to Judah, and no predictions concerning the Gentiles. The sins charged against the people are lying, perjury, drunkenness, lust, robbery, murder, treason, and regicide. The worship of Jehovah was corrupted with idolatry and profaned by formality.

Third, the SPIRITUAL APPLICATION (i.-xiv.). If Amos emphasises the "severity" of God, Hosea emphasises His "goodness" (Rom. xi. 22). There are passages here which, for pathos and love, are unrivalled (ii. 14, 15, 19, 20 ; iii.; xi. 3, 4, 8 ; xiv.). This Book emphasises the shame of sin, the fruit of backsliding, the love of the Lord, and the con- ditions of restoration. Special chapters are the third and the fourteenth. In chapter iii. is a remarkable prophecy, verse 4, telling of the present, and verse 5, of the future of God's people, Israel. Chapter xiv. is the greatest in the Bible for the backslider. Mark carefully the speakers in the several verses : Prophet, 1-3 ; Lord, 4-7 ; Ephraim, 8a ; Lord, 8b ; Ephraim, 8c ; Lord, 8d ; Prophet, 9.

The leading note of Hosea's utterances is an impassioned tenderness, in harmony with the personal experiences which he describes.

Analysis of Hosea

I. PERSONAL AFFLICTION (i.-iii.).

The Faithless Wife and her Faithful Husband.

1. The CHILDREN, or Signs, ... i. 1-ii. 1.
   - (i.) First Sign : Gomer.
   - (ii.) Second Sign : Jezreel.
   - (iii.) Third Sign : Lo-ruhamah.
   - (iv.) Fourth Sign : Lo-ammi.

2. The WIFE, or Backsliding, ... ii. 2-23.
   - (i.) The Grievance of Love.
   - (ii.) The Severity of Love.
   - (iii.) The Goodness of Love.

3. The HUSBAND, or Deliverance, ... iii.
   - (i.) Command, ... 1.
   - (ii.) Obedience, ... 2, 3.
   - (iii.) Significance, ... 4, 5.

II. NATIONAL REFLECTION (iv.-xiv.).

The Faithless Nation and the Faithful Lord.

1. The TRANSGRESSION of Israel is Prominent, ... iv.-viii.
   Key : ii. 1-5.
   - (i.) Idolatry.
   - (ii.) Anarchy.

2. The VISITATION of Israel is Prominent, ... ix.-xi. 11.
   Key : ii. 6-13.
   - (i.) Egypt. West.
   - (ii.) Assyria. East.

   The RESTORATION of Israel is Prominent, ... xi. 12-xiv
   Key : ii. 14-23.
   - (i.) Retrospect.
   - (ii.) Prospect.

ISAIAH

Keyword—SALVATION. CHAPTERS : **66.**

Prophet No. 5. *Southern Kingdom.* *Pre-Exilic.*

Assyrian Period. DATE : 758-698.

THE name Isaiah means "Yahweh is Salvation,"
or "Salvation of Yahweh." The prophet
received his call in the last year of the reign of
Uzziah (756 B.C.), and continued until the time of
Hezekiah, a period of not less than forty years.
His contemporaries were Hosea and Micah. We
are told that he was married (viii. 3), and had two,
possibly three, sons (vii. 3 ; viii. 1-4). The scene
of his labours was chiefly, if not exclusively, Jerusalem. He is rightly called the Evangelical Prophet,
and by common consent is one of the greatest of the
prophets in splendour of intellectual endowments.
He takes an unchallenged place among the very
great writers whom humanity has produced. His
power of vivid, luminous visualization of truth,
touched with extraordinary depth of emotion is
unmatched. He is equally distinguished for intensity and for majesty of utterance. The chapters
of the second division of the Book easily take their

place in the very great literature of the world. Isaiah and Job are poets of superlative greatness.

The prophet stands midway between Moses and Christ, and begins to prophesy 217 years after the division of the United Kingdom. His ministry includes the last years of the Northern Kingdom.

The Book falls into three distinct parts. The first is Prophetic (i.-xxxv.); the second is Historic (xxxvi.-xxxix.); and the third is Messianic (xl.-lxvi.). The keynote of the first part is, we may say, Condemnation; of the second, Confiscation, and of the third, Consolation. In the first part Assyria is central; in the third part it is Babylon, and the second part points back to the one and forward to the other. Isaiah says that he and his children were for "signs" (viii. 18), and this is very suggestive. Maher-shalal-hash-baz, means "speed to the spoil, hurry to the prey," and represents chapters i.-xxxix.; Shear-jashub means "a remnant shall return," and represents chs. xl.-lxvi.; and Isaiah, which means "Salvation of the Lord," represents the whole Book.

For about a century the Isaianic authorship of chs. xl.-lxvi., has been not only questioned, but denied, and such terms as "the Deutero-Isaiah," "the Babylonian Isaiah," and "the Great Unnamed" have become commonplaces in this field of study.

The question, as Prof. A. B. Davidson has said, "is one of fact and criticism exclusively, and not a matter either of faith or practice." It is most important to observe the different view-points of the two main divisions. In chs. i.-xxxix., the prophet is addressing his own generation, but, if he wrote chs. xl.-lxvi., he is addressing a generation a century and a half after his time, the captives in Babylon. If prediction be once admitted as an element in prophecy, the Spirit of God could well have used Isaiah to speak to a distant generation. The unity of the Book has been learnedly argued, and certainly must not be airily dismissed.

What matters, of course, is the substance of this great Book. In part one, mark specially the Great Indictment (ch. i.); the Prophet's Call and Commission (ch. vi.); the Book of Burdens (xiii.-xxiii.); the Book of Songs (xxv.-xxvii.); and the Book of Woes (xxviii.-xxxii.).

Part two (xxxvi.-xxxix.) is very valuable for the light it throws on the character and time of Hezekiah. His Songs (xxxviii. 20) are, in all likelihood, the Songs of Degrees, Psalms cxx.-cxxxiv.

Part three (xl.-lxvi.) is one grand Messianic poem, the Rhapsody of Zion Redeemed, and is peerless literature. It is in three divisions of nine chapters each, and each division consists of three sections, and chapter liii. is the central chapter of the central section of the central division, and the central verses of this central chapter enshrine the central truth of the Gospel (5, 6). These divisions and sections are: A (*a*) xl.; (*b*) xli.; (*c*) xlii. 1-xliii. 13; (*a*) xliii. 14-xliv. 5; (*b*) xliv. 6-23; (*c*) xliv. 24-xlv. 25; (*a*) xlvi.; (*b*) xlvii.; (*c*) xlviii. B (*a*) xlix.; (*b*) l. ; (*c*) li. (*a*) lii. 1-12 ; (*b*) lii. 13-liii. ; (*c*) liv. (*a*) lv. ; (*b*) lvi. 1-8 ; (*c*) lvi. 9-lvii. 21. C (*a*) lviii.; (*b*) lix.; (*c*) lx.; (*a*) lxi.; (*b*) lxii.; (*c*) lxiii. 1-6. (*a*) lxiii. 7-lxiv. 12; (*b*) lxv. ; (*c*) lxvi.

The greatest chapters are the sixth and fifty-third.

NOTE 39

The Unity of Isaiah Demonstrated by Its Structure.

A. i. 2-v. 30. Exhortations: REPREHENSORY. Prophetic.

   B. vi. 1-13. The VOICE from the TEMPLE. The Scattering.

      C. vii. 1-xii. 6. HISTORIC. Events and Prophecies (Ahaz).

         D. xiii. 1-xxvii. 13. BURDENS. Alternated with ISRAEL'S Blessings.

         D. xxviii. 1-xxxv. 10. WOES. Alternated with JEHOVAH'S Glories.

      C. xxxvi. 1-xxxix. 8. HISTORIC. Events and Prophecies (Hezekiah).

   B. xl. 1-11. The VOICE from the WILDERNESS. The Gathering.

A. xl. 12-lxvi. 24. Exhortations. PROMISSORY. Prophetic. (E. W. BULLINGER).

Analysis of Isaiah

DIVISION I.—PROPHETIC (i.-xxxv.).

Keynote: CONDEMNATION.
Outlook : ASSYRIAN.

1. Prophecies Concerning Judah and Israel (i.-xii.).

2. Predictions Against Foreign Nations (xiii.-xxiii.)

THE BOOK OF BURDENS.

3. Announcements of Judgments and Deliverances (xxiv.-xxxv.).

(iv.) The Future of the Nations and of Israel
      Contrasted, ...   **xxxiv.-xxxv**
  (*a*) Desolation (**xxxiv.**).
  (*b*) Restoration (**xxxv.**).

DIVISION II.—HISTORIC (xxxvi.-xxxix.).
    Keynote :   CONFISCATION.
    Outlook :   ASSYRIAN AND BABYLONIAN.

1. **Looking Backward : Assyrian (xxxvi.-xxxvii.).**

  (i.) Hezekiah's Trouble, ... **xxxvi.**

  (ii.) Hezekiah's Triumph, ... **xxxvii.**

2. **Looking Forward : Babylonian (xxxviii.-xxxix).**

  (i.) Hezekiah's Sickness, ... **xxxviii.**

  (ii.) Hezekiah's Sin, ... **xxxix.**

DIVISION III.—MESSIANIC (xl.-lxvi.).
    Keynote :   CONSOLATION.
    Outlook :   BABYLONIAN.

1. **The Deliverance,** ... ... **xl.-xlviii.**
    God and the gods : Israel and the Heathen
    compared.

2. **The Deliverer,** ... ... **xlix.-lvii.**
    The Sufferings and the Glory of Jehovah's
    Servant compared.

3. **The Delivered,** ... ... **lviii.-lxvi**
    The Faithful and the Unfaithful, and
    their respective Ends compared.

MICAH

Keyword—ARRAIGNMENT.   CHAPTERS : 7.

Prophet No. 6.   *Northern and Southern Kingdoms.*

Pre-Exilic.   *Assyrian Period.*

DATE : 740-695 B.C.

M ICAH is a combination of three Hebrew
     words which together mean "Who is like
Yah !"

THE PROPHET AND HIS TIME.

Of the man himself we do not know much, but
through the medium of his message we may judge
of his personal qualities, and of his power as a
preacher. His style is rapid, bold, and vivid. The
introduction tells us that he ministered in the days
of Jotham, Ahaz, and Hezekiah of the Southern
Kingdom, and that means, during the reigns of
Pekah and Hoshea of the Northern Kingdom. These
reigns cover a period of fully sixty years, and these
were years of political unrest and social decay.
Micah is the only prophet whose ministry was
directed to both the Kingdoms, and the conditions
in each gave shape to his message. His contemporaries were Hosea, a prophet in the North, and
Isaiah, in the South, and he combined the dominant

notes of each, with striking contrasts of detail and style.

THE PROPHET AND HIS TASK.

Isaiah's prophetism had in it a political element ; he was concerned on account of the attempt of Israel and Syria to force Judah into an alliance with them against Assyria ; but Micah has nothing to say about this. Isaiah was a prophet of the Court and city, but Micah was a country prophet. He was much occupied with the moral and social condition of the people, and of this he writes graphically. No class was exempt from the prevailing corrupting influences : princes, priests, prophets, and people were all victims of social disorder and moral decay (ii. 2, 8, 9, 11 ; iii. 1-3, 5, 11). Micah shows that, notwithstanding this state of things, they clung to religious ordinances and spiritual forms, and he exposes the futility of this (vi. 7, 8).

THE PROPHET AND HIS TESTIMONY.

It was no easy task which Micah had, but he brought to it strong qualities and a great belief in God and righteousness. He tears aside the veil which hid their sin and shame from view, and he denounces their iniquities in scathing terms. In short sharp sentences he brings his whip down upon the venal judges, the corrupt priests, and the hireling prophets, and makes them smart beneath the lash. He tells them also of coming judgment (iii. 12 ; iv. 10 ; vi. 16). But, like his prophet brothers, he looks beyond, to a time of restoration. In the storm he sang a song; in the night he caught a glimpse of the morning. With his threats are mingled promises (iv. 1-8, cf. 1. 9-16; v. 7, 8 ; iii. 6, 7, 12 ; with ii. 12 ; iv. 10 ; v. 8, 6).

The classic passage in this Book is vi. 8 ; of which Huxley wrote: "In the eighth century before Christ, in the heart of a world of idolatrous polytheists, the Hebrew prophet put forth a conception of religion which appears to me as wonderful an inspiration of genius as the art of Phidias, or the science of Aristotle. If any so-called religion takes away from this great saying of Micah, I think it wantonly mutilates ; while if it adds thereto, I think it obscures the perfect ideal of religion."

NOTE 40
Isaiah and Micah Compared.

Micah	Isaiah	Micah	Isaiah	Micah	Isaiah
i. 9-16	x. 28-32	iii. 5-7	xxix. 9-12	v. 2-4	vii. 14
ii. 1, 2	v. 8	iii. 12	xxxii. 14	v. 6	xiv. 25
ii. 6, 11	xxx. 10, 11	iv. 1	ii. 2	vi. 6-8	lviii. 6, 7
ii. 11	xxviii. 7	iv. 4	i. 20	vii. 7	viii. 17
ii. 12	x. 20-23	iv. 7	ix. 7	vii. 12	xi. 11
		iv. 10	xxxix. 6		

Analysis of Micah

I. THE PEOPLE SUMMONED TO ATTEND (i.-ii.)
"Hear, all ye people" (i. 2).

1. A Declaration of Impending Judgment, ... i. 2-16.
2. A Rehearsal of the Reasons for this Judgment, ii. 1-11.
3. A Promise of Blessing Beyond the Judgment, ii. 12, 13.

II. THE LEADERS SUMMONED TO ATTEND (iii.-v.).
"Hear, O heads of Jacob" (iii. 1).

1. The Sin of the Leaders, and the Consequence, iii.
2. A Promise of Restoration and Blessing, ... iv. 1-8.
3. Israel's sure Travail, but ultimate Triumph, ... iv. 9-v. 15.

III. THE MOUNTAINS SUMMONED TO ATTEND (vi.-vii.).
"Hear ye, O mountains" (vi. 1-9).

1. The Lord Expostulates with His People, ... vi. 1-9.
2. The Indictment and Sentence against the People, vi. 10-16.
3. The Hope of the People, and the Answer of God, vii.

NAHUM

NAHUM, which means "Compassion," or "Consolation," directs his message against Nineveh. About 130 years before Jonah had delivered a message there, and with what results we know (Jonah iii. 5-10). Now, the doom of the city is proclaimed. The dates between which Nahum predicted are 663 B.C., when Thebes fell (iii. 8-10), and 606 B.C., when Nineveh fell ; in all likelihood this prophecy belongs to the year 650 B.C., or there about.

As to its literary form, Dr. R. Moulton says that the Prophecy "hovers between the Doom Song and the Rhapsodic Discourse " ; and as to its quality, De Wette observes that "It is a classic in all respects. It is marked by clearness, by its finished elegance, as well as by fire, richness, and originality. The rhythm is regular and lively." How brilliant and spirited is his description of a battle (iii. 2, 3). Two things characterise the Prophecy ; first, the prophet does not allude to the sin of his people, nor to any impending wrath to be visited upon them (cf. i. 12, 13, 15) ; and second, his gaze is fixed upon the enemies of Judah. At the time of this pronouncement Nineveh appeared to be impregnable, with walls 100 feet high, and broad enough for three chariots to drive abreast on them ; with a circumference of 60 miles, and adorned by more than 1200 towers. But what are bricks and mortar to God ! The mighty Empire which Tiglath-Pileser, Shalmaneser, Sargon, Sennacherib, Esarhaddon, and Asshur-banipal had built up, the Lord threw down at a stroke, and that beyond all recovery. In the second century after Christ, not a vestige of it remained, and its very site was long a matter of uncertainty.

This is a prophecy of doom, and we may not look here for the spiritual element which we find in HOSEA, MICAH, and ISAIAH, though the majesty and mercy of God in i. 1-8, should be carefully studied.

NAHUM is a Book which should bring much comfort in these days to all lovers of righteousness. In our time, as then, proud civilizations, so-called, are staking everything upon the strength of their fighting power on land and sea and in the air, and their boast, as we might expect, is characterized by a monstrous disregard of God, His righteousness and sovereignty; but again, as long ago, men and nations will have to learn that God is on the Throne, and that "His Kingdom ruleth over all."

NOTE 41

Nineveh and Thebes.

NINEVEH. Assyrian city on the left bank of the Tigris, opposite Mosul. Its walls, enclosing 1800 acres, with 15 gates and many towers, were protected on three sides by a moat leading to the Tigris. Nineveh owed its chief renown to Sennacherib (2 Kings xix), who created a majestic palace at Kuyunjik and an arsenal at Nebi Yunus, and also laid out a park wherein he acclimatised exotic animals and plants. Esarhaddon widened the streets and built a palace at Nebi Yunus. The fall of the city, foretold by Nahum and Zephaniah, was achieved by the Medes and Babylonians, B.C. 606, and a Sassanian village grew upon the mounds.

THEBES. The No of chap. iii. 8; Jer. xlvi. 25; Ezek. xxx. 14-16, is Thebes, the ancient capital of Upper Egypt. It lies on the banks of the Nile. 450 miles from Cairo. Of prehistoric foundation, it provided the 11th and 12th dynasty kings, and after the Hyksos expulsion flourished again. It was said to have 100 gates.

Analysis of Nahum

I. JUDGMENT UPON NINEVEH DECLARED (i.).

1. The Character and Power of the Lord, ... 1-8.

2. The Destruction of Nineveh, and the Peace of Judah, ... 9-15.

II. JUDGMENT UPON NINEVEH DESCRIBED (ii.).

1. The Siege and Capture of the City, ... 1-8.

2. The Utter Sack of the City, ... 9-13.

III. JUDGMENT UPON NINEVEH DEFENDED (iii.).

1. Because of her sin she shall be overthrown, ... 1-7.

2. Her great wealth and strength cannot suffice to save her, ... 8-19.

ZEPHANIAH

Keyword—VINDICATION.   CHAPTERS : **3.**

Prophet No. 8   *Southern Kingdom.*   *Pre-Exilic.*

Assyrian Period.   DATE : 640-610 B.C.

ZEPHANIAH means "He whom Jehovah hides," or "Jehovah is hidden." The prophet was, most probably, the great-great-grandson of Hezekiah, and he prophesied in the early years of Josiah's reign, and his words promoted, no doubt, the revival which took place in the eighteenth year of that king's rule. Zephaniah ministered between Nahum and Jeremiah ; was contemporary with the former, and, possibly, with the latter also. This Prophecy reflects the dark days which followed the reigns of Manasseh and Amon. It follows the main prophetic line, denouncing sin, pronouncing judgment, and announcing restoration. These predictions refer not only to the Chosen People, but also to the nations, as in ISAIAH and EZEKIEL. The whole earth is the theatre where the Divine Judge displays the grandeur of His law and the glory of His love.

The dominating note of this Book is "The Day

of the LORD," an expression which, in all the Prophetic Writings, points to a time of judgment.

From a literary point of view, ZEPHANIAH is much inferior to NAHUM, yet its descriptions are vivid. Two contrasted passages are worthy of special attention, namely, i. 14-18, describing judgment, and iii. 14-17, describing blessing.

NOTE 42
The "Day of the LORD" in Zephaniah.

MUCH prophetic material is condensed into small space. "If anyone wishes all the secret oracles of the prophets to be given in a brief compendium, let him read through this brief Zephaniah."

This is essentially the prophecy of *The Day of the* LORD. Nowhere is this Day pictured more vividly than in chap. i. 14-18. It is most important in the study of prophecy and the prophets to discover in what directions their messages con-verge, and to distinguish the various ages which constitute the prophetic plan. While it is true that' this Day of the LORD spoken of by Joel, Amos, Hosea, Micah, Isaiah, and other prophets, had a partial fulfilment when the Chosen People were taken into servitude, and subsequently, it should also be seen that these occasions did not exhaust the passages referred to, but still await such fulfilment. In part, Zephaniah's prophecy reaches on to a time yet to come. It was given to those ancient prophets to soar above the earth-born mists which becloud human vision, and see God's purposes rising majestically against the clear firmament of His righteous sovereignty, like sunlit Alpine peaks against the azure sky; but it was not given to them to see how many an obstacle must be surmounted, how many a disappointment suffered, ere the longed-for goal could be attained. This Day, then, is a time when judgment will be visited upon all the peoples of the earth because of their sins; when the fury of Jehovah will sweep the world and whirl down upon the heads of the wicked. This period is already begun, and will be consummated when Christ returns to the earth in glory. That time of sobs will be fol-lowed by songs (iii. 14-20).

Analysis of Zephaniah

I. A DECLARATION OF RETRIBUTION (i.).

INTRODUCTION (1).

1. **The Scope of Judgment** (2, 3).

2. **The Cause of Judgment** (4-6).

(i.) Idolatry, ...	4, 5a.
(ii.) Oscillation, ...	5b.
(iii.) Apostasy, ...	6.

3. **The Subjects of Judgment** (7-13).

(i.) Princes, ...	8.
(ii.) Oppressors, ...	9, 10.
(iii.) Merchants, ...	11.
(iv.) The Indifferent, ...	12, 13.

4. **The Nature of Judgment** (14-18).

II. AN EXHORTATION TO REPENTANCE (ii. 1-iii. 8a).

1. **The Call to Judah** (ii. 1-3).

2. **The Doom of the Nations** (ii. 4-15).

(i.) West : Philistines, ...	4-7.
(ii.) East : Moabites and Ammonites, ...	8-11.
(iii.) South : Ethiopians, ...	12.
(iv.) North : Assyrians, ...	13-15.

    3. The Sin of Jerusalem (iii. 1-5).
    4. The Fate of the Obdurate (iii. 6-8a).

III. **A PROMISE OF REDEMPTION** (iii. 8b-20).
     1. The Conversion of the Nations (8b-10).
     2. The Restoration of Israel (11-13).
     3. The Day of Jubilation (14-17).
     4. The Reproach Rolled Away (18-20).

HOLD thy peace at the presence of the Lord God;
    For the Day of the LORD is at hand:
For the LORD hath prepared a sacrifice,
    He hath sanctified His guests.

The great Day of the LORD is near:
    It is near and hasteth greatly!
Even the voice of the Day of the LORD;
    The mighty man crieth there bitterly!

That Day is a day of wrath,
    A day of trouble and distress,
A day of wasteness and desolation,
    A day of darkness and gloominess.

A day of clouds and thick darkness,
    A day of the trumpet and alarm
Against the fenced cities,
    And against the high battlements!

Seek ye the LORD, all ye meek of the earth,
Which have wrought His judgment;
      Seek righteousness,
      Seek meekness:
      It may be ye shall be hid
      In the Day of the LORD's anger.

JEREMIAH

Keyword—WARNING.   CHAPTERS : 52.

Prophet No. 9.   *Southern Kingdom.*   *Pre-Exilic and Exilic.*

Assyrian and Babylonian Periods.   DATE : 627-585 B.C.

JEREMIAH seems to mean "Whom Yah casts or appoints." This Book is of immense importance, alike on autobiographical, historical, and prophetical grounds, but all we can do within our present limits is to suggest how the study of it may be approached.

THE TIME OF JEREMIAH.

In the prophetic office he was preceded by Joel, Jonah, Amos, Hosea, Isaiah, Micah, and Nahum ; and he was contemporary with Zephaniah, Habakkuk, and Obadiah in the Land, and, for a time, with Ezekiel and Daniel in the East. He saw five kings upon the throne of Judah : Josiah, Jehoahaz, Jehoiakim, Jehoiachin, and Zedekiah ; and he was to Josiah what Isaiah had been to Hezekiah. Five years after Jeremiah's call the Book of the Law was found in the Temple (2 Kings xxii.), the reading of which led to widespread confession and apparent reformation, but the work was not deep, and with the death of Josiah, Judah's last hope passed away. The condition of things is reflected in chapters x.-xii; and it was at such a time as this that the prophet was called to his thankless but necessary task.

THE PERSON OF JEREMIAH.

This Book has been called "A Prophetic Auto-biography," for, in these pages, the prophet himself stands revealed; timid, sensitive, sympathetic, loyal, courageous, plaintive, retiring, tender, severe, and patient. None of the other prophets comes so near to us in a human way as Jeremiah, and as a sufferer perhaps no other character comes so near to the Man of Sorrows.

THE TASK OF JEREMIAH.

He was told at the beginning what he had to do and what he might expect, and he was promised Divine support (i. 10-19). He had in a decadent age and to a stiff-necked people to proclaim un-welcome truth, and he had his full share of the consequences that generally accompany such a task.

His message passed through certain well-defined stages. There is first the note of DENUNCIATION. Jehovah had delivered this people from Egyptian bondage, had led them through the wilderness, and had wonderfully revealed Himself to them, and His will for them, but they had forsaken Him, they had walked after vanity and become vain. Following on this is the note of VISITATION. Sin must be punished ; with evil comes its inevitable and just reward (xvi. 9, 13 ; xxv. 11).

But these people were "the dearly beloved of Jehovah's soul" (xxi. 7), and so there is added the note of INVITATION. While there is life there is hope ; upon repentance will come blessing. God is both just and gracious ; and so the people are called upon to amend their ways (vii. 3 ; xviiii. 7-10).

One other note is struck, the note of CONSOLA-TION. Beyond rebellion will be repentance, and glory will follow the gloom (xxx.-xxxiii.). During the storm a vision is caught of coming calm, the dawning of a better day. These predictions include the restoration from Babylonian captivity, but they go beyond that, to the time of Christ's next Advent and the final recovery of Israel.

THE BOOK OF JEREMIAH.

Much ingenuity has been spent in the endeavour to place chronologically the various utterances of this prophet, but finality in this need not be expected. It is clear that his messages are not in chronological order in his Book, but seem to be presented according to some group scheme. It

will be well, however, for us to re-arrange the
material so that we may follow the historical course
of events.

The ministry of Jeremiah falls into three main
divisions, separated by long silences, and corresponding to the reigns of the three chief kings
under whom he prophesied. The first period was
under Josiah, and was mainly one of appeal, enforced by declaration of coming visitation. The
second period was under Jehoiakim, and was one
of warning, deepening into irrevocable judgment.
The third period was under Zedekiah, and was one
of reconstruction, seeking to establish a new order
amid the ruins of the old. These three periods
cover forty-five years ; the first, twenty years,
628-608 B.C.; the second, eleven years, 608-597
B.C. ; and the third, fourteen years, 597-583 B.C.
The substance of Jeremiah's messages in these
periods is indicated in the following analysis.

THE INTEREST OF JEREMIAH.

This Book yields to none in the Bible in its
intensely human interest. There is a BIOGRAPHICAL
interest : the characters of the period—Jeremiah,
Baruch, Josiah, Jehoiakim, Zedekiah, Necho, Nebuchadnezzar. There is a HISTORICAL interest : the
stirring events of the period—finding the Book of

the Law, the Reformation, Battles of Megiddo and Carchemish, Nebuchadnezzar's invasion of Judah, Jeremiah's Rolls and Jehoiakim's Vandalism, Destruction of Jerusalem. There is a PROPHETICAL interest—the seventy years' captivity, the future of Babylon and of Israel. There is a DOCTRINAL interest—Jeremiah's teaching on God, the Kingdom, Sin, Repentance, Judgment, the Messiah, the New Covenant. Personal Responsibility, Redemption, Destiny. This is a Book to be known and loved.

NOTE 43
The Prophet Jeremiah.

"TO understand Jeremiah implies such a profound insight into human character, into the lessons of the past and the facts of the present, into the religious history of the race and the perils of to-day, as our happy circumstances and prosperous material civilisation with difficulty allow. To understand Jeremiah is to understand the world's need of Christ."

(BALLANTINE).

"Jeremiah is the most misunderstood of all the great men of history. To be one of the healthiest of men and to be thought morbid, to be one of the strongest and to be thought weak, to be one of the bravest and to be thought faint-hearted, to be a titan and to be thought a pigmy, has been his hard fortune."

(BALLANTINE).

"Keep in mind in your study of Jeremiah that his natural temperament was such that in order to perform the work required of him, he passed through the most intense anguish of spirit. Was the wisdom of God manifest in this? Could a man of different temperament have done this work to which Jeremiah was called? Would the wicked kings and people have listened to announcements of coming judgments from other than tear-filled eyes?" (W. W. WHITE).

Circumstances do not change one; they simply develop what is in one.

Analysis of Jeremiah

(Chronologically Arranged).

INTRODUCTION : Chapter i.

THE PROPHET'S CALL AND COMMISSION.

I. PROPHECIES BEFORE THE FALL OF JERUSALEM.

1. Prophecies in the Reign of Josiah.

(i.) FIRST MOVEMENT, ... **ii.-vi.**
Judah's Sin ; A Call to Repentance ;
Prediction of Judgment.

(ii.) SECOND MOVEMENT, ... **vii.-ix.**
Indictments, Threatenings, the Pro-
phet's Grief, and Wailing called for.

(iii.) THIRD MOVEMENT, ... **x.-xii**
Idolatry, Disobedience, Treachery;
The Lord's Disappointment with
His People.

2. Prophecies in the Reign of Jehoiakim.

(i.) ORDER. Chs. xxvi.; xlvi.-xlix. 33; xxv.;
xxxvi. 1-8; xlv.; xxxvi. 9-32; xiv.-xv.;
xvi.; xvii.; xviii.-xix. 13; xix. 14-xx.;
xxxv.; xxii.-xxiii. 8 ; xxiii. 9-40 ; xiii.

(ii.) SUBSTANCE. Jeremiah predicts judgment
against the nations and Judah ; re-
proves false prophets ; foretells the
Babylonian invasion ; and suffers for
his message.

3. Prophecies in the Reign of Zedekiah.

(i.) ORDER. Chs. xxiv.; xxvii.; xxviii.-xxix.;
xlix.34-li.; xxi.; xxxiv.; xxxvii.-xxxviii.;
xxxix. 15-18 ; xxxii.; xxxiii.; xxx.;
xxxi.; xxxix. 1-14.

(ii.) SUBSTANCE. Great Prediction against Babylon ; Jeremiah's imprisonment ; Prophecies of restoration ; Jerusalem taken, and Zedekiah's fate.

II. PROPHECIES AFTER THE FALL OF JERUSALEM.

1. **The Remnant in Judah,** ... ... xl.-xliii. 3.

2. **The Remnant in Egypt,** ... ... xliii. 4-xliv.

CONCLUSION : Chapter lii.
Historical Supplement.

NOTE 44

Structure of the Book of Jeremiah.

A. i. 1-3. Introduction.

 B. i. 4-19. Jeremiah's Commission given.

  C. ii. 1-xx. 18. Prophecies addressed to Jews.

   D. xxi. 1-xxxv. 19. History, etc. Jehoiakim (not chronological).

    E. xxxvi. 1-32. Baruch's Mission to Jehoiakim.

   D. xxxvii. 1-xlv. 5. History, etc. Zedekiah (not chronological).

  C. xlvi. 1-li. 64. Prophecies addressed to Gentiles.

 B. li. 64. Jeremiah's commission ended.

A. lii. 1-34. Conclusion.   (E. W. BULLINGER).

HABAKKUK

Keyword—JUSTICE.   CHAPTERS : 3.

Prophet No. 10.   *Southern Kingdom.*   *Pre-Exilic.*

Babylonian Period.   DATE : 608-598.

HABAKKUK, which means "Embracing," was contemporary with Jeremiah at home, and with Daniel abroad ; and he prophesied, almost certainly, in the reigns of Jehoahaz and Jehoiakim. The state of things recorded in chapter i. 2-4, reflects the conditions in Jehoiakim's time, and the threatened invasion of the Chaldeans answers to the facts recorded in 2 Kings xxiv.-xxv.

The literary form of the Prophecy is unique among the prophetic Writings. The prophet casts his thought into a dramatic representation, with Jehovah and himself as the speakers. His first complaint is because of the apostasy of Judah, and his second is that the LORD could and would use as the instrument of chastisement such a wicked people as the Chaldeans. The Divine reply to the latter complaint is the heart of the Book (ii. 4). It announces the Divine principle of righteousness which, in effect, is "The unjust shall die : the just shall live." This principle is applied, first to the Chaldeans (ii. 5-20), and then to Judah (ch. iii.). In the first application a five-fold "Woe" is pronounced against the Chaldeans, and the second application is a sublime Theophany and its effect. The text of the effect (iii. 16-19) is one of the finest things in the Bible.

The central thought of the Prophecy is quoted three times in the New Testament, but with varying emphasis. In Rom. i. 17, the emphasis is on "Just;" in Gal. iii. 11, it is on "Faith"; and in Heb. x. 38, it is on "Live."

The Theophanic Ode (iii) was set to music and sung at public worship by the Jews.

NOTE 45
Faith in Habakkuk.

Faith Tested,	.....	..	The Problem: i. 1-ii. 1.
Faith Taught,	.....	.....	The Solution: ii. 2-iii. 15.
Faith Triumphant,		.....	The Issue: iii. 16-19.

NOTE 46
The Woes in Habakkuk.

1. Of Cruel Rapacity, ii. 6-8.
2. Of Reckless Pride, ii. 9-11.
3. Of Relentless Tyranny, ii. 12-14.
4. Of Cunning Baseness, ii. 15-17.
5. Of Insensate Idolatry, ii. 18, 19.

Analysis of Habakkuk

I. THE COMPLAINT (i. 1-11).

1. The Indictment against Judah (2-4).

2. The Invasion of the Chaldeans (5-11).

II. THE APPEAL (i. 12-ii. 20).

1. The Remonstrance (i. 12-ii. 1).

   (i.) The Challenge, ... i. 12-14.

   (ii.) The Charge, ... i. 15, 16.

   (iii.) The Conclusion, ... i. 17-ii. 1

2. The Reply (ii. 2-20).

   (i.) The Principle of Righteousness Announced to the Prophet, ... 2-4.

   (ii.) The Principle of Righteousness Applied to the Chaldeans, ... 5-20.

III. THE SONG (iii.).

1. The Cry for Revival (2).

2. The Vision of Jehovah (3-15).

3. The Effect on the Prophet (16-19).

DANIEL

Keyword : DOMINION.   CHAPTERS : 12.

Prophet No. 11.   *God's Universal Kingdom.*   *Exilic.*

Babylonian and Medo-Persian Periods.   DATE : 606-534 B.C.

DANIEL, which means "God is my Judge,"
spoke and wrote in exile, as did Ezekiel and
John. He, with others, was deported from Judah
in 606 B.C., being then about twenty years of age,
and three years later his recorded ministry began.
As this ministry continued into the Persian period,
Daniel must have been over ninety years of age at
his death. His contemporaries were Jeremiah,
Habakkuk, Ezekiel, and Obadiah.

This Book is not among the Prophets in the
Hebrew Bible, but is one of the five "Latter Writings" (Kethubim), the others being EZRA, NEHE-
MIAH, 1 and 2 CHRONICLES. In its contents the
Book is historical, prophetical, and apocalyptical.
About half of it is history, and about half is pro-
phetic-apocalypse. The first half is narration, and
the second half is revelation. It was written for
the Jews in captivity, and for generations unborn.
The subject is the Trend and End of "the Times
of the Gentiles" (Luke xxi. 24), and the Universal

Kingdom of God's Appointed King. The focus of the Book is "the time of the end" (ii. 28, 29, 45 ; viii. 17, 19, 23, *et al.*). The period covered is 72 years. In chs. i.-vi., Daniel is spoken of, third person ; and in chs. vii.-xii., Daniel speaks, first person.

The chronological order of the chapters is, with their dates : i. (606), ii. (603), iii. (?), iv. (?), vii. (541), viii. (538), v. (538), ix. (537), vi. (537), x. (533), xi. (533), xii. (533). Chapters ii. 4-vii. 28, are in Aramaic, and i. 1-ii. 3, viii.-xii., are in Hebrew.

The Book of Daniel is a Prophetic Philosophy of History, and is the greatest book in the Bible on Godless Kingdoms and the Kingdom of God. These are portrayed in chapter ii., from the human standpoint, by a dream ; and in chapter vii., from the Divine standpoint, by visions. In the one view the world's kingdoms are likened to a powerful Colossus, and in the other view, to four vicious Beasts.

In addition to these two great revelations are the vision of the Two Beasts in chapter viii., the prophecy of the Seventy-Sevens in chapter ix., and the unveiling of the Scripture of Truth in chapters xi. 1-xii. 4.

The two heathen monarchs of the Book are

Nebuchadnezzar and Belshazzar. The Empires introduced are the Babylonian, Medo-Persian, Grecian, and Roman. The portrait of Daniel himself is one of the values of the Book, and his prayer in chapter ix. is one of its great passages.

NOTE 47
Themes in Daniel.

Hebrews at a Heathen Court. Chap. i.
A Dream of Destiny. Chap. ii.
Faithfulness Tested by Fire. Chap. iii.
The Tragedy of a Tree. Chap. iv.
The Feast and the Fingers. Chap. v.
The Lion-hearted among the Lions. Chap. vi.
Godless Kingdoms and the Kingdom of God. Chaps. vii.-viii.
A Prophet at Prayer. Chap. ix.
The Mystery of a Man. Chap. x.
A Struggle for Sovereignty. Chaps. xi. 1-xii. 4.
A Vision of Victory. Chap. xii. 5-13.

NOTE 48
Daniel's Age in the Chapters of His Book.

Order of Chapters.	Age of Daniel.
i.	19
ii.	22
iii.	?
iv.	?
vii.	84
viii.	87
v.	87
ix.	88
vi.	88
x.	92
xi.	92
xii.	92

Analysis of Daniel

I. HISTORICAL (i.-vi.).

EZEKIEL

Keyword—GLORY.   CHAPTERS : 48.

Prophet No. 12.   *Exilic.*   *Babylonian Period.*

DATE : 592-572 B.C.

EZEKIEL, which means "God Strengthens," was taken into Babylonian captivity with Jehoiachim in 599 B.C., being about twenty-three years of age, and seven years later he began his prophetic ministry and continued for twenty years. Like Jeremiah, he was a priest as well as a prophet. Of the three Major Prophets, Isaiah was the great poet, Jeremiah was the great preacher, and Ezekiel was the great artist. Isaiah had blown the silver trumpet over Jerusalem, Jeremiah was playing the mournful flute in Judah, and Ezekiel was striking the iron harp by the Chebar. This prophet has not the sustained flight of Isaiah, nor the tenderness or Jeremiah, but there is a directness which is common only to stern strong natures.

The style and method of Ezekiel are unique. Symbolic action often supplies the text for his message, as in the Mimic Siege of Jerusalem (ch. iv.).

In addition to this Emblem Prophecy, are Visions,

as in ch. viii. ; Similitudes, as in ch. xvi. ; Parables, as in ch. xvii. ; Poems, as in ch. xix. ; Proverbs, as in ch. xii. 22, 23 ; xviii. 2 ; Allegories, as in chs. xvi., xxiii. ; and Prophecies, as in chs. vi., xx., xl.-xlviii. No artist has given us pictures so inspiring, so mysterious, so charming and so terrifying as these.

The dominating notes of his ministry are Sin, Punishment, Repentance, and Blessing. To destroy false hopes and to awaken true ones was the burden of his soul.

The Book falls into three distinct parts. 1, Predictions *before* the Siege of Jerusalem : chs. i.-xxiv ; B.C. 592-588 ; 4½ years. 2, Predictions *during* the Siege of Jerusalem : chs. xxv.-xxxii ; 588-586 B.C. ; 2 years. 3, Predictions *after* the Siege of Jerusalem : chs. xxxiii.-xlvii ; 586-572 B.C. ; 14 years. The subjects treated in these parts are, the Denunciation of Judah ; the Visitation of the Nations ; and the Restoration of Israel.

The Book begins with Heavenly Glory, in the Cherubic Vision (ch. i.) ; it ends with Earthly Glory, in the vision of the New Order (chs. xl.-xlviii.) ; and in between, it tells of the Departing Glory (viii. 4 ; ix. 3 ; x. 4, 18, 19 ; xi. 22, 23). The idea of Glory runs through the whole Prophecy, and, in a sense, characterises it.

Ezekiel has been called "the prophet of recon-struction," and this he was. He saw a great future not for Judah only, but for the whole Nation, when it shall have been reunited and purified (chs. xxxvi.-xxxvii.). With Jeremiah, he shares in the distinction of promulgating the doctrine of individual responsibility, but he gives it an emphasis which is all his own (cf. Jer. xxxi. 29, 30 Ezek. xviii.).

NOTE 49
Ezekiel and His Book.
STUDY OUTLINE.

THE PROPHET HIMSELF.
    Earliest Influences.
    Personal Details.
    Call and Commission.
HIS PROPHETIC MISSION.
    Ezekiel in Judea.
    Ezekiel in Chaldea.
HIS PROPHETIC MESSAGE.
    Outline of his Prophecies.
        Denunciation of Judah, i.-xxiv.
        Visitation of the Nations, xxv.-xxxii.
        Restoration of Israel, xxxiii.-xlviii.
    Dominant Notes of his Ministry.
        Sin, Punishment, Repentance, Blessing.
HIS PROPHETIC METHOD.
    The Simple Method.
        By Proverbs, *e.g.*, chap. xviii.
        By Parables, *e.g.*, chaps. xv., xvii., xxiv.
        By Allegories, *e.g.*, chaps. xvi., xxiii.
    The Complex Method.
        By Sustained Imagery, *e.g.*, chaps. xxix.-xxxii.
        By Gesture Language, *e.g.*, chap. iv. 1-3.
        By Vision, *e.g.*, chap. xxxvii.

Analysis of Ezekiel

I. DENUNCIATION OF JUDAH (i.-xxiv.)

Predictions BEFORE the Siege of Jerusalem.
4½ years, 592-588 B.C.

II. VISITATION OF THE NATIONS (xxv.-xxxii.).

Predictions DURING the Siege of Jerusalem.
2 years. 588-586 B.C.

1. Against Ammon (xxv. 1-7).
2. Moab (xxv. 8-11).
3. Edom (xxv. 12-14).

4. Philistia (xxv. 15-17.)
5. Tyre (xxvi.-xxviii. 19).
6. Sidon (xxviii. 20-26).

7. Seven Predictions against Egypt (xxix.-xxxii.).

III. RESTORATION OF ISRAEL (xxxiii.-xlviii).

Predictions AFTER the Siege of Jerusalem.
14 years. 586-572 B.C.

1. **Predictions of New Life to be Bestowed.**
   (xxxiii.-xxxix.).

   (i.) The Watchman and the Shepherds, ... xxxiii.-xxxiv.
   (ii.) Restoration of Israel, Moral and Corporate, ... xxxv.-xxxvii.
   (iii.) Judgment against Gog and Magog, ... xxxviii.-xxxix.

2. **Descriptions of the New Order to be Established (xl.-xlviii.).**

   (i.) The Vision of the Temple, ... xl.-xliii. 12.
   (ii.) The People and the Temple, ...:. xliii. 13-xlvi.
   (iii.) The Land and the Temple, ... xlvii.-xlviii.

OBADIAH

Keyword—RETRIBUTION.   CHAPTER : I.

Prophet No. 13.   *Exilic.*   *Babylonian Period.*

DATE : 586-583. B.C.

OBADIAH, which means "Servant of Jehovah,"
received this "vision" about the time of
Judah's overthrow in 586. Of the prophet we know
nothing, and although his message is short it is
significant. His contemporary was Jeremiah. His
word is against Edom, as Nahum's was against
Nineveh. The Edomites were the posterity of
Esau, and consistently were Israel's enemies. The
quarrel between the two brothers was reflected in
their posterity. When Jerusalem fell, the Edomites
rejoiced (cf. Lam. iv. 21, 22 ; Psa. cxxxvii. 7).

The overthrow of this people, it is said, is certain
(1-9). They will be unseated from their security
(3, 4), plundered by enemies (5, 6), deserted by
allies (7), and stripped of wisdom and might (8, 9).
The reason for this is given (10-14) ; namely, for
her bitter hostility to Jacob her brother (10), for
her shameful alliance with Judah's foes (11), and
for the part she played at the time of Judah's

overthrow (12-14).   In consequence of this,
Edom will be overthrown; her punishment will be
retributive (15, 16).

On the other hand, Israel will be delivered, and
"possess their possessions" (17-21).   Some think
that the Prophet speaks here not of the calamity
in 586 B.C. but of the capture and plunder of
Jerusalem by the Philistines and Arabians in 848-
844 B.C.   Obadiah's message is a rebuke of pride
and unbrotherliness, and an affirmation of the law
of retribution (cf. Jer. xlix. ; Ezek. xxv.).

In form the prophecy is lyric exultation with
Divine monologue.

NOTE 50
Esau and Edom.

Read the history of Edom in a good Bible Dictionary.
Study the history of Esau in Genesis.
Locate the land of Edom, and learn what you can about its
extent and topography.
Connect Amos ix. 2 and Obadiah 4.
Mark the places where *Esau* and *Edom* are used in the
prophecy.
See what Amos, Joel, and Obadiah say about Edom.
Compare Obadiah and Psalm cxxxvii.

Analysis of Obadiah

I. THE DOOM OF EDOM (1-16).

1. The Certainty of the Overthrow, ... 1-9.
2. The Reason for the Overthrow, ... 10-14.
3. The Character of the Overthrow, ... 15, 16.

II. THE DELIVERANCE OF ISRAEL (17-21).

1. The Triumph of Israel, ... 17-18.
2. The Possessions of Israel, ... 19, 20.
3. The Establishment of Israel, ... 21.

HAGGAI

Keyword—CONSIDER.   CHAPTERS : 2.

Prophet No. 14.   *To the Jews.   Post-Exilic.*

Medo-Persian Period. DATE : 520.

A^T this point we enter upon a new prophetic period. The history of the people of Israel, as to government, is divisible into three periods : (1) Israel under Judges, Moses to Samuel ; (2) under Kings, Saul to Zedekiah ; and (3) under Priests, Joshua to the Destruction of Jerusalem in 70 A.D. Viewed in relation to the captivity, the periods are: (1) Pre-Exilic ; (2) Exilic ; and (3) Post-Exilic. Or, viewed in relation to the world Empires, the periods are : (1) the Assyrian ; (2) the Babylonian ; and (3) the Medo-Persian. Haggai, Zechariah, and Malachi ministered in the third of each of these periods.

Haggai, which means "Festal," and who prophesied in 520 B.C., was, no doubt, born in captivity, and returned to the Land under Zerubbabel. The foundation of the Temple had been laid, but the work had for long been at a standstill, and it was to urge the people to complete it that Haggai prophesied. His ministry lasted for about four months, during which time he delivered four messages, which are dated. Sixth month, first day ; i. 2-11. Seventh month, twenty-first day ; ii. 1-9. Ninth month, twenty-fourth day ; ii. 10-19. Ninth month, twenty-fourth day ; ii. 20-23. The message of the Book to us is : Do the duty which lies to hand, with unwavering faith and steady perseverance, in spite of opposition. "Be strong and work."

NOTE 51
The Prophecies of Haggai.

THE Book is a series of four Prophecies to the Builders of the Temple, each exactly dated.

i. The hard times suffered by the community connected with their caring for their own houses before giving themselves to the building of the Temple.

ii. Depression at the sight of the restored Temple combated; the latter glory shall be greater than the former.

iii. An analogy: the touch of pollution defiles, the touch of holiness does not make holy; their two months' zeal has not yet brought the blessing, but it shall come.

iv. Zerubbabel shall be the signet of God (the position forfeited by Jehoiachin (or Jeconiah); cf. Jer. xxii. 24-30).   (Prof. RICHARD MOULTON).

Analysis of Haggai

I. THE WORD OF REPROOF (i.).

1. The Temple of the Lord is Unfinished, ... 1-6.
2. The Trouble of the People is Explained, ... 7-11.
3. The Testimony of the Prophet is Heeded, ... 12-15.

II. THE WORD OF SUPPORT (ii. 1-9).

1. The Depression of the People, ... 1-3.
2. The Promise of the Lord, ... 4, 5.
3. The Glory of the Temple, ... 6-9.

III. THE WORD OF BLESSING (ii. 10-19).

1. The Diffusive Character of Evil, ... 10-13.
2. The Uncleanness of the People, ... 14-17.
3. The Certainty of the Blessing, ... 18, 19.

IV. THE WORD OF PROMISE (ii. 20-23).

ZECHARIAH

Keyword—Consummation.   Chapters : 14.

Prophet No. 15.   *To the Jews.*   *Post-Exilic.*

Medo-Persian Period.   Date : 520-518.

ZECHARIAH, which means "One whom Jehovah remembers," was contemporary with Haggai, was his junior in years (ii. 4), and spoke for the same purpose. He, too, no doubt, was born in captivity, and returned under Zerubbabel. He and Haggai both prophesied in the second year of Darius Hystaspes, and their ministries were eminently effective.

The Prophecy falls into two main divisions, chs. i.-viii. and ix.-xiv. ; and each of these is in two parts. The authorship of chs. ix.-xiv. is uncertain, and in Matt. xxvii. 9, 10, a quotation from this division is attributed to Jeremiah. The style differs from that of chs. i.-viii ; the circumstances are wholly changed ; visions have ceased, and prophecy rises to a more solemn strain. The following analysis indicates the subject of the four parts.

Zechariah saw eight visions in one eventful night :

The Angelic Horsemen (i. 7-17); The Four Horns and the Four Smiths (i. 18-21); The Man with the Measuring Line (ii.); Joshua the High Priest (iii.); The Candlestick and the Olive Trees (iv.); The Flying Roll (v. 1-4); The Ephah and the Woman (v. 5-11); and The Four Chariots and Horses (vi. 1-8).

The Symbolic Act which follows (vi. 9-15), is designed to show that the promised Branch will exercise, as did Melchisedec, the double office of Priest-King, when He returns to the earth to set up His Millennial Kingdom. In chs. vii.-viii., in reply to an inquiry as to whether certain Fasts were now to be observed (vii. 1-3), a fourfold answer is given: (1) They should discover their motive in fasting, and remember the former years (vii. 4-7); (2) the Lord requires inward righteousness rather than outward forms (vii. 8-14); (3) the Lord will restore to His people what they had lost (viii. 1-7); and (4) the Fasts will be turned into Feasts of gladness (viii. 8-23).

In division two (chs. ix.-xiv.) are two Burdens (ix. 1; xii. 1). The first Burden is to the effect that Israel will be reunited and restored; and the second is to the effect that before this restoration there will be judgment on Israel because of their rejection of the Messiah; but all their enemies will be overthrown, and they at last shall be characterised by "Holiness unto the Lord."

Three great ideas characterise this Book, namely, an universal purpose, a Messianic hope, and Divine sovereignty.

NOTE 52

The Author of Zechariah ix.-xiv.

IT must not just be assumed that chapters ix.-xiv. of this Prophecy were not written by Zechariah. The differences in style between these chapters and chapters i.-viii. may be explained by the difference of subject and the probable interval of thirty or forty years in the prophet's life. The predictions of chapters ix.-xiv. require a different style from the visions of chapters i.-viii. The early part of the Book was meant to encourage Israel while building the Temple, but the latter part consists of woes upon the enemies of God's people, and promises of blessing upon Israel. Therefore the reassuring "thus saith the Lord" is appropriate to the early but not to the later part of the Book. The characteristic mark of prediction, "in that day," is rare in the early chapters because prediction is rare, and common near the end of the Book because that part is almost entirely predictive. We would not expect many literary marks of a common authorship between prophecies so totally different in occasion and purpose, one uttered by a young man, and the other by an old man; yet compare chapters ii. 10 and ix. 9; viii. 8 and xiii. 9.

Analysis of Zechariah

I. THE CHOSEN PEOPLE AND THE TEMPLE.
Chapters i.-viii.

1. The Visions of the Seer (i.-vi.).

2. The Fasts and the Feasts (vii, viii.).

II. THE MESSIANIC KING AND THE KINGDOM.
Chapters ix.-xiv.

FIRST BURDEN.

1. The Final Restoration of Judah and Israel (ix.-xi.).

SECOND BURDEN.

2. The World-Drama of Judgment and Redemption (xii.-xiv.).

MALACHI

Keyword—Apostasy.　　　　Chapters : 4.

Prophet No. 16.　*To the Jews.*　*Post-Exilic.*

Medo-Persian Period.　　Date : 433-425 B.C.

MALACHI means "My Messenger," and
whether it is the name of the author of this
Book, or a title employed to express his mission,
is not certain (cf. iii. 1). This is the last of the Old
Testament Prophecies. The setting of it is in the
stirring time of Nehemiah, and Malachi was to
that reformer what Haggai and Zechariah had been
to Zerubbabel.

Following on a period of religious revival (Neh.
x. 28-39), the people became religiously indifferent
and morally lax, and it is this state of things which
Malachi rebukes (cf. Neh. xiii. 4-31).

The attitude of the people is exhibited in the
sevenfold "wherein" (i. 2, 6, 7 ; ii. 17 ; iii. 7, 8, 13),
and the charge which Malachi brought against them
is fourfold, relating to things religious, moral,
social, and material. Religiously, they were guilty
of profanity and sacrilege ; morally, of sorcery,
adultery, perjury, fraud, and oppression ; socially,
they were untrue to their family responsibilities ;

and materially, they were "robbing God" of the
tithes due to Him.

The Prophecy ends with a reference backward to
Moses, and forward to Elijah, that is, John the
Baptist. The heart of hope in the Prophecy is
chapter iii. 10, 16-18.

Malachi's message is eminently necessary and
appropriate to-day, for these abuses have their
equivalents in the modern Church. How prevalent
is "a form of godliness," the power being denied ;
how weak are multitudes of Christians with regard
to great moral questions ; how frequent is alliance
in marriage of saved and unsaved ; and how shame-
fully lax are Christians in the matter of giving of
their substance for the maintenance of God's work.
To this situation Malachi still speaks.

At the end of the first Book of the Old Testament we read of a "coffin," and at the end of the
last Book we read of a "curse," indicating that, till
then, all was failure ; but the Second Man, the
Lord from Glory, having come, the New Testament
opens and closes in better terms ; Grace triumphant
at last.

Analysis of Malachi

I. RELIGIOUS DECLENSION (i.-ii. 9).

1. Expression of Jehovah's love for Israel, ... i. 1-5.
2. Expostulation with the Priests for their offences, ... i. 6-14.
3. Execration of the Priests for their indifference, ... ii. 1-9.

II. SOCIAL DEBASEMENT (ii. 10-16).

Condemnation of the Priests and the People.

      (*a*) For Alien Marriages.

      (*b*) For Cruel Divorces.

III. MORAL DEFLECTION (ii. 17-iv. 6).

1. The Coming of the Lord for Judgment, ... ii. 17-iii. 6.
2. The Charge preferred against the People, ... iii. 7-12.
3. The Contrast between the righteous and the wicked. ... ... iii. 13-iv. 6.

Concluding Note

THE period of about four centuries between the
Testaments is of immense importance for a
right understanding of the New Testament. The
Old Testament closed in the Medo-Persian period,
and the New Testament opens in the Roman
period, and between these is the great Grecian
period. Between the Testaments the seat of World
Empire moved from the East to the West, from
Asia to Europe. In this period arose Greek cities
in Palestine, bearing Greek names, and the Hebrew
Scriptures were translated into Greek (LXX).
Also in this period arose the sects of the Pharisees,
the Sadducees, and the Essenes, and the Sanhedrin
came into existence. In Malachi's time the Temple
of Zerubbabel was standing, but in Matthew's time,
the Temple of Herod. Synagogues also arose in
this period, which are so prominent in the New
Testament. To this period also we are indebted
for the fourteen Writings of the Apocrypha, some
of which, such as the two MACCABEES, the WISDOM
OF SOLOMON, and ECCLESIASTICUS, are of great
literary and historical importance. It was also in
this period that the doctrine of immortality was

taught by Plato. While these Apocryphal Writings are not regarded as Holy Scripture, they must not be neglected by the Bible student. Though we have no inspired writings of this period, God was not inactive, and the fulfilment of His redeeming purpose was progressing towards "the fulness of the time," when Christ would appear.

NOTE 53
Personalities and Events Between the Testaments.

B.C.

399 Death of Socrates.
384 Birth of Aristotle (d. 322)
382 Birth of Demosthenes (d. 322).
356 Birth of Alexander the Great (d. 323).
347 Death of Plato.
341 Birth of Epicurus (d. 270)
323 Alexander the Great dies
306 Alexander's dominion divided into four kingdoms as foretold by Daniel.
287 Birth of Archimedes (d. 212).
285 Version of the LXX commenced at Alexandria.
    Palestine alternately subject to the Ptolemies of Egypt and the Seleucidae of Syria.
180 Probable date of *Ecclesiasticus*.
175 Great persecution of the Jews by Antiochus Epiphanes, predicted by Daniel.

B.C.

167 Noble revolt of Mattathias and his five sons.
146 Carthage destroyed by Scipio.
106 Births of Pompey and Cicero.
100 Birth of Julius Caesar (d. 44).
95 Birth of Lucretius (d. 55).
75 Birth of Hillel.
70 Birth of Virgil (d. 19).
63 Pompey takes Jerusalem.
59 Birth of Livy (d. A.D. 17).
48 Murder of Pompey in Egypt.
44 Caesar assassinated.
43 Birth of Ovid (d. A.D. 18).
40 Herod appointed King of the Jews.
30 Deaths of Antony and Cleopatra.
17 Herod begins to rebuild the Temple.
4 JESUS CHRIST IS BORN.

THE NEW TESTAMENT

NOTE 54
The Divisions of the New Testament.

IN earliest times the New Testament was divided into three parts: 1. The Gospels, *To Euangelion*; 2. The Epistles, *To Apostolikon*; and, 3. Revelation, *Hē Apokalupsis*.

1. *The Gospels* are divisible into two parts:
   (i) *The Synoptic Gospels.*   (ii) *The Fourth Gospel.*

The first three Gospels are called *synoptic*, because they present the same general view or outline, from *sun*, with, and *opsis*, seeing, *i.e.* seeing together.

2. *The Epistles* are divisible into two parts:
   (i) *The Pauline Epistles.*   (ii) *The Catholic Epistles.*

The Epistles which are not Pauline are called Catholic or General, because they are not addressed to single Churches. This designation dates from the second century. Though Second and Third John are not "general," they are viewed under cover of the First Epistle.

3. *The Revelation* is the only book of its class in the New Testament. The word *apokalupsis* means unveiling, disclosing, making known, from *kalupsis*, a covering, with *apo*, away from, *i.e.* an uncovering. At the time this book was written its contents were almost wholly related to the future, and many think they still are.

It should not be considered fanciful to see in words of our Lord, spoken in the Upper Room, references to each of these divisions of the N.T.

The Gospels : 'He (the Spirit) shall bring to your remembrance all that I said unto you."

The Epistles : "He shall guide you into all the truth."

The Revelation: "He shall declare unto you the things that are to come."—(John xiv. 26; xvi. 13).

THE NEW TESTAMENT

Introduction

"TESTAMENT" means "Covenant," and wherever there is a covenant there must be two parties. In this case the parties are Divine and human, God and man.

But this is a *New* Covenant, and that implies that there was something before. There are two words in our Version which are translated "new"; one of them means new *as to time* (*neos*, Heb. xii. 24), and the other means new *as to quality* (*kainos*, Heb. ix. 15), and both are used and are true of this collection of Writings which we call the New Testament. It is new as to time because it follows the Old Testament, and it is new as to quality because it is better than the former Covenant.

The Old Covenant centres in and circles round the Law, but the New Covenant, in and round the Gospel (John i. 17). The New Covenant is the superstructure of which the Old is the foundation. The Old is foreshadow, and the New is fulfilment. The Old is promise, and the New is performance.

The Old is a problem, and the New is a solution. The Old is a commencement, and the New is a consummation. These Covenants cannot be rightly understood apart.

In the Old Testament are thirty-nine Writings, and in the New there are twenty-seven. The broadest classification of the latter gives us two main divisions, the Evangelical Writings, and the Apostolical, four and twenty-three respectively. They may also be classified as Historical, five; Doctrinal, twenty-one; and Apocalyptical, one. The GOSPELS relate to the past; the ACTS and EPISTLES to the present; and the REVELATION to the future. In the GOSPELS Christ is Prophet, in the ACTS and EPISTLES He is Priest, and in the REVELATION He is King. Israel gives complexion to the GOSPELS, the Church to the ACTS and EPISTLES, and the World to the REVELATION. In the GOSPELS we see the Founder of revealed religion; in the ACTS and EPISTLES we have the fundamentals of it; and in the REVELATION the fulfilment of it. In the first group is introduction; in the second is application; and in the third is realisation. "The truths found in germ in the GOSPELS, are historically illustrated in the ACTS, doctrinally unfolded and applied in the EPISTLES, and symbolically presented in the Apocalypse."

This collection of Writings came into existence during the second half of the first century of our era (50-100 A.D.), and the period represented is a century. There are eight authors, and possibly a ninth for HEBREWS. The *chronological* order of the Books is the order in which they were written, probably as follows : JAMES, MARK, 1-2 THESS., 1-2 CORINTHIANS, GALATIANS, ROMANS, MATTHEW, LUKE, EPHESIANS, COLOSSIANS, PHILEMON, PHILIPPIANS, 1-2 PETER, ACTS, HEBREWS, JUDE, 1 TIM., TITUS, 2 TIM., REVELATION. JOHN'S GOSPEL, 1-3 EPISTLES OF JOHN. The order in our Bible is the *logical*, first the Christ, then the Church, and finally the Consummation.

The value of these Writings, historical and spiritual, is out of all proportion to their number and length, and their influence upon life and history is incalculable. Here is the noontide of the day which began to dawn in Eden. The Christ of Prophecy in the Old Testament becomes the Christ of History in the Gospels ; the Christ of Experience in the Epistles ; and the Christ of Glory in the Revelation.

The Ministry of Jesus the Christ.

	I. PREPARATION		II. MINISTRATION						III. CONSUMMATION
					GALILEAN				
	1	2	3	4			5	6	7
	THE 30 YEARS	OPENING EVENTS	JUDÆAN	FIRST PERIOD	SECOND PERIOD	THIRD PERIOD	PERÆAN	CLOSING EVENTS	THE 40 DAYS
MARK	—	i. 1-13	—	i. 14—iii. 6	iii. 7—vii. 23	vii. 24—ix. 50	x. 1-52	xi. 1—xv. 47	xvi. 1 - 20
LUKE	i. 1—ii. 52	iii. 1—iv. 13	—	iv. 14—vi. 11	vi. 12—ix. 17	ix. 18-50	ix. 51—xix. 28	xix. 29—xxiii. 56	xxiii. 56—xxiv. 53
MATTHEW	i. 1—ii. 23	iii. 1—iv. 11	—	iv. 12—xii. 14	xii. 15—xv. 20	xv. 21—xviii. 35	xix. 1—xx. 34	xxi. 1—xxvii. 66	xxviii. 1 - 20
JOHN	i. 1-18	i. 19—ii. 12	ii. 13—iv. 42	iv. 43—v. 47	vi. 1-71	vii. 1—viii. 59	ix. 1—xii. 11	xii. 12—xix. 42	xx. 1—xxi. 25

EVANGELICAL WRITINGS

INTRODUCTION

NOTE 56

The Synoptic Problem.

THAT there is such a problem is a fact, and it should not be ignored by the average student of the Gospels. No one can read these Gospels without observing that there are resemblances and differences, and the problem consists in the harmonising of these, and so of determining the relation of the Synoptics to one another. These records are compilations, and behind them are sources upon which they have drawn, and the question is, what were these sources ?

In the main there are three hypotheses:

1. **The Oral Tradition Hypothesis.** This assumes that each of the Evangelists wrote independently of the others, and derived the substance of his writing not from written sources but from oral narratives of sayings and doings of Jesus which, by virtue of repetition, had assumed a relatively fixed form.

2. **The Mutual Use Hypothesis.** In this view the problem can be accounted for by assuming that one of these Gospels was used by the other two, and each of the three has been regarded as the source of the others.

3. **The Documents Hypothesis.** This is the theory which almost all scholars hold at the present time, with differences of opinion as to how many such documents there were. Most scholars are agreed upon two such sources:

(*a*) Mark's Gospel, and (*b*) a now non-existent document which is called "Q," from the German *quelle*, meaning *source*. But the facts necessitate the assumption of other sources.

The Synoptic Problem, therefore, has to account for (1) what is common to all the Gospels, (2) what is common to any two of them, and (3) what is peculiar to each.

The EVANGELICAL WRITINGS
Introduction

TITLE.

WHAT are called the Gospels, MATTHEW, MARK, LUKE and JOHN, are really four records of one Gospel. The word "Gospel" means "Good News," and this meaning sufficiently indicates the scope, content, and value of these Records. All the Biblical Writings give news, but they do not all give good news. This Good News is that God has manifested Himself in time and in flesh for the redemption of mankind. Each of the four Gospels records this Good News.

ORIGIN AND SOURCES.

The origination of these Writings is one of the problems of the New Testament, and must be left to the New Testament critical scholar. That behind our Gospels were sources which were drawn upon there can be little doubt (cf. Luke i. 1-4). There is material which is common to MATTHEW, MARK, LUKE, and each of these has material which is peculiar to itself. Differences there are, but these are not necessarily discrepancies; contrasts do not necessarily mean contradictions.

The first three Records are called *synoptic*, which means that they give the same general view or outline. The fourth Record is *autoptic*, and quite distinct in viewpoint and time.

DATE AND ORDER.

It is not possible to fix with certainty the dates of these Records, but the earliest, we may say, was not before 50 A.D., and the latest was not after 95 A.D. Unquestionably the first to appear was MARK, and the last, JOHN, and of the other two, MATTHEW is prior to LUKE.

AUTHORSHIP.

There is no reason to doubt that these Records came from the men whose names they bear, MATTHEW, the taxgatherer ; MARK, the son of Mary ; LUKE, "the beloved physician ;" and JOHN, the fisherman. Concerning the authorship of the Fourth Gospel much criticism has raged, but Bishop Westcott's evidence for the Johannine authorship is unanswerable.

CHARACTER.

It is difficult to classify the Gospels as literature. They are not history, nor are they biography, as we commonly understand these terms, and yet they are more than miscellaneous notes concerning

Jesus' life, teaching, and work. Perhaps *Memoirs* is as good a designation as any.

NUMBER AND CHARACTERISTICS.

Not all that has been written on this point has been profitable, and some of it has been absurd. The number of Gospels recognised as genuine has always been four. As early as 150 A.D., Tatian, a Syrian, made a harmonic arrangement of these four from a Syriac translation of them then in existence.

The reason for there being four, and four only, must be significant, and this significance we must look for in the answer which Christ is to the need of mankind ; to the Jew in MATTHEW, to the Roman in MARK, to the Greek in LUKE ; and to the Church in JOHN. There is the need ; and the answer is Christ, the Sovereign in MATTHEW, the Servant in MARK, the Man in LUKE, and God in JOHN. These presentations are inclusive and final. The first two are official, and the last two are personal.

With these distinctions there are other characteristics of these Records which help us to understand why there are only four. MATTHEW is specially related to the Past, MARK to the Present, LUKE to the Future, and JOHN to all Eternity. The Cherubic figures of Ezekiel have a symbolic significance which is reflected in these Records : MATTHEW being Lion-like ; MARK, Ox-like ; LUKE, Man-like ; and JOHN, Eagle-like. Matthew is the preacher, Mark is the chronicler, Luke is the historian, and John is the philosopher.

VALUE.

We are entirely dependent upon these four Records for our knowledge of the Redeemer. Had these not been written it is probably true that the Church would not have survived.

That behind the human authors and sources was a Divine superintending providence cannot be doubted. These unschooled men were unconscious artists, and were guided by the Spirit of God to portray a character which neither they nor any other could have created. The value of these brief pamphlets is beyond all price.

In the brief introduction to each of these Gospels, reference will be made to seven particulars, namely, authorship, readers, place of writing, date, style, purpose, and features. These particulars should be followed out in detail by a careful reading of the Records, together with some reliable INTRODUCTION.

MARK

Keyword : MINISTRY.　　　　　"BEHOLD MY SERVANT."

WRITTEN IN ROME.　　WRITTEN FOR ROMANS.

OX-LIKE ASPECT.　　THE GOSPEL OF WORK.

DATE : 50-55 A.D.

THE AUTHOR.

JOHN MARK was the son of Mary, who lived in Jerusalem (Acts xii. 12). His name occurs eight times in the New Testament. JOHN was his Jewish, and MARK, his Roman name. At the beginning of Paul's missionary life, and at the end of it, Mark was with him, and, it would appear, he was with Peter between these periods.

That Mark wrote this GOSPEL is a very ancient tradition, going back to the time of Papias, 120 A.D., who speaks of him as "the interpreter of Peter." In Acts x. 34-43, is a summary of Peter's preaching, and Mark's Gospel is substantially the full text of Peter's oral messages. By "interpreter," in all likelihood Papias meant "translator," that is, that Mark translated into Greek the Aramaic in which Peter would preach.

THE READERS.

The view has strong support that Mark wrote

for Roman readers. The evidence for this is both external and internal. There is a general absence of Old Testament quotations. Words the meaning of which a Roman would not have known are translated (*e.g.*, iii. 17 ; v. 41 ; x. 46, etc.). Jewish customs are explained (*e.g.*, vii. 2 ff ; xv. 42). The Mount of Olives is located (xiii. 3). There is no mention of the Jewish law. Latin words occur which are not in the other Records (*e.g.* vi. 27 ; vii. 4 ; xii. 42, etc.).

THE PLACE OF WRITING.

It has been held that Mark wrote in Egypt, in Antioch, in Syria, and in Cæsarea, but the preponderance of testimony looks to Rome as the place of writing. This view finds warrant and confirmation in 1 Peter v. 13, if "Babylon" there means Rome.

THE DATE.

It may be assumed that this Gospel was written before the destruction of Jerusalem, in 70 A.D. It is also certain that this is the first of the Four Records, and as Luke's Gospel would be written about 56-60 A.D., Mark's must have been before 56 A.D., and, says Dr. A. T. Robertson, the most probable date is 50 A.D., the earliest of the New Testament Writings, with the possible exception of JAMES.

THE STYLE.

Of all the GOSPELS, Mark's is the most graphic, the most simple and direct. His words are little pictures. His favourite tenses are the imperfect and the historical present, which set before us the action and movement of real life (cf. i. 30, 37). Mark's style, says Dr. Morrison, "is unclassical, provincial, and destitute of every species of ' the wisdom of words.' It is homely, unadorned, and devoid of literary artifice or art." This artlessness is no small part of its charm.

THE PURPOSE.

The opening words may be taken to indicate the purpose (i. 1), namely, to present Jesus as He had been in daily actual life, living and working among men, in the fulness of His energy, the Servant Who stooped to conquer (Zech. iii. 8 ; Isa. lii. 13-liii. 12). Chapter x. 45 summarizes the Gospel : "The Son of Man came . . . to minister, " chaps. i.-x.; "and to give His life a ransom for many," chaps. xi.-xvi.

FEATURES.

In these the Gospel is rich, and only a few can be named. Here are eighteen miracles, two of which are exclusively Mark's ; and four parables, one of which is peculiar to this Gospel. None of these parables is developed, and there are here no long discourses. Mark alone says, and says twice, that the Apostles "had no leisure so much as to eat." Forty-one times he uses a word (*eutheōs*) which is variously translated "immediately," "anon," "forthwith," "by and by," "straightway," "as soon as," and "straitly." He alone tells us of not less than eleven occasions amid His work on which Christ retired, either to escape from His enemies, or to refresh His soul with prayer. He alone tells us that Jesus was "the carpenter," so flashing a light over the obscure years in Nazareth. Emphasis by repetition is characteristic of Mark (*e.g.*, i. 45; iv. 8; xiv. 68, *et al.*). Also he is rich in detail (*e.g.*, iii. 16; x. 46; v. 13; vi. 7; i. 35; iv. 35; xi. 4; xii. 41; vi. 32; i. 41, 43; viii. 12, 23, etc.). These details, and such like, refer to names, number, time, place, colour, and feeling.

NOTE 57
Mark in Matthew and Luke.

OF Matthew's 1068 verses (R.V.) about 500 are from Mark's 661 verses; and of Luke's 1149 verses (R.V.) about 320 are from Mark. Only from 20 to 30 verses of Mark are not to be found in either Matthew or Luke.

Analysis of Mark

As MARK'S Gospel was the first of the four to be written, and is almost completely incorporated in MATTHEW and LUKE, a very detailed analysis of it is given, showing that it consists of 112 paragraphs. The seven parts of the Day fall in three pairs with the Consummation as centre and crown.

(a) ACCLAMATION
   (b) OPPOSITION
      (c) SEPARATION
         (d) CONSUMMATION
      (c) INSTRUCTION
   (b) CONDEMNATION
(a) CRUCIFIXION

THE DIVINE SERVANT AND HIS DAY OF SERVICE.
Key Text, x. 45.

The Thirty Years of Preparation (No Record).

The Opening Events of Christ's Ministry (i. 1-13).

1. Introduction, … … … … ..	1.
2. John the Baptist and his Ministry, … …	2-8.
3. The Baptism and Dedication of Jesus, …	9-11.
4. The Temptation of Jesus, … … …	12-13.

The Judæan Ministry (No Record).

THE GALILEAN MINISTRY.
FIRST PERIOD (i. 14-iii. 6).

Dawn and Acclamation (i. 14-45).

5. First Words, … … … … …	14, 15.
6. Fellow-Workers, … … … …	16-20.
7. The Cure of a Demoniac, … … …	21-28.
8. The Healing of Simon's Mother-in-law, …	29-31.
9. Ministry after Sunset, … … …	32-34.
10. Prayer, Interruption, and Renewed Service,	35-39.
11. The Cleansing of a Leper, … … …	40-45.

THE GALILEAN MINISTRY.
THIRD PERIOD (vii. 24-ix. 50).

Afternoon and Instruction (viii. 27-x. 52).

THE PEREAN MINISTRY (x. 1-52).

THE CLOSING EVENTS OF CHRIST'S MINISTRY
(xi. 1-xv. 47).
JERUSALEM.

Evening and Condemnation (xi. 1-xiii. 37).

SUNDAY.
THE DAY OF APPROACH.

MONDAY.
THE DAY OF JUDGMENT.

TUESDAY.
THE DAY OF CONFLICT.

THE OLIVET PROPHECY (xiii.).

Night and Crucifixion (xiv. 1-xv. 47).
TUESDAY still, or WEDNESDAY.

NOTE 58
Mark xvi. 9-20.

BIBLICAL Criticism has two great branches, Textual Criticism and Historical Criticism. The latter concerns itself with questions as to the composition, authorship, date, and historical value of an ancient document, as these may be judged from internal evidence. On the other hand, Textual Criticism concerns itself with the state of the text, seeking to ascertain its original form, freed from the errors which are incidental to the transmission of ancient manuscripts. Whether or not the last twelve verses of Mark's Gospel are genuine, that is, are the work of Mark, is a matter not for sentiment, but for Textual Criticism, and perhaps the fairest thing to say about this Ending, in view of the long and heated conflict over it on the part of the experts, is that while its genuineness is influentially challenged, it is not finally disproved. The two oldest and best Greek MSS., the Vaticanus, and the Sinaiticus stop at verse eight, but many valuable MSS., both Greek and Latin, have the Ending (9-20). Whether this question will ever be settled no one can say, but until it is, we may say with one of the experts (Dr. Gregory), "A Christian may read, enjoy, ponder these verses, and be thankful for them as much as he pleases."

MATTHEW

Keyword : SOVEREIGNTY.   "BEHOLD THY KING."

WRITTEN IN JUDAEA.   WRITTEN FOR JEWS.
LION-LIKE ASPECT.   THE GOSPEL OF POWER.
Date : 52-56 A.D.

THE AUTHOR.

MATTHEW was one of the twelve Apostles. He is mentioned but once in addition to the four records of his apostolic appointment, namely in connection with his call to discipleship. He had been a farmer of Roman taxes, and, therefore, was much despised by his fellow-countrymen. His name means "the gift of God." Antiquity is unanimous in the belief that he wrote the Gospel which bears his name.

THE READERS.

Internal evidence shows that he wrote mainly for his own countrymen, the Jews. Evidence of this is found in his references to Jerusalem, to David, to the Kingdom ; in his sixty-five references to the Old Testament ; in his view of the then present as the fulfilment of prophecy ; and in his tracing the genealogy of the Christ back to Abraham, and no further. Only Jews could appreciate such references.

THE PLACE OF WRITING.

In the absence of anything to the contrary we must assume that Matthew wrote his Gospel in Judæa.

THE DATE.

It is impossible to determine exactly the date of this composition, but it is practically certain that it was before the destruction of Jerusalem in 70 A.D.; and if, as seems to be the case, it preceded Luke's Gospel and certainly followed Mark's, it may be placed between 52-56 A.D., and possibly later.

THE STYLE.

The Record is characterized by what Archdeacon Farrar has called "antique simplicity," and "monumental grandeur." There is here an art which is all the more effective from its simple unconsciousness. How could the unlettered Galilean publican have written, unaided, a book so immeasurably effective? How could he have sketched out a tragedy which, by the simple divineness of its theme, dwarfs the greatest of all earthly tragedies? How could he have composed a Passion-music which, from the flute-like strains of its sweet overture to the "multitudinous chorale" of its close, accumulates with unflagging power the mightiest elements of pathos and of grandeur? Why would the world lose less from the loss of "Hamlet," and the "Divina Commedia," and the "Paradise Lost" together, than from the loss of this brief book of the despised Galilean? Because this book is due not to genius, but to revelation; not to art, but to truth. The greatness of the work lay, not in the writer, but in Him of Whom he wrote; and in this, that without art, without style, without rhetoric, in perfect and unconscious simplicity, he sets forth the facts as they were. He is "immeasurably effective" because he nowhere aims at "effectiveness."

PURPOSE.

The purpose of this GOSPEL is disclosed in part by the fact that it was written for Jewish readers, and is thoroughly Jewish in complexion. The object of the writer seems to have been to connect the Law with the Gospel; to show the relation of the Old Dispensation to the New; "to connect the memories of his readers with their hopes; to show that the Lord of the Christian was the Messiah of the Jew."

Though not the first of the Four to be written, it is placed first as being most intimately connected with the Old Testament.

The object, as Prof. Work has said, is to present the Person of Jesus Christ to the world against the sky of the Past, to make His face stand out so clearly against the background of Promise, Prophecy, Type, and Symbol, that men may recognise in Him the fulfilment of the Voice of the Past in the actuality of the Present. It was Matthew's design or the Spirit's design through him, to show that in the Old Testament the New was prefigured; that the New emerged from the Old, and vastly transcended it; that in Jesus the Old had its conclusion, and the New, its commencement. This is true of Matthew's Record as it is not of any of the others.

FEATURES.

This GOSPEL, which is about as long as Luke's, contains fourteen entire sections which are found in it alone. Among the peculiarities are ten parables, two miracles, four events of the Infancy, seven incidents connected with the Passion and Resurrection, and not a few great passages in our Lord's discourses. One fourth of the whole Gospel is taken up with the actual words of the Son of Man.

Matthew alone calls Jerusalem the "Holy City," and the "Holy Place," and the "City of the Great King." Seven or eight times he calls our Lord "the Son of David."

He traces Jesus' genealogy, not to Adam, as does Luke, but to Abraham, the founder of Israel. He alone speaks of "the consummation of the age," and he alone speaks of the "Church." Characteristic phrases and expressions are, "That it might be fulfilled"; "The Kingdom of the Heavens" (33 times); "Our Heavenly Father" or "Father in the Heavens" (about 22 times); "Lo, behold" (about 60 times); the indefinite particle of transition (*tote*) is used by him ninety times. There are some seventy words used by Matthew that are found nowhere else in the New Testament. Seven, ten, and twelve, with their multiples, repeatedly appear. There are five great continuous discourses — the Sermon on the Mount, the Address to the Apostles, the Parables on the Kingdom of Heaven, the talk on the Church, and the Olivet Discourse.

NOTE 59
The Authorship of the First Gospel.

THE Gospel itself does not say who its author was, and while we may assume that he was Matthew the Apostle, we cannot finally prove this. Papias (second century) says that "Matthew wrote the Oracles in Hebrew, and each one interpreted them as he could," but the majority of scholars believe that this does not refer to our canonical Gospel, but to *Logia*, or Sayings of Jesus, which were in existence before the Gospel was written, and which the author of the Gospel incorporated into his record, which, on this account, came to be known as Matthew's.

Analysis of Matthew

I. THE PERSON OF THE KING (i. 1-iv. 11).

1. His Ancestry (i. 1-17).
    (i.) Abraham to David, ...   1-6.
    (ii.) David to Zedekiah, ...   6-11.
    (iii.) Zedekiah to Jesus, ...   11-17.

2. His Advent (i. 18-ii. 23).
    (i.) His Divine Origin, ...   i. 18-23.
    (ii.) His Human Birth, ...   i. 24, 25.
    (iii.) His Early Infancy, ...   ii.

3. His Ambassador (iii. 1-12).
    (i.) The Man, ...   1-4.
    (ii.) His Mission, ...   5, 6.
    (iii.) His Message, ...   7-12.

4. His Advance (iii. 13-iv. 11).
    (i.) The Condescension, ...   iii. 13-15.
    (ii.) The Consecration, ...   iii. 16, 17.
    (iii.) The Conflict, ...   ·...   iv. 1-11.

II. THE PURPOSE OF THE KING (iv. 12-xvi. 12).

1. The Enunciation of His Principles (iv. 12-vii. 29).
    (i.) The Inception of the Kingdom, ...   iv. 12-25.
    (ii.) The Manifesto of the King, ...   v.-vii.

2. The Demonstration of His Authority (viii. 1-ix. 34).
    (i.) First Cycle of Credentials, ...   viii. 1-22.
    (ii.) Second Cycle of Credentials, ...   viii. 23-ix. 17
    (iii.) Third Cycle of Credentials, ...   ix. 18-34.

3. The Promulgation of His Message (ix. 35-xi. 30).
    (i.) The Need, ...   ix. 35-38.
    (ii.) The Call, ...   x. 1-4.
    (iii.) The Charge, ...   x. 5-42.
    (iv.) The Difficulties, ...   xi.

4. **The Opposition to His Claims** (xii. 1-xvi. 12).

    (i.) In its Commencement, ... xiii.

    (ii.) In its Consequence, ... xii. 1-52.

    (iii.) In its Culmination, ... xiii. 53-xvi. 12.

III. THE PASSION OF THE KING (xvi. 13 - xxviii. 20).

1. **The Revelation of His Person** (xvi. 13-xvii. 21).

    (i.) The Confession, ... xvi. 13-16.

    (ii.) The Claim,... ... ... xvi. 17-28.

    (iii.) The Confirmation, ... xvii. 1-21.

2. **The Instruction of His Disciples** (xvii. 22-xx. 28).

    (i.) Their Relation to Heavenly Things, ... xvii. 22-xviii.

    (ii.) Their Relation to Earthly Things, ... xix. 1-xx. 28.

3. **The Rejection of His Messiahship** (xx. 29-xxiii. 39).

    (i) The Public Claims, ... xx. 29-xxi. 17.

    (ii). The Final Conflict, ... xxi. 18-xxii. 46.

    (iii.) The Great Indictment, ... xxiii.

4. **The Consummation of His Work** (xxiv.-xxviii.).

    (i.) His Vision of the End, ... xxiv.-xxv.

    (ii.) His Passion for the World, ... xxvi.-xxvii.

    (iii.) His Victory through the Grave, ... xxviii.

NOTE 60

The Discourses in Matthew.

IT is worthy of notice that there are in this Gospel five considerable discourses, each ending with the formula, "It came to pass when Jesus finished" (vii. 28; xi. 1; xiii. 53; xix. 1; xxvi. 1); and there is a sixth but without this formula (xxiii). These discourses are:

The Sermon on the Mount (v.-vii.); the Charge to the Twelve (x.); the Parables of the Kingdom (xiii.); Teaching on Greatness and Forgiveness (xviii.); Denunciation of the Pharisees (xxiii.); and the Great Apocalypse (xxiv.-xxv.). These it is supposed were taken from the "Oracles" to which Papias refers, which were written by Matthew the Apostle in the Hebrew tongue (see Note 59).

LUKE

Keyword : HUMANITY.   "BEHOLD THE MAN."

WRITTEN IN CÆSAREA. WRITTEN FOR THE WORLD.

MAN-LIKE ASPECT.   THE GOSPEL OF SYMPATHY.

DATE : 56-60 A.D.

THE AUTHOR.

THERE is no difference of opinion among scholars to-day as to the authorship of the third Gospel. LUKE is mentioned only three times in the New Testament, all occurrences being in the Prison Epistles (Col. iv. 14 ; Philemon 24 ; 2 Tim. iv. 11). By profession he was a medical doctor, and from the some seventeen nautical terms which he uses in his Record it has been inferred that he exercised his art in the crowded merchant ships which were incessantly coasting from point to point of the Mediterranean. His professional knowledge is reflected in many medical terms in both the GOSPEL and the ACTS. He may well have been one of the earliest Gentile converts, and one of the earliest evangelists in Europe (Acts xvi. 10, "we"). Luke's association with Paul is a fact of outstanding importance, both for Luke and Paul, and also for the Christian Church.

Peter and Mark, Luther and Melanchthon, Calvin and Beza, are among other "holy and beautiful friendships in formative epochs of the Church."

THE READERS.

Mark wrote for Romans, Matthew for Jews, and Luke for Greeks (i. 1-4 ; Acts i. 1), and these represent the three great history-shaping Peoples of that time, the Romans on the side of the Law, the Jews on the side of Religion, and the Greeks on the side of Literature and Art. Theophilus, of whom we know nothing, may have been addressed as representing the Gentile world.

THE PLACE OF WRITING.

As Luke was with Paul during his two years of detention in Cæsarea, he would have ample opportunity to make the investigations to which he makes reference in his Prologue (i. 1-4). We may believe, therefore, that this Gospel was written in Cæsarca.

THE DATE.

If the above be a right inference, it helps us with the date, for Paul was in Cæsarea in 58-60 A.D. It is believed that Luke's Gospel is the latest of the three, so that, if Mark wrote between 50-55 A.D., and Matthew between 55-57 A.D., Luke may well have followed before 60 A.D., having Mark's

Gospel and the "Logia" to draw upon. Later dates are claimed for all the Synoptic Records, but these are quite as likely, perhaps more likely than those.

THE STYLE.

Luke's is the most literary of the Gospels ; the writer was master of a good Greek style, his Writing is more classical than any of the others.

THE PURPOSE.

Luke's design is fully stated in his unique Prologue (i. 1-4), wherein are set forth his motives and his method. As to his *method*, he "traced the course of all things accurately from the first," and wrote "in order," that is, in chronological sequence ; and as to his *motive*, it was that his readers "might know the certainty concerning the things wherein (they were) instructed." Luke's design was to make prominent the universal scope of the Gospel, and herein he reflects the spirit and the mission of Paul, whose companion he was.

FEATURES.

The characteristics of each of the Gospels are in keeping with their design. This is eminently evident in MATTHEW and LUKE. The one is unmistakably Jewish, and the other unmistakably Gentile in complexion.

Luke, writing for mankind, traces Jesus' genealogy back to Adam. In pursuance of the purpose
to present Jesus the Saviour of the World, it is
worthy of notice that he alone records the parables
of the Two Debtors, the Good Samaritan, the Lost
Piece of Silver, the Prodigal Son, Dives and Lazarus,
the Pharisee and the Publican, and five others;
and he only records the miracles of the Ten Lepers,
and the Miraculous Draught of Fishes, and four
others.

Luke alone preserves the first Christian hymns,
the *Benedictus*, the *Magnificat*, the *Nunc Dimittis*,
the *Ave Maria*, and the *Gloria in Excelsis*. He
gives special prominence to prayer, recording six
occasions, omitted by the others, on which our
Lord prayed, and three of the parables peculiar
to this Gospel concern prayer.

The universality of the Good News is emphasised
by such words as "grace" (eight times), "to tell
glad tidings" (ten times); "Saviour," or "salvation," or "saved" (fourteen times). The "beloved
physician" presents the Great Physician to all
sin-sick souls. Christ is "a Light to lighten the
Gentiles;" "all flesh shall see the salvation of
God;" repentance and remission of sins should
be preached "unto all nations."

This Gospel also takes special notice of the

grace and tenderness of Jesus to women, as may be seen in his references to Elizabeth, Mary, Martha, Jesus' mother, the widow, the women who accompanied Jesus, the weeping women on the way to Calvary, and Jesus' address to the "Daughters of Jerusalem." Also, in this Gospel, special notice is taken of poor and humble people, of the despised, and of the lost. Much, also, is said of angelic appearances.

The first two and last chapters are of outstanding importance and beauty, and the great section peculiar to Luke, chaps. ix. 51-xviii. 14, is of engaging interest and historical value ; it has been called the "Journal of Travel," and the "Great Insertion."

Such are some of the distinctive features of this Record wherein "a profound, loving, gentle, and mighty humanity everywhere delights us." Even a notorious unbeliever has said that it is "the most beautiful book ever written" ("*le plus beau livre qu'il y ait*").

Analysis of Luke

III. THE ATONEMENT AND ASCENSION OF THE SON OF MAN (xix. 28-xxiv.).

NOTE 61

Luke's Use of his Material.

IT is remarkable that the Marcan and non-Marcan material in Luke's Gospel alternate, and Canon Streeter has pointed out that if one eliminates all the Marcan passages, what remains is a unity, and this was probably the first sketch of the Gospel, called by the experts Proto-Luke.

The non-Marcan passages are : i. 1-iv. 30; vi. 20-viii. 3; ix. 51-xviii. 14; xix. 1-27; xxii. 14-xxiv. 53.

The Marcan passages are, of course, what remains: iv. 31-vi. 19; viii. 4-ix. 50; xviii. 15-43; xix. 28-xxii. 13.

Read these two separately and see with what impression it leaves you.

JOHN

Keyword : DEITY.   "BEHOLD THY GOD.

WRITTEN IN EPHESUS.   WRITTEN FOR THE CHURCH.

EAGLE-LIKE ASPECT.   THE GOSPEL OF WISDOM.

DATE : 90-100 A.D.

THE AUTHOR.

OVER a hundred years ago discussion began concerning the authorship of the Fourth Gospel, and it has continued to our time, but in spite of all the learned argument and guesses which would discredit the Johannine authorship, the facts declare, as Godet, Westcott, Lightfoot, Sanday, and others have shown, that the author was the Apostle John, the "beloved disciple." One of the first to appear on the scene of the Gospel Story, he is the last to leave it ; his apostolic life covers about seventy years of the first Christian century. A cousin of Jesus, he was brought up, it would appear, in Capernaum, and he spent his last years in Ephesus.

THE READERS.

Paul speaks of "the Jews, the Gentiles (and) the Church of God" (1 Cor. x. 32), and that is an exhaustive analysis. Matthew wrote for the Jews,

Mark and Luke for the two great representatives of the Gentiles, the Romans and the Greeks, and from among Jews and Gentiles the Christian Church was to be called, and for such is the Fourth Gospel written. This is accounted for in part by its date, and it accounts in part for its contents.

THE PLACE OF WRITING.

Seeing that John, according to reliable tradition, spent his later years in Ephesus, almost certainly this Gospel was written there, either before or after his banishment to Patmos.

THE DATE.

From the evidence which the Gospel itself supplies, a late date must be given to it. The difference between the Synoptics and the Fourth Gospel is apparent to all, and the advance of the latter upon the former finds its natural explanation in the advance of the thought of the Church, which must have progressed in apprehension with the lapse of time. The selection of the material in this Gospel is affected unmistakably by the time at which it was written. There is here a maturity which does not attach to the Synoptics, and it is accounted for by nearly thirty years of Christian history from the time of the Synoptists.

THE STYLE.

John's style differs greatly from that of the Three Synoptists. The language is Greek, but the style is Hebrew. John uses fewer words than any of the Synoptists, but he uses them to great purpose. His essential thoughts and images are few, but he repeats these again and again with strange impressiveness. The order is not chronological, but is determined by the author's purpose. The Gospel is essentially philosophical, theological, mystical, spiritual, but this is not to say that it is not reliably historical.

THE PURPOSE.

John's *theme* is clearly outlined in his Prologue (i. 1-18), and his *motive* is as clearly indicated in his concluding words (xx. 31 ; chap. xxi. is an Appendix). From the latter we learn that the Gospel was written to show that Jesus is God, with a view to the creation of faith in the readers, and the impartation of eternal life to them. This purpose dominates the Record so distinctively that Godet divides it into three main parts, which answer to the three parts of the Prologue (i. 1-5 ; 6-11 ; 12-18) ; The Incarnate Word (i.-iv.) ; Jewish Unbelief (v.-xii.) ; Christian Faith (xiii-xvii), followed by the consummation of Unbelief (xviii-xix), and of Faith (xx).

John's *Gospel* is designed to show that Jesus was the Divine Son ; his *First Epistle* is designed to set forth the Divine Son as Jesus ; and his *Apocalypse* unfolds the power and glory of Jesus Christ, the Divine Son. Than these three Writings nothing is more profound or sublime, so awe-inspiring and comforting.

FEATURES.

Almost all the features of this Gospel are distinctive. John alone gives us a glimpse into the first year of our Lord's ministry (ii-iv) ; he alone records the great Discourses on the New Birth, the Living Water, the Bread of Life, the Good Shepherd, and the Light of the World ; he alone records at length the momentous Upper Room Discourse and events, and the great Intercessory Prayer (xiii-xvii).

There are here no genealogy, no birth, no boyhood, no growth, no baptism, no temptation, and no Gethsemane. Everything is directed to the end in view, to prove that Jesus was God. "Witness" is one of the keywords of the Book, occurring about fifty times, and calls attention to the word of the Baptist, of the Evangelist, of Philip, of Nathaniel, of Nicodemus, of the Samaritan Woman, of the Nobleman, of Martha, of the Scriptures, of the Works, of Christ Himself, and of the Father, in attestation of our Lord's Divinity.

There are in this Gospel no scribes, no lepers, no publicans, and no demoniacs. John does not narrate a single parable ; and of the eight miracles recorded five are peculiar to this Gospel. John regards all subjects in the light of their absolute antitheses : light and darkness, life and death, spirit and flesh, heaven and earth, truth and error, love and hate, Christ and devil, God and world. In the use of the title "the Logos" for Christ, John stands alone.

The arrangement of the Book is throughout constructed with reference to the sacred numbers three and seven. "Jesus is thrice in Galilee, thrice in Judea, twice three feasts take place during His ministry, and particularly three Passover feasts. He works three miracles in Galilee, and three in Jerusalem. Twice three days is He in the neighbourhood of John ; three days are covered by the narrative of Lazarus, and six by the fatal Passover. He utters three Sayings on the Cross, and appears thrice after the Resurrection." Seven times He says "I am," culminating in the thrice-repeated "I am" in viii. 24, 28, 58.

Outstanding words in JOHN are :

Light (23 times), Darkness (9), Truth (25), Love, to love (18),

Glory, Glorify (42), World (78), Eternal Life (15), Abide (18), Judge, Judgment (30), Believe (98), Know (55), Works (23), Name (25), Signs (17).

The most frequently quoted verse of the Bible, John iii. 16, contains the four most important words of Christianity, "world," "gave," "believeth," and "life," and, incidentally, the initial letters of the words in this verse, "God," "only-begotten," "Son," "perish," "eternal," and "life," spell Gospel.

NOTE 62
The Key to the Fourth Gospel.

THREE words furnish us with this key, *Revelation, Rejection*, and *Reception*. All three are in the Prologue: *Revelation* of Jesus the Word (i. 1-5a); *Rejection* through unbelief (i. 5b-11), and *Reception* by faith (i. 12-18). All that follows is a development of this outline :

2. The First Manifestations of the Word (Revelation), and the Beginnings of Faith (Reception), and Unbelief (Rejection), i. 19-iv. 54.

3. The Development of Unbelief (Rejection) in Israel, v.-xii.

4. The Development of Faith (Reception) in the Disciples, xiii.-xvii.

5. The Consummation of Unbelief (Rejection) in Israel, xviii.-xix.

6. The Consummation of Faith (Reception) in the Disciples, xx.

7. The Manifestation of the Lord (Revelation) for the Correction of Unbelief (Rejection), and the Confirmation of Faith (Reception), xxi.

Analysis of John

PROLOGUE. THE PAST. (i. 1-18).
(*a*) The DIVINE LIFE Revealed (1-5).
(*b*) THE DIVINE LIGHT Displayed (6-13).
(*c*) The DIVINE LOVE Expressed (14-18).

PART A.
THE REVELATION OF GOD AS LIFE TO THE WORLD (i. 19-xii. 50).

I. THE LIFE ANNOUNCED (i. 19-ii. 22).
1. The Witness of the Baptist (i. 19-34).
2. The Witness of the First Disciples (i. 35-51).
3. The Witness of the Works (ii. 1-22).

II. THE LIFE ACKNOWLEDGED (ii. 23-iv. 54).
1. In Judæa, South (ii. 23-iii. 36).
2. In Samaria, Centre (iv. 1-42).
3. In Galilee, North (iv. 43-54).

III. THE LIFE ANTAGONISED (v.-xii.).
1. The Controversy Aroused (v. 1-47).
      (i.) Love Displayed, ... 1-18.
      (ii.) Light Revealed, ... 19-47.
      (iii.) Life Presented, ... 39-40.
2. The Controversy Developed (vi.-x.).
      (i.) The Life Despised, ... vi.
      (ii.) The Light Refused, ... vii.-ix.
      (iii.) The Love Outraged, ... x.
3. The Controversy Concluded (xi.-xii.).
      (i.) The Love Sympathising, ... xi. 1-37.
      (ii.) The Light Saving, ... xi. 38-xii. 11.
      (iii.) The Life Shining. ... ... xii. 12-50.

PART B.
THE REVELATION OF GOD AS LIGHT TO THE DISCIPLES (xiii.-xvii.).

I. INTRODUCTION TO THE LIGHT FOR THEM
(xiii. 1-30).
1. The Light Expressing Love (1-20).
2. The Light Exposing Hate (21-30).

II. IMPARTATION OF THE LIGHT TO THEM
(xiii. 31-xvi. 33).

III. INTERCESSION FOR THE LIGHT IN THEM
(xvii.).

PART C.
THE REVELATION OF GOD AS LOVE TO ALL (xviii.-xx.).

I. THE TRIAL OF DIVINE LOVE (xviii. 1-xix. 16).

II. THE TRAGEDY OF DIVINE LOVE (xix. 17-42).

III. THE TRIUMPH OF DIVINE LOVE (xx.).

EPILOGUE. THE FUTURE (xxi).

THE APOSTOLICAL WRITINGS

INTRODUCTION

THE HISTORY—THE ACTS

NOTE 63
The Apostolical Writings.

THE HISTORY. Book of the ACTS.
THE LITERATURE. The EPISTLES.

I. The Pauline Epistles.
GROUP 1. 1-2 *Thessalonians.*
GROUP 2. 1-2 *Corinthians, Galatians, Romans.*
GROUP 3. *Colossians, Philemon, Ephesians, Philippians*
GROUP 4. 1 *Timothy, Titus,* 2 *Timothy, Hebrews* (?).

II. The Catholic Epistles.
GROUP 1. Jacobean. *James, Jude.*
GROUP 2. Petrine. 1-2 *Peter.*
GROUP 3. Johannine. 1-2-3 *John, Revelation.*

I. The Pauline Epistles.

GROUP 1. Eschatological: The Last Things: 1 Thess..
A.D. 52. 2 Thess., A.D. 53.

GROUP 2. Soteriological: Free and Full Salvation by Christ's
Cross. 1-2 Cor., A.D. 57. Gal., A.D.
57-58. Rom., A.D. 58.

GROUP 3. Christological: The Doctrine of Christ. Col.,
Philemon, Eph., A.D. 62. Phil., A.D. 63.

GROUP 4. Ecclesiological: The Church and Congregation.
1 Tim., A.D. 65-67. Titus, A.D. 65-67.
2 Tim., A.D. 67-68. Hebrews (?), A.D.
64-68.

II. The Catholic Epistles.

James. A.D. 44-49.   Jude. A.D. 65-68.
1 Peter. A.D. 62-64.   2 Peter. A.D. 68.
1-2-3 John. A.D. 90-98.   Revelation. A.D. 68-70.

The
APOSTOLICAL WRITINGS
Introduction

THE New Testament is divisible into three or two main parts. The three parts are the Historical, the Didactical, and the Prophetical Writings ; and these are, respectively, MATTHEW to ACTS ; ROMANS to JUDE ; and the REVELATION. But these books also fall into two main parts ; the Evangelic Writings, MATTHEW to JOHN ; and the Apostolic Writings, ACTS to REVELATION. The subject of the first of these two parts is The Christ ; and of the second, The Church, in the most comprehensive sense of this word. The first tells of the introduction of the Gospel into the world ; and the second, of the promulgation and progress of the Gospel in the world. The subject of the first is, Christ for us ; and of the second, Christ in us. In the first, Christ is revealed historically, and in the second, He is revealed mystically.

These two parts, consisting of twenty-seven Writings, constitute our New Testament. It is natural to ask what distinguishes these Writings from those of the Sub-Apostolic Age, the period immediately following that of the Apostles. Canon Bernard in his invaluable book on "The Progress of Doctrine in the New Testament," has something to say on this subject. In effect it is this. In the Evangelic Writings we have revelation without interpretation ; that is, the Evangelists are inspired to record, but they do not attempt to interpret the things they put on record ; there is no record of their apprehension of those things. But when we come to the Apostolical Writings we find both revelation and interpretation ; we have Paul's apprehension, and Peter's, and James', and Jude's, and John's, of the things of which they speak. So evident is this, that we speak of Pauline theology, and Petrine theology, and Johannine theology. By these terms we do not mean that we have in the Epistles conflicting theologies, but that there was varied apprehension of the revelation of God which was made in Christ Jesus our Lord ; and this apprehension was inspired.

But when we come to the Sub-Apostolic Writings, we find, as in those which preceded them, apprehension and interpretation, but revelation and inspiration have ceased. The Councils which fixed the Canon of the New Testament did not include any of these Sub-Apostolical Writings. From the close of the Apostolical Age until now there have been apprehension and interpretation, but no Biblical revelation or inspiration.

The position, then, is this, that in the Evangelic Records we have revelation but not interpretation ; in the Apostolic Writings we have revelation plus interpretation ; and in the Sub-Apostolic Literature we have interpretation without revelation. One factor, revelation, is in the first Group ; another factor, interpretation, is in the third Group ; and both factors are in the second Group. The period covered by the New Testament Writings is the period of the New Covenant revelation. The record of the introduction of that revelation, in the Gospels, is without the touch of human inter-pretation ; but the record of the development of that revelation, in the Epistles, has interwoven with it divinely-inspired interpretation.

Christian doctrine is based on the facts concern-ing Christ, so, of course, there could be no doctrinal interpretation before or during the historical manifestation. The cry of "Back to Christ from the teaching of Paul," that is, back from sophistry to simplicity, is singularly wanting in spiritual understanding, and, incidentally, is a virtual denial of the divine inspiration of the Epistolary

Scriptures. A distinguished American lecturer has recently written, "I have always experienced great difficulties in getting at Him (Christ), because His figure was completely obscured by the dark shadow of that Paul of Tarsus, who in his Pharisaic self-righteousness and arrogance had undertaken to explain Him to the rest of the world as he thought He ought to be explained ... Like myself, millions of other people very likely would have become good Christians if only Paul had let them." Our theologians would not put the matter in that crude and blatant way, but in its essence it does represent what some of them think, and such thinking is an entire misconstruing of the significance of the New Testament. Paul is Christ's chief interpreter, and he interprets Him not as a clever Rabbinic scholar, but as a divinely-inspired Christian. Unless we get this point of view the whole perspective of the New Testament will be thrown out.

With this as the broad background we approach the Apostolical Writings, ACTS to REVELATION. These divide into History, the ACTS ; Doctrine, ROMANS to JUDE ; and Apocalypse, the REVELATION. In the second of these divisions are twenty-one of the twenty-three Apostolical Writings, and they are from the hands of five authors, James, Paul,

Peter, Jude, and John ; and their respective lines of interpretation, which are complementary and not contradictory, are called by theologians the Jacobean, the Pauline, the Petrine, and the Johannine. On and from Christ this Temple of Christian Truth rests and rises.

These are wonderful Writings. Charles Reade said that the Book of the ACTS is one of the most graphic and forceful bits of writing anywhere to be found. Only by reading it at a sitting, and reading it often in this way, can one appreciate its power. Some of the Epistles are incomparable literature in their class. ROMANS is acknowledged to be a masterpiece. For profoundness of thought, moral force, spiritual insight, logical precision, and intellectual grasp, is there anything that can be compared with it ? The little Note to PHILEMON is a literary and spiritual gem. COLOSSIANS and EPHESIANS are perfect specimens of spiritual Philosophy and Christian Ethics. And there are parts of other of Paul's Letters which have not only never been excelled, but have never been equalled. Of such passages, it will readily be admitted, are the thirteenth and fifteenth chapters of 1 CORINTHIANS.

Equally rich in quality, though of a different order, is John's First Epistle. So simple, yet so profound, at once lucid and eluding, severe and tender. The Epistle to the HEBREWS is also a masterpiece of writing, in which Hebraic truth is cast in Hellenic mould to set forth the Christian Gospel in its widest meaning.

The Book of the REVELATION is in a class by itself in the New Testament, and is our only specimen of inspired symbolic writing. Its appeal is to the imagination rather than to the intellect, and to hope rather than to love.

These are the writings which now we are to consider one by one.

NOTE 64

The Gospels and the Acts.

THERE are three Synoptic Gospels, and the Acts is in three parts. On examination it will be seen that these facts are related to one another in a way which cannot be accidental. The relations are, Matthew and Acts i.-vii. Mark and Acts viii.-xii. Luke and Acts xiii.-xxviii. Matthew was written for Jews, and in Acts i.-vii. the Church was Jewish. Mark wrote for Romans, and in Acts viii.-xii. we see the Gospel reaching Romans through Jews (cf. ch. x.).

Luke wrote for Greeks, and in Acts xiii.-xxviii. we see a world-wide mission, and a protracted Gospel witness in Greece (cf. chs. xvii.-xviii.).

As the Fourth Gospel was written for the Church of God it is related to the whole of the Acts. These facts are impressive and important.

The
APOSTOLICAL WRITINGS

The History—The Acts.
Keyword : Witness.

IT is no exaggeration to say that the Book of the Acts is one of the most graphic pieces of writing in all literature, and what makes it this, we must endeavour, briefly, to see.

The Title.

The Book has no inspired title, and has been denominated in various ways. There are here thoughts as well as deeds, and the thinkers and doers are by no means the Apostles only, or chiefly. The Book is really a record of the Mind and Might of the Holy Spirit.

The Author.

It is perfectly clear that "Luke, the beloved physician," was the writer of this record, and for the following among other reasons :

(1) It is evident that the Third Gospel and this Book are from the same hand, for the same style, language, and method characterise them both. The Gospel treats of the Person and Work of the Christ, and the Acts treats of the Origin and Progress of the Church ; and chapter i. 1 links the two.

(2) The employment in the Book of a number of medical terms in a technical sense, points to a doctor as the author.

(3) The writer was one of Paul's companions ; and Luke was such (xvi. 10-17 ; xx. 5-15 ; xxi. 1-18 ; xxvii. 1-xxviii. 16 ; the "We" sections).

(4) Luke's name does not occur in the record, which it certainly would have done, had anyone else written it. A parallel case is John and the Fourth Gospel (i. 37, 40 ; xiii. 23 ; xx. 2 ; xxi. 7, 20).

(5) The Author of the Acts was with Paul at Rome, and Luke was there with him (xxvii. 1-xxviii. 16 ; 2 Tim. iv. 11).

The Date.

The precise date of this Book is not known, but it may fairly be assumed that it was at the place and time at which its record closes, that is, at Rome, about 63 A.D. At the time of writing Paul had been two years in captivity, and nothing is said of his release, which, almost certainly, took place in 63 A.D. The abrupt conclusion of the narrative suggests a change of circumstances. Either the great fire of Rome, in 64 A.D., or want of opportunity, or political discretion, or Luke's death, would account for the incompleteness of the record.

The Sources.

That Luke had recourse to sources of information is certain, so that the only question is as to what these were. The answer to this inquiry may be summarised as follows :

(1) The "We" sections, already referred to, are Luke's, as an eye-witness.

(2) Everything from chapter xiii, in addition to the "We" sections, Luke would get from Paul, with whom he was at Cæsarea, and Philippi, and Malta, and Rome, and, as Zahn says, nothing is more natural than that the great missionary should have communicated to his beloved friends the record of his work and experience in great heathen centres of commercial life like Corinth, Ephesus, and Athens.

(3) What is related in chapter xii, he might well have got from Mark, to whose house Peter went after his release from prison, and who was with Luke in Rome (2 Tim. iv. 11).

(4) Cornelius, who lived at Cæsarea (x. 1) could have given Luke the information for the major parts of chapters ix.-xi, for Luke was at Cæsarea with Paul.

(5) Paul, who witnessed the martyrdom of Stephen, could, and no doubt would, have given to Luke the details of chapters vi-vii.

(6) Philip, who lived at Cæsarea (vi. 5 ; xxi. 8), where Luke was for so long, could have given him the particulars of chapter viii.

(7) What is recorded in chapters i-v, may well have been supplied by Peter, Barnabas, and Philip, who were known to Luke.

It is not to be supposed that the ACTS is a collection of reports, but only that Luke, who assimilated his materials and wrought them into a unity of record, derived these materials from authentic sources.

THE CHRONOLOGY.

There is no continuous system of Chronology in the "Acts," and we are, therefore, dependent upon such notes of time of Jewish or Roman history, as may be found in it, and in the Epistles.

Of such, there are chiefly ten. (1) The reign of Aretas of Damascus (ix. 25, cf. 2 Cor. xi. 32). (2) The reign and death of Herod Agrippa I (xii). (3) The famine under Claudius (xi. 28-30 ; xii. 25). (4) The proconsulship of Sergius Paulus in Cyprus (xiii. 7). (5) The Expulsion of Jews from Rome under Claudius (xviii. 2). (6) The proconsulship of Gallio in Achaia (xviii. 12). (7) The reign of Herod Agrippa II, and marriage of his sister Drusilla to Felix (xxiv. 24 ; xxv. 13-xxvi. 32). (8) The procuratorships of Felix and Festus (xxi. 38 ; xxiii. 24 ; xxiv. 10, 27). (9) The days of Un-leavened Bread (xx. 6, 7). (10) The Persecution under Nero. Of these notes of secular history Lightfoot regards the dates of two as fixed. "The first of these is St. Paul's second visit to Jerusalem (xi. 30 ; xii. 25), which is obviously synchronous, or nearly so, with the death of Herod Agrippa (xii. 23) ; but this latter event is known to have happened in A.D. 44. The second is St. Paul's appearance before Festus, and consequent voyage to Rome (xxvi. 32 ; xxvii. 1). It appears that the deposition of Felix, and the accession of Festus, most probably happened in A.D. 60, and must certainly have happened close upon that year." From this last date it is possible to work back, and obtain a good idea of the times of the chief events of this history. The principal chronologists vary from one to two years in their schemes, but here we follow Lightfoot's, which, in the main, is most widely accepted.

LIGHTFOOT'S DATES OF FOURTEEN EVENTS.

EVENT.	CHAP.	A.D.
1. Ascension of Christ, ...	i. 9	30
2. Conversion of Saul, ...	ix. 1-19	34-36
3. Paul's First Visit to Jerusalem, ...	ix. 26	37, 38
4. Paul at Antioch, ...	xi. 26	44
5. Paul's Second Visit to Jerusalem,	xi. 30	45
6. Paul's First Missionary Journey,	xiii. 4	48
7. The Great Council at Jerusalem,	xv. 1-29	51
8. Paul's First Visit to Corinth, ...	xviii. 1	52
9. Paul's Fourth Visit to Jerusalem,	xviii. 22	54
10. Paul leaves Ephesus, ...	xx. 1	57
11. Paul's Arrest in Jerusalem, ...	xxi. 33	58
12. Paul reaches Rome, ...	xxviii. 16	61
13. Close of the "Acts,"	xxviii. 30, 31	63
14. Paul is Martyred, ...		67

From this table we see that the period covered by the "Acts" is approximately thirty-three years, the same as that covered by the Gospel narrative (B.C. 4, A.D. 30). When we conceive of the history as within such limits, we begin to realise how great were the agents, and how intense the activities of this first generation of Church history. Had the later generations of the Church followed the example of the first, the world would have been evangelised fifty times by now.

10

The main divisions of this chronology are as follows : (1) Chaps. i-ix. 25 ; A.D. 30-37, seven years. (2) Chaps. ix. 26-xii. 24, A.D. 37-44, seven years. (3) Chaps. xii. 25-xv. 35, A.D. 44-51, seven years. (4) Chaps. xv. 36-xxi. 16, A.D. 51-58, seven years. (5) Chaps. xxi. 17-xxviii. 31, A.D. 58-63, five years. (6) Release to death of Paul, A.D. 63-67, four years. The history should be followed from point to point with the aid of these dates, until the mind has thoroughly grasped its sequence and scope.

THE OBJECT.

The design of the writer of this Book was, as he says (i. 1), to show that and how the risen Lord was continuing to do from Heaven what He had commenced on earth. He had said to His Apostles : "I will build My Church" (Matt. xvi. 18), and in the ACTS we see Him doing it. Throughout, Christ is the Author and Authority of the work, and all others are His agents (i. 24 ; ii. 33 ; iii. 16 ; iv. 10 ; v. 14, 31, 32, 42 ; vii. 56 ; viii. 4, 5, 35 *et al*). How the Redeemer's design was advanced in the generation A.D. 30-63, is shown in this enthralling narrative with consummate skill. The record of progress is presented in what almost amounts to a refrain (cf. ii. 47 ; v. 14-16 ; vi. 7 ; ix. 31 ; xiii. 24 ; xvi. 5 ; xix. 20), and we are shown how the light which dawned in Bethlehem brightened and spread from Jerusalem to Antioch, to Ephesus, to Troas, to Philippi, to Athens, to Corinth, and to Rome. Hill top after hill top is caught by the rising sun, until they flame like beacon fires from the capital of Judaism to the capital of Paganism.

The Plan.

That the record proceeds upon a definite plan is clearly indicated in Chap. i. 8 : "Ye shall receive power, after that the Holy Spirit is come upon you : and ye shall be witnesses unto Me, both in Jerusalem, and in all Judæa, and in Samaria, and unto the uttermost part of the earth." From this passage we learn four things. First, that the central subject of Christian witness is Christ ; second, that the exclusive source of Christian witness is the Church ; third, that the widening sphere of Christian witness embraces the world ; and fourth, that the unfailing secret of Christian witness is the Holy Spirit. The Book may be analysed according to the third of these particulars, and each division illustrates the other three. Chaps. i-vii, tell of the witness in Jerusalem, the City; Chaps. viii-xii, tell of the witness in Judæa and Samaria and beyond, the Provinces ; and Chaps. xiii-xxviii, tell of the witness "to the uttermost part of the earth," the World. The witness in the first of these periods was devoted to the Jews ; in the third, it was chiefly to the Gentiles ; and in the second was the transition from the first to the third. In each of these ministries Christ is the theme, the Church is the means, and the Spirit is the power. In the first, Jerusalem is the centre ; in the second, Antioch ; and in the third, Rome. In the first period Peter dominates ; in the third, Paul is supreme ; and in the second, Barnabas represents the transition from Peter to Paul. These three movements are one in intent and design, and show how, on the human side, a town carpenter and a handful of illiterate men out-lived because they out-loved the Roman Empire ; and how, on the divine side, the Son of God and His Church established a spiritual Kingdom in this world.

VALUES.

Many and great are the values of the ACTS. Its *Historical* value is now placed beyond all question. The veracity and accuracy of Luke are no longer challengeable.

Its *Doctrinal* value is inestimable. All the notes of the Christian Gospel are here sounded, and they peal forth in rapturous harmony. The Message, though presented by many, and in varying terms, is always the same. Jesus was the promised Messiah, the Son of God, and the Redeemer of the world. His death was atoning. He rose from the dead, and ascended into Heaven, and by the Holy Spirit He is ever present with His people. He forgives sins, and empowers for holy life and noble service. There is here no attempt to systematise truth. Creedal formulation awaited the age of criticism and controversy, but here all is simple, natural and passionate.

And the *Biographical* value of the ACTS is immense. Here, indeed, is a crowded platform! Some of the characters are portrayed at length, but the most of them, briefly; Jews and Gentiles, Christians and Pagans, rulers and subjects, philosophers and artisans are here.

The mere recital of the names fires the imagination and moves the heart. The outstanding personalities are, of course, Peter and Paul, and these are in the fellowship of a host of Christians, most of whom are unnamed. And there are here foes as well as friends, and women as well as men. What a gallery! Aeneas, Agabus, Agrippa, Alexander, Ananias, Annas, Andrew, Apollos, Aquila, Aristarchus, Augustus, Bar-Jesus, Barnabas, Barsabas, Bartholomew, Bernice, Blastus, Caiaphas, Candace, Caesar, Claudius, Cornelius, Crispus,

Damaris, Demetrius, Dionysius, Dorcas, Drusilla, Erastus, Eutychus, Felix, Festus, Gaius, Gallio, Gamaliel, Herod, Janus, Jason, Jesus, John Mark, John, Lucius, Lydia, Manaen, Mary, Matthew, Matthias, Mnason, Nicanor, Nicolas, Niger, Parmenas, Priscilla, Prochorus, Publius, Rhoda, Sapphira, Sceva, Sergius Paulus, Secundus, Silas, Simeon, Simon, Sopater, Sosthenes, Stephen, Tabitha, Theophilus, Theudas, Timon, Timotheus, Trophimus, Tychicus, Tyrannus, and possibly others. This is, indeed, a stirring scene, and to know these people is to know the history of the Christian Church from A.D. 30-63.

Then, how great is the *Missionary* value of this Book! It is the authorised Missionary Manual of the Church, and the greatest missionary story ever told. If the names of people in these pages stir one, scarcely less so must the names of places. Athens, Antioch, Amphipolis, Antipatris, Apollonia, Assos, Attalia, Azotus, Berea, Corinth, Cæsarea, Cenchrea, Chios, Clauda, Cnidus, Cos, Crete, Cyprus, Damascus, Derbe, Ephesus, Gaza, Iconium, Jerusalem, Joppa, Lystra, Lydda, Melita, Miletus, Mitylene, Myra, Mysia, Neapolis, Paphos, Patara, Perea, Philippi, Ptolemais, Puteoli, Rome, Regium, Rhodes, Salamis, Samaria, Samos, Samothrace, Seleucia, Sidon, Syracuse, Tarsus, Thessa-

lonica, Tyre, Troas, and other places—every one
of which tells a bit of the story of the first Planting
of Christianity—take us over land and sea, north
and south, from the Jordan to the Tiber, and
represent the intellectual, political, and commercial
life of the ancient world. We are made to see, by
this record, that the first missionary principle was
to evangelise city centres so that from these the
Gospel might radiate to all surrounding places ;
hence, such strategic places as Antioch, Iconium,
Lystra, Derbe, Ephesus, Philippi, Thessalonica,
Corinth, and Rome dominate the narrative. Nothing that is relevant to world evangelisation is
omitted in this narrative ; indeed, the story deter-
mines what is relevant.

And how immense is the *Dispensational* value of
the ACTS. It is the most important dispensational
book in the Bible because it tells us how the great
change-over from Judaism to Christianity was
made. It enables us to see the distinction between
the Messianic Kingdom and the Christian Church ;
between the earthly and the heavenly, between the
temporal and the eternal. Here the ends of ages
meet, the one terminal, and the other germinal.
Two dispensations swing on these hinges, one
door closing, and the other opening. There is the
same kind of difference between Peter's sermon at

Jerusalem (Chap. ii.) and Paul's at Antioch, in Pisidia (Chap. xiii.), that there is between the Sermon on the Mount (Matt. v-vii) and the Upper Room Discourse (John xiii-xvi).

And interpenetrating all these other values is the *Spiritual*. The ACTS is essentially a record of the activities of the Holy Spirit, and here He is seen related to every aspect of the believer's and the Church's life and work. He is the Spirit of Promise (Chap. i.), of Power (ii.), of Healing (iii.), of Boldness (iv.), of Judgment (v.), of Administration (vi.), of Steadfastness (vii.), of Evangelism (viii.), of Comfort (ix.), of Guidance (x.), of Prophecy (xi.), of Deliverance (xii.), of Missions (xiii.), of Protection (xiv.), of Councils (xv.), of Restraint and Constraint (xvi.), of Opportunity (xvii.), of Revelation (xviii.), of Purpose (xix.) ; indeed, the Spirit dominates the whole story. The ACTS is the record of a Spirit-begotten, Spirit-filled, and Spirit-guided Church. Other great notes in this spiritual symphony are Prayer and Faith, Joy and Courage, Sacrifice and Victory. No language can describe the power of this record ; it is something that must be felt.

The ACTS is a Book of Origins. Here are the beginnings of the Christian Church, of apostolic miracles, of apostolic sermons, of Christian persecution, of Christian martyrs, of Gentile converts, of disciplinary judgment in the Church, of Church Synods, of Foreign Missions, of Christian Communism; the beginnings of Deacons and Bishops, of Christian Baptism and Christian Assemblies, and of the denomination "Christian." ACTS is a dawn, a glorious sunrise, a bursting forth in a dark world of eternal light; it is a Book precious beyond all price.

NOTE 65
Words Peculiar to Luke's Gospel and the Acts.

THE diction and style of the Third Gospel and the Acts prove identity of authorship. The following are some of the words peculiar to these two Writings:

WORD.	LUKE.	ACTS.	WORD.	LUKE.	ACTS.
Cause. Fault	xxiii. 4, 14, 22	xix. 40	Show. Appoint	x. 1	i. 24
Seek	ii. 44, 45	xi. 25	Draw up. Pull out	xiv. 5	xi. 10
Find	ii. 16	xxi. 4	Receive	viii. 40	xv. 4 et al.
Shake off	ix. 5	xxviii. 5	Perplexed. Doubt	ix. 7	ii. 12. v. 24
Keep	ii. 51	xv. 29	Confidently affirm	xxii. 59	xii. 15
Judge	xii. 14	vii. 27, 35	Pass through	viii. 1	xvii. 1
Lay wait for	xi. 54	xxiii. 21	Next day	vii. 11. ix. 37	xxi. 1. xxv. 17
Set on	x. 34	xxiii. 24	Cry against	xxiii. 21	xxii. 24 et al.
Take in hand	i. 1	xix. 13	Devout	ii. 25	ii. 5
Mightily	xxiii. 10	xviii. 28	Preserve	xvii. 33	vii. 19
Heal. Cure	xiii. 32	iv. 22, 30	Order	i. 3	xviii. 23
Let down	v. 19	ix. 25 et al.	Shut up	iii. 20	xxvi. 10

There are twenty-one or twenty-two in addition to these.

Analysis of Acts

BECAUSE of the tremendous importance of this First Chapter of Church History, and in order to show the relation of the Epistles to it, it is here presented in great detail.

I. THE JEWISH PERIOD OF THE CHURCH'S WITNESS
(i. 1-viii. 3). A.D 30-37. THE CHURCH FOUNDED.
Central City, JERUSALEM.

Trouble Without.

1. Founding of the Church (i. 1-ii. 13).
(i.) The Days of Preparation, ...	i. 1-26.
(ii.) The Days of Pentecost, ...	ii. 1-13.

2. Testimony of the Church (ii. 14-47).
(i.) THEIR SIMPLE CREED, ...	14-41.
The Discourse of Peter.	
(ii.) THEIR SANCTIFIED CONDUCT, ...	42-47.
A Description of the First Church.	

3. Opposition to the Church (iii. 1-iv. 31).
(i.) The Occasion of it, ...	iii. 1-26.
(ii.) The Expression of it, ...	iv. 1-22.
(iii.) The Sequel to it, ...	iv. 23-31.

Trouble Within.

4. Discipline in the Church (iv. 32-v. 16).
(i.) The Originating Circumstances, ...	iv. 32-37.
(ii.) The Specific Occasion, ...	v. 1-10.
(iii.) The Salutary Effect, ...	v. 11-16.

Trouble Without.

5. Testing of the Church (v. 17-42).
(i.) The Detention and Deliverance of the Apostles, ...	17-21a.
(ii.) The Trial and Triumph of the Apostles, ...	21b-42.

Trouble Within.

6. Administration in the Church (vi. 1-6).
(i.) The Complaint of the Disciples, ...	1.
(ii.) The Conference of the Church, ...	2-4.
(iii.) The Choice of Deacons, ...	5-6.

1. **Paul's Tireless Activities** (xiii. 1-xxi. 16).
   A.D. 47-58 = 11 years

  (i.) THE FIRST MISSIONARY JOURNEY. 4 years.
    3 chapters (xiii.-xv.). Chapters xiii. 1-
    xv. 35. A.D. 47-51.

(a) The Call and Consecration at Antioch, ...	xiii. 1-3.
(b) The Circuit in Asia Minor, ...	xiii. 4-xiv. 28.
(1) The Outward Journey, ... A.S.S.P.P.A.I.L.D.	xiii. 4-xiv. 20.
(2) The Inward Journey, ... L.I.A.P.A.A.	xiv. 21-28.
(c) The Conference at Jerusalem, ...	xv. 1-35.

  (ii.) THE SECOND MISSIONARY JOURNEY
    (xv. 36-xviii. 22). A.D. 51-54 = 3 years.
    3 chapters (xvi.-xviii.).

(a) Apostolic Labours in Asia Minor, A.S.C.D.L.P.G.T.	xv. 36-xvi. 10
(b) Apostolic Labours in Macedonia, S.N.P.A.A.T.B.	xvi. 11-xvii. 15
(c) Apostolic Labours in Achaia, ... A.C.C.E.C.J.A.	xvii.16-xviii.22

    1 Thessalonians, A.D. 52.   From Corinth.
    2 Thessalonians, A.D. 53.   From Corinth.

  (iii.) THE THIRD MISSIONARY JOURNEY.
    (xviii. 23-xxi. 16). A.D. 54-58 = 4 years.
    3 chapters (xix.-xxi.).

(a) Paul's Activities in Asia, ... A.G.P.E.	xviii.23-xix. 41

    1 Corinthians. A.D. 57. From Ephesus.

(b) Paul's Experiences in Europe, ... M.A.P.	xx. 1-5.

    2 Corinthians. A.D. 57. From Macedonia.
    Galatians.   A.D. 57. From Corinth.
    Romans.   A.D. 58. From Corinth.

(c) Paul's Journey to Jerusalem, ... T.A.M.C.S.M.C.R.P.T.P.C.J.	xx. 6-xxi. 16.

2. Paul's Fruitful Captivities (xxi. 17-xxviii. 31).
A.D. 58-63 = 5 years.

(i.) At Jerusalem (xxi. 17-xxiii. 35.) = 1 year.
3 chapters (xxi.-xxiii.). A.D. 58.

(a) The Apostle's Detention, ...   xxi. 17-36.
(b) The Apostle's Defence, ...   xxi. 37-xxiii. 11
(c) The Apostle's Danger, ...   xxiii. 12-22.

(ii.) At Caesarea (xxiv.-xxvi.). A.D. 58-60.
2 years. 3 chapters (xxiv.-xxvi.).

(a) Paul before Felix, ...   xxiv.
(b) Paul before Festus, ...   xxv. 1-12.
(c) Paul before Agrippa, ...   xxv. 13-xxvi. 32

(iii.) At Rome (xxvii.-xxviii.). A.D. 61-63.
2 years. 2 chapters, xxvii.-xxviii.

(a) On the Sea, ...   xxvii.
(b) At the Island, ...   xxviii. 1-10.
(c) In the City, ...   xxviii. 11-31.

Ephesians, A.D. 62.   Colossians, A.D. 62.
Philemon, A.D. 62.   Philippians, A.D. 63.

Released from First Roman Imprisonment, A.D. 63-67.
1 Timothy, A.D. 66-67.   From Macedonia.
Titus, A.D. 66-67.   From Ephesus.

Re-arrested, Taken to Rome, Martyred, A.D. 68, 2 Tim., A.D. 68.

See Note 64, on Page 274.

NOTE 66

Paul's Visits to Jerusalem.

First.   Stays with Peter for fifteen days. Acts ix. 26-30., Gal. i. 18

Second.   On a charitable mission. Acts xi. 30.

Third.   At the first Church Conference. Acts xv. 1-29, Gal. ii. 1-10.

Fourth.   At the close of the second missionary journey, on his way from Caesarea to Antioch. Acts xviii. 22.

Fifth.   Observed the Feast of Pentecost. Arrested in the Temple by the Jews. Acts xxi. 17-xxiii. 30.

The chronology of the Acts presents a difficult problem, but the dates given by Ramsay for the above visits are: first, A.D. 34; second, A.D. 45; third, A.D. 50; fourth, A.D. 53; fifth, A.D. 57.

NOTE 67

List of Paul's Speeches.

1. At Antioch of Pisidia. The Messiahship of Jesus. Acts xiii. 16-41.
2. At Lystra. The sin of idolatry. Acts xiv. 15-17.
3. At Athens. The true God and the worship of Him. Acts xvii. 22-31.
4. At Miletus. His ministry and example. Acts xx. 18-35.
5. At Jerusalem. His defence before the Jews. Acts xxii. 1-21.
6. At Caesarea. His defence before Felix. Acts xxiv. 10-21.
7. At Caesarea. His defence before Festus and Agrippa II. Acts xxvi. 1-29.
8. At Rome. His defence before the Jews. Acts xxviii. 17-20.

THE APOSTOLICAL WRITINGS

The Literature—The Epistles
Introduction

NOTE 68

Chronology of New Testament Literature.

DECADE.	WRITING.	DATE.	PLACE.	PERIOD.
A.D. 40 - 50	James	44 - 49	Jerusalem	
50 - 60	1 Thessalonians 2 Thessalonians 1 Corinthians 2 Corinthians Galatians Romans	52 53 57 57 58 58	Corinth Corinth Ephesus Macedonia Corinth Corinth	Initial
50 - 70	Mark Luke Matthew	50 - 55 58 - 61 60 - 66	Rome Cæsarea Judea	
60 - 70	Ephesians Colossians Philemon Philippians 1 Peter Acts Hebrews 2 Peter Jude 1 Timothy Titus 2 Timothy Revelation	62 - 63 62 - 63 62 - 63 63 62 - 64 63 - 64 64 - 68 64 - 68 65 - 68 65 - 67 65 - 67 67 - 68 68 - 70	Rome Rome Rome Rome Babylon ? Rome Rome ? Rome ? Jerusalem Macedonia Ephesus ? Rome Patmos	Central
90 - 100	John's Gospel John's Epistles	90 - 95 90 - 98	Ephesus Ephesus	Final

THE APOSTOLICAL WRITINGS

Introduction

THE New Testament is divisible into three distinct parts ; the first four Books are Evangelical, the next twenty-two are Apostolical, and the last one is Apocalyptical : or, we may speak of the first five Writings as Historical, of the next twenty-one as Didactical, and the last as Prophetical. Either way the Epistles form a distinct group, and they constitute the major part of the New Testament, twenty-one of its twenty-seven Books.

LETTERS

Now the first thing that must impress the thoughtful reader of these Epistles is that they *are* Epistles, that is, Letters. The deepest truths and the highest arguments of our religion are conveyed to us in the most familiar form of writing known to us, for letters are the most personal form of literature. How different would have been the reception of these pages if their truths had been presented in the form of theological essays, or of doctrinal treatises. The appeal of such a form would have been very limited, but letters bring home the Divine revelation "to our business and to our bosoms."

Letters have at least a threefold advantage over a treatise, or other formal writing ; first, they admit of a freer handling of a subject ; second, the individuality of the writers finds fuller expression ; and third, ampler use can be made of the actual circumstances of the reader. We can discern all these advantages in the Letters of the New Testament.

The Gospel comes to us individualised in these Letters. However we regard inspiration we cannot claim that the employment of it destroys the individuality of the writers of Holy Scripture. On the subject of inspiration three attitudes are taken : in the first, the Divine element is too exclusively considered ; in the second, undue prominence is assigned to the human agency ; and in the third, both these elements are recognised in their proper sphere, and are harmoniously combined. The Bible is at once a Divine and a human Book ; it is Divine thought in human language ; it is heaven in terms of earth. "A body hast Thou prepared me ;" the spirit is Divine, but the body is human.

So we find the free play in these Letters of the

individuality of their authors. The distinctiveness severally of the Writings of Paul, and John, and James is quite unmistakable. Indeed, we may say that by his Letters we learn more about Paul than from all that is told us of him in the ACTS. The man Paul is behind his Letters ; not obtrusively or egotistically, but irresistibly ; and the other writers also are wrought into their Writings; the "natural manliness" of Peter, the "uncompromising moral forthrightness" of James, and the "brief quivering sentences" of the Apostle John, and these characteristics are part of their message.

Just because Christianity is not an abstract theory, a mere philosophy, a cold ethic, but a life and a power, we must look for it in the common ways and things of men, in people, in places, and in events. Theological discourses could not so present it, but Letters can and do. Observe, for instance, how full these Letters are of personalities, the people who wrought in the first stages of Gospel history. Here we meet with a galaxy of names and faces of persons far sundered, and of many social ranks, both of men and women.

"Many of them are names of slaves and artisans, undistinguished and ordinary persons," says Dean Farrar. "Some of them, like Tryphena and Tryphosa ('the wanton,' 'the luxurious'), could have been little less than insulting; Nereus, Hermes, Phœbe, were names of heathen deities in whom men believed no longer, grotesquely bestowed on slaves; Stachys 'wheat-ear,' Asyncritus 'incomparable,' Persis, a poor slave girl brought from the Persian slave-market—all these names, even when not ridiculous, involved more or less of a stigma. The salutations sent to these poor persons have no more inherent importance than the salutations which any modern clergyman might send in a letter to any poor pensioners or aged widows in his flock." But how eloquent are these names! Their significance is derived from their relation to the Gospel, and the Gospel is demonstrated by these names. And there are many others, and better known, such as Timothy, and Titus, and Luke, and Epaphroditus, and Philemon, and Epaphras, and Onesimus. Here we have Christianity in life and action in the record of Letters.

The Writers.

These twenty-one Letters come, in unequal numbers, from five or six writers : one from James, one from Jude, two from Peter, three from John, thirteen from Paul, or fourteen, if he wrote HEBREWS, otherwise, there is a sixth writer. Of these five only Peter and John were of the Apostolate

of Jesus, and two others were Jesus' brothers according to the flesh ; but Paul stands out among them
like Jupiter or Venus in the sky.   This panel of
writers is surprising, and some of them would not
have been chosen by any Theological Faculty, but
the Holy Spirit chose them because of those
qualities in them which together enabled Him to
communicate a full revelation.

Phillips Brooks has defined preaching as "Truth
through Personality," and that is just what we have
in these Letters.   No one presentation of Christianity could have been adequate, and so through
no one mind did the Spirit work.   For Christianity
doctrinal and logical He chose Paul ; for Christianity ethical He chose James and Jude ; for
Christianity experimental He chose Peter ; and for
Christianity mystical He chose John.   These
characteristics are not exclusive to the respective
writers, but they are distinctive.

To these Apostolical Writings must, of course,
be added the ACTS, and another writer,
Luke.   Further reasons for this providential
selection are found in a following paragraph.

EPISTOLARY GROUPS.

Looking at the ACTS and Epistles we observe
that they fall into five groups, which we may call

the Jacobean, the Pauline, the Lucan, the Petrine, and the Johannine. In the first are two Books, in the second are thirteen (or fourteen), in the third is one, in the fourth are two, and in the fifth are three. Luke's Writings are the "Gospel," biographical, and the ACTS, historical, and they stand in a category by themselves, the one being in the Evangelical group, and the other in the Apostolical group.

The other Writings are generally classified as the Pauline and the Catholic Epistles. The former of these designations needs no comment, but a word will be said about the latter in the Introduction to these Letters. Other particulars of all these Letters will be found in their respective Introductions.

RELATIONS.

In a preceding paragraph reference is made to why five (or six) men were chosen to write these portions of Holy Scripture. But the mental characteristics of these are closely related to, and, indeed, are chosen for the sake of the substance of these Writings.

Christianity is manifold, and its meaning has been communicated to us by means of differing mental moulds, and these must be viewed together if we would discern the whole truth. The Pauline and Catholic Epistles are not contradictory, but complementary. It has been well said : "We see Christianity from the first in its manifold diversity, as well as in its blended simplicity. We can judge of it as it appeared to men of differing temperaments and as it was understood in divergent yet harmonious schools of thought. In the Letters of St. Peter we see it in its moderate, its conciliating, its comprehensive, its Catholic aspect. In St. James and St. Jude it is presented in its more limited and more Judaic phase. In the Epistle to the Hebrews we see how it was regarded by the philosophic school of Alexandrian students. In the Letters of St. Paul we have the Christianity of freedom, of complete emancipation from Levitic externalism—the Gospel to the Gentile world. In those of St. John we have Christianity in its intensest spirituality, in its abstractest essence, as the religion of spiritual purity, love, and adoraation."

Paul is the Apostle of Gentile Christianity; James and Jude, of Jewish Christianity ; Peter, of Catholic Christianity; and John, of Mystical Christianity. Lange has pointed out that each of these writers stands in a peculiar relation to Christianity, as the fulfilment of different aspects of Old Testament revelation. Paul teaches Christianity as the fulfilment of the Old Covenant, and of the Sacraments of the Old Testament; hence, such expressions as, "the new covenant," "the true circumcision," and "the true passover."

James teaches Christianity as the fulfilment of the Law of the Old Testament; hence such expressions as, "the royal law of love," and "the law of liberty." Peter teaches Christianity as the fulfilment of the Theocracy of the Old Testament; hence such expressions as "a royal priesthood," and "a holy nation." John teaches Christianity as the fulfilment of the Symbolism of the Old Testament; hence such expressions as "the true light," "the true life," and "the true love." Thus do these Apostles mutually support and supplement each other, and their Writings constitute a full development of the religion of Christ. Paul is prominently the Apostle of Faith; James, of Works; Peter, of Hope; Jude, of Loyalty; and John, of Love. These Apostolical Writings bear a distinct relation to the Evangelical Writings, JAMES, JUDE, and HEBREWS, with MATTHEW; 1-2 PETER, with MARK; the Letters of Paul, with LUKE, and the Letters of JOHN, and the REVELATION, with his Gospel.

This, then, is the New Testament, simple, yet profound; ancient, yet modern; local, yet universal; personal, yet collective; human, yet Divine.

THE PAULINE EPISTLES

INTRODUCTION

GROUP 1:
INTRODUCTION
1 THESSALONIANS
2 THESSALONIANS

GROUP 2:
INTRODUCTION
1 CORINTHIANS
2 CORINTHIANS
GALATIANS
ROMANS

GROUP 3:
INTRODUCTION
COLOSSIANS
PHILEMON
EPHESIANS
PHILIPPIANS

GROUP 4:
INTRODUCTION
1 TIMOTHY
TITUS
2 TIMOTHY
HEBREWS (?)

NOTE 69
St. Paul.
Himself.

The Pharisee (Phil. iii. 4-6. Acts xxiii. 6; xxvi. 4, 5). *The Roman* (Acts xxii. 25-29). *The Christian* (Phil. iii. 7-14). *The Undiscourageable* (2 Cor. ii. 14; Acts xxiv. 16; 2 Tim. i. 3). *The Sufferer* (2 Cor. xi. 23-28). *The Bible Student* (2 Tim. iii. 15-17; Acts xxiv. 14). *The Friend* (Rom. xvi. 1-16). *The Orator* (see his speeches, Note XIV). *The Man of Prayer* (Phil. i. 3-11; Eph. vi. 18; 2 Tim. i. 3, 4; 1 Thess. i. 2, 3; ii. 13; 2 Thess. i. 3, 11, 12; ii. 13-15). *The Missionary* (Acts ix. 15; xiii. 47; xviii. 6; xxii. 21; xxvi. 16-18; see *Missionary Journeys* in Analysis of Acts).

His Circle.

1. *Distinguished.* Luke, Barnabas, Mark, Timothy, Titus, Silas, Stephen, Aquila, Apollos, Philemon.

2. *Obscure.* Ananias, Tychicus, Epaphras, Epaphroditus, Onesimus, Demas, Hymenaeus, Dionysius.

3. *Official.* Gallio, Lysias, Felix, Festus, Agrippa.

See also Acts xiii. 1; xvii. 9; xx. 15-17; xxvii. 1-3; xxviii. 7. Phil. iv. 2, 3. Rom. xvi. 1-16. Col. iv. 7-17; 2 Tim. iv. 9-21; Titus iii. 12-15.

His Metaphors.

Architecture (Acts xvii. 24, 29; xx. 32; Rom. xv. 1, 2, 20; Gal. ii. 9, 18; 1 Cor. iii. 9-17; viii. 1, 10; Eph. ii. 20-22; iv. 16; Col. ii. 6, 7; 1 Tim. iii. 14, 15).

Agriculture. (1 Cor. iii. 6-9; ix. 7, 9, 10; xv. 35-38, 42-44; Gal. vi. 7, 8; 2 Cor. ix. 6-11; Col. i. 6; Phil. i. 11; Rom. vii. 4, 5; xi. 16-24; 1 Tim. v. 17, 18; 2 Tim. ii. 4-6).

Law Courts (Rom. vii. 3, 4; Gal. iii. 15; iv. 1).

Athletics (Acts xiii. 25; xx. 24; 2 Thess. iii. 1; Rom. ix. 15, 16; Gal. ii. 2; v. 7; Phil. ii. 16; iii. 12-14; 1 Thess. ii. 2; Col. iv. 12; 1 Cor. ix. 24-27; 1 Tim. iv. 7; 2 Tim. ii. 5; iv. 7, 8).

Soldiers and Armies (Rom. vii. 23; xiii. 11-13; 2 Cor. ii. 14-16; vi. 7; x. 3-6; 1 Thess. v. 5-8; Eph. vi. 10-17; 2 Cor. vii. 5; Phil. iv. 7; 1 Cor. xv. 23, 52; Col. ii. 15; 2 Tim. ii. 3, 4).

THE PAULINE EPISTLES

Introduction

PAUL'S Letters being two-thirds in number of the Epistolary Writings of the New Testament require a separate introduction, because of their special features and qualities.

LOST LETTERS.

It is obvious that Paul must have written hundreds, perhaps thousands of letters. The further he travelled the larger did his correspondence become, for he kept in touch with the Churches he founded and visited, and with numberless individuals. Surely such correspondence is embraced in the reference to the care of all the churches which came upon him daily (2 Cor. xi. 28).

But of all the letters he wrote, only thirteen or fourteen have been preserved ; the others have perished. We have no reason to believe that those which we have are of more value than those which are lost, or, to put it in another way, that those which are lost were of less value than those which are preserved.

We are not left to guess as to the fact of lost

letters, for in 1 Cor. v. 9 Paul refers to a Letter which he previously had written to this Church, so that the so-called *first* Epistle must be the *second* at least, and the expression "my letters," in 2 Cor. x. 9, 10, certainly has reference to more than two. The reference in Col. iv. 16, may be to Ephesians, which, no doubt, was a circular Letter, but Eph. iii. 3 may well allude to a lost letter.

Furthermore, Paul's unfailing courtesy and gratitude led him to acknowledge all kindnesses shown to him, and as he wrote to the Philippians once to thank them for help received (iv. 10), we must conclude that in like manner he acknowledged previous gifts (iv. 16). And when he sent deputies, as Timothy to Athens (1 Thess. iii. 5), almost certainly he would have sent letters also : and when he speaks in 2 Thess. iii. 17, of his signature in *"every* letter," he must have been referring to more than the two we have of his messages to this Church.

LETTER FORM.

It would seem that even at this early date there was an ordinary form of correspondence which was to some extent fixed. At any rate, there is in Paul's Letters a general identity of structure— first, a greeting ; second, a thanksgiving ; third, a doctrinal section; fourth, a practical section; fifth, salutations and an autograph conclusion. That an epistolary form was commonly observed is evident also in the Letters to the Asian Churches (Rev. ii.-iii).

DESTINATION.

Of Paul's thirteen Letters nine were sent to Churches, one to Rome, two to Corinth, one to the Galatian group of Churches, one to Ephesus, one to Philippi, one to Colossae, and two to Thessalonica (Salonica); and four were sent to individuals, one to Philemon, one to Titus, and two to Timothy. The field of these Letters reaches from eastern Asia Minor to the Imperial Capital. It is a wonder that of the hundreds he must have written to individuals, only four have been preserved.

ORDER.

These Letters may be read in two orders, their chronological order, and that in which they are found in our Bibles. The latter order Dr. Marcus Dods has said, "is meaningless," and Dean Farrar has called it "haphazard and accidental," but is this so? Dr. E. W. Bullinger saw considerable meaning in the Biblical arrangement of these Letters. The following is a summary of his view.

There are three pivotal Epistles, "Romans," "Ephesians," and the "Thessalonians," and these treat respectively of

Justification, Sanctification, and Glorification, or Christ Crucified, Christ Risen, and Christ Coming Again.

All failure on the part of believers relates to one or other, or all of these great truths. Of the first, "Romans," Justification, "1 Corinthians" represents *practical* failure, leaven in conduct (v. 6) ; and "2 Corinthians" represents *doctrinal* failure, leaven in creed (v. 9).

Of the second, "Ephesians," Sanctification, "Philippians" represents *practical* failure, not keeping the unity (iv. 2) ; and "Colossians" represents *doctrinal* failure, not holding the Head (ii. 19).

Of the third, "Thessalonians," Glorification, there is no failure in creed or conduct in the Glory, hence no Church Epistles follow.

If this be thought to be somewhat artificial, it should be remembered that the sum of truth is more than the values of its separate parts. At any rate, it is significant that the first of Paul's Epistles, 1-2 Thessalonians, which are eschatological, are placed last, and that that one which treats of the first great evangelical truth, Justification, though the sixth to be written, is placed first. Our Bible order of the Books is not "meaningless."

But there is another order, the chronological, which reveals the development of the Apostle's thought and the sequence of the circumstances which made the Letters necessary. The writing of these Letters covered about sixteen years, from A.D. 52 to A.D. 68, and the order of them is, 1-2 Thessalonians, 1-2 Corinthians, Galatians, Romans, Philippians, Ephesians, Colossians, Philemon, 1

Timothy, Titus, and 2 Timothy. When the Apostle wrote the first of these Letters about sixteen years after his conversion, he was about forty-six years of age, and when he wrote the last of them he was about sixty-two. The significance of the chronological order will be seen in what follows.

GROUPS.

That the Letters of this Apostle fall into several well-defined groups, no careful reader can fail to observe. Of such groups there are four. The first comprises 1-2 Thessalonians ; the second, 1-2 Corinthians, Galatians, and Romans ; the third, Philippians, Ephesians, Colossians, and Philemon ; and the fourth, 1 Timothy, Titus, and 2 Timothy. Between each of these groups is a period of not less than four years.

The dates of the first are A.D. 52, 53 ; of the second, A.D. 57, 58 ; of the third, A.D. 62, 63 ; and of the fourth, A.D. 67, 68.

The first group falls in the period of the second missionary journey ; the second, of the third missionary journey ; the third, of the first Roman imprisonment ; and the fourth in the period of release from Rome, and of the second captivity, which ended in death.

Each of these groups has its own characteristic,

or dominating complexion. Of the first, the theme is the Coming ; of the second, the Cross ; of the third, Christ ; and of the fourth, the Congregation. In theological terms, the first group is Eschatological, the second is Soteriological, the third is Christological, and the fourth is Ecclesiological.

Of this Pauline literature, Bishop Lightfoot regards the first group as a Prologue, and the fourth as an Epilogue, and groups two and three as setting forth the main teaching of the Apostle ; the second, stressing the truth, *Christ died for us,* and the third, stressing the truth, *We must die with Christ.* The one is the answer to Judaism and formalism, and the other is the answer to Hellenism and antinomianism ; the one shows the true ground of Christian hope, and the other shows the true motive of Christian life.

VALUE.

Much has been written on the inestimable value of these Writings, and no praise of them can be exaggerated. Two tributes may here be quoted. The first is from Schaff, in his History of the Christian Church :

"Tracts for the time they were tracts for all time. Children of the fleeting moment, they contain truths of infinite moment. They compress more ideas into fewer words than any other Writings, human or Divine, except the Gospels. They discuss the highest themes which can challenge an immortal mind. And all this before humble little Societies ! And yet they are of more real and general value to the Church than all the systems of theology, from Origen to Schleiermacher."

The second tribute is from Ewald, who says :

"Considering these Epistles for themselves only, and apart from the general significance of the great Apostle of the Gentiles, we must still admit that, in the whole history of all centuries and of all nations, there is no other set of Writings of similar extent, which, as creations of the fugitive moment, have proceeded from such severe troubles of the age, and such profound sufferings of the author himself, and yet contain such an amount of healthfulness, serenity, and vigour of immortal genius, and touch with such clearness and certainty on the very highest truths of human aspiration and action. From the smallest to the greatest they seem to have proceeded from the fleeting moments of this earthly life only to enchain all eternity; they were born in anxiety and bitterness of human strife to set forth in brighter lustre their superhuman grace and beauty."

NOTE 70

Paul's Epistles Classified.

GROUP I.   Prologue. 1-2 Thessalonians.

GROUP II.   Theological. Objective. Christ died for us.
            The true ground of Christian hope: answer-
              ing Judaism.
            1-2 Corinthians, Galatians, Romans.

GROUP III. Experimental. Subjective. We must die with
              Christ.
            The true power of Christian life: answer-
              ing Hellenism.
            Colossians, Philemon, Ephesians, Philippians.

GROUP IV.   Epilogue. 1 Timothy, Titus, 2 Timothy.

NOTE 71—The Setting and Character of Paul's Epistles.

THE SETTING.

LETTER.	PERIOD.	"ACTS."
1 Thessalonians.	Second Missionary Journey.	xviii. 11
2 Thessalonians.	Second Missionary Journey.	xviii. 11
1 Corinthians.	Third Missionary Journey.	xix. 20, 21
2 Corinthians.	Third Missionary Journey.	xx. 1
Galatians.	Third Missionary Journey.	xx. 2, 3
Romans.	Third Missionary Journey.	xx. 2, 3
Ephesians.	First Roman Captivity.	xxviii. 30
Colossians.	First Roman Captivity.	xxviii. 30
Philemon.	First Roman Captivity.	xxviii. 30
Philippians.	First Roman Captivity.	xxviii. 30
1 Timothy.	Fourth Missionary Journey.	1 Tim. i. 3
Titus.	Fourth Missionary Journey.	Titus 1. 5
2 Timothy.	Second Roman Captivity.	2 Tim. iv. 20

THE CHARACTER.

GROUP.	LETTER.	CHARACTERISTIC.
i. Preface. A.D. 52 - 53	1 - 2 Thessalonians.	Prophetical. Christian Hope. The Coming. Perfecting of Salvation.
ii. The Cross. A.D. 57 - 58	1 - 2 Corinthians. Galatians. Romans.	Polemical. Christian Faith. The Conflict. Plan of Salvation.
iii. The Christ. A.D. 62 - 63	Ephesians. Colossians. Philemon. Philippians.	Philosophical. Christian Love. The Conquest. Privileges of Salvation.
iv. Postscript. A.D. 65 - 68	1 Timothy. Titus. 2 Timothy.	Pastoral. Hope. Faith. Love. The Congregation. Purpose of Salvation.

THE PAULINE EPISTLES

GROUP I.

INTRODUCTION
1 THESSALONIANS
2 THESSALONIANS

NOTE 72
"The Lord's Return" in the Thessalonian Epistles.

OF Paul's Epistles those which are first *chronologically* are last *experimentally;* that which was first taught will be the last to be fulfilled.

1. **References.**
   1 Thess. i. 10; ii. 19; iii. 13; iv. 13-18; v. 1-11, 23.
   2 Thess. i. 5-10; ii. 1-12.
2. **Words Employed.**
   (a) *Apokalupsis*: from *apo*, and *kalupsis*, an uncovering, unveiling; referring to the visibility of the Lord at His return (cf. Acts i. 11). "The *apokalupsis* of the Lord Jesus from heaven" (2 Thess. i. 7).
   (b) *Parousia.* This means *personal presence* (cf. 2 Cor. x. 10; Phil. ii. 12), and so teaches that the coming again of Christ will not be spiritual but personal (1 Thess. ii. 19; iii. 13; iv. 15; v. 23; 2 Thess. ii. 1, 8, 9).
   (c) *Epiphaneia*: from *epi*, and *phaneia*, shining upon, and so, appearance, manifestation, with reference to the *glory* of the Second Advent; 2 Thess. ii. 8.

The words (b) and (c) are used together in 2 Thess. ii. 8: "The *brightness* of His *presence.*"

NOTE 73
Paraphrase of 1 Thessalonians iv. 13-18.

THIS passage is the first doctrinal revelation of the Second Advent. The following is Dr. George Milligan's paraphrase:

"With regard, moreover, to that other matter which we understand is causing you anxiety, the fate, namely, of those of your number who are falling on sleep before the coming of the Lord, we are anxious, Brothers, that you should be fully informed. There is no reason why you should sorrow, as those who do not share in your Christian hope cannot fail to do. For as surely as our belief is rooted in the death and resurrection of Jesus, even so we are confident that God will bring along with the returning Jesus those who have fallen on sleep through Him. Regarding this, we say, we are confident, for we have it on the direct authority of the Lord Himself that we who are surviving when the Lord comes will not in any way anticipate those who have fallen asleep. What will happen will rather be this. The Lord Himself will descend from heaven with a shout of command, with the voice of an archangel, and with the trumpet-call of God. Then those who died in Christ, and in consequence are still living in Him, shall rise first. And only after that shall we who are surviving be suddenly caught up in the clouds with them to meet the Lord in the air. Thus shall we ever be with the Lord. Wherefore comfort one another with these words."

THE PAULINE EPISTLES

GROUP 1.   ESCHATOLOGICAL.

    1 THESSALONIANS.   2 THESSALONIANS.

Introduction

THIS is the Eschatological Group, the Epistles
of the Second Advent of Christ. The first to
be written of Paul's preserved Letters, they are
placed last of the Church Epistles, because that is
their place in historical fulfilment.

They are the Letters of the Second Missionary
Journey, and are valuable, among other reasons,
for the picture they present of one of the first
Christian Churches in Europe.

Thessalonica was founded in B.C. 315, by Cassander, who gave it the name of his wife, a sister
of Alexander the Great. It is now called Salonika,
and is the capital of Greek Macedonia, and one of
the principal seaports of South-Eastern Europe.
The population in 1926 was a quarter of a million.
In the Great War (1914-1918) the Allies landed
an Expeditionary Force there. It is nearly 1890
years since these Letters were written, and they
retain their fascination and power unimpaired,
and undiminished.

1 THESSALONIANS

GROUP 1.

Keyword : ADVENT.   ESCHATOLOGICAL.

Place of Writing : CORINTH.   DATE: 52 A.D.

THE FIRST LETTER IN POINT OF ORDER.

THE READERS.

THESSALONICA, the modern Salonika, was the capital of Macedonia. Thither Paul went on his Second Missionary Journey, and what happened there and then is told in Acts xvii. 1-9. From the preaching of the Gospel a Christian Assembly was established. It was a small community (ii. 11), composed chiefly of Gentiles (Acts i. 9, 10 ; xvii. 4), and these were mainly slaves and artisans (iv. 11, 12). From Acts xx. 1-3, it would appear that Paul was twice again in this city during his Third Missionary Journey. It was the Apostle's policy to establish Churches in and to write letters to radiating centres, from which less important places could be reached ; hence his ministry at Philippi, Thessalonica, Corinth, Ephesus and Rome.

THE DATE.

Paul's Second Missionary Journey was in the years 51-54 A.D. (Acts xv. 36-xviii. 22). Driven out of Thessalonica, he went to Berea, Athens, and Corinth, and it was during his eighteen months' stay in this last city (Acts xviii. 11) that he wrote the two Letters to Thessalonica, following on the report which Timothy brought him from and of the Church there (iii. 1-8). The First Epistle, then, was written from Corinth in A.D. 52, and it has the distinction of being the first of the Pauline Letters which have been preserved. It was written about sixteen years after his conversion and when he was about forty-six years of age.

THE OCCASION AND OBJECT.

As Paul, who had been driven from Thessalonica (Acts xvii. 10), could not yet revisit the Church there (ii. 18), on receiving news from Timothy (iii. 6), he wrote this Letter to encourage the Church in the midst of persecution (ii. 14); to defend his own conduct whilst with them, against slanderous charges (ii. 1-10); to assure them of his love for them, of his desire to see them, and of his delight at what Timothy had told him (ii. 17-20; iii. 6-8); to warn them against their former heathen vices (iv. 1-8); to rebuke indolence on the part of some (iv. 11, 12, cf. 2 Thess. iii. 10-12); to comfort and reassure those who were perplexed about their loved ones who had died (iv. 13-18); to exhort them to watchfulness, in view of Christ's Return (v. 1-11); and to encourage spiritual concord (v. 12-24).

NOTES.

This Letter, more than any other of Paul's, is characterised by simplicity, gentleness, and affection. Later on the Apostle was in controversy with Judaizers, persons who sought to graft Christianity upon Judaism, and later again, he was in conflict with Gnosticism; but here there is no controversy. Later on Paul had to defend his Apostolic Commission (2 Corinthians), to prove the abrogation and annulment of the Law by the coming of the Gospel (Galatians), and to define and establish the doctrine of justification by faith (Romans), but he does none of these things here.

Though in this Epistle there is no formal statement of doctrine, as there is, for example, in ROMANS, yet, it has considerable doctrinal value. The Trinity is assumed (i. 1, 5); God is Father (i. 1); Christ is the Son of God (i. 10); and the Spirit is personal (v. 19).

In a great passage, purity is enjoined "with stainless delicacy, yet with absolute precision" (iv. 1-8).

The twin ideas of the Epistle are "affliction" and "advent." Each of the five chapters ends on the note of Christ's Second Coming (i. 10 ; ii. 19 ; iii. 13 ; iv. 16 ; v. 23) ; and the great passage, iv. 13-18, is the first revelation of the Lord's Advent for His Church.

There is not a single quotation from the Old Testament in the Epistle.

There are many notable verses in this Letter. For example, Chap. i. 3, faith, love, and hope, linked with work, labour, and patience. In Rev. ii. 2, the latter are without the former.

Chap. i. 9, 10 ; "ye turned," past ; "to serve," present ; "and to wait," future. The first may be associated with faith, the second, with love, and the third, with hope.

Chap. ii. 10, "holily," in relation to God ; "righteously," in relation to men ; and "unblameably" in relation to himself.

There are in this Epistle many striking words and phrases. For example,

"No need" (i. 8 ; iv. 9 ; v. 1) ; "gentle as a nurse" (ii. 7) ; "as a father with his own children" (ii. 11) ; "the rest" (iv. 13 ; v. 6) ; "asleep," "sleep" (iv. 13 ; v. 6 ; two words in the Greek) ; "through Jesus" (iv. 13) ; "without ceasing" (i. 5 ; ii. 13 ; v. 17) ; "praying exceedingly" (iii. 10) ; "more and more" (iv. 1, 10) ; "taught of God to love" (iv. 9) ; "know" (i. 4 ; ii. 1, 9, 11 ; iii. 3 ; iv. 2) ; "coming" (*parousia*, ii. 19 ; iii. 13 ; iv. 15 ; v. 23) and mark in chapter v. 12-22, those "little arrow-flights of sentences, unique in their originality, and pregnant in meaning."

In chap. v. 23, is the earliest passage in which the

trichotomy of our human nature is recognised in Scripture.

The Letter abounds with germs of thought which are developed in later Epistles; for example, "armour," v. 8, with Eph. vi. 13-17; and the duty towards ministers, v. 12, with 1 Cor. ix. 2-15; 2 Cor. xi. 8-10. Well may Dean Farrar say that we would not consent to part with this Epistle for all the letters written from the time of Cicero to that of Carlyle.

The following seventeen words occur in this Epistle and nowhere else in the New Testament.

"Blamelessly" (ii. 10; iii. 13; v. 23); "to await" (i. 10); "having been bereaved" (ii. 17); "disorderly" (v. 14); "I adjure" (v. 27); "has-sounded-out" (i. 8); "taught-of-God" (iv. 9); "a shout of command" (iv. 16); "flattery" (ii. 5); "faint-hearted" (v. 14); "wholly" (v. 23); "yearning-over" (ii. 8); "remain" (iv. 15, 17); "be-moved" (iii. 3); "countrymen" (ii. 14); "a nurse" (ii. 7); "exceedingly" (v. 13).

In addition to these, there are seventeen words in this Letter which do not occur in any other of Paul's Letters.

Analysis of 1 Thessalonians

INTRODUCTION (chap. i. 1).

I. A WORD OF EXULTATION (i. 2-10).

1. Because of the Love that Served (2-4).
2. Because of the Faith that Received (5-7).
3. Because of the Hope that Waited (8-10).

II. A WORD OF EXPLANATION (ii., iii.).

1. The Slander and Suffering (ii. 1-16).
2. The Tidings and Thanksgiving (ii. 17-iii. 10).
3. The Prayer and Purpose (iii. 11-13).

III. A WORD OF EXHORTATION (iv.-v. 24).

1. With Respect to Christian Conduct (iv. 1-12).
2. With Respect to Christian Comfort (iv. 13-v. 11).
3. With Respect to Christian Concord (v. 12-24).

CONCLUSION (v. 25-28).

NOTE 74

The Christology of 1 Thessalonians.

"THE Christology of the Epistle appears only incidentally, and for that reason is all the more decisive. In four places (i. 3, v. 9, 23, 28) we have the full expression, 'our Lord Jesus Christ.' The frequent title 'the Lord,' implies a great deal. Side by side with the Father, 'our Lord Jesus' is addressed in prayer (iii. 11). He 'died for us' (v. 10; cf. ii. 15), and 'was raised from the dead' (i. 10; iv. 14). He is in Heaven, whence He will come again to gather to Himself both quick and dead (iv. 16-18)."—Dr. ALFRED PLUMMER.

2 THESSALONIANS

GROUP 1.

Keyword : JUDGMENT.   ESCHATOLOGICAL

Place of Writing : CORINTH.   DATE : 53 A.D.

THE SECOND LETTER IN POINT OF ORDER.

THE READERS.

THE same as of the First Epistle.

THE DATE.

This Letter was written from Corinth some months after the former one, and probably in the Spring of A.D. 53.

THE OCCASION AND OBJECT.

Shortly after Paul had written his first Letter to Thessalonica he received further news of the Church there, and although, on the whole, it was favourable, there were two matters about which he felt directed by the Spirit to write to them. One of these was their misapprehension on a point of teaching, concerning the Lord's Return, teaching which he had given them both orally, and in his first Letter (ii. 5) ; and the other related to the result, in the conduct of some, of that misapprehension. These two matters are dealt with here, the one doctrinal, in chap. ii., and the other practical, in chap. iii.

As to the doctrinal error, Paul had said in his first Letter, "we that are alive, that are left" (iv. 17), and this had been interpreted to mean that Christ would return in Paul's life-time ; and this idea had been fostered (ii. 2) (*a*) by some among them professing to speak under inspiration, or with the gift of tongues, "spirit" ; (*b*) by some rumoured expression of the Apostle's opinions, "word," and, (*c*) apparently, by a forged communication, "letter as from us." The result of this was that these young Christians were being "shaken," or unsettled, and Paul would reassure them.

The way in which he does so, follows in this chapter (ii.). He says that "the Day of the Lord" will not be "present" until two events occur, first, "the apostasy" ; and second, "the apocalypse of the man of sin" (ii. 3).

As to the practical error, the Letter makes it clear that, following the misapprehension of Paul's teaching, some had ceased to work and were not comporting themselves as Christians should (iii. 11). These he rebukes, and instructs the Church as to what should be its attitude towards them (iii. 6-15).

NOTES.

This is the shortest of the Pauline Epistles, excepting the note to Philemon. The subject of the First Epistle, the Second Advent, is the subject of this one also, but with an important difference of view-point. In each is an outstanding passage (I Thess. iv. 13-18 ; 2 Thess. ii. 1-12). The first of these is for the comfort and encouragement of Christ's saints, and the second, tells of coming judgment on Christ's foes ; the first relates to the Church, and the second, to the World : the first speaks of the *Parousia* (iv. 15), and the second, of the *Apocalupsis* (i. 7) : the first reveals that Christ will come to the *air*, and the second, that He will come to the *earth* : the first points to "the Day of Christ" (cf. Phil. i. 10), and the second, to "the Day of the Lord" (ii. 2, R.V.). Failure to distinguish these view-points will result in much confusion.

In this Epistle is the celebrated passage about the Man of Sin (ii. 1-12), who is also called "the son of perdition," and "the lawless one" (ii. 3, 8). This is the Antichrist, the *alter Christus*, Satan's Messiah, and, perhaps, should be identified with the "little horn," of Dan. vii, viii ; and with the "beast out of the earth" of Rev. xiii, xvi ; (cf. John v. 43 ; I John ii. 18).

Another important passage relates to the "restrainer" (ii. 6, 7). Volumes have been written on this subject, and it, or he, has been identified with the Roman Empire and the Emperor, the fabric of Civil Society, and the Holy Spirit and the Christian Church. Each of these views should be examined before any of them is rejected. Special attention should be given to the last of these views, that which relates to the Holy Spirit.

The last dispensation ended in rejecting the true Christ. The present dispensation will end in accepting the Antichrist. Every dispensation has ended in apostasy and failure. The "mystery of lawlessness" is opposed to the "mystery of godliness" (ii. 7 and 1 Tim. iii. 16).

In this Epistle are important differences of rendering in the Revised Version : notably in i. 10, 11 ; ii. 1, 2, 3, 4, 6, 7, 8, 10, 12 ; iii. 1, 2, 3, 5, 9, 10, 12, 16, which should be carefully compared with the Authorised Version.

There are here four prayers ; two of them beginning in the same way (i. 11, 12 ; ii. 16 ; iii. 5 ; iii. 16), and one request for prayer (iii. 1).

Chap. iii. 6-15, is a weighty passage on dutifulness, attending to one's present responsibility, doing the work which lies to one's hand, free from religious excitement and intrusive curiosity. Neither yesterday nor to-morrow is ours, but only to-day, therefore we should do well and "be not weary in well-doing" (13). Making a business of being busybodies is here condemned (11, Gr.).

It is true that Christians at this time expected Christ to return almost immediately. This only need be said about it, that while their perspective was wrong, their hope was right.

Striking expressions in this Epistle are, "faith groweth exceedingly," "flaming fire," "eternal destruction," "the glory of His might," "to be marvelled at," "every good pleasure of goodness," "shaken from your mind," "the mystery of lawlessness," "the Lord Jesus shall slay with the breath of His mouth," "the working of Satan," "them that are perishing," "eternal comfort," "good hope," "unreasonable men," "all have not the faith," "the patience of Christ," "disorderly," "imitate us," "peace at all times in all ways."

The following eleven words occur in this Epistle and nowhere else in the New Testament.

"Flame" (i. 8) ; "behaved-not-disorderly" (iii. 7) ; "disorderly" (iii. 6, 11) ; not the same word as in 1 Thess. v. 14 ; "a manifest token" (i. 5) ; "to be glorified" (i. 10, 12) ; "boast" (i. 4) ; "well-doing" (iii. 13) ; "being busy-bodies" (iii. 11) ; "mark" (iii. 14) ; "suffer" (i. 9) ; "increases exceedingly" (i. 3).

In addition to these, there are nine words in this brief Letter which do not occur in any other of Paul's Letters.

Analysis of 2 Thessalonians

INTRODUCTION (chap. i. 1-2).

I. PRELIMINARY (i. 5-12).

INSPIRATION FOR THE OPPRESSED.

1. Thanksgiving (3-4).
2. The Second Advent and The Recompense of Men (5-10).
3. Prayer (11-12).

II. PROPHETICAL (ii. 1-17).

INSTRUCTION FOR THE PERPLEXED.

1. The Second Advent and The Course of Events (1-12).
2. Thanksgiving and Exhortation (13-15).
3. Prayer (16, 17).

III. PRACTICAL (iii. 1-16).

INJUNCTIONS FOR THE DISORDERLY.

1. Request (1-2).
2. Assurance (3-4).
3. Prayer (5).
4. The Second Advent and The Present Duty (6-15).
5. Prayer.

CONCLUSION (iii. 17, 18).

NOTE 75

The Cities of Paul's Epistles.

GROUPS I. AND II.

GROUP I. **Thessalonica, now Salonika.**

A large and important Macedonian city. It was named after the wife of Cassander, Thessalonica, the sister of Alexander the Great, about 315 B.C. Under the Romans it became the capital of one of the four districts into which Macedonia was divided, and afterwards the virtual capital of the whole province. It was at one time the headquarters of Pompey and his senate. Cicero spent seven months of exile in it. Seeing the strategic importance of the city Paul made it the scene of one of his missionary campaigns, and from thence "sounded forth the Word of the Lord" (i. 8). Members of the Church of Thessalonica whose names are known are Jason, Gaius, Secundus, Aristarchus, and perhaps Demas.

GROUP II. **Corinth.**

This city was the commercial capital of Greece, and became a great maritime power. Its western harbour, Lechaeum, received the shipping of Italy, Sicily, and Spain; and its eastern port, Cenchreae, the shipping of Asia Minor, Syria, Phoenicia, and Egypt. At the zenith of its power it had a population of 200,000 freed men and half a million slaves. It was destroyed by the Romans in 146 B.C., and lay desolate for a century. Julius Caesar refounded it in 46 B.C. To the city, which was a centre of commerce, a shrine of art, and a vortex of iniquity, Paul came in 50 A.D. He lived with Aquila and Priscilla, and with them wrought at tent-making (Acts xviii. 2, 3). Here he was tried, at the instigation of the Jews, before Gallio, the brother of Seneca, and was acquitted. At the time of his trial he had been in Corinth for eighteen months, and after it, "he tarried yet many days" (Acts xviii. 11, 18). At Corinth Paul wrote his two letters to Thessalonica, the Roman Epistle, and possibly the Galatian letter. To the Church at Corinth he sent the two canonical Epistles, and apparently two others, referred to in 1 Corinthians v. 9; 2 Corinthians ii. 4, vii. 8; one of which may be fragmentarily preserved in 2 Corinthians vi. 14-vii. 1, while the other is perhaps to be found,

{Continued on page 330

THE PAULINE EPISTLES

GROUP 2

INTRODUCTION

1 CORINTHIANS

2 CORINTHIANS

GALATIANS

ROMANS

(*Continued from page 328*)

in whole or in part, in 2 Corinthians x.-xiii.   It was in this city that
ecclesiastical divisions began (1 Cor. i. 10; xi. 18; xii. 25).

In the Second Great War the Germans occupied Corinth in April,
1941, and the Allies recaptured it in October, 1944.

The Galatian Churches.

Where these Churches were is one of the vexed questions of N.T.
exegesis (Acts xvi. 6) see pages 148-150.   The restricted Northern
area is advocated by Lightfoot, Jowett, Wendt, Godet, Findlay,
Moffatt, and others; and the Southern, or great Roman Province of
Galatia, is advocated by Renan, von Soden, J. Weiss, Gifford, Bacon,
Ramsay, and others.   A detailed summary of both views is given in
Moffatt's *Introduction to the Literature of the New Testament*,
pp. 90-101.

Rome.

Even to summarise the history of this great city great erudition
would be required.   Jerusalem, Athens, and Rome have been the
greatest cities in the world, alike for values religious, political, legal,
artistic, and literary.

Rome, a city of rulers and builders from Julius Caesar to Musso-
lini; Augustus, Nero, Vespasian, Domitian, Trajan, Hadrian, Marcus
Aurelius, Septimius Severus, Diocletian.   A city of great buildings;
its Temple of Jupiter; its magnificent Forum, with its Temples,
Arches, and Churches; its Colosseum; its Law Courts, and its
Pantheon.   A city associated with the names of great prose writers:
Cicero, and Caesar; of great poets: Virgil, Horace, Ovid; of great
historians: Livy, Tacitus, and Suetonius; of orators and philosophers:
Cato, Seneca, and Quintilian.   But for the Christian the chief
interest of Rome is related to the Christians there, to the Letter
which Paul wrote to them, to Paul's imprisonment and execution
there, to Peter's presence and martyrdom there, and to the many
Christian martyrs whose monument is in the Catacombs.

In the Second Great War the Germans occupied Rome in Sept.,
1943, and the Allies captured it in June, 1944.

THE PAULINE EPISTLES

GROUP 2.   SOTERIOLOGICAL.

   1 CORINTHIANS.   2 CORINTHIANS.

   GALATIANS.   ROMANS.

Introduction

THIS is the Soteriological Group, the Epistles of Free and Full Salvation by the Cross of Christ. Not only can their importance not be exaggerated, it cannot fully be estimated. They are Paul's most powerful, most argumentative, and most impassioned Epistles. Prof. G. G. Findlay says : "They furnish us with an impregnable fortress of our faith, planted in the midst of the New Testament ; and they supply a fixed starting-point and indubitable test for the examination of all questions touching the origin and nature of Christianity, and the history of the apostolic age."

The atmosphere and tone of them are entirely different from that of the First Group, which was written between four and five years earlier. The reason for this is to be found on the one hand, in the character and circumstances of the Thessalonian Church at that time, and, on the other hand, in the situation which had been created between the second and third Missionary Journeys by the collision of Paul with Peter at Antioch (Gal. ii. 11-21). This controversy precipated "a momentous epoch in apostolic history, the whole future of Christianity was involved in it," and the echoes and effects of it were heard and felt for a century afterward, and the matter, in its essence, is not a dead issue even now.

The question which was raised at that time, and which the Letters of this Group answer, was whether Christianity was but a phase or development of Judaism, or whether it was something entirely new, superseding Judaism. Out of that Antioch discussion emerged the widespread effort to Judaize Gentile Christianity, to place Gentile converts in the yoke of the Mosaic Law, and so, in effect, to rob Christians of their freedom in Christ, and to destroy the distinctive truths of Christianity.

Salvation was either by faith, or by the works of the law, but it could not be by both. Defeated at the Council of Jerusalem (Acts xv), the Judaizers later followed Paul, and endeavoured to inoculate his converts with their legalistic doctrine, supporting their propaganda by affirming that Paul had no apostolic standing (Gal. ii. 6-10 ; 2 Cor. xi. 5).

This controversy was at its height when Paul was in the vigour and maturity of his powers, in the sixth decade of the first century. It was the great controversy of his life, and these Letters of the second group are the product and monument of it. The answer to the Judaizers was the Cross of Christ. At every turn in these Epistles we are face to face with the Crucified Christ. Every question, doctrinal, ethical, ecclesiastical, social, practical, and personal, is here confronted with the work wrought on Calvary. In these Letters Paul fought out and won, for all time, the battle of full and free salvation.

NOTE 76

References to Christ's Sacrifice in Group II. of Paul's Epistles.

Cross. 1 Cor. i. 17, 18; Gal. v. 11; vi. 12, 14.

Crucify. 1 Cor. i. 13, 23; ii. 2, 8; 2 Cor. xiii. 4; Gal. ii. 20; iii. 1; v. 24; vi. 14; Rom. vi. 6.

Blood. 1 Cor. xi. 27; x. 16; Rom. iii. 25; v. 9.

Death. 2 Cor. v. 14; 1 Cor. xv. 12; Gal. ii. 21; Rom. vi. 8, 11; vii. 4; x. 7; 1 Cor. xi. 26; xv. 21; Rom. v. 6, 10; vi. 3, 4, 5, 9; Rom. vii. 9; viii. 34; xiv. 9, 15; 1 Cor. xv. 3; 2 Cor. v. 14, 15; iv. 10.

1 CORINTHIANS

GROUP 2.

Keyword : CALVARY.   SOTERIOLOGICAL.

Place of Writing : EPHESUS.   DATE : 57 A.D.

THE THIRD LETTER IN POINT OF ORDER.

THE READERS.

STANDING on Grecian soil, Corinth was a
Roman Colony, the capital of Achaia, founded
by Julius Cæsar in B.C. 46, and it was at once the
seat of Roman government and the centre of Greek
commerce. Beautifully situated, and by reason of
its occupations and recreations, its wisdom and
wealth, its luxury and licence, it drew to itself a
heterogeneous population of Jews, Greeks, Romans,
Asiatics, and Phœnicians. It was, says Farrar,
"the Vanity Fair of the Roman Empire ; at once
the London and Paris of the first century of Christianity ; so famous for its infamy, its debauchery
and drunkenness, that the name ' Corinthian,'
became a synonym for profligacy."

In such a city a Christian Church was established
by the Apostle Paul, during his eighteen months'
sojourn there, in the years 52-53 A.D. (Acts xviii.
1-17), during which time he wrote his two Letters
to Thessalonica. It would appear that the Church

334

was composed largely of Gentiles, and mainly from the poorer and unlearned strata of society (1 Cor. i. 26-28). These, then, were the readers of this Letter.

THE DATE

Leaving Corinth in A.D. 53, Paul returned by Ephesus (Acts xviii. 19) and Jerusalem, to Antioch (Acts xviii. 21, 22), from whence, after a while, he set out on his Third Missionary Journey. This would be in the year 53-54 A.D. Passing through Galatia and Phrygia, and "the upper coasts" (Acts xviii. 23 ; xix. 1) 54-57 A.D., Paul came to Ephesus, where he ministered for "three years" (Acts xix. 1 ; xx. 31). From a combination of references we gather that it was in 57 A.D. that he wrote this First Letter to Corinth, during his sojourn at Ephesus. Its place in the ACTS is between verses 20 and 21 of chapter xix. About four years elapsed between the writing of the second Letter to Thessalonica and this one to Corinth.

THE OCCASION AND OBJECT.

As to the occasion, the facts seem to be as follows : (1) During his sojourn in Ephesus Paul paid a visit to Corinth. This seems clear from the reference in 2 Cor. xii. 14 ; xiii. 1, 2, to "the third time." While on this visit he witnessed certain tendencies in the Church which greatly grieved him, in consequence of which (2) after his return to Ephesus, he wrote to them a short Letter, forbidding them to "company with fornicators" (1 Cor. v. 9). What, therefore, we call the First Letter to Corinth is, in fact, the Second, and the Second is the Third.

Not without reason is it supposed that two fragments of the first lost Letter survive. The first of these is 1 Cor. vi. 12-20, and the second is 2 Cor. vi. 14-vii. 1. Both these passages are almost certainly interpolations, as the following fact shows. (3) In the lost Letter certain matters were referred to which raised questions in the minds of the Christians at Corinth, so they wrote to Paul, asking for light on these and kindred subjects. In chap. v. 9-13, he explains what he had said about companying with fornicators ; and in chaps. vii-xii, he answers other questions which they had asked : observe "now concerning" in vii. 1 ; viii. 1 ; xii. 1. A reference again to the supposed two fragments of the lost Letter will show that the subjects of them are those about which the Corinthians inquire in the letter they wrote to Paul. 1 Cor. vi. 13, occasioned the question about "things sacrificed to idols," which the Apostle answers in viii. 1-xi. 1 ; chap. vi. 14, occasioned the question about the resurrection of the body, which is answered in chap. xv. 35 ; chap. vi. 20, occasioned the question about slavery, which is answered in chap. vii. 21-24 ; and 2 Cor. vi. 14-vii. 1, occasioned the question about mixed marriages which Paul answers in 1 Cor. vii. 12-14.

(4) Certain men from Corinth visited Paul at Ephesus, and, perhaps, brought with them the letter which the Church had written to the Apostle (1 Cor. xvi. 17, 18). (5) About the same time he heard from another source (1 Cor. i. 11) tidings which revived his worst fears. Thus, the occasion of this Letter was the condition of things in the Corinthian Church, the divisions and disorders among them, their domestic and social difficulties, and certain doctrinal matters ; and Paul's object in writing was to rebuke the disorders, and to resolve the difficulties.

This he does in a Letter which is the longest, "and in some respects the most magnificent, of his Epistles." In chaps. i-vi he deals with the disorders ; and in chaps. vii-xv, with the difficulties. Paul at this time was at the height of his powers, and "nowhere," says Prof. Findlay, "does his inspired sagacity, his moral insight and practical sense, shine with more luminous effect than in 1 Corinthians." About a dozen subjects are handled with unstudied naturalness and ease, and while some of these are, for us, irrelevant, the underlying principles of the Letter, and its spiritual power, are of priceless and abiding worth.

The disorders in the Church relate to party factions, want of discipline, litigation before heathen tribunals, impurity, indecorous behaviour on the part of the women, and abuse of the Lord's Supper. The difficulties relate to marriage and celibacy, eating meats offered to idols, the exercise of the spiritual gifts, order in public worship, the matter of a bodily resurrection, and the offertory for the poor at Jerusalem.

The Christians at Corinth were dear to Paul, because he was their "father" (iv. 15), and he well knew that if they rejected his authority in the matters of this Letter, Corinth would be lost, and his work would have been in vain. Hence the passion with which he rebukes and pleads.

NOTES.

We may discern the intellectual vigour of Paul at this time in the fact that in I CORINTHIANS he employs 236 words which do not occur again in any of his Epistles, and of these, about 100 do not occur anywhere else in the New Testament.

The central idea of the Epistle is the Cross of Christ, and to it he relates every subject which he handles. Dr. A. T. Pierson puts this fact in a slightly different form. He says: "The nuptial union between Christ and the Church is the key to the main divisions of I Corinthians. *Factions in the Church* dishonour it. *Impurity* is destructive of it. *Marriage* illustrates it, and is hallowed by it. *Identification with idols* profanes it. The *Lord's Supper* expresses and emblemizes it. *Disorderly Assemblies* disgrace it. *The Resurrection* consummates and crowns it."

There are fourteen direct references in the Epistle to Calvary, by "cross," "crucified," "died," "blood," and "sacrificed." Prof. Findlay says that this "is the Epistle of the doctrine of the Cross in application." Amongst the four evangelical Epistles it holds a place in the practical sphere similar to that of ROMANS in the theoretical and theological. In I CORINTHIANS the Gospel proves itself to be the "power of God," and in ROMANS, "the wisdom of God." The theology of I Cor. is not the product of Paul's brain, but a development of the revelation of the Evangelical Records. The Christ of Paul, and the Jesus of the Gospels, are one and the same Person. Paul's doctrine of the Cross is an exposition of the historical facts.

This Epistle, better perhaps than any other, gives us an insight into the inner life and proceedings

of an early Christian Society, and of the difficulties and dangers to which the Christians were
exposed. Especially does it disclose the seriousness of the problems of living a Christian life
in a city so notorious for vice as was Corinth,
and where a believer could hardly buy meat in
the market, or go to any social entertainment,
without being confronted with the matter of idol-
offerings.

The Letter presents a striking picture of what
Farrar calls the "turbulent, conceited, party-
shaken, clever, restless, backsliding Church of
Corinth." Paul begins with a reference to their
enrichment "in all utterance, and all knowledge"
(i. 5), and later, he says, somewhat sarcastically,
"we know that we all have knowledge" (viii. 1),
and in several places he asks "know ye not?" with
all your knowing!

Six times in this Epistle, and once in the Second,
the Apostle speaks of these people being "puffed
up," or inflated with conceited opiniativeness;
and his argument in chap. viii is that love is better
than knowledge.

Writing on "The Apostle Paul," Sabatier says:
"While the Epistle to the Galatians was the founda-
tion of *Christian Dogma*, the two Epistles to the
Corinthians, signalising as they do the emancipa-

tion of the regenerate conscience, are the beginning of *Christian Ethics*.

Though the whole Letter is wonderful, there are some passages of outstanding impressiveness. Of these must be named that which speaks of the apparent foolishness of the Gospel and the Church (i-ii); the reference to the Lord's Supper (xi), which is the fullest, to this Ordinance, in the New Testament; the Church, the Body of Christ, displaying unity in diversity (xii); and the incomparable passages on Love (xiii), and the Resurrection (xv).

In this Epistle there are 236 words used which do not occur in any other of Paul's Letters, and of these 100 do not occur anywhere else in the New Testament. The latter are as follows:

"Unmarried" (vii. 8, 11, 32, 24); "low-born" (i. 28); "without expense" (ix. 18); "uncertainly" (ix. 26); "obscurely" (xiii. 12); "uncovered" (xi. 5, 13); "unwillingly" (ix. 17); "immovable" (xv. 58); "unworthy" (vi. 2); "unworthily" (xi. 27); "quit-yourselves-like-men" (xvi. 13); "helps" (xii. 28); "freedman" (vii. 22); "without distraction" (vii. 35); "demonstration" (ii. 4); "architect" (iii. 10); "wander-without-a-home" (iv. 11); "behaves unseemly" (vii. 36; xiii. 5); "uncomely" (xii. 23); "an instant" (xv. 52); "pipe" (xiv. 7); "lifeless things" (xiv. 7); "noose" (vii. 35); "husbandry" (iii. 9); "are naked" (iv. 11); "diversities" (xii. 4); "interpreter" (xiv. 28); "wherefore" (viii. 13; x. 14); "bring-into-servitude" (ix. 27); "takes" (iii. 19); "defamed" (iv. 13); "have-self-control" (vii. 9; ix. 25); "idol-temple" (viii. 10); "hindrance" (ix. 12); "awake-up" (xv. 34); "abortion" (xv. 8); "operations" (xii. 6, 10); "shame" (vi,

5 ; xv. 34) ; "put-out" (v. 13) ; "celebrate-the-feast" (v. 8) ;
"appointed-to-death" (iv. 9) ; "desirers" (x. 6) ; "become
uncircumcised" (viii. 18) ; "interpretation" (xii. 10 ; xiv. 26) ;
"other-tongues" (xiv. 21) ; "devoted" (vii. 35) ; "manners"
(xv. 33) ; "fought with beasts" (xv. 32) ; "healing" (xii.
9, 28, 30) ; "offered-in-sacrifice" (x. 28) ; "straw" (iii. 12) ;
"covered" (xi. 6) ; "they were strewed" (x. 5) ; "using-as-
their-own" (vii. 31 ; ix. 18) ; "muzzle" (ix. 9) ; "have long-
hair" (xi. 14, 15) ; "long hair" (xi. 15) ; "governments" (xii.
28) ; "cymbal" (xiii. 1) ; "collection" (xvi. 1, 2) ; "railer"
(v. 11 ; vi. 10) ; "to be loosed" (vii. 27) ; "market" (x. 25) ;
"Maranatha" (xvi. 22) ; "drunkard" (v. 11 ; vi. 10) ; "much
more then" (vi. 3) ; "foolishness" (i. 18, 21, 23 ; ii. 14 ; iii.
19) ; "by" (xv. 31) ; "be babes" (xiv. 20) ; "victory" (xv.
54, 55, 57) ; "destroyer" (x. 10) ; "companionship" (xv. 33) ;
"smelling" (xii. 17) ; "to play " (x. 7) ; "consolation" (xiv.
3) ; "sitting near" (attending) (ix. 13) ; "passing" (xvi. 7) ;
"persuasive" (ii. 4) ; "refuse" (iv. 13) ; "off-scouring" (iv.
13) ; "vainglorious" (xiii. 4) ; "birds" (xv. 39) ; "I combat"
(ix. 26) ; "twinkling" (xv. 52) ; "race-course" (ix. 24) ;
"profit" (vii. 35 ; x. 33) ; "consent" (vii. 5) ; "permission"
(vii. 6) ; "disputer" (i. 20) ; "partake" (ix. 13) ; "rank" (xv.
23) ; "typically" (x. 11) ; "beyond prime" (vii. 36) ; "con-
tentious" (xi. 16) ; "Minds" (xiv. 20) ; "made of dust" (xv.
47, 48, 49) ; "is kind" (xiii. 4) ; "as" (xv. 8) ; "intelligible"
(xiv. 9) ; "comeliness" (xii. 23).

Analysis of 1 Corinthians

2 CORINTHIANS

GROUP 2.

Keyword : VINDICATION.   SOTERIOLOGICAL.
Place of Writing : MACEDONIA.   DATE : 57 A.D.
THE FOURTH LETTER IN POINT OF ORDER.

THE READERS.

THE same as of the First Epistle, which see under this heading.

THE DATE.

If the First Epistle was written from Ephesus in the Spring of A.D. 57, this one must have been written in the Autumn of the same year, and, it would appear, from somewhere in Macedonia, at Philippi, or Thessalonica.

THE OCCASION AND OBJECT.

Peculiar difficulties, historical and literary, attach to this Epistle, as it is well nigh impossible to say with confidence what Paul's movements and actions were in relation to Corinth, in this year.

It is influentially held that the Apostle wrote not fewer than four Letters to this Church (1) the lost Letter of 1 Cor. v. 9 ; (2) Our 1 Corinthians ; (3) a stern Letter (2 Cor. ii. 3 ; vii. 12), which, it is thought, cannot be our 1 Corinthians, but rather

2 Cor. x. 1-xiii. 10 ; and (4) a glad Letter, which would be our 2 Cor. i-ix ; xiii. 11-14. No one can read 2 CORINTHIANS with any care and not be struck with the difference in outlook and tone between chaps. i-ix, and chaps. x-xiii. The former division is jubilant and conciliatory, but the latter is sad and severe, and it is widely felt that these two notes could not possibly have been sounded in the same Letter, and that, therefore, to the Letter chaps. i-ix, has got attached a fragment at any rate, of a previous Letter, chaps. x-xiii. 10. This seems possible and reasonable ; but while it would resolve some difficulties, it would create others. Dr. Archibald Robertson rightly asks : "Can we suppose that interpolations so serious (vi. 14-vii. 1 ; ix, and x-xiii. 10) as to amount to the formation of an entire Epistle out of hetero-geneous fragments—or even the interpolation of any one of the passages in question—can have taken place without leaving so much as a ripple upon the stream of textual tradition ?" (Hasting's Bible Dict., i. 497).

Moreover, though still not without difficulties, there is another explanatory view, which two verses suggest. First, the Epistle is addressed, not only to the members of the Church at Corinth, but also to "all the saints that are in the whole of

Achaia" (i. 1) ; and second, in chap. ii. 6, we read
of "punishment which was inflicted by the *more*,"
which indicates that what was done, was not done
unanimously ; in other words, that there were in
the Church a majority and a minority. If these
two verses are a clue, then chapters i-ix, would be
written to the majority, and chapters x-xiii, with
reference to the minority and all whom they
represented in Achaia.

The bearing of this upon the occasion and object
of the Letter is obvious. If we assume that the
latter of these two views is correct, then the occasion
of the Letter was twofold : (*a*) the report which
Titus brought to Paul in Macedonia (ii. 13 ; vii.
5, 6) of the repentance and goodwill of the majority
of the Church members (ii. 6, 7) ; and (*b*) a further
report that there was in the Church an opposing
minority (x. 10, "they say"). That being the
occasion, the object also would be twofold : (*a*) to
express thanksgiving to God and gratitude to the
majority, and (*b*) to answer the assaults of the
minority.

But who were the latter ? Evidently "certain
persons" with "letters of commendation" (iii. 1 ;
x. 13-17), obtained in all probability from Jerusalem
(Acts xv. 1, 24 ; Gal. ii. 12), had arrived at Corinth,
and were gravely disturbing the young believers

there, firstly, by preaching a pseudo-gospel (xi. 3, 4), and secondly, by denying Paul's Apostolic authority (xi. 5, 13, 23). These were of the Judaistic agitators who dogged the footsteps of Paul across Asia Minor and into Europe, impugning his message and attacking his person. The division x-xiii, of this Epistle was not yet written *to* these mischief-makers, but *of* them, and Paul's purpose was to present facts and truths which would discredit their perilous propaganda.

That Paul clearly distinguishes in this Letter between these two parties in the Church, the majority, and the minority, and that he believed the majority were now loyal to him, is seen in his frequent use of "all," or "you all" for the majority (ii. 3-5 ; iii. 18 ; v. 10 ; vii. 13 ; xiii. 13), and "some" for the minority (iii. 1 ; x. 2, 7, 12 ; xi. 4 ; xii. 21).

NOTES.

The Epistle consists of an Introduction, Three Divisions, and a Conclusion. See the Analysis. It is the least systematic, as 1 CORINTHIANS and ROMANS are the most systematic, of all Paul's Letters.

This Epistle is the most personal of the Writings of Paul ; nowhere else is he portrayed so intimately ; nowhere is his rich humanity so in evidence. To appreciate the Letter one must understand the situation.

Between the writing of First and Second Corinthians, there occurred the riot recorded in Acts xix ; (2 Cor. i. 8-10). Paul had intended to visit Corinth, but the news he had received from there led him to change his plan (i. 15-17). Titus had been sent instead, and Paul, driven out of Ephesus, went to Troas, where he expected to meet Titus, and to learn from him how his former letter had been received (ii. 1, 3, 4, 9, 12). Titus did not arrive, and Paul, who obviously was ill from his recent experience in Ephesus (i. 8, 9), and was restless in spirit (ii. 13), proceeded to Macedonia, probably to Philippi (ii. 13 ; Acts xx. 1), and there he met Titus, who gave him a report which, in part, cheered him greatly, and, in part, caused him much anxiety (ii. 14-17). Behind the writing of this Letter was the darkest hour in Paul's life. Evidence of this is seen in such passages as vii. 5 ; iv. 7-v. 4 ; vi. 4-10, in addition to the passages already referred to. Such, then, was the situation out of which this Letter came, and it accounts for the form in which it is cast.

The personal element in it is one of its outstanding features, and is one of its chief values. Here Paul is a minister of Christ, and a man among men ; none the less so truly human because he was so spiritual. What would hurt us, hurt him, and nerves affected him, as they affect us. The whole Epistle pulsates with emotion : "it enables us, as it were, to lay our hands upon his breast, and feel the very throbbings of his heart." His feelings oscillate between the extremes of satisfaction and indignation : "explanation, defence, protestation, appeal, reproach, invective, threatening, with a vein of subduing pathos blended with the most subtle irony" run through the whole. It is this fact which makes analysis difficult, for "feeling cannot be reduced to system ; it vanishes under the dissecting knife."

Paul's detractors and calumniators made a three-fold assault upon him ; they attacked his person, his teaching, and his character ; and his defence is along these three lines. For the first attack see x. 1, 10 ; xi. 6 ; and the defence, x. 7 ; xiii. 4. For the second attack see x. 12-18 ; xi. 7-12 ; xii. 13 ; xi. 4 ; ii. 17 ; and the defence, ii. 17 ; iv. 2, 5 ; x. 12-18 ; xi. 1-4 ; xi. 22-30 ; xii. 1-12. For the third attack see i. 15-17 ; x. 9-11 ; xi. 16-19 ; xii. 16-19 ; and the defence, iii. 1-6 ; x. 18 ; i. 15 24 ; xii. 14-18 ; vii. 2-4 ; v. 13 ; xi. 16-19. It has well been called Paul's *Apologia pro Vita Sua*.

He was accused of fickleness (i. 17, 18, 23), of

pride and boasting (iii. 1 ; v. 12), of obscurity in preaching (iv. 3), of weakness (x. 10), of rudeness of speech (xi. 6), of being contemptible in person (iv. 7-10) ; vi. 4-10 ; x. 10 ; xii. 7-10) of being dishonest (xii. 16-19), of being hardly sound of mind (v. 13 ; xi. 16-19 ; xii. 6), and of being no Apostle (xi. 5 ; xii. 12) ; and this Letter is largely an answer to these charges.

But though the Epistle is predominantly per-sonal, it is by no means without great doctrinal value. The contrast between the Old Covenant and the New (iii.) ; Christ's substitutionary work (v. 21) ; the Gospel of reconciliation (v. 18-20) ; the nature of the world, and the duty of Christians to separate themselves from it (vi. 14-vii. 1) ; the glory of the Gospel (iv. 5, 6) ; and the life after death (v. 1-10), are among the more important passages, to which must be added all references to God, Christ, and the Holy Spirit.

Among the specially impressive passages are the following : iv. 7-12 ; iv. 16-18 ; v. 1-10 ; v. 17-21 ; vi. 4-10 ; viii. 9 ; ix. 8; xi. 23-33 ; xii. 1-10 ; xiii. 14.

To compare the two Letters to Corinth will prove instructive. The First gives insight into the character and condition of the early Churches ; the Second, into the life and character of the Apostle Paul. The First is objective and practical ;

the Second is subjective and personal. The First is systematic ; the Second is not. The First is deliberate ; the Second is impassioned. The First warns against Pagan influences ; the Second, against Judaic influences. The two together are valuable beyond all estimate for an understanding of the problems of first century Christians, and for an appreciation of the greatest missionary of the Christian era.

It is worth noticing that in portions of this Letter the mind of the Apostle works around a certain word, or words. For example :

In chapter i, "comfort" ten times ; "affliction" and "suffering," eight times ; "deliver," three times in verse 10 ; "acknowledge," three times in verses 13, 14 ; "yea," six times ; "nay," four times. In chapter ii, "sorrow," eight times ; "forgive," six times ; "savour," four times. In chapter iii, mark "sufficient" and "ministration" ; "veil." Other repeated words in this letter are "glory," "exceeding," "clothed," "know," "knowing," "good courage," "manifest," "reconciliation," "grace," "earnest," "love," "all," "measure," "commend," "foolish," "perils," "weakness," and "boast," "boasting," about thirty times.

As words are the expression of thoughts, recurring words make certain thoughts emphatic. These words are characteristic of the extreme emotion of mind in which the Letter was written.

This Epistle tells us things about Paul which are not hinted at anywhere else. For example, his escape from Damascus (xi. 32, 33), his revelations and visions (xii. 1-4) ; his "thorn in the flesh" (xii. 7) ; the five Jewish scourgings, two Roman scourgings, three shipwrecks, and many perils (xi. 23-27). Thus, though Paul speaks much about "boasting," he certainly was not a boaster, or he would have told Luke all about these experiences, and Luke would have recorded them in the ACTS.

The Epistle teaches us many lessons. We should always be ready to forgive (ii. 10). We should be grateful for good news (ii. 13, 14). We should be courageous and hopeful (iv. 8-10). We should recognise that affliction is a road to glory (iv. 16-18). We should have a true "aim" (v. 9). We should see that there are two sides to life (vi. 10).

We should have a concern to help Church members who are poor (viii-ix). We should not be eager to defend ourselves against the assaults of others, but there are times when it is desirable and necessary (x-xi). We should be glad to suffer if God wills (xii. 8-10). We should be strictly honest (viii. 16-22 ; xii. 17-18).

In this Epistle are 171 words which do not occur in any other of Paul's Letters ; and of these 91 do not occur again in the New Testament. The latter are as follows :

"Burdensome" (xi. 9) ; "indignation" (vii. 11) ; "pureness" (vi. 6 ; xi. 3) ; "watchings" (vi. 5 ; xi. 27) ; "abundance"

(viii. 20); "beyond measure" (x. 13, 15); "unveiled" (iii. 14, 18); "indescribable" (ix. 15); "unprepared" (ix. 4); "renounced" (iv. 2); "sentence" (i. 9); "I have espoused" (xi. 2); "unutterable" (xii. 4); "to beam forth" (iv. 4); "willing of themselves" (viii. 3. 17); "Belial" (vi. 15); "deep" (xi. 25); "thirst" (xi. 27); "falsifying" (iv. 2); "giver" (ix. 7); "evil report" (vi. 8); "ethnarch" (xi. 32); "will-receive" (vi. 17); "will-be-utterly-spent" (xii. 15); "from home" v. 6, 8, 9); "frightening" (x. 9); "did-not-lack" (viii. 15); "lightness" (i. 17); "at home " (v. 6, 8, 9); "rank among" (x. 12); "walk among" (vi. 16); "having-been engraven" (iii. 7); "for-us-to-despair" (i. 8 ; iv. 8); "I listened-to" (vi. 2); "to-be-clothed-upon" (v. 2, 4); "longing" (vii. 7, 11); "may-dwell" (xii. 9); "rebuke" (ii. 6); "diversely-yoked" (vi. 14); "good report" (vi. 8); "to reach," "reaching" (x. 13, 14); "when" (iii. 15, 16); "competent" (iii. 5); "cheerful" (ix. 7); "overthrow" (x. 4, 8 ; xiii. 10); "veil" (iii. 13, 14, 15, 16); "making-gain-by-corrupting" (ii. 17); "did-not-burden" (xii. 16); "condemnation" (iii. 9 ; vii. 3); "did-lazily-burden" (xi. 9 ; xii. 13, 14); "perfecting" (xiii. 9); "beholding as-in-a-mirror" (iii. 18); "participation" (vi. 14); "defilement" (vii. 1); "blame" (vi. 3 ; viii. 20); "a night and a day" (xi. 25); "strong-holds" (x. 4); "crafty" (xii. 16); "momentary" (iv. 17); "as being beside myself" (xi. 23); "poor" (ix. 9); "a year ago" (viii. 10 ; ix. 2); "purposes" (ix. 7); "have-before-sinned" (xii. 21 ; xiii. 2); "began-before" (viii. 6, 10); "foreannounced" (ix. 5); "completely-filling-up" (ix. 12 ; xi. 9); "offence" (vi. 3); "became-poor" (viii. 9); "basket" (xi. 33); "tabernacle" (v. 1, 4); "thorn" (xii. 7); "more-diligent" (viii. 17, 22); "straitened" (iv. 8 ; vi. 12); "de-spoiled" (xi. 8); "concord" (vi. 15); "sent-with" (xii. 18); "agreement" (vi. 16); "sent-with" (viii. 18, 22); "labouring-together" (i. 11); "commendatory" (iii. 1); "above" (xi. 23); "above-measure" (xi. 23); "beyond" (x. 16); "do-we-over-stretch" (x. 14); "surpassing degree" (xi. 5); "sparingly" (ix. 6); "puffings up" (xii. 20); "radiancy" (iv. 4); "false apostles" (xi. 13); "whisperings" (xii. 20).

Analysis of 2 Corinthians

INTRODUCTION (i. 1-11).
    (*a*) Address and Greeting (1-2).
    (*b*) Thanksgiving for Comfort and Trouble (3-7).
    (*c*) The Nature of the Trouble (8-11).

PART I. CONSOLATION (i. 12-vii. 16).

1. The Minister of the Gospel.

AN EXPLANATION (i. 12-ii. 11).

(i.) The Ground of Appeal for Sympathy, ...		i. 12-14.
(ii.) The Change of Plan Explained, ...	...	i. 15-ii. 4.
(iii.) The Treatment of the Offender, ...	...	ii. 5-11.

2. The Ministry of the Gospel.

AN EXPOSITION (ii. 12-v. 21).

(i.) Praise for Good News, ...		ii. 12-17.
(ii.) The Source of Satisfaction and Sufficiency,		iii. 1-6.
(iii.) Two Ministries Contrasted, ...		iii. 7-18.
(iv.) The Glory of the Gospel Ministry, ...		iv. 1-6.
(v.) The Frailty of the Messengers, ...		iv. 7-15.
(vi.) The Preacher's Hope, Here and Hereafter,		iv. 16-v. 10.
(vii.) The Minister's Devotion to his Message,		v. 11-21.

3. The Ministered Unto by the Gospel.

AN EXHORTATION (vi. 1-vii. 16).

(i.) The Method and Condition of Apostolic Ministry, ...		vi. 1-10.
(ii.) Paul's Appeal for Frankness and Affection,		vi. 11-vii. 4.
(iii.) The Object and Effect of a Previous Letter,		vii. 5-16.

PART II. SOLICITATION (viii.-ix.).

1. **Liberality of the Macedonian Churches** (viii. 1-5).
2. **Appeal to the Corinthians for Generosity** (viii. 6-15).
3. **Commendation of the Fund Delegates** (viii. 16-24).
4. **Plea for the Fulfilment of Promise** (ix. 1-5).
5. **Reward and Results of Bountiful Giving** (ix. 6-15).

NOTE 77

An Example of Paul's Compressed Thought (2 Cor. ix. 8).

I. INFLOW. "God is able to make to abound towards you all grace."
   1. *Power*. "God is able."
   2. *Provision*. "Grace."
   3. *Prodigality*. "To make to abound all grace."

II. POSSESSION. "Ye always having all-sufficiency in all things."
   1. *Fulness*. "All-sufficiency."
   2. *Range*. "In all things."
   3. *Duration*. "Always."

III. OUTFLOW. "That ye may abound to all good work."
   1. *Motive*. We *should* abound, *because* God has abounded towards us.
   2. *Means*. We *can* abound, *for* He has abounded towards us.
   3. *Measure*. We *must* abound, *as* He has abounded towards us.

GALATIANS

Keyword : LIBERTY.   SOTERIOLOGICAL.
Place of Writing : MACEDONIA.   DATE : 57 A.D.
THE FIFTH LETTER IN POINT OF ORDER.

THE READERS.

WHO the readers of this Letter were depends
upon which of two theories is correct, the
North Galatian, or the South Galatian, as they
are called. The North Galatian theory locates
the Churches to which this Letter was sent in the
north-east of Asia Minor ; the South Galatian
theory locates them in the south-east. The Northern
theory limits the reference to Galatia proper, a
broad strip of land over two hundred miles in
length, stretching from north-east to south-west,
the chief cities of which were Tavium, Ancyra,
and Pessinus. The Southern theory refers to the
Roman Province of Galatia, wherein, in addition to
the above were Lycaonia, Isauria, Phrygia, and a
portion of Pisidia, in which area lay Antioch,
Iconium, Lystra, and Derbe.

If the Northern theory is right, Paul founded
these churches when on his Second Missionary
Journey ; but if the Southern theory is right, it

was when on his First Missionary Journey that he founded the churches in the south-east. The Northern theory is championed by Bishop Lightfoot, and the Southern theory by Professor Ramsay, and, it may be said, the former is the generally accepted view.

Assuming, then, the North Galatian theory, the readers of this Letter would be chiefly Gauls, whose forebears poured into Asia Minor in the third century B.C., and also Jews, who had settled in considerable numbers in that Province. Roman writers tell us that the Gallic Celts were characterised by mental alertness and ready impressibility ; that they were generous, inconstant, impulsive, vehement, treacherous in their dealings, easily discouraged by failure, and quarrelsome. These features are reflected in the Letter before us. "They were ever in extremes, first receiving the Apostle as an angel, and ready to pluck out their eyes and give them to him (iv. 15), but ' soon removing ' by false teachers ' to another Gospel '" (i. 6), and then under the influence of the same ardour beginning to "bite and devour one another" (v. 15). Eight out of the fifteen "works of the flesh" enumerated in chap. v. 20, 21, are sins of strife.

But while the majority of believers in these churches were Gauls, there certainly were Jews there, for not a little of this Letter assumes an acquaintance with the Old Testament which converted heathen could not be expected to have, except under Jewish instruction.

Outside of this Epistle there are only five references to Galatia ; 1 Cor. xvi. 1 ; 2 Tim. iv. 10 ; 1 Peter i. 1 ; Acts xvi. 6 ; xviii. 23, and in the last two passages Luke calls it "the Galatic Land."

The Date.

This also depends on whether the North or South Galatian theory is the correct one. The Northern theory would require the autumn of 57 A.D. for the writing of the Letter, but the Southern theory would place it several years earlier.

The Occasion and Object.

While Paul was in Macedonia (Acts xx. 1), and on his way to Corinth, he got word of the state of things in the Galatian Churches, and at once wrote this Letter. The trouble, as in Corinth, was two-fold, and emanated from the same quarter. Judaizers claiming authority from Jerusalem were endeavouring to place the Gentile Christians in the yoke of the Mosaic Law, and their method was to deny Paul's apostolic standing, and to impugn his teaching. Both these factors are in evidence in 2 Corinthians and Galatians, only in the former it is the personal aspect which is dominant, and in the latter, it is the doctrinal aspect. In 2 CORINTHIANS Paul defends his apostolic authority, and in this Epistle he expounds the unique character of the Gospel, showing that it is not auxiliary to the Law, but entirely distinct. Farrar says that these false teachers "wanted to substitute external badges for inward faith ; legal bondage for Christian freedom ; observance of practices for holiness of heart. They were striving to put the new, rich, fermenting wine of Christianity into the old and bursten wine-skins of Levitism. In their hands Christianity would have decayed into exclusiveness, self-congratulation, contempt of others, insistence upon the outward, indifference to the essential—a Christianity of the outward platter, a Christianity of the whitened grave." It was for ever to settle this matter that the Apostle wrote GALATIANS, in which he makes it crystal clear that the Gospel did not mean that the Gentiles were to be converted into Jews, that a man could not become a perfect Christian without becoming a partial Jew.

Divinely inspired, he renders this service in a Letter which Professor Findlay has spoken of as presenting "the most profound, condensed, and powerful argument ever expressed in writing."

The object of the Letter was not only to discredit the Judaizers and re-establish the Galatians, but to state in final terms, and for all time, what Christianity is. No one can understand what it is who does not distinguish clearly between the Law and the Gospel, and between Works and Faith. These contrasts and their accompaniments are sharply made in this Epistle, especially in chapters iii.-iv ; but it is shown that the Law is not opposed to the Gospel, but was a preparation for it, holding us "as wards in discipline, till such time as Christ came." On this subject Paul and James are not at variance. Paul believes in works, and James believes in faith ; the difference in their viewpoint is just this, that Paul's "faith" is a means of justification, and James' "works" is an evidence of it. Paul's message is to the sinner, and James' message is to the saint. Neither Apostle teaches that we must work in order to believe ; but both teach that we must believe in order to work.

NOTES.

In the Text of Westcott and Hort there are in GALATIANS approximately 2400 words, the length of a small pamphlet, and yet, as Professor Sabatier says : "There is nothing in ancient or modern language to be compared with this Epistle. All the powers of Paul's soul shine forth in its few pages. Broad and luminous view, keen logic, biting irony, everything that is most forcible in argument, vehement in indignation, ardent and tender in affection, is found here, combined and poured forth in a single strain, forming a work of irresistible power."

Assuming that GALATIANS comes between 2 CORINTHIANS and ROMANS, it is not difficult to see its relation to each. It finishes what 2 CORINTHIANS begins, and it begins what ROMANS finishes, and is the transition from the one to the other. The personal factor dominates in 2 CORINTHIANS; the doctrinal factor dominates in ROMANS, and in GALATIANS they are in about equal proportion (i-iv), with the doctrinal in the ascendant. The *feeling* of 2 CORINTHIANS runs over into GALATIANS, and the *thought* of GALATIANS runs over into ROMANS.

If GALATIANS was written in Macedonia, and ROMANS in Achaia, they must both have been written within the limits of a few months (Acts xx. 1-3), a good quarter's work. Indeed, it may be said that GALATIANS is the rough draft of which ROMANS is the full text.

Bishop Lightfoot has tabulated many of the parallels between the two Epistles. Compare the following : Gal. iii. 6-22 with Romans iv.; Gal. iv. 4-7 with Romans vii. 15-17 ; Gal. iii. 10 with Rom. iv. 15 ; Gal. iii. 11 with Rom. iii. 21 ; Gal. iii. 12 with Rom. x. 5 ; Gal. ii. 16 with Rom. iii. 20 ; Gal. ii. 19, 20 with Rom. vii. 4, vi. 6 ; Gal. v. 16, with Rom. viii. 4 ; Gal. ii-v with Rom. i-viii. The relation between the Letters is minute and fundamental. Both are the charter of evangelical faith, and the basis and ground-plan of the theology of salvation, the Magna Charta of spiritual emancipation. The difference between them is that GALATIANS was written in deep emotion, and ROMANS with calm, mature reflection.

It is little wonder that Martin Luther loved GALATIANS. He said of it : "The Epistle to the GALATIANS is my Epistle. I have betrothed myself to it. It is my wife." "In this Epistle," says Godet, "Luther found the secret of his own deliverance. Taking this as his weapon, he plunged into the fearful conflict with the Papistry and religious materialism of his time." Of Luther's Commentary on GALATIANS Dr. Agar Beet says : "It is my deliberate judgment that, for the purpose for which the Epistle was written, and for its chief practical worth now, Luther has caught and reproduced the inmost thought of St. Paul more richly than has any other writer, ancient or modern."

GALATIANS was the battle axe which Luther brought down with terrific and telling force upon the helmets of his foes.

The thought of "*Liberty*" occurs in these few chapters eleven times, more often than in all the other Epistles put together. And as this freedom is in *Christ*, we need not be surprised to find this name forty-three times in this Epistle. Other words which are of the essence of the Letter are, "Law," thirty-one times ; "Flesh," eighteen times ; "Spirit," fifteen times ; "Faith," twenty-two times ; "the Promise," ten times ; "Bondage," and related words, eleven times ; "the Cross," six times.

Most important is it to mark the point of chapter i. 6, 7. In the Greek two words are used for "another ;" the first is *heteros*, which means *different*, and from which we derive our word heterodoxy ; the second is *allos*, and means *another of the same kind or quality* ; and so Paul could say that the "another" Gospel of the Judaists was not "another."

It is claimed that about 300 different interpretations have been given of chapter iii. 20 : "Now a mediator is not a mediator of one, but God is one." The meaning appears to be as follows : A mediator implies two parties, between whom the mediation is carried on. The law is a contract between two parties, God on the one hand, and the Jewish

people on the other. But in the giving of the
promise there is no mediator. It depends on God
alone, and He gives the promise directly. There
are not two contracting parties, and so, no need of
mediators, men or angels. Paul's argument is,
that "it is better to depend upon an unconditional
promise of God, than upon a covenant made
between God and man ; for, in the latter case, the
conditions of the covenant might be broken by
man (as they had been), and so the blessings
forfeited ; whereas, in the former case, God being
immutable, the blessings derived from His promise
remain steadfast for ever. The passage is parallel
with Rom. iv. 13-16" (Conybeare and Howson).

The passage, chapter ii. 11-16, is of the most
tremendous importance. Between the First and
Second Missionary Journeys the Council of
Jerusalem was held (Acts xv), at which, by the
decision of the Apostles, Gentile Christians were
exempt from the Mosaic ceremonial (Acts xv.
23-29), and a letter to this effect was sent to the
Church at Antioch (xv. 22). Between the Second
and Third Missionary Journeys occurred the
incident recorded in Gal. ii. 11-16, the controversy
of Paul with Peter, over the very matter which
had been pronounced upon at the Council of
Jerusalem. Peter, by his action at Antioch, did

not discern, as Paul did, that the issue raised was
absolutely fundamental ; it was a question of
whether Christianity was to be a development of
Judaism, and an extension of the domain of the
Mosaic Law, or whether it was to free men from
legal bondage, from the vain effort after righteousness by works, and to give them freedom and
power, by faith in a crucified and risen Christ. By
his action at Antioch, Peter sought a compromise
of that issue ; but Paul would have none of it, he
"withstood him to the face, because he was to be
blamed" (ii. 11). For this, the Judaizers never
forgave him, and for this, Protestant Christians
have never ceased to bless him, and with him to
bless Wycliff, and Huss, and Luther, and Tyndale,
and Knox, and Wesley, and Spurgeon.

Linger on these passages : i. 15, 16a ; ii. 16 ;
ii. 20 ; iii. 3 ; iii. 8 ; iii. 13 ; iv. 4-6 ; v. 1 ; v. 14 ;
v. 22, 23 ; v. 25 ; vi. 2, 5 ; vi. 7 ; vi. 14.

In this Epistle there are 78 words which do not
occur in any other of Paul's Letters, and of these,
32 do not occur again in the New Testament.
The latter are as follows :

"Agar" (iv. 24, 25) ; "allegorized" (iv. 24) ; "bewitched"
(iii. 1) ; "bite" (v. 15) ; "nation-like" (ii. 14) ; "gave-place"
(ii. 5) ; "rejected with contempt" (iv. 14 ; "adds thereto"
(iii. 15) ; "cursed" (iii. 10, 13) ; "to have a-fair-appearance"
(vi. 12) ; "to Judaize" (ii. 14) ; "Jewishly" (ii. 14) ; "Judaism"

(i. 13, 14); "to-make-acquaintance" (i. 18); "to-spy-out"
(ii. 4); "vainglorious" (v. 26); "shall-have-been-formed"
(iv. 19); "is mocked" (vi. 7); "Walk-uprightly" (ii. 14);
"Brought-in-stealthily" (ii. 4); "of fathers" (i. 14); "per-
suasion" (v. 8); "before-announced, glad-tidings" (iii. 8);
"time-before-appointed" (iv. 2); "provoking" (v. 26);
"confirmed-beforehand" (iii. 17); "conferred" (i. 16);
"brands" (vi. 17) ; "contemporaries" (i. 14) ; "be-in-the-same-
rank-with" (iv. 25) ; "conjointly-dissembled" (ii. 13); "de-
ceives" (vi. 3).

NOTE 78
Some Characteristics of Galatians.

Oneness of Purpose.—Many subjects are treated of in
1 Corinthians (see Analysis, pp. 343–345), but in Galatians
Paul devotes himself to the task of combating one error and
establishing one truth. He shows that the Gospel is not a
Judaized Christianity, but something entirely new.

Severity of Tone.—In Philippians, except for a few slight
cautions, there is nothing but commendation, but Galatians
contains no commendation, no salutations, no praise, but
almost continuous reproof from beginning to end. This
severity, however, is mixed with tenderness (iv. 12-16, 19, 20).

The Person and Work of Christ.—In this Epistle there
are not fewer than forty-seven references to Christ, and these
are made by eight designations or titles. The Son (i. 16;
iv. 4, 6), The Son of God (ii. 20), Jesus (vi. 17), Jesus Christ
(i. 1, 12; ii. 16; iii. 1, 14, 22; v. 6), Christ Jesus (ii. 4; iii. 26, 28;
iv. 14; ii. 16; iii. 14; v. 6, 24), Christ (i. 6, 7, 10, 22; ii. 16, 17,
20, 21; iii. 13, 16, 24, 27, 29; iv. 19; v. 1, 2, 4, 24; vi. 2, 12),
Lord (i. 19; v. 10), Lord Jesus (vi. 17). These references
constitute a full Christology, telling of the Divinity and
humanity of Christ, of His atoning death and triumphant
resurrection, and of His power to save.

Analysis of Galatians

INTRODUCTION (i. 1-10).

1. **The Address** (1-2).
   - (i.) The Writer, ... 1-2a.
   - (ii.) The Readers, ... 2b.

2. **The Blessing** (3-5).
   - (i.) Its Nature, ... 3a.
   - (ii.) Its Origin, ... 3b-5.

3. **The Occasion** (6-10).
   - (i.) The Apostasy of the Galatians, ... 6-7.
   - (ii.) The Anathema of the Perverters, ... 8-9.
   - (iii.) The Apostle of the Gospel, ... 10.

I. A PERSONAL NARRATIVE (i. 11-ii. 21).
Paul Vindicates his Apostolic Authority.

1. **His Claim to Divine Illumination** (i. 11-12).

2. **His Conduct Before his Conversion** (i. 13-14).

3. **His Commission at his Conversion** (i. 15-16a).

4. **His Course After his Conversion** (i. 16b-17).

5. **His Contact with the Apostles** (i. 18-ii. 10).
   - (i.) The First Visit to Jerusalem, ... i. 18-24.
   - (ii.) The Second Visit to Jerusalem, ... ii. 1-10.

6. **His Controversy with Peter at Antioch** (ii. 11-16).

7. **His Conclusion of the Whole Matter** (ii. 17-21).

II. A DOCTRINAL ARGUMENT (iii.-iv.).
Justification is by Faith in Christ Alone.

1. **The Doctrine Expounded** (iii.).
   - (i.) Proved from Past Christian Experience, ... 1-5.
     - (a) Conversion through Christ.
     - (b) Reception of the Spirit.
     - (c) Persecution for Testimony.
   - (ii.) Proved from the Covenant of God with
     Abraham, ... 6-18.

369

III. A PRACTICAL EXHORTATION (v. 2-vi. 10).
Enter into the Full Consequences of your Emancipation.

ROMANS

GROUP 2.

Keyword : RIGHTEOUSNESS. SOTERIOLOGICAL.
Place of Writing : CORINTH. DATE : 58 A.D.
THE SIXTH LETTER IN POINT OF ORDER.

THE READERS.

THAT there were Gentiles in the Church at
Rome is evident from such references as i. 6,
13 ; xi. 13, 25, 28, 30 ; xv. 15-21 ; and that there
were Jews there is equally clear from such passages
as ii. 17 ; iv. 1 ; vii. 1 ; and that the Church was
composed of both elements is further evinced from
such portions as xv. 7-13 ; and xvi. 17-19 ; and it
is a reasonable inference from such verses as i. 5, 6,
13-15 ; xv. 15-21, as well as from the whole argument of chapters ix-xi, that the Gentile portion
of the Church was in the ascendancy, both in
numbers and doctrinal influence. For a sidelight
on these particulars see Acts xxviii. 17-28.

But the question confronts us, Who founded the
Church at Rome ? The Roman Catholic Church
says that the Apostle Peter founded it ; but for
that claim there is no foundation whatever ; on the
contrary, the historical evidence points the other
way, though, in consequence of the almost unani-

mous tradition of the early Church, we may assume that he was martyred at Rome.

It is equally clear that Paul did not found the Church there, as, at the time of writing, he had never been in the Capital (i. 8-15 ; xv. 23, 24). We have no certain knowledge of the origin of this Church, but it is highly probable that of the Jews and proselytes from Rome who were present at Jerusalem on the day of Pentecost (Acts ii. 10), some were included in the 3000 converts (ii. 41), and on their return to Rome would carry with them the glad tidings of the Gospel of Jesus Christ. And in any case, the news of the Gospel would soon have reached Rome, on account of the frequent communication between that City and great centres of population such as Jerusalem, Antioch, Thessalonica, Philippi, Corinth, and Ephesus. No doubt Paul's converts were continually arriving at Rome. The list of names recorded in Rom. xvi. 3-16, names of former disciples and helpers of Paul tends to substantiate this view ; and these, no doubt would have taken a prominent part in organising the Church in the Capital.

With reference, however, to this last remark, it is only fair to say that there is some reason for thinking that ROMANS was an encyclical Letter, and was sent with varying terminations to other

Churches, and that several of these terminations are brought together at the end (xv. 33-xvi. 20, 24, 27). Certainly chapter xvi presents a number of as yet unsolved problems.

THE DATE.

It is practically certain that this Letter was written by Paul at Corinth (xvi. 1), in the spring of A.D. 58, while on his Third Missionary Journey, and during the "three months" referred to in Acts xx. 3 ; just before his last visit to Jerusalem (Acts xx. 3-21).

THE OCCASION.

In order to understand this it will be well to get a clear view of the background. Paul was converted within the years 33-36 A.D. (Acts ix). The First Missionary Journey and the Council of Jerusalem (Acts xiii-xv) belong to the years 47-51 A.D. The Second Missionary Journey (Acts xv-xviii), to the years 51-54 A.D. The Third Missionary Journey (Acts xviii-xxi), to the years 54-58 A.D., which last year brings us to the date of the Roman Epistle. Paul had, therefore, been evangelising for more than ten years, and had covered ground, east of the Ægean Sea, from Jerusalem to Troas, and most of the Ægean Sea, from Philippi to Corinth. To him had been com-

mitted "the Gospel of the uncircumcision" (Gal.
ii. 7), that is, he was a missionary to the Gentiles.
And to him had been revealed the mystery of the
Church, the Body of Christ (Gal. i. 12 ; Rom.
xvi. 25, 26 ; Eph. iii. 1-12), the truth that all
social and national distinctions are done away in
Christ ; and that He being the fulfilment of the
Law (Rom. x. 4 ; Col. ii. 17) liberates us from the
bondage of the Law (Gal. iii. 16-29), so that we are
not debtors to do the Law (Gal. v. 2-4), but are
called in freedom to a life in the Spirit (Gal. v. 1,
25)

The very essence of Paul's teaching was
vigorously assailed. Judaizers, Jews who taught
that Gentile converts must be circumcised and
keep the Law of Moses, followed Paul from place
to place and unsettled the minds of his converts
by attacking his person, and denying his teaching.
This is what happened in the Galatian Churches,
and at Corinth, as the Letters to these make abundantly clear ; and, no doubt, the influence of these
mischievous propagandists was widespread, reaching even to Rome. In 2 CORINTHIANS Paul had
fully answered the attack upon his person, on his
standing as an Apostle, and in GALATIANS he had
defended and expounded his distinctive teaching.
But life was passing ; he was now nearly sixty years

of age, and nearly worn out, and, as yet, he had made no attempt to systematize his teaching. In 2 CORINTHIANS and GALATIANS the personal and emotional elements figure largely, and aspects of Paul's "Gospel" are defended, but there is no attempt to present a constructive and comprehensive statement of his theology. But now the time for such an effort had come. He was expecting to visit the Capital of the Empire, and he would send before him a Letter which would embody what he meant by Christianity.

"The Epistle," say Sanday and Headlam, "is the ripened fruit of the thought and struggles of the eventful years by which it had been preceded. It is natural that he should cast back his glance over the years which had passed since he became a Christian, and sum up the result as he felt it for himself. The momentum of his past experience guides his pen." Here, then, we find the occasion for this Letter.

THE OBJECT.

This already has been anticipated. Occasion and object go together. Some have said that the Apostle's object was polemical ; others, that it was dogmatic ; and others, that it was apologetic ; but surely we may find all three strains in this sublime harmony. Paul would now deliberately and logically fix in writing what he so deeply feels in his heart, and in doing so he cannot but be polemical, dogmatic, and apologetic.

To Paul Christianity was profound philosophy, and he, under the guidance of the Spirit, handled his theme 'profoundly. To Paul philosophy was not the guesses of the Schools, but the wisdom of God, and God's wisdom exhibited in man's salvation, revealed in human history, and evidenced in Christian character. The Apostle unfolds these aspects of Divine Philosophy in the three great divisions of this Epistle ; Philosophy of Salvation, in chapters i-viii ; Philosophy of History in chapters ix.-xi ; and Philosophy of Conduct in chapters xii-xv. The three questions which here are answered are : How can man be just with God ? What is the significance of Israel in history ? What are the practical evidences of Christian character ? These are not questions of local and transient importance, as are some of the matters dealt with in some of the Epistles, but are of vital and abiding moment. How thoroughly they are handled in this Letter the analysis following will indicate.

SUMMARY.

In ROMANS are an Introduction, three main Divisions, and a Conclusion. In the introduction

the Theme of the Epistle is disclosed (16, 17).
It is the Righteousness of God ; and this is viewed
in the first division (i-viii), in relation to sin and
sins ; in the second division (ix-xi), in relation to
the calling of Israel ; and in the third division
(xii-xv), in relation to every-day life ; and in each
of these divisions its theme is presented construc-
tively. The first division is Doctrinal, the second
is Dispensational, and the third is Practical.

(1) In the Doctrinal division (i. 18-viii 39), the
Righteousness of God is set before us in relation
to sin and sins in the Christian Message (i. 18-v.
21), and the Christian Life (v.-viii). This sequence
is most important. The Message precedes the
Life ; the Life should follow the Message. Christian character is the Christian Gospel. Spiritual
life is not something evolved from natural life, but
is a "new creation." What, then, is the Message ?
it is that condemned souls (i. 18-iii. 20), may be
justified (iii. 21-v. 11). If men are not condemned
there is no need for them to be justified. If justification is offered to us, it is because we are condemned. This section is concluded by tracing
Condemnation and Justification to their historical
sources in Adam and Christ (v. 12-21).

But Justification is not all. Why are men justified ?
It is that they may be sanctified. We are given

"eternal life" that we might live it, and for ever, here, and hereafter; and so the Christian Life is set before us in chapters vi-viii, in its two great aspects of Sanctification (vi. 1-viii. 11), and Glorification (viii. 12-30), and all is concluded with a Triumphant Song, which celebrates the whole wonderful revelation and experience (viii. 31-39). The heart of the Christian Message is Redemption; and the heart of the Christian Life is Holiness. (2) In the Dispensational division (ix-xi) the Righteousness of God is viewed in relation to the Calling of Israel, and here the whole history of this People is presented, their Election, in chapter ix; their Rejection, in chapter x; and their Conversion, in chapter xi; the first, in the past; the second, in the present; and the third, in the future.

(3) In the Practical division (xii. 1-xv. 13) the Righteousness of God is related to human conduct. First of all the Problems are considered (xii-xiii), and then, the Principles (xiv-xv. 13). Our conduct Problems, as Christians, lie in three spheres: in the Church (xii. 3-13); in the World (xii. 14-21); and in the State (xiii); that is, our duties are religious, social, and civil. How are we to discharge these? Christian Principles of Action are laid down in chapters xiv. 1-xv. 13. In summary

they are, personal freedom to act ; individual
accountability to God ; and relative responsibility
to help. The Conclusion (xv. 14-xvi. 27) treats of
various matters.

NOTES.

The values of this Epistle can never be estimated.
Its *intellectual* value is in the demand it makes, by
reason of its form and substance, upon the thoughtful mind. Its *historical* value is in the light it
throws upon Christianity and the world of Paul's
day. Its *theological* value is in the profoundness
and comprehensiveness of its terms and teaching.
Its *spiritual* value is in the revelation of the scope,
secret, and strength of the Christian life. And its
practical value is in the fruits of the Epistle in the
believing soul, and in the Christian Church.

The connection between the first and third
divisions should not be overlooked. Paul is no
theorist, or dry theologian. What he believes and
teaches he relates to life ; he weds the doctrinal to
the practical. These God has joined together,
and no man should put them asunder. Doctrine
and practice, creed and conduct, faith and works,
thought and action are related to one another as
cause to effect, as root to fruit, as centre to circumference.

The great words of this Epistle are :

"Law," 78 times ; "All," 71 times ; "Righteousness," 66 times ; "Faith," 62 times ; "Sin," 60 times ; "Death," 42 times ; "in Christ," 33 times ; "Flesh," 20 times ; "Impute," 19 times ; "God forbid," 10 times.

These figures include cognate words.

There are more quotations from the Old Testament in this Epistle than in all the other Epistles together. There are at least seventy direct quotations : these are from at least fourteen of the Old Testament Books ; and the Writings most quoted are the PSALMS and ISAIAH.

Chapter iii. 25, 26, has been called "The Acropolis of the Christian Faith."

To know and believe the teaching of this Book is to be grounded and settled in the Faith. It is by common consent a masterpiece of argument, and for insight and power it has no rival. Of the Epistle, Luther said : "It is the chief book of the New Testament, and the purest Gospel. It can never be too much read or studied ; and the more it is handled the more precious it becomes, and the better it tastes." And Godet said : "It is the greatest masterpiece which the human mind has ever conceived ;" and Coleridge : "It is the most profound extant ;" and Meyer : "It is the greatest and richest of all the apostolic works."

ROMANS was not the first Letter which Paul

wrote to a Christian Church, but it is put first in
the Biblical order because it is the foundation
document of the whole Pauline system of truth
and teaching; as the THESSALONIANS are put last,
because they take us to Glory.

Here is a Letter written by a Hebrew, in a Greek
city, to Romans. This reminds us that the inscrip-
tion on the Cross was in Hebrew, and Greek and
Latin; the languages of religion and culture and
government. The Epistle to the Romans represents
them all.

In this Epistle there are no less than 219 words
which do not occur in any other of Paul's Letters;
and of these, 94 do not occur anywhere else in the
New Testament. Here are the latter:

"Wild olive tree" (xi. 17, 24); "inexpressible" (viii. 26);
"impenitent" (ii. 5); "proportion" (xii. 6); "without excuse"
(i. 20; ii. 1); "unmerciful" (i. 31); "unsearchable" (xi. 33);
"coals" (xii. 20); "without law" (ii. 12); "forbearance"
(ii. 4); "warring against" (vii. 23); "abhorring" (xii. 9);
"severity" (xi. 22); "cursing" (iii. 14); "infirmities" (xv. 1);
"asps" (iii. 13); "perfidious" (i. 31); "come abroad" (xvi.
19); "become unprofitable" (iii. 12); "righteous judgment"
(ii. 5); "used deceit" (iii. 13); "in bondage" (vi. 19); "a
hundred years" (iv. 19); "barned" (i. 27); "were-broken-
out" (xi. 17, 19, 20); "stretched-out" (x. 21); "grafted-in"
(xi. 17, 23, 19, 24); "reminding" (xv. 15); "are-covered"
(iv. 7); "a longing" (xv. 23); "art-named" (ii. 17); "in-
ventors" (i. 30); "whether" (vi. 16); "divinity" (i. 20);
"hateful to God" (i. 30); "a trap" (xi. 9); "commit-sacri-
lege" (ii. 22); "administering-in-sacred-service" (xv. 16);
"cheerfulness" (xii. 8); "are perceived" (i. 20); "newness"

(vi. 4; vii. 6); "evil dispositions" (i. 29) "a good olive tree" (xi. 24); "condemnation" (v. 16, 18; viii. 1); "slanderers" (i. 30); "slumber" (xi. 8); "dug down" (xi. 3); "throat" (iii. 13); "remnant" (xi. 5); "became vain" (i. 21); "changed" (i. 25, 26); "lawgiving" (ix. 4); "lust" (i. 27); "oldness" (vii. 6); "is present with" (vii. 18, 21); "passing-by" (iii. 25); "thing formed" (ix. 20); "that-had-before-taken-place" (iii. 25); "first-gave" (xi. 35) "are-we-better ? " (iii. 9) ; "going-before" (xii. 10) ; "forefather" (iv. 1) ; "reception" (xi. 15) ; "succourer" (xvi. 2) ; "prophetic" (xvi. 26) ; "reverenced" (i. 25) ; "hardens" (ii. 5) ; "counsellor" (xi. 34) ; "conjoined" (vi. 5) ; "strive-together-with" (xv. 30) ; "may-be-refreshed-with" (xv. 32) ; "may-be-glorified-to-gether" (viii. 17) ; "delight" (vii. 22) ; "bow-down" (xi. 10) ; "bearing-witness-with" (ii. 15 ; viii. 16 ; ix. 1) ; "to-be-com-forted-together" (i. 12); "groans-together" (viii. 22); "cutting-short" (ix. 28) ; "ruin" (iii. 16) ; "consent" (vii. 16) ; "travails-together" (viii. 22) ; "slaughter" (viii. 36) ; "more boldly" (xv. 15); "married" (vii. 2); "makes-intercession" (viii. 26); "we-more-than-overcome" (viii. 37); "to-be-high-minded" (xii. 3) ; "under-judgment" (iii. 19) ; "remnant" (ix. 27) ; "was left" (xi. 3) ; "kindly-affectioned" (xii. 10) ; "divine-answer" (xi. 4) ; "kind-speaking" (xvi. 18) ; "lie" (iii. 7) ; "whisperers" (i. 29).

NOTE 79

The Old Testament in Group II. of Paul's Epistles.

IN 1 Corinthians are about thirty references to the Old Testament; in 2 Corinthians, about twenty; in Galatians, about thirteen; and in Romans, about seventy-four, that is, upwards of one hundred and forty references in this Group of Epistles, and they are taken chiefly from Genesis, Deuteronomy, Isaiah, and the Psalms.

Analysis of Romans

PROLOGUE (i. 1-17).

PART A.
DOCTRINAL. PHILOSOPHY OF SALVATION.
(i. 18-viii. 39).
The Righteousness of God in Relation to Sins and Sin.

I. THE CHRISTIAN MESSAGE (i. 18-v. 21).
PROPITIATION, FOUNDATION.
CHRIST FOR US. Key: i. 16-17.

1. Theme: **Condemnation** (i. 18-iii. 20).

2. Theme: **Justification** (iii. 21-v. 11).

Supplementary—v. 12-21.
Condemnation and Justification traced to their historical sources
in Adam and Christ.

II. THE CHRISTIAN LIFE (vi.-viii.).
IDENTIFICATION, SUPERSTRUCTURE.
CHRIST IN US. Key: v. 9, 10.

3. Theme: **Sanctification** (vi. 1-viii. 11).

NOTE 80

"In Christ" in Paul's Epistles.

THE catacombs show that the early Christians had passwords which were understood among one another, brief but pregnant, and of these none was more significant than *En Christō*, "In Christ."

An examination of Paul's Epistles will show that this word is the key to each of them, and this is not to be wondered at as the object of these Epistles is to show the quality of the life which Christians should live. Following the canonical order we see that :

In *Romans* we are *Justified* "in Christ" (iii. 24). Though Romans was the sixth Letter to be written it is placed first, because it treats of the first great thing in the new life—Justification.

In 1 *Corinthians* we are *Sanctified* "in Christ" (i. 2). Paul rebukes the ethical and theological errors of the Church by showing them that what is judicially true of Christians should also be practically true.

In 2 *Corinthians* we are *Vindicated* "in Christ" (xii. 19). There do arise times when "in Christ" it is our duty to defend ourselves.

In *Galatians* we are *Liberated* "in Christ" (ii. 4). This Epistle is the great Charter of our emancipation from the Law, wherein it is shown that we are dead to the Law, to self, and to the world "in Christ" (ii. 19, 20; v. 24; vi. 14).

In *Ephesians* we are *Exalted* "in Christ" (i. 3; ii. 6); by His death, burial, resurrection, and ascension, the believer is dead, buried, raised, and seated in heavenly places.

In *Philippians* we are *Exultant* "in Christ" (i. 26). This is the Epistle of Christian joy, and it is shown that joy is normal Christian experience "in Christ."

[Continued on page 388

THE PAULINE EPISTLES

GROUP 3

INTRODUCTION

COLOSSIANS

PHILEMON

EPHESIANS

PHILIPPIANS

"In Christ" in Paul's Epistles.

(*Continued from page 386.*)

IN *Colossians* we are *Complete* "in Christ" (ii. 9, 10). All of God is in Christ, and all of Christ is for us, so that being already complete in Him, we may become complete by the gracious operations of the Holy Spirit.

In *Philemon* we are made *Gracious* "in Christ" (15, 16). The spirit of forgiveness and forgetfulness of wrong done to us takes possession of us, because "in Christ" wrongs are righted, and crookednesses are evened out.

In *1 Thessalonians* we are *Hope-full* "in Christ" (i. 3). The Flaming of His Advent Feet is all across the pages of this Epistle. He is our prospect. There will be one generation of Christians that will not die, for Christ will come for them.

In *2 Thessalonians* we are *Glorified* "in Christ" (i. 12; ii. 14). The "day of Christ" is to precede the "day of the Lord," and the gathering of the saints unto Him is to be accomplished before Antichrist is revealed. Though first to be written these two Epistles are put last of the Church Epistles, because they treat of the final experience, the glorification of the saints.

In *1 Timothy* we are made *Faithful* "in Christ" (i. 18, 19); faithful to the doctrine, to the worship, and to the oversight of the Church; faithful in personal walk and work.

In *Titus* we are made *Exemplary* "in Christ" (ii. 7, 8); in all things showing ourselves a pattern of good works.

In *2 Timothy* we are *Triumphant* "in Christ" (iv. 6-8), and though persecuted we are at last brought forth in triumph, a good fight fought, the race run, and the faith kept.

THE PAULINE EPISTLES

GROUP 3.   CHRISTOLOGICAL.
COLOSSIANS.   EPHESIANS.
PHILEMON.   PHILIPPIANS.

Introduction

THE Epistles of Paul have been classified in various ways, and each of these is of interest from its own standpoint. The classification we have adopted here is that of the Four Groups. But another, which is suggestive, relates the Letters to the first Roman imprisonment, and is threefold —before, during, and after that event. *Before* the imprisonment were six Epistles, 1-2 THESSALONIANS, 1-2 CORINTHIANS, GALATIANS, and ROMANS ; *during* it were four, COLOSSIANS, PHILEMON, EPHESIANS, and PHILIPPIANS ; and *after* it were three, 1 TIMOTHY, TITUS, and 2 TIMOTHY. In the pre-prison period were two groups, with two Epistles in the first, and four in the second.

The relation of these groups to one another is a fascinating study. The first may be regarded as a Prologue (1-2 Thess.), and the last as an Epilogue (1 Tim., Titus, 2 Tim.), and the two middle groups as presenting the substance of Paul's

Epistolary ministry, the first of them being controversial (1-2 Cor., Gal., Rom.), and the second
being contemplative (Col., Philemon, Eph., Phil.).
The essence of the Controversial Epistles is *Christ
for us* ; and of the Contemplative Epistles, *Christ
in us*.

The difference between these two central groups
is due to Paul's changed circumstances. When
he wrote the Controversial Epistles he was an
unresting missionary, preaching the Gospel,
founding Churches, teaching converts, and answering enemies all the way from Antioch to Corinth ;
but when he wrote the Contemplative Epistles he
was a prisoner at Rome, and instead of two continents for a sphere of labour, he had "a hired
house." The change of circumstances gave the
Apostle an opportunity which a busy travelling
ministry did not afford ; his tireless activity was
followed by fruitful captivity.

No one can read the Prison Epistles without
feeling that they have in them an element which
is wanting, for the most part, in the previous
group. The creative is followed by the consoli-
dating period. There is here a change, not of subject
but of standpoint, a change not of attitude, but of
atmosphere. The sword has not been laid down,
but the trowel is prominent. Controversy is not

altogether at an end, but it is subordinate. The personal element is not wanting, but it is here not defensive but appreciative.

Between the writing of ROMANS and EPHESIANS, Paul travelled from Corinth to Jerusalem by Philippi and Ephesus. At Miletus he gave a charge to the Ephesian Elders (Acts xx. 17-38). At Jerusalem he had a conference with the Church, conformed to Jewish ritual, was seized by the mob, was rescued by the Roman garrison, addressed the multitude, addressed the Sanhedrin, learned of a conspiracy to kill him, and was sent to Cæsarea where he remained in captivity for about two years (Acts xxi. 23-xxiii. 35), after having appeared before Felix, Festus, and Agrippa (Acts xxiv-xxvi). This was in the years 57-60 A.D. Having appealed to Cæsar, Paul was sent to Rome, arriving there in 61 A.D., where he remained a prisoner until 63 A.D. It was during these two years that he wrote this group of Epistles.

Addressing the Ephesian Elders (Acts xx. 17-35), Paul described his ministry in three expressions which, says Prof. Findlay, "define admirably the principles and method of his teaching." He had "gone about heralding the *kingdom* ;" he had "testified *the gospel* of the grace of God ;" and he had not shunned "to declare all *the counsel* of God." May it not be said that 1-2 THESSALONIANS represent the first of these claims ; GALATIANS and ROMANS, the second ; and 1-2 CORINTHIANS the third. But, in this same address he foresaw trouble (Acts xx. 29, 30), and we may expect that he would relate himself to it when it arose, which, indeed, he does, in this third group of Letters. What the trouble was, and how he dealt with it, we shall see.

Looking at these four Letters, we discern readily that they fall into two pairs, one pair being doctrinal, EPHESIANS, COLOSSIANS, and one pair, personal, PHILIPPIANS, PHILEMON. In each of these pairs there are differences. In the first, COLOSSIANS was sent to the Church at Colossae, whereas it is practically certain that EPHESIANS was a Circular Letter. In keeping with this, COLOSSIANS deals with a specific subject, but EPHESIANS is in much more general terms. But there is here unity as well as diversity. Both these Letters treat of Christ and the Church, but in COLOSSIANS the emphasis is on the Lordship of Christ, whereas, in EPHESIANS, it is on the Nature and Unity of the Church. COLOSSIANS treats of the union of believers with Christ in His exalted heavenly life ; and EPHESIANS, of the unity of believers in the Holy Spirit.

The structure of these two Letters is the same; half of each being doctrinal, and half practical; and, it has been pointed out, they are alike in diction.   Seventy-eight verses out of 155 have the same phrases.   But diversity as well as unity characterises these two Letters; neither is a copy or a mere echo of the other.   Nothing like Eph. vi. 10-17 occurs in COLOSSIANS, and nothing like Col. ii. occurs in EPHESIANS.   These Epistles are related to one another much as are GALATIANS and ROMANS.   "GALATIANS and COLOSSIANS are specific, impassioned and polemical: ROMANS and EPHESIANS are calm and independent expositions of the truths involved in the Letters which had immediately preceded them."   EPHESIANS and COLOSSIANS are alike as twin sisters might be, and yet, like twin sisters, each is distinct and independent.   The topic of COLOSSIANS is *Christ in All;* and the topic of EPHESIANS is *All in Christ.*

As to the other pair, both are personal, but PHILEMON is addressed to an individual, and PHILIPPIANS to a Church; the one is private, and the other is public; the one is to make a request, and the other, to acknowledge a favour; the complexion of the one is hope, and of the other, joy.

PHILEMON and PHILIPPIANS are homely and human; EPHESIANS and COLOSSIANS are sublime and superhuman.   The first pair reveal Paul's heart, but the second pair disclose his mind.

In PHILEMON Paul is the gentleman, in PHILIPPIANS he is the saint ; in COLOSSIANS he is the apologist, and in EPHESIANS he is the theologian. These Epistles are not Eschatological as are 1-2 THESSALONIANS ; nor Soteriological as are 1-2 CORINTHIANS, GALATIANS, and ROMANS ; but they are pre-eminently Christological ; the Person of Christ dominates them ; in PHILEMON and PHILIPPIANS, Christ in the individual ; in EPHESIANS and COLOSSIANS, Christ in the Church ; in the first pair, the individual in Christ, and in the second pair, the Church in Christ.

NOTE 81

Colossae.

COLOSSAE was an ancient Phrygian city on the south bank of the Lycus river, an affluent of the Maeander. It was one of the three sister cities which received the Gospel about the same time, the other two being Laodicea and Hierapolis (iv. 13). It was a city of importance, being traversed by the great trade-route between Ephesus and the Euphrates. The Church was not directly founded by Paul, and there is no evidence that he ever preached in any of the cities of the Lycus valley; but during his three years' residence in Ephesus, "all they that dwelt in Asia heard the Word of the Lord," and it was probably at this time that the Churches of the Lycus were founded. Citizens of Colossae were Epaphras and Philemon, Apphia, Archippus, and the slave Onesimus.

COLOSSIANS

GROUP 3.

Keyword : FULNESS.   CHRISTOLOGICAL.

Place of Writing : ROME.   DATE : 62 A.D.

THE SEVENTH LETTER IN POINT OF ORDER.

THE DATE.

THERE is no reason to doubt that Paul wrote this Letter, and PHILEMON, EPHESIANS, and PHILIPPIANS at his "hired house" in Rome, during his first imprisonment there, in the years 61-63 A.D. What we cannot be so sure about is the order in which he wrote these Epistles. Lightfoot and Moule advocate the view that PHILIPPIANS was written first, but others argue that, of the four, it was written last. The reasons for this latter we shall refer to in the introduction to PHILIPPIANS. The matter is not of great importance.

Then there is the question of whether COLOSSIANS was written before or after EPHESIANS. That they were written at about the same time seems clear, and the nature of their contents seems to harmonise best with the opinion that COLOSSIANS was written first. It stands much in relation to EPHESIANS as GALATIANS does to ROMANS. It is the germ of which the Ephesian Letter is a more elaborate expansion. Psychological reasons would lead us to the view that the calm of EPHESIANS would follow and not precede the controversy of COLOSSIANS, that the general address would follow the particular, and that the most advanced teaching would come last. Assuming this, we follow the order COLOSSIANS, PHILEMON, EPHESIANS, and PHILIPPIANS, and place the first three in the year 62 A.D.

THE READERS.

In chapter iv. 13, three towns are named, Colossae ("you"), Laodicea, and Hierapolis. These were in Phrygia, and were located in the valley of the Lycus, a tributary of the Meander. They lay in the form of a triangle, Colossae and Laodicea being the base, and Hierapolis the apex. Colossae and Hierapolis were on the north of the river, and Laodicea was on the south. Laodicea was about nine miles from Colossae, and Hierapolis was about thirteen miles distant, while the distance between Hierapolis and Laodicea was about six miles. Of these three towns Laodicea was the richest and most influential, and Colossae was the least important. Yet, it was to little Colossae that this marvellous Letter was sent.

In Acts xix. 10, we read that during Paul's sojourn at Ephesus "all they who dwelt in Asia heard the Word of the Lord Jesus, both Jews and Greeks." No doubt Colossians would hear and receive the Gospel at Ephesus, which was about a hundred miles away, and would carry it back to their homes, and publish it among their friends, and so a Church would be formed. Among the converts there were Epaphras, who seems to have been the minister of this group of Churches (i. 7), and Philemon, evidently well-to-do, and Apphia his wife, and Archippus his son, who also was a minister (iv. 17 ; Philemon 1, 2). These, it would seem, Paul knew personally, and later Onesimus, though he had not himself been to Colossae (ii. 1). No doubt there were Jews in the Assembly there, but the Epistle treats the Church as specifically Gentile.

The Occasion.

Epaphras, who was minister at Colossae "on the behalf" of Paul, paid a visit to the Apostle in his prison-house at Rome (i. 7). The reason for this visit would seem to have been twofold—to convey the sympathetic greetings of the Colossians whom the Apostle knew, and to report a danger which was threatening the Church there (ii. 8).

The nature of this danger is made sufficiently clear in chapter ii, which is the heart of the Letter, and accounts for what precedes and what follows it. "The Colossian Heresy," as Lightfoot calls it, was twofold. Jewish Christians imbued with heathen philosophy were leading the converts astray in two directions, doctrinally and practically, theologically and ethically. On the one hand they were substituting inferior and created beings, angelic mediators, for the Divine Head Himself; and, on the other hand, they were insisting on ritual and ascetic observances as the foundation of their moral teaching. The one error was intellectualistic, and the other was ritualistic; mysticism characterised the one, and formalism the other. The complexion of the one heresy was Judaic, and of the other, Gnostic. These two elements are so closely interwoven in Paul's refutation that it is almost impossible to separate them (ii. 8-23), and yet they are clearly distinguishable.

The Judaic element is seen in the references to meats and drinks, Sabbaths and new moons, circumcision and other ordinances (ii. 11, 16, 21, 22). The Gnostic element is seen in references to philosophy, voluntary humility, angel-worship, pride, prohibitions, will-worship (ii. 8, 18-23). The Gnostic error, which culminated in the early part of the second century, is here seen in embryo. Gnosticism laid great stress upon knowledge, which was the exclusive privilege of the select few. It taught that evil had its origin and abode in matter, in the material, sensible world ; and to explain how God, Who is perfect, could create matter, which is evil, it maintained that there were certain successive evolutions or emanations of God, in which the Divine element became more and more feeble, until at length contact with matter was possible, and creation ensued. These emanations were called aeons, or angels. This heresy is one of the most fantastic productions of the human brain, and it was the first attempt to bring Christianity under the influence of heathen speculation.

The report of this menace at Colossae was the occasion of this Epistle.

THE PURPOSE.

The object of Paul, in writing the Letter, was to refute this double error, and he does so by affirming the supremacy of Christ and the completeness of the Church in Him. These two great truths are found in two verses at the centre of the Epistle (ii. 9, 10) ; "In Him dwelleth all the fulness of the Godhead bodily, and ye are in Him being fulfilled." That is the reply alike to Judaic perversion and Gnostic speculation.

Paul shows that wrong views as to the true nature of the Lord mean wrong views about everything else throughout the universe, for Christ is the full and final revelation of God; the Creator of all things (i. 16), the Head of the Church (i. 18); and the Fulness of Deity (i. 19; ii. 3, 9).

The two great passages then of the Epistle, which reveal the purpose for which it was written, are chapters ii. 8-23; and i. 13-20. The first describes and refutes the Colossian heresy, and the second expounds the Person and Work of Christ. In the Letter the heresy is answered before it is mentioned; it is destroyed before it is described.

Nothing could be more profound or sublime than the passage, chapter i. 13-20; where Christ is seen to be the Image of God (15), the Creator of the Universe (15-17), the Head of the Church (18), the Fulness of God (19), and the Redeemer of the World (20). There are only two other comparable Christological passages in Paul's Writings, and these also are in the Prison Epistles— Eph. i. 20-23; and Phil. ii. 6-11.

A true Christology is the final answer to every heresy that ever has been, or ever will be.

NOTES.

The richness of COLOSSIANS may be judged of from the fact that there are here fifty-five words which occur in none of Paul's other Epistles, and thirty-four of these occur nowhere else in the New Testament. The thirty-four are the following:

"Disheartened" (iii. 21); "foul language" (iii. 8); "cousin" (iv. 10); "I am filling up" (i. 24); "recompense" (iii. 24); "having-stripped" (ii. 15; iii. 9); "putting-off" (ii. 11); "using" (ii. 22); "pleasing" (i. 10); "unsparing-treatment" (ii. 23); "let-preside" (iii. 15); "subject-yourselves-to-decrees" (ii. 20); "voluntary-worship" (ii. 23); "having-made-peace" (i. 20); "intruding-into" (ii. 18); "thankful" (iii. 15); "Godhead" (ii. 9); "defraud-of-the-prize" (ii. 18); "being-moved-away" (i. 23); "complaint" (iii. 13); "new-moon" (ii. 16); "visible" (i. 16); "consolation" (iv. 11); "persuasive-speech" (ii. 4); "satisfaction" (ii. 23); " ye-heard-of-before" (i. 5); "having-nailed" (ii. 14); "holding-the-first-place" (i. 18); "Scythian" (iii. 11); "firmness" (ii. 5); "makes-a-prey-of" (ii. 8); "bodily" (ii. 9); "philosophy" (ii. 8); "hand-writing" (ii. 14).

Other notable words are :

"Mystery" (i. 27; ii. 2; iv. 3), which, in the New Testament, never means that which cannot be understood, but that which is understood only by the initiated, an open secret, "a truth which was once hidden but now is revealed," "a truth which without special revelation would have been unknown."

"Full knowledge" (i. 9, 10; ii. 2; iii. 10; *epignosis*, a stronger word than *gnosis*). The use of the word in COLOSSIANS is interesting because of the *Gnostic* (knowledge) heresy. "Fulness," *pleroma* (i. 19; ii. 9), means, says Farrar, "the brimmed receptacle and the total contents of all the gifts and attributes of God;" "the whole glorious total of what God is," says Moule. Related words here are, "to fill," "to fulfil" (i. 9, 24, 25; ii. 10; iv. 12). "All," "every" (i. 10, 15, 28; i. 6, 9, 10, 11, 19, 28; ii. 2, 9, 10, 19; iii. 16; iv. 12; iii. 17, 23; i. 4; ii. 3, 13, 22; iii. 8, 11, 14, 17; iv. 7; i. 16, 17, 20; iv. 20, 22; iv. 9). Also, "riches," "wisdom," "understanding."

COLOSSIANS and EPHESIANS have been called

"twin" Epistles, and when the two are compared we realise how apt this description is. Not only is the main theme of each the same, Christ and the Church, but whole sections are parallel, for example, the Christian Family (Col. iii.-iv ; Eph. v-vi) ; many sentences are the same (*e.g.*, Col. i. 14 ; Eph. i. 7), and many words occur in each which are not found again in the New Testament (*e.g.*, "alienated," Col. i. 21 ; Eph. ii. 12 ; "quickened-together," Col. ii. 13 ; Eph. ii. 15 ; and seven other words). Seventy-eight verses out of 155 have the same phrases. For full lists see Paley's "*Horae Paulinae*," pp. 91-103 ; and Westcott's "*Ephesians*," pp. 42-46.

Yet, this likeness notwithstanding, each Epistle has its own individuality. There is a controversy in COLOSSIANS, but not in EPHESIANS. A certain danger is in view in COLOSSIANS, but not in EPHESIANS. In COLOSSIANS Paul's mind is perturbed, but not in EPHESIANS. COLOSSIANS is addressed to a single Church, but EPHESIANS is not (cf. Col. iv. 16 : "the Epistle from Laodicea is, almost certainly, the Ephesian Letter).

Of these Epistles Farrar says : "They are twin sisters of close resemblance yet marked individuality, whose faces, alike, yet different, can only be explained by their common parentage."

Analysis of Colossians

Theme : CHRIST AND HIS PEOPLE.

INTRODUCTION (i. 1-14).

(a) Salutation, ... 1-2.
(b) Thanksgiving, ... 3-8.
(c) Intercession, ... 9-14.

PART A. DOCTRINAL. CHRIST (i. 15-ii. 3).

I. THE PERSON OF CHRIST (i. 15-19).

1. His Relation to God (15a).
2. His Relation to Creation (15b-17).
3. His Relation to the Church (18-19).

II. THE WORK OF CHRIST (i. 20-ii.3).

1. The Glorious Purpose (i. 20).
2. The Partial Accomplishment (i. 21-23).
   (i.) The Objects, ... 21a.
   (ii.) The Work, ... 21b.
   (iii.) The Means, ... 22a.
   (iv.) The End, ... 22b.
   (v.) The Condition, ... 23a.
3. The Chosen Instrument (i. 23b-ii. 3).
   (i.) Paul's Solemn Charge, ... i. 24-27.
   (ii.) Paul's Loving Care, ... i. 28-ii. 3.
   (a) For all Men, ... i. 28, 29.
   (b) For the Colossians, ... ii. 1-3

PART B. POLEMICAL. THE CHURCH (ii. 4-iii. 4).

I. THE POSITION OF THE CHURCH (ii. 4-15).

1. The Threatening Danger (4-7).
   (i.) A Subtle Enticement, ... 4.
   (ii.) A Hearty Encouragement, ... 5.
   (iii.) A Profound Exhortation, ... 6, 7.
2. The Saving Doctrine (8-15).
   (i.) The Need for it, ... 8.
   (ii.) The Nature of it, ... 9-15.
   (a) God's Fulness is in Christ. ... ... 9.

PHILEMON

GROUP 3.

Keyword : BROTHERHOOD.   CHRISTOLOGICAL.
Place of Writing : ROME.   DATE : 62 A.D.
THE EIGHTH LETTER IN POINT OF ORDER.

THIS Letter is absolutely unique, not only in the Pauline literature, but in all literature. Though it has but 334 words (Westcott-Hort Text), yet, Franke says, it "far surpasses all the wisdom of the world." The relevant facts are quickly told.

THE DATE.

This Note was written at the same time as the Letter to Colossae, and was sent to the same town. This would be in 62 A.D.

THE OCCASION.

The occasion of the Letter was the presence in Rome of a slave from Colossae. His name was Onesimus, a Phrygian, and, in some way, possibly by robbery (18), he had wronged his master, Philemon, who, at this time, was a member of the Colossian Church (2, 10 ; Col. iv. 9, 17). Somehow this run-away slave got into touch with Paul in Rome, with the result that he became a Christian. For a short time he rendered Paul some service

(11-13), but the Apostle did not feel it was right to retain him, but that he should return to his master. That conviction was the occasion of the Letter.

THE OBJECT.

The design of the Apostle in writing was to persuade Philemon to receive, forgive, and re-instate Onesimus, and to do so in a way entirely new, "not now as a slave, but above a slave, a brother beloved" (16). Paul more than hints that he had the right to make this request, with every reason to expect its fulfilment (19-21). Yet, he does not use the language of command, but of entreaty (8-10), and bases his appeal on Philemon's Christianhood (5-8), and on his own circum-stances (9) ; and he supports his request by express-ing the hope that he may ere long visit Philemon (22), a subtle and powerful support to his entreaty.

NOTES.

This Note to a friend has been universally praised, and none too much. Luther says : "This Epistle showeth a right noble, lovely example of Christian love." Calvin, referring to Paul, says : "Though he handleth a subject, which otherwise were low and mean, yet, after his manner he is borne up aloft unto God." Ewald pronounces it

"surpassingly full and significant." Sabatier says :
"We have here only a few familiar lines, but so
full of grace, of salt, of serious and trustful
affection, that this short Epistle gleams like a pearl
of the most exquisite purity in the rich treasure of
the New Testament." Baur says : "It is penetrated
with the noblest Christian spirit." Holtzmann
pronounces it to be "a pattern of tact, fine feeling,
and graciousness." Ellicott calls it, "This exquisite and interesting Epistle, alike a masterpiece
of persuasive tact and delicacy, and an enduring
model of truest Christian courtesy." Lightfoot
says, "The Epistle to Philemon stands unrivalled."
And Maclaren says : "That must have been a
great intellect, and closely conversant with the
Fountain of all light and beauty, which could
shape the profound and far-reaching teachings of
the Epistle to the Colossians, and pass from them
to the graceful simplicity and sweet kindliness of
this exquisite Letter ; as if Michael Angelo had
gone straight from smiting his magnificent Moses
from the marble mass, to incise some delicate and
tiny figure of love or friendship on a cameo."

Notwithstanding the shortness of this Letter,
there are no less than eight words which do not
occur in any other of Paul's Letters, and five of
these do not occur anywhere else in the New

14

Testament. These five are, "unserviceable" (11), ; "voluntary" (14) ; "may have profit" (20) ; "thou owest also" (19), and "I will repay" (19).

The last of these words is of great interest. It is a stereotyped formula in papyri documents, the promise to pay back borrowed money. In a note-of-hand belonging to the first century, and with reference to a hundred silver drachmae, one named Papus wrote on behalf of two people who could not write : "Which we will also repay . . . with any other that we may owe . . ." The same expression, though another Greek word, occurs in Matt. xviii. 26, 29.

Another word is here which figures in the papyri. Paul says : "I, Paul, wrote it with mine own hand" (19). The word "hand-writing" (*cheirographon*) occurs in Col. ii. 14, "having blotted out the hand-writing." In the famous Florentine papyrus of A.D. 85, the Governor of Egypt gives this order in the course of a trial : "Let the hand-writing be crossed out."

These words are interesting as showing that Christianity did not coin them, but that the New Testament was written in the *Koinē*, or common language of the people.

Other interesting words are : "bowels" (7, 12, 20), which the R.V. translates "heart," The ancients regarded this physical part as the seat of the affections. In two places there is a play upon words. "Onesimus" means "Profitable," and in verse 20, Paul says, "may I have *profit* of thee in the Lord (*onaimēn*). Again, in verse 11, he says, and again with reference to the meaning of "Onesimus," "once to thee *unserviceable* (*achrēston*), but now serviceable (*euchrēston*) to thee and to me."

Farrar finds a parallel to this in George Whitefield's pulpit appeal to the comedian Shuter, who had often played the character of Ramble. "And thou, poor Ramble, who has so often rambled from Him, oh, end thy ramblings, and come to Jesus."

Short as this Letter is, no fewer than eleven persons are mentioned in it ; five at the beginning ; five at the end ; and Onesimus, the central figure. Of these eleven, Timothy, Mark, and Luke are outstanding characters.

This is the only private letter that has been preserved of Paul's private correspondence, which must have been considerable. Many of the letters of Cicero, of Seneca, and of Pliny have been preserved, models of grace and eloquence ; but how willingly would we sacrifice these for some more of Paul's !

This Letter and one written by Pliny the Younger have often been compared and contrasted. They should be read together. Here is Pliny's.

The Letter of Pliny the Younger to Sabinianus
on behalf of an offending freedman.

"C. Plinius, to his Sabinianus, greeting—

"Your freedman, with whom, as you had told me, you were vexed, came to me, and, flinging himself at my feet, clung to them as though they had been yours. He wept much, entreated much, yet at the same time left much unsaid, and, in short, convinced me that he was sincerely sorry. I believe that he is really reformed, because he is conscious of his delinquency. You are angry, I know ; justly angry, that too I know ; but gentleness is most praiseworthy exactly where anger is most justifiable. You loved the poor fellow, and I hope will love him again ; meanwhile, it is enough to yield to intercession. Should he ever deserve it, you may be angry again, and all the more excusably by yielding now. Make some allowance for his youth, for his tears, for your own kindly disposition.

Do not torture him, lest you torture yourself as well, for it is a torture to you when one of your kindly nature is angry.

I fear you will think that I am not asking but forcing you if I join my prayers to his ; I will, however, do so, and all the more fully and unreservedly in proportion to the sharpness and severity with which I took him to task, sternly threatening that I would never say a word for him again. *That* I said to him because he needed to be well frightened ; but I do not say it to you, for perhaps I shall say a word for him again, and again gain my point ; provided only my request be such as it becomes me to ask, and you to grant. Farewell ! "

Both these letters are classic, but there are striking contrasts. Pliny's is for a freedman ; Paul's is for a slave. Pliny has doubt about the future good conduct of the freedman ; Paul has no doubt about the slave's. Pliny assumes that Sabinianus is and will be angry ; Paul does not assume that

Philemon is or will be angry. Pliny begs that torture will not be resorted to ; Paul asks that the slave be treated as a brother beloved. Pliny severely scolded the freedman ; there is no word of Paul scolding the slave. Pliny's letter is frozen kindness ; Paul's melts and glows with Christian love.

This little Note has immense values. There are at least seven. Its Personal value consists in the light which it throws upon the character of Paul. Its Ethical value consists in its balanced sensitiveness to what is right. Its Providential value consists in its underlying suggestion that God is behind and above all events. Its Practical value consists in its application of the highest principles to the commonest affairs. Its Evangelical value consists in the encouragement it supplies to seek and to save the lowest. Its Social value consists in its presentation of the relation of Christianity to slavery and all unchristian institutions. And its Spiritual value consists in the analogy between it and the Gospel Story.

With reference to this last, Luther says : "Even as Christ did for us with God the Father, thus also doth St. Paul for Onesimus with Philemon ; for Christ also stripped Himself of His right, and by love and humility enforced the Father to lay aside His wrath and power, and to take us to His grace for the sake of Christ, Who lovingly pleadeth our cause, and with all His heart layeth Himself out for us. For we are all His Onesimi to my thinking."

Before we pass from these three Letters destined for Western Asia Minor, a word must be said about Tychicus. He accompanied Paul on his Third Missionary Journey (Acts xx. 4), and, during Paul's release from his first Roman imprisonment, was sent to Ephesus (2 Tim. iv. 12), and to Crete (Tit. iii. 12). But the greatest service of his life was the bearing of COLOSSIANS and EPHESIANS to their destinations (Col. iv. 7 ; Eph. vi. 21). Not only did he carry these Letters over the Adriatic and Ægean Seas, as Phœbe carried the Letter to Rome, but he had messages to communicate orally, including, no doubt, instructions as to the circularising of the Ephesian Letter.

The Letter to Philemon was entrusted to and delivered by Onesimus, who accompanied Tychicus on the journey. What a time they must have had together over all those miles of ocean !

Analysis of Philemon

INTRODUCTION (1-3).

1. **Superscription,** ... ... 1-2.
   - (i.) The Writer.
   - (ii.) The Readers.

2. **Benediction,** ... ... 3.
   - (i.) The Blessings.
   - (ii.) The Blessers.

I. COMMENDATION.
PAUL'S PRAYERS FOR PHILEMON (4-7).

1. **Paul's Thanksgiving,** ... ... 4, 5, 7.
   - (i.) The Cause of it.
   - (ii.) The Motive of it.

2. **Paul's Supplication,** ... ... 4, 5, 6.
   - (i.) The Occasion of it.
   - (ii.) The Purport of it.

II. APPROACH TO THE OBJECT OF THE LETTER (8-9).

1. **Paul might Enjoin.**
   - (i.) His Right.
   - (ii.) His Reason.

2. **Paul but Entreats.**
   - (i.) The Ruling Principle.
   - (ii.) The Personal Plea.

III. DISCLOSURE OF THE OBJECT OF THE LETTER (10-19).

1. **The Request** ... ... 10-12.
   - (i.) Father and Son, ... 10.
   - (ii.) Past and Present, ... 11.
   - (iii.) Sent to be Received, ... 12.

2. **The Desire,** ... ... 13-14.
   - (i.) I would have kept, but— ... ... 13.
   - (ii.) You had not given, ... 14.

EPHESIANS

GROUP 3.

Keyword : VOCATION.   CHRISTOLOGICAL.
Place of Writing : ROME.   DATE : 62 A.D.
THE NINTH LETTER IN POINT OF ORDER.

THE DATE.

FOUR of Paul's Letters are known as the "Prison Epistles." These are COLOSSIANS, PHILEMON, EPHESIANS, and PHILIPPIANS. But Paul was in prison three times, once in Cæsarea, for about two years, 58-60 A.D., and twice in Rome, the first time for about two years, 61-63 A.D., and the second time in 67 A.D. Some commentators have held that these four Epistles were written during the Cæsarean imprisonment, but that view is not commonly accepted, though it has recently been revived. We may assume that the time of writing was during the first Roman imprisonment.

There is difference of opinion as to the order in which these Letters were written, some putting EPHESIANS before COLOSSIANS, and some *vice versa;* some putting PHILIPPIANS first, and some putting it last. The order is not of great importance, though of considerable interest ; and here, without dogmatism, we follow the order, COLOSSIANS, PHILEMON, EPHESIANS, and PHILIPPIANS, and for reasons to which we shall refer.

EPHESIANS, then, was written by Paul during his first Roman imprisonment in the years 61-63 A.D., and, probably, in the year 62 A.D.

THE READERS.

Of course the Colossian Letter was sent to the Colossians, and the Galatian Letter, to the Galatians; surely, then, the Ephesian Letter was sent to the Ephesians! The matter, however, is not as simple as that. If you read this Epistle with care, certain things must impress you. For instance, though Paul had spent three years ministering in Ephesus (Acts xx. 31) there is in this Letter no trace of local colouring, which we would expect to find; and personal tidings and greetings are wanting. This latter fact is the more remarkable, in view of Paul's long association with the Church, seeing that there are personal tidings and greetings in the Colossian Letter (iv. 7-18), though Paul had never been to Colossae (ii. 1). Further, there is not a single word of familiarity or endearment in the whole Letter, no "beloved," as in Phil. iv. 1 ; or "faithful brethren," as in Col. i. 2 ; ("my brethren," in vi. 10, is omitted in the R.V., but

see verse 23). And again, the benediction in chap.
vi. 23, 24, is given in the third person, and not,
as everywhere else (Col. iv. 18 ; Phil. iv. 23), in
the second person. "There is," says Prof. Findlay,
"an official distance and formality in the writer's
attitude, such as we find in no other Epistle, and
very different from Paul's manner toward his
friends and disciples." Furthermore, in the two
oldest manuscripts, the Vatican and Sinaitic, both
of the fourth century, the words in chapter i. 1,
"at Ephesus" are omitted, though all other MSS.
and the ancient Versions have these words. Add
to all this the teaching and form of the Epistle,
and we are driven to the conclusion that this was
a Circular Letter, written for a group of Churches
of which that of Ephesus ranked as chief, and that
copies were prepared in which the name was
inserted of each particular Assembly. The original
letter would be the property of the Ephesian Church
and copies of it would be made there. Such a
solution of the problem is confirmed by Col.
iv. 16, where we read of "the Epistle from Laodicea."
We know of no Epistle which was sent expressly
to that Church, but, almost certainly it is this
Ephesian Epistle which is referred to. The opening
words of Paul's Letter would read : "To the saints
which are——," a blank being left for the name

of each Church of the Asian group, for which the Letter was intended. The Letter has well been described as "The general Epistle of Paul to Ephesus and its daughter Churches."

The readers, then, were the members of the Churches in Western Asia Minor, the Churches to which the Risen Lord, through the Apostle John, sent Messages (Rev. ii. -iii).

But this fact should not divert our attention from Ephesus, and the Church there.

EPHESUS.

This was one of the three great cities of the Mediterranean Lands, the others being, Antioch in Syria, and Alexandria in Egypt, and it was the Metropolis of Proconsular Asia. At the close of his Second Missionary Journey Paul spent a week-end at Ephesus, bringing Priscilla and Aquila with him, and leaving them there, and promising that he himself would return (Acts xviii. 18-21).

This promise he fulfilled at the beginning of the Third Missionary Journey, and he remained there for about three years (Acts xix ; xx. 31). On his last voyage to Jerusalem he touched at Miletus, some thirty miles south of Ephesus, and there he gave a pathetic charge to the Elders of the Ephesian Church (Acts xx. 17-38).

Tradition says that the Apostle John spent the latter part of his life in Ephesus, and died there ; also that the Virgin Mary died_and was buried there. By the close of the first century the Church at Ephesus had begun to decline (Rev. ii. 4).

THE OCCASION.

The occasion of most of Paul's Epistles is obvious. He wrote 1 CORINTHIANS to answer inquiries and to rebuke errors. He wrote 2 CORINTHIANS to encourage the repentant, and to defend his apostleship. He wrote GALATIANS to warn the Churches in that Province against apostasy. He wrote PHILIPPIANS to thank the Church there for their kindness to him. But we find nothing of this in EPHESIANS. Being a Circular Letter it was not called forth by any particular circumstances, and is directed, not to the Church of any one place, nor to the Churches of any one generation, but to the universal Church in every age.

THE PURPOSE.

The purpose of this Letter must be gathered largely from the time and circumstances of its production, that is, its contents must be read in the light of these. In A.D. 62, Paul was not far from his journey's end. He had weathered a rough sea, and there was one more stormy bit before he anchored in the landlocked bay where tempests will rave no more for ever. His life and its controversies lay, for the most part, behind him. No longer was he condemning schisms, as in 1 CORINTHIANS, no longer was he defending his apostleship, as in 2 CORINTHIANS ; no longer was he rebuking fickleness, nor controverting the teaching of the Judaizers, as in GALATIANS ; and no longer was he battling with Gnosticism, as in COLOSSIANS. Important as these matters were, they now, for him, were past ; and at last, from a glorious height, he surveys the purposes of God from eternity to eternity. This Epistle bids us look behind and beyond, into the infinite. It has such phrases as "before the foundation of the world," "a dispensation of the fulness of the times," "in the ages to come," "the purpose of the ages which He purposed in Christ Jesus," "to head up all things in Christ," phrases which are fathomless in their significance.

But here is no wandering of sublime thought. These transcendent truths have their focus in time, and in the Christian Church. "As in ROMANS," says Bishop Moule, "so here, Paul addresses himself to the mighty theme of the whole Gospel ; from the point of view not now of the justification of the saints, but of their life in and union with their Redeeming Head, and the consequent oneness of the whole organism of the true Church in time and in eternity."

The theme of both COLOSSIANS and EPHESIANS is Christ and the Church, but whereas in the former the emphasis is on Christ, in the latter it is on the Church. Christ, says Paul, is "Head over all things to the Church which is His Body, the fulness of Him Who all in all is being fulfilled" (i. 23). What an astounding and sublime thought! The passage implies, indeed declares, that without the Church Christ is not complete; that the Head finds completeness only in the Body, and that in His Church He is moving towards a completeness absolute and all-inclusive. Thus Origen interpreted the passage. He says: "Wherefore Christ is fulfilled in all that come unto Him, whereas He is still lacking in respect of them before they have come."

Another wonderful passage is in chapter ii. 19-22, where the Church is likened to "an Holy Temple . . . builded for an habitation of God." And the Church which has been likened to a Body and a Building, is likened, in chapter v. 32, to a Bride.

If we would know what the Christian Church is, viewed ideally, we must turn to EPHESIANS, where the revelation is most fully set forth. The unity, the beauty, and the function of the Christian Church are here presented in struggling terms, that is, in language which struggles to express the inexpressible. Prof. Findlay says that EPHESIANS is "the most laboured" of Paul's Epistles, and the reason is not far to seek. The Apostle has reached the final note of his music, he has come to the last word of his message, and it is the music and message of *Christ Completed in His Church*.

This truth about the Church was something absolutely new. Paul says that "in other ages (it) was not made known unto the sons of men," but that "it is now revealed unto His holy Apostles and prophets by the Spirit (iii. 5; cf. Rom. xvi. 25, 26; Col. i. 26). The Church is no more a development of the Temple or the Synagogue than Christianity is a development of Judaism.

It is the great New Testament "Mystery"; something which does not appear at all in the Old Testament; something absolutely new. The subject of the Old Testament prophets was the *Kingdom*; but the subject of the New Testament Apostles is the *Church*; and in EPHESIANS Church truth blazes forth in fulness of glory.

The Church of history is a very different thing, and yet, through all these centuries, God, in spite of us, if not by means of us, has been fulfilling His matchless design. Through all declensions and perversions, through all caricatures and compromises, Christ has been building His Church, and is building it, and one day He will "present it to Himself a glorious Church, not having spot, or wrinkle, or any such thing" (v. 27).

The Church is not Jewish or Gentile, not Catholic or Protestant, not Episcopal or Dissenting; but it is the aggregate of all believing men, women, and children, throughout this Christian dispensation, a holy, wonderful, glorious thing.

This, then is the message of EPHESIANS. Paul will yet write a letter of thanksgiving to Philippi, and will give instructions on certain matters to Titus and Timothy, but here he reaches the zenith of his ministry, and here he expresses the fulness of his soul.

NOTES.

The richness of EPHESIANS may be judged of from the fact that there are here forty-two words which occur nowhere else in the New Testament. These are :

"Without God" (ii. 12); "filthiness" (v. 4); "He led captive" (iv. 8); "to be renewed" (iv. 23); "opening" (vi. 19); "having-cast-off-all-feeling" (iv. 19); "unwise" (v. 15); "darts" (vi. 16); "nourishes," "bring-up" (v. 29; iv. 4); "less-than-the-least" (iii. 8); "unity" (iv. 3. 13); "may-be-fully-able" (iii. 18); "let-set" (iv. 26); **"shall-shine-upon"** (v. 14); "preparation" (vi. 15); "good-will" (vi. 7); "jesting" (v. 4); "shield" (vi. 16); "perfecting" (iv. 12); "lower" (iv. 9); "obtained-an-inheritance" (i. 11); "being-tossed" (iv. 14); "world-rulers" (vi. 12); "in-secret" (v. 12); "sleight" (iv. 14); "greatness" (i. 19); "systematizing," "artifices" (iv. 14; vi. 11); "middle-wall" (ii. 14); "foolish-talking" (v. 4); "wrestling" (vi. 12); "provocation" (iv. 26); "multifarious" (iii. 10); "have-foretrusted" (i. 12); "per-severance" (vi. 18); "wrinkle" (v. 27); "joint-partakers" (iii. 6; v. 7); "fellow-citizens" (ii. 19); "fitted-together" (ii. 21; iv. 16); "being-built-together" (ii. 22); "joint-body" (iii. 6); "long-lived" (vi. 3); "salvation" (vi. 17). In addition to these words, there are eleven others which are used again only in Colossians, in the New Testament, four nouns, one adjective, and six verbs: "men-pleasers" (vi. 6); "alienated-from" (ii. 12; iv. 18); "might-reconcile" (ii. 16); "increases" (ii. 21; iv. 15); "increase" (iv. 16); "joint" (iv. 16); "eye-service" (vi. 6); "being-rooted" (iii. 18); "raised-up-together" (ii. 6); "quickened-with" (ii. 5); "hymns" (v. 19). And in addition to all the above there are in Ephesians forty-three words which do not occur in any other of Paul's letters.

Other outstanding words in this Epistle are:

"Will" (God's), "predestinated," "afore-prepared," "grace," "the heavenlies," "Spirit," and "spiritual," "mystery," "ful-ness," "glory," compounds in "exceedingly" (i. 19, 21; iii. 19, 20; iv. 10; ii. 7), and in "together" (iii. 6; ii. 22; ii. 19; iii. 6; v. 7; ii. 21; iv. 16), "riches," and "in Christ."

It may be said that all EPHESIANS is notable, but mark especially the amazing passage in chapter i. 3-14. No better word has been spoken of these verses than that of Dr. Armitage Robinson. He says: "These twelve verses baffle our analysis. They are a kaleidoscope of dazzling lights and shifting colours: at first we fail to find a trace of order or method. They are like the preliminary flight of the eagle, rising and wheeling round, as though for a while uncertain what direction in his boundless freedom he shall take. So the Apostle's thought lifts itself beyond the limits of time and above the material conceptions that confine ordinary men, and ranges this way and that in a region of spirit, a heavenly sphere, with no course as yet marked out, merely exulting in the attributes and purposes of God.

"At first we marvel at the wealth of his language : but soon we discover, by the very repetition of the phrases which have arrested us, the poverty of all language when it comes to deal with such topics as he has chosen. He seems to be swept along by his theme, hardly knowing whither it is taking him. He begins with God—the blessing which comes from God to men, the eternity of His purpose of good, the glory of its consummation. But he cannot order his conceptions, or close his sentences. One thought presses hard upon another, and will not be refused. And so this great doxology runs on and on: "in Whom ... in Him ... in Him, in Whom ... in Whom ... in Whom ... !"

Then, note the two prayers (i. 15-23 ; iii. 14-21) ; the great passage on the Mystery (iii. 2-12) ; and on the unity, endowment, function, and prospect of the Church (iv. 1-16) ; and on the Christian family (v. 22-vi. 9) ; and on the Christian armour (vi. 11-17).

"In the depth of its theology," says Dean Farrar, "in the loftiness of its morals, in the way in which the simplest moral truths are based upon the profoundest religious doctrines—the Epistle is unparalleled."

NOTE 82
Ephesus.

THIS city was situated about the middle of the western coast of Asia Minor. It was a large and important city, and in Paul's time had a population of about 340,000. The Temple of Artemis or Diana was there, and the Ephesians were proud that their city was the warden of it. It was the city of the philosophers Thales and Heraclitus, and was a place of rich culture. "With its oriental religion, its Greek culture, its Roman government, and its world-wide commerce, it stood midway between two continents, being on the one hand the gateway of Asia to crowds of western officials and travellers, and on the other hand the rendezvous of multitudes of Eastern pilgrims coming to worship at Artemis' shrine. Traversed by the great imperial highway of intercourse and commerce, it had all nationalities meeting and mingling in its streets." With this city were associated Aquila and Priscilla, Apollos, Tychicus, and Timothy, and it was greatly privileged to have the protracted ministries of the Apostles Paul and John, and to receive a Letter from Heaven (Rev. ii.).

Analysis of Ephesians

Theme : THE CHURCH IN CHRIST.

INTRODUCTION (i. 1, 2).

PART A. DOCTRINAL (i. 3-iii. 21).
THE CHRISTIAN AGE.

I. THE ORIGIN OF THE CHURCH (i. 3-14).

1. **The Divine Purpose (3-6).**
   Election by the Father, ... Theological.

2. **The Divine Plan (7-10).**
   Redemption by the Son, ... Historical.

3. **The Divine Process (11-14).**
   Salvation by the Spirit, ... Experimental.

II. THE GLORY OF THE CHURCH (i. 15-23).

1. **The Occasion of the Prayer (15, 16).**

2. **The Object of the Prayer (17-19a).**
   (i.) Preparative : "That," ... ... 17, 18a.
   (ii.) Progressive : "That," ... ... 18b-19a.

3. **The Outlook of the Prayer (19b-23).**
   (i.) Christ's Resurrection, ... 19b-20a.
   (ii.) Christ's Enthronement, ... 20b-21.
   (iii.) Christ's Authority, ... 22, 23.

III. THE CHARACTER OF THE CHURCH (ii. 1-10).

1. **Our State by Nature : The Past,** ... ... 1-3.
   (i.) The Condition, ... 1.
   (ii.) The Characteristics, ... 2, 3a.
   (iii.) The Consequence, ... 3b.

2. **Our Standing by Grace : The Present,** ... 4-10.
   (i.) That God hath Wrought, ... 4, 5a.
   (ii.) What God hath Wrought, ... 5b, 6.
   (iii.) Why God hath Wrought, ... 7.
   (iv.) How God hath Wrought, . .. 8-10.

427

IV. THE PROGRESS OF THE CHURCH (ii. 11-22).

1. Our Former Alienation (11, 12).

(i.) In Respect of the Covenants of Promise, ... 11.
(ii.) In Respect of the Christ of God, ... 12a.
(iii.) In Respect of the Course of History, ... 12b.

2. Our Present Unification (13-18).

(i.) The Announcement of it, ... 13.
(ii.) The Accomplishment of it, ... 14-16.
(iii.) The Assurance of it, ... 17, 18.

3. Our Ultimate Destination (19-22).

(i.) In Respect of the City : Ours the Freedom, ... 19a.
(ii.) In Respect of the Household : Ours the
Fellowship, ... 19b.
(iii.) In Respect of the Sanctuary : Ours the
Fulness ... ... 20-22.

V. THE FUNCTION OF THE CHURCH (iii. 1-13).

1. The Revelation to Men Concerning the Mystery (2-6).

(i.) The Time of it ... ... 5.
(ii.) The Channel of it, ... 3, 4.
(iii.) The Nature of it, ... 6.

2. The Commission of Paul to Preach the Mystery (7-9).

(i.) His Glorious Mission, ... 8, 9.
(ii.) His Divine Authority, ... 7a, 8a.
(iii.) His Perfect Equipment, ... 7b.

3. The Intention of God by Means of the Mystery (10-13).

(i.) The Revelation of Eternal Purpose, ... 11, 12
(ii.) The Exhibition of Infinite Wisdom, ... 10b.
(iii.) The Instruction of Celestial Beings, ... 10.

VI. THE FULNESS OF THE CHURCH (iii. 14-21).

1. The Approach to Prayer (14, 15).

(i.) The Occasion.
(ii.) The Posture.
(iii.) The Address.
(iv.) The Compass.

2. The Appeal for Plenitude (16-19).

(i.) The Conditions of this Fulness, ... 16, 17.
(a) The Empowering of the Spirit (16).
(b) The Indwelling of Christ (17).

    (ii.) The Purpose of this Fulness, ... **18, 19a.**
        (*a*) Apprehension. (*b*) Knowledge.
    (iii.) The Measure of this Fulness, ... **19b.**
        (*a*) Immediately, "into." (*b*) Eternally, "unto."

3. The Ascription of Praise (20, 21)

    (i.) The Object of our Worship.
    (ii.) The Strength of Our Confidence.
    (iii.) The Reason of Our Gratitude.
    (iv.) The Duration of Our Thanksgiving.

PART B. PRACTICAL (iv.-vi. 20).
THE CHRISTIAN LIFE.

I. THE CALLING OF THE CHRISTIAN (iv. 1-16).

1. The Ground of our Greatness (1-6).
    (i.) Our Exalted Vocation, ... **1-3.**
    (ii.) Our Spiritual Unity, ... **4-6.**

2. The Variety of our Gifts (7-13).
    (i.) The Special Service, ... **7-11.**
    (ii.) The Common Service, ... **12, 13.**

3. The Secret of our Growth (14-16).
    (i.) Fixity of Principle, ... **14.**
    (ii.) Richness of Power, ... **15, 16.**

II. THE CONDUCT OF THE CHRISTIAN (iv. 17-vi. 9)

1. Personal Conduct (iv. 17-32).
    (i.) Contrasted Principles of Life, ... **17-24.**
    (ii.) Contrasted Practice in Living, ... **25-32.**

2. Social Conduct (v. 1-21).
    (i.) Love Excluding Lust, ... **1-5**
    (ii.) Light Excluding Darkness, ... **6-14.**
    (iii.) Wisdom Excluding Folly, ... **15-21.**

3. Domestic Conduct (v. 22-vi. 9).
    (i.) Wives and Husbands : Submission and Love, **v. 22-23**
    (ii.) Children and Parents : Honour and Discipline, **vi. 1-4.**
    (iii.) Servants and Masters ; Obedience and Justice, **vi. 5-9.**

III. THE CONFLICT OF THE CHRISTIAN (vi. 10-20).

1. The Christian Warrior (10, 11).
2. The Christian Warfare (12).
3. The Christian Weapons (13-20).

CONCLUSION (vi. 21-24).

PHILIPPIANS

GROUP 3.

Keyword : JOYFUL.   CHRISTOLOGICAL.

Place of Writing : ROME.   DATE : 63 A.D.

THE TENTH LETTER IN POINT OF ORDER.

THE DATE.

OF the place of PHILIPPIANS, in this group of
Letters, each of two views is influentially
held ; one, that it was the first of the four to be
written ; and the other, that it was the last. The
argument on each side is interesting, though not
of vital importance. For the former view, Farrar,
following Lightfoot, Moule, and Beet, says :
"Seeing the delicate susceptibility of St. Paul's
mind, and its tenacity of recent phrases and im-
pressions, I hold it to be a psychological impossibility that he should have written PHILIPPIANS
after COLOSSIANS and EPHESIANS, and yet have
shown no traces of the special thoughts with which
he had been so recently and so powerfully occupied."
On the other hand, Ellicott, Findlay and others
argue for the later date on the ground that Paul
expects an imminent trial, which, he hopes, will
issue in his release (i. 25, 26 ; ii. 24).

If the early view is correct, this Letter was

written late in 61 A.D., or early in 62 A.D. If
the late view, it would be written in 63 A.D., at the
close of which year he was released from his first
Roman imprisonment.

THE READERS.
Paul and Philippi.

Philippi was a city of Macedonia which was
raised to the rank of a Roman military colony by
Julius Cæsar, who gave the people the privileges
of a Roman city, which included the franchise
(Acts xvi. 12). Its outstanding distinction is in
the fact that it was the first place in Europe which
received the Gospel. The Church there was
founded by Paul when he was on his Second
Missionary Journey, in 52 A.D. (Acts xvi. 12-40).
At the close of his Third Missionary Journey,
after his leaving Ephesus, in 57 A.D., he went into
Macedonia (Acts xx. 1 ; 2 Cor. ii. 12, 13 ; vii.
5, 6), where he wrote his Second Letter to the
Corinthians, and it is practically certain that he
spent some time at Philippi (Acts xx. 2). Three
or four months later, on his return from Greece,
he evidently spent the Passover at Philippi (Acts
xx. 6).

This, then, was the city to which this Letter
was conveyed by Epaphroditus.

The Church at Philippi.—Paul's going to Philippi was the result of a vision (Acts xvi. 6-12). There appears to have been no synagogue in the city, which implies, perhaps, that there were not many Jews there ; but on the Sabbath a prayer meeting was held on the banks of the Ganges, to which Paul and Silas resorted. The audience was composed mostly of women, whom Paul addressed. By that talk was secured the first convert to Christianity in Europe, a woman from Asia, and well-to-do (Acts xvi. 14). Other converts followed, and the Church was commenced (Acts xvi. 15), which became specially dear to Paul (iv. 1), and which in turn greatly loved him (iv. 14-16).

The Occasion.

The Church at Philippi was almost quite free from those errors which beset so many of the Churches of that day. The claim is qualified on account of the singular outburst in chapter iii. 2, 3, 17-19. The whole of chapter iii. from verse 2, is a digression, and chapter iii. 1, connects with chapter iv. 1. The reason for this severe passage is unknown, but it seems like "the spent wave, the dying echo of the Judaic controversy."

Otherwise the Epistle is calm and joyful. The Philippians had sent to Paul, by Epaphroditus

(ii. 25), a gift of money (iv. 10, 14). This they had done three times before, twice when Paul was at Thessalonica, and once when he was at Corinth (iv. 15, 16 ; 2 Cor. xi. 9). In their generosity is to be found the occasion of the Letter.

THE OBJECT.

Paul's purpose in writing was twofold, gratefully to acknowledge the kindness of this Church, and gently to promote concord among some of the members who were in disagreement (iv. 2). Except for the digression of chapter iii. 2-21, these are the dominating notes of the Letter. It differs from all Paul's other Letters in its charming spontaniety. It shows the Apostle in some of the sweetest aspects of his character. "This is an epistle of the heart," says Prof. Findlay, "a true love letter, full of friendship, gratitude, and confidence ; it makes those intimate revelations of the soul's history and emotions which the deepest sympathy and mutual affection alone are wont to elicit."

NOTES.

The Philippian Letter reveals what, in God's good purpose, normal Christian experience should be—an experience of abiding joy in one's own soul, and of gracious harmony with fellow-

Christians. The keynotes here, are *joy* and *unity*.

Says Bengel: "I rejoice! do you rejoice? is the sum of the Letter." The word "rejoice" and its equivalents, occur sixteen times in these four chapters, but the whole Letter exudes joy. And lest it be thought that this state of heart was induced by circumstances, let us remember that Paul was in prison, chained day and night to a soldier, with few friends, and not a few enemies (ii. 20, 21 ; i. 15, 16). Christian joy is more and better than happiness, because it does not depend on what happens.

The note of unity also, sounds throughout the Epistle, but two sections emphasise it, i. 27-ii. 18 ; and iv. 1-9. Christian experience, and the experience of Christians, are not always in harmony. Too much of the latter is sad and discordant ; the former is glad and harmonious.

In exhorting to unity, the Apostle gives us one of the greatest passages in all his writings (ii. 6-11). This is all the more impressive as the occasion was not theological but ethical. The great Christological passages in Paul are in the Prison Epistles ; here, and Col. i. 14-20 ; and Eph. i. 20-23. Every word in the passage before us is heavy with meaning ; it is one of the profoundest and sublimest statements ever uttered.

The *kenōsis* controversy is based on ii. 7. Much that has been spoken and written on the subject has been grievous or irrelevant. The passage refers not to Christ's *knowledge* but to His *glory*.

Other striking passages are, i. 19-26, respecting the choice of life or death : iii. 7-11, revealing Paul's devotion to Christ : iii. 12-16, disclosing his progress and purpose in the Christian life : iv. 8, describing the things which we should think about ; iv. 11-13, declaring the Apostle's independence and contentment "in Christ."

In this comparatively short Letter there are no fewer than sixty-five words which do not occur in any other of Paul's writings ; and of these, thirty-five do not occur again in the New Testament. The latter are the following :

"Purely" (i. 16) ; "intelligence" (i. 9) ; "were-lacking-opportunity" (iv. 10) ; "the less sorrowful" (ii. 28) ; "ye revived" (iv. 10) ; "absence" (ii. 12) ; "rapine" (ii. 6) ; "content" (iv. 11) ; "genuinely" (ii. 20) ; "out-resurrection" (iii. 11) ; "stretching-out" (iii. 13) ; "longed-for" (iv. 1); "differently" (iii. 15) ; "good report" (iv. 8) ; "may-be-of-good-courage" (ii. 19) ; "like-minded" (ii. 20) ; "concision" (iii. 2) ; "under-the-earth" (ii. 10) ; "vain-glory" (ii. 3) ; "receiving" (iv. 15) ; "greatly" (iv. 10) ; "initiated" (iv. 12) ; "eighth day" (iii. 5) ; "having disregarded" (ii. 30) ; "consolation" (ii. 1) ; "like" (ii. 27) ; "commonwealth" (iii. 20) ; "being-frightened" (i. 28) ; "refuse" (iii. 8) ; "being conformed" (iii. 10) ; "striving-together" (i. 27 ; iv. 3) ; "yoke-fellow" (iv. 3) ; "imitators-together" (iii. 17) ; "joined-in-soul" (ii. 2) ; "highly-exalted" (ii. 9).

Other words or phrases to be studied are : "brethren,"

"beloved," "to depart," "the form of God," "He emptied Himself," "counted it not a prize," "dogs," "the mark," "the goal," "whatsoever," "bishop," "deacons," "keep," "to live is Christ," "lowliness of mind," "the body of our humiliation," "moderation," "remain" and "remain-with," "the things that are excellent," "bonds."

This concludes the Third Group of Paul's Writings, with their great notes of Fulness in Christ, Christian Brotherhood, Holy Calling, and Abiding Joy.

NOTE 83

Philippi.

THIS city, situated in the east of Macedonia, was re-founded in the middle of the fourth century B.C., by Philip of Macedon. By "first of the district" (Acts xvi. 12) is probably meant that that was the Roman colony's estimate of its own importance. There does not seem to have been a synagogue here, probably because a military colony did not offer the same attractions to the Jews as a commercial city would do, but there was a place of prayer, to which Paul resorted (Acts xvi. 13, 16), and it was here, in green pastures and beside still waters, that he won his first European convert, the proselyte Lydia (Acts xvi. 14).

It was at Philippi that Paul and Silas were beaten and imprisoned, an outcome of which was the conversion of the jailer and his family. In the Acts the change in chapter xvi. from "they" to "we" favours Ramsay's view that "the man of Macedonia" whom Paul saw in a vision, and in response to whose call he crossed the Aegean, was Luke the physician.

Analysis of Philippians

INTRODUCTION (i. 1-2).

THE JOYFUL REPOSE OF THE CHRISTIAN LIFE.
(i. 3-26).

1. Repose in the Promise of the Past (3-11).
    (i.) Praise for Progress, ... 3-7.
    (ii.) Prayer for Perfecting, ... 8-11.

2. Repose in the Purpose of the Present (12-18).
    (i.) By Means of his Bonds, ... 12-14.
    (ii.) By Means of his Foes, ... 15-18.

3. Repose in the Plan of the Future (19-26).
    (i.) Paul's Ambition, come Life or Death, ... 19-20.
    (ii.) Paul's Attitude towards Life and Death, ... 21-26.

THE LOFTY IDEAL OF THE CHRISTIAN LIFE.
(i. 27-ii. 30).

1. The Standard Appointed (i. 27-ii. 16).
    (i.) Steadfastness in Suffering, ... i. 27-30.
    (ii.) Harmony by Humility, ... ii. 1-11.
    (iii.) Effectiveness through Earnest Effort, ... ii. 12-16.

2. The Standard Approached (ii. 17-30).
    (i.) The Example of Paul, ... 17-18.
    (ii.) The Example of Timothy, ... 19-24.
    (iii.) The Example of Epaphroditus, ... 25-30.

THE DEVOUT ENERGY OF THE CHRISTIAN LIFE.
(iii. 1-iv. 1).

1. Christianity is Opposed to Judaism (iii. 1-16).
    (i.) The Peril of the Christian, ... 1-6.
    (ii.) The Passion of the Christian, ... 7-11.
    (iii.) The Progress of the Christian, ... 12-16.

2. Christianity is Opposed to Antinomianism
    (iii. 17-iv. 1).
    (i.) The Course to Pursue, ... 17-19.
    (ii.) The Claim of Faith, ... 20-21.
    (iii.) The Call to Stand Fast, ... iv. 1.

THE GRAND UNIQUENESS OF THE CHRISTIAN LIFE
(iv. 2-20).

1. **Its Selflessness (2-7).**
   (i.) Unity of Mind and Purpose, ... 2-3.
   (ii.) Unreserved Delight in God, ... 4-7.

2. **Its Spirituality (8-9).**
   (i.) The Heart's Employment,... ... ... 8.
   (ii.) The Heart's Encouragement, ... 9.

3. **Its Sufficiency (10-20).**
   (i.) Satisfaction in Christ, ... 10-13.
   (ii.) Supply through Christians, ... 14-20.

CONCLUSION (21-23).

NOTE 84
Women in the Church of Philippi.

"THE prestige of women in the Church of Philippi, as in the other Macedonian Churches (Acts xvii. 4, 12) is a striking fact, only to be compared with their prominence at an earlier date in the personal ministry of our Lord " (Lightfoot). St. Paul's first Philippian audience consisted entirely of women (Acts xvi. 13); his first convert was a woman of influence, whose *familia* was baptised with her, and who became his hostess (14, 15); and the only element in the Philippian Church which called for reproof in his letter was the variance of two prominent Christian ladies, both of whom he remembered gratefully as his fellow-workers in the Gospel (Phil. iv. 2, 3)."

—Dr. JAMES STRAHAN.

NOTE 85
Ignatius and Philippi.

DURING the Trajan persecution, about 116 A.D. Ignatius was arrested and sent from Antioch to Rome where he was to die in the arena. On the way he stopped at Philippi, and made so deep an impression on the Church there that they asked the martyr's young friend Polycarp to send them copies of Ignatius' own letters. Polycarp's *Epistle to the Philippians* was the response, and it is still extant.

THE PAULINE EPISTLES

GROUP 4

INTRODUCTION

1 TIMOTHY

TITUS

2 TIMOTHY

HEBREWS (?)

NOTE 86

The Pastoral and the Recognised Pauline Epistles.

OF all the letters which profess to have come from the Apostle Paul those to Timothy and Titus are the most disputed, but the affinities between these and Paul's other letters are more than sufficient to override the objections which have been raised to their Pauline authorship.

1 Timothy	Romans	2 Timothy	Romans	Titus	Romans
i. 8, 9 i. 17 ii. 1, 2	vii. 12 xvi. 27 xiii. 1	i. 7 i. 8, 12 i. 9, 10	viii. 15 i. 16 xvi. 26	i. 1·4 ii. 13 iii. 10	xvi. 25, 26 v. 2 xvi. 17, 18
	1 Corinthians		**1 Corinthians**		**1 Corinthians**
i. 20 ii. 11, 12 ii. 13, 14	v. 5 xi. 8, 9; xiv. 34 xi. 3	i. 2·6; ii. 1, 2 iii. 10, 11	iv. 17 xvi. 10, 11	i. 7 ii. 13 iii. 3	iv. 1 i. 7 vi. 11
	Ephesians		**Ephesians**		**Ephesians**
iii. 5, 15 iii. 15, 16 iv. 1	ii. 19, 20 iv. 21 ii. 2	i. 9, 10 ii. 8 ii. 9	iii. 3, 5, 9, 10 i. 19, 20 iii. 1, 13	i. 1·4 ii. 14 iii. 3	i. 9, 10 i. 7, 14; v. 2, 25-27 ii. 2; v. 8
	Philippians		**Philippians**		**Philippians**
i. 12 i. 18 ii. 1	iv. 13 ii. 25 iv. 6	i. 3 i. 8·13 iii. 10-14	iii. 5 { i. 29, 30 ii. 19·22 iii. 10, 11, 17 iv. 9 }	ii. 13 iii. 2 iii. 5, 7	iii. 20 iv. 5 iii. 9
	Colossians				
i. 1·4, 11, 12; iii. 15, 16	i. 23·27	i. 12	i. 20		

These references are selected from Dr. R. A. Falconer's article on the Pastoral Epistles in Hastings' Dictionary of the Apostolic Church, p. 591.

THE PAULINE EPISTLES

GROUP 4.   ECCLESIOLOGICAL.

I TIMOTHY.   TITUS.   2 TIMOTHY.

HEBREWS (?)

Introduction

FOR an understanding of the revelation communicated by the Apostle Paul it is of great
importance that we study his Letters chronologically, and in groups. The chronological order is
that of revelation, and the canonical order is, in
general, that of experience. This explains why
ROMANS comes first, and THESSALONIANS, last. In
experience we begin at the point of justification,
and end at the point of glorification. But the
order of revelation is different. It begins, in the
THESSALONIANS, with our future prospect, and
ends, in the Pastoral Epistles, with our present
duties.

The writing of these Letters covers a period of
fifteen or sixteen years, 52-68 A.D., and between
each of the four groups is a period of from four
to five years.

Group 1, A.D. 52, 53 ; Group 2, A.D. 57, 58 ;
Group 3, A.D. 62, 63, and Group 4, A.D. 67, 68.

The first represents the morning of Paul's ministry ; the second represents the noontide ; the third represents the afternoon ; and the fourth represents the evening. The day proceeds from the morning brightness of hope, to the noontide of conflict with error, to the afternoon calm of reflection, to the evening attention to duty.

The prospect of Christ's return is in both the first and last groups, but in the latter, the imminence of the advent has receded. It is still the Church's hope, but in the Pastoral Letters room is left for the Lord to tarry for "a long time" (Matt. xxv. 19). To say, as some have, that Paul changed his views on the subject of a second advent of Christ, is not true. At the end as definitely as at the beginning he loved and looked for His appearing (2 Tim. iv. 8), but there is a change of emphasis.

These Epistles are called Pastoral because they are written to individuals, whereas all the others, except the note to Philemon, are written to Churches. The note to Philemon, concerned as it is with strictly personal matters, could not be called pastoral, but these three Letters concern the affairs of the universal Church, and so the benedictions are plural in form, "you," not "thee" (1 Tim. vi. 21 ; Titus iii. 15 ; 2 Tim. iv. 22).

The authenticity of these Letters has been more

questioned than that of any other of the Apostle's Writings, and the challenge has been on four grounds; first, that they cannot be fitted into the history of Paul's travels as recorded in the ACTS ; second, that the particular heresies referred to in them belong to the second century, and not to the first ; third, that they reveal a more developed Church organisation than we find in the rest of the New Testament ; and fourth, that the language of these Letters differs in many ways from that of Paul's other Writings.

Over against these objections let us place the weighty statement of Prof. G. G. Findlay that, "There is not a shred of historical evidence against the Letters. The witness of the Early Church to their place in the New Testament Canon and their Pauline authorship is as clear, full, and unhesitating as that given to the other Epistles. It is only on grounds of internal criticism that objections of real weight can be raised." This "internal criticism" refers to the fourth objection, that of language, but in the light of all the facts, that also becomes invalid.

It is true that in these Letters are many words which occur nowhere else in the New Testament. In the three Epistles (thirteen chapters) Prof. Van Oosterzee and Dr. Gloag say there are 188 such words : Prof. Findlay says (excluding proper names) 171 ; and Prof. David Smith says there are 146 such words.

In reply to the objection raised on this ground, let two things be said. First, that similarly objection might be taken to all Paul's Epistles, for the following are the number of words which do not occur again in the New Testament : in 1 Thess., 17; 2 Thess., 11 ; 1 Cor., 100 ; 2 Cor., 91 ; Gal., 32 ; Rom., 94 ; Eph., 42 ; Phil., 35 ; Col., 34 ; and Philemon, 5 ; 461 in all. Is it, then, inconceivable that in the remaining three Epistles Paul should use many words not employed before ? "The Apostle's vocabulary," says Prof. Findlay, "was uncommonly fresh ; he was inventive and original in language ; and the habit of using novel and singular expressions grew upon him." Second, this peculiarity of language can well be accounted for by a consideration of the date of the Epistles, the peculiar nature of the subjects discussed, and "the plain, substantial accordance in all main points with the Apostle's general style" (Ellicott).

This last point is of great importance. It has been said that these Letters are characterised by poverty of sentiment, and so are unworthy of the Apostle Paul. But so far from this being the case, we may trace in these three Epistles connections

with all the other Pauline Letters. Here, as in
THESSALONIANS, is the Second Advent (2 Tim.
iv. 1, 8 ; Titus ii. 13). Here, as in 1 CORINTHIANS,
are references to women (1 Cor. xi. 2-16 ; 1 Tim.
ii. 9-15), and the resurrection (1 Cor. xv. ; 2 Tim.
ii. 18). Here, as in GALATIANS and ROMANS, are
references to the Law, Christ's death, and salvation
(1 Tim. ii. 6 ; Titus i. 2, 3 ; ii. 11 ; iii. 4-7). Here,
as in EPHESIANS, is reference to gifts of ministry
bestowed upon the Church (Eph. iv. 11, 12 ; 1 Tim.
iii). Here, as in COLOSSIANS, are references to
Judaistic, and possibly, to Gnostic errors (Col.
ii. 20-23 ; 1 Tim. iv. 3-5 ; Col. ii. 9-15 ; 1 Tim.
ii. 5-7 ; Col. ii. 2-4, 8, 16, 22 ; 1 Tim. vi. 3, 4, 20,
21 ; Titus i. 13-16). And here, as in PHILIPPIANS,
Paul refers to his approaching death (Phil. i. 20-23 ;
ii. 17 ; 2 Tim. iv. 5-8, 18). If specific doctrines
are subordinate in these Epistles it is because Paul
is not now, as in GALATIANS, and ROMANS, and
COLOSSIANS, declaring and defending the doctrines
of the Person of Christ, the relation of the Law to
Christianity, or the ground and fruits of justification. The great truths of his other Epistles are
assumed, and it now remains only for him to
exhort these and all ministers and believers to
"guard the deposit against all assaults, especially
those of the Jewish Gnostics," to maintain a

pure ministry and worship, and to live a godly life.

These brief Letters are the Minister's Manual, setting forth the Pastoral Office, Qualifications, and Duties.

If groups two and three of these Letters present respectively the combative and contemplative substance of the Gospel, groups one and four respectively present a prologue and an epilogue, a preface and a postscript.

NOTE 87
Genuineness of the Pastoral Epistles.

"THESE Epistles stand or fall together. Even the most 'advanced' and hostile critics are prepared to admit the genuineness of the Second Epistle to Timothy. But if that be genuine, St. Paul must have been liberated before the Neronian persecution, and the case in favour of the two other Epistles is greatly strengthened. The power, beauty, and value of the Epistles is their best attestation. Dr. Wace says truly that 'the sacred writings are throughout characterized by a wonderful combination of the loftiest faith in the mysteries of godliness with profound practical wisdom; and it is a combination of which no instance can be shown in those apocryphal and forged productions among which it has been attempted to range these Epistles.'"

—Archdeacon FARRAR, in *The Messages of the Books.*

1 TIMOTHY

GROUP 4.

Keyword : MINISTRATION.   ECCLESIOLOGICAL.

Place of Writing : MACEDONIA (?)   Date : 66-67 A.D.

THE ELEVENTH LETTER IN POINT OF ORDER.

TIMOTHY.

TIMOTHEUS, which is said to mean "honouring God," or "honoured by God," was Paul's most intimate and best loved disciple and friend. His mother was a Jewess, his father was a Greek, and the family lived at Derbe, or Lystra. Paul, on his First Missionary Journey brought Timothy, who was then a boy, to a saving knowledge of Christ (Acts xiv. 6, 7), and on his Second Journey, Timothy was circumcised, ordained, and left home to travel with the great Apostle (Acts xvi. 1-3 ; 1 Tim. iv. 14 ; 2 Tim. i. 6), and of all Paul's companions he was the most constant and faithful (Phil. ii. 19-22). It has been well said that "Timothy was one of the magnificent compensations Paul enjoyed for the cruel treatment he received at Lystra" (Acts xiv. 8-21 ; xvi. 1-2).

The name of the young evangelist is connected with each of the four groups of Paul's Letters (Thess., Cor., Phil.), and, for the most part, he was

constantly with his great master. Such confidence
had Paul in him that he delegated to him most
difficult and delicate tasks in Thessalonica, Corinth,
and Ephesus (1 Thess. iii. 1-2 ; 1 Cor. iv. 17 ;
xvi. 10 ; 1 Tim. i. 3). What he accomplished is
the more remarkable seeing that he was of a nervous
temperament, and physically weak (1 Cor. iv. 17 ;
xvi. 10, 11 ; 1 Tim. iv. 14-16 ; v. 20, 21, 23 ; vi.
11-14 ; vi. 20 ; 2 Tim. i. 14 ; ii. 1-7 ; iv. 1, 2). As
Paul drew near to the end of his course, it was
Timothy he wanted to have with him, and for whom
he sent (2 Tim. iv. 9, 13).

To this young man, still young in A.D. 67 (1 Tim.
iv. 12), perhaps about thirty years of age, Paul
wrote two of his thirteen Letters. Each has its
own circumstantial significance, in that the First
was the first Letter which Paul wrote after his
release from his first Roman imprisonment, and
the Second was certainly the last he ever wrote,
shortly before his martyrdom.

THE DATE.

One of the arguments against the authenticity
of this Letter, and it applies to the other two
Pastorals, is that there is no place for it in the
history of the ACTS. This is perfectly true, but the
history there is not complete. From scattered

references (Philemon 22 ; Phil. ii. 24 ; Rom. xv. 24 ; 1 Tim. i. 3 ; Titus iii. 12 ; 2 Tim. iv. 9, 10, 12, 13, 21), the course of events appears to have been as follows :

In A.D. 63 Paul was released from his first Roman imprisonment, which accounts for no reference being made to the great fire of Rome, in A.D. 64, and he would then fulfil his promise to Philemon and his Philippian friends to revisit them. After that he *may* have taken the contemplated voyage to Spain (but this is doubtful). The above references allude to the Apostle having been recently at Miletus, Troas, Crete, and possibly, Corinth, and to his intention to winter in Nicopolis ; but he was rearrested, taken back to Rome, and, probably in the Spring of A.D. 68, was martyred. This means that the Pastoral Letters were written in the years 66-67 A.D.

THE PURPOSE.

The occasion of writing was twofold, the spread of error, and the Apostle's consciousness that his end was near ; and the object also was twofold, to caution and to confirm ; to warn against false teaching in its many forms, and to encourage Timothy, and every minister, and every Christian, to continue in the truth, and to live a holy life. These two strands of thought constitute the pattern of the Letter, the general and the particular, the relative and the personal, correct doctrine and practical piety.

Paul had predicted that heresies would menace the Church at Ephesus (Acts xx. 28-30), and they were now present (1 Tim. i. 3-7 ; iv. 1-3 ; vi. 3-10, 20, 21). Gnostic Judaists, by their asceticism and Scriptural jargon, were likely to impress superficial minds, and the Apostle writes to warn them. These are the "grievous wolves" of the prediction. The Gnostics believed in a succession of emanations, a hierarchy of æons mediating between God and the world, and, no doubt, this is what is meant by "endless genealogies" in chapter i. 4. The Gnostics also, and consequently, reduced Christ to the rank of an æon, but Paul affirms, "there is one Mediator between God and man, the Man Christ Jesus" (ii. 5). Further, the Gnostics taught that matter was inherently evil, but Paul declares that "every creature of God is good" (iv. 4, 5). These, and kindred errors are what Paul calls "profane babblings and incongruities of the ' knowledge ' (gnōsis), falsely so named" (vi. 20), and he warns Timothy against them, and bids him warn others against them.

But the Apostle's exhortations are eminently practical. One of the most effective ways of excluding error from the Church, or neutralising its influence in the Church, was to have as the Church's leaders men competent and approved. This is the significance of chapter iii, which details the qualifications of bishops and deacons. And again, it was of supreme moment that "the angel of the Church" (Rev. ii. 1), Timothy himself, should be beyond reproach, true, faithful, and courageous (iv. 12-16). Timothy evidently was discouraged, and disposed to withdraw from his difficult task, but this, Paul definitely vetoed: "Stay on at Ephesus," he says (i. 3).

The contents of this Epistle may be briefly summed up in three chief topics; first, a pure Gospel; second, a worthy worship; and third, a faithful ministry.

NOTES.

In these six chapters there are 118 words which Paul does not use in any other of his Epistles, and of these, 73 do not occur again in the New Testament. The latter are as follows:

"Purity" (iv. 12; v. 2); "uncertainty" (vi. 17); "modesty" (ii. 9); "recompense" (v. 4); "men-stealers" (i. 10); "irreproachable" (iii. 2); "oppositions" (vi. 20); "ransom" (ii. 6); "interminable" (i. 4); "to-be-rejected" (iv. 4); "acceptable" (ii. 3; v. 4); "acceptation" (i. 15; iv. 9); "treasuring-up" (vi. 19); "unapproachable" (vi. 16); "to-exercise-authority" (ii. 12); "degree" (iii. 13); "hurtful" (vi. 9); "old wives" (iv. 7); "exercise" (iv. 8); "constant quarrellings"

(vi. 5); "sustenance" (vi. 8); "double-tongued" (iii. 8); "persecutor" (i. 13); "base" (iii. 15); "descendants" (v. 4); "investigation" (i. 4); "intercessions" (ii. 1; iv. 5); "being-nourished" (iv. 6); "impart-relief" (v. 10, 16); "perjurors" (i. 10); "sharply-rebuke" (v. 1); "to-teach-other-doctrines" (i. 3; vi. 3); "liberal-in-distributing" (vi. 18); "tranquil" (ii. 2); "fear-of-God" (ii. 10); "let-be-put-on-the-list" (v. 9); "guise" (ii. 9); "may-have-grown-wanton-against" (v. 11); "being cauterized" (iv. 2); "ready-to-communicate" (vi. 18); "modest" (ii. 9; iii. 2); "decently" (ii. 9); "disputes-of-words" (vi. 4); "vain-talking" (i. 6); "reception" (iv. 3); "smiters-of-mothers" (i. 9); "left-alone" (v. 5); "novice" (iii. 6); "sick" (vi. 4); "entertain-strangers" (v. 10); "to-rule-the-house" (v. 14); "confessedly" (iii. 16); "smiters-of-fathers" (i. 9); "pierced" (vi. 10); "plaitings" (ii. 9); "gain" (vi. 5, 6); "meekness-of-spirit" (vi. 11); "prejudice" (v. 21); "partiality" (v. 21); "expressly" (iv. 1); "coverings" (vi. 8); "stomach" (v. 23); "to-bear-children" (v. 14); "child-bearing" (ii. 15); "brought-up children" (v. 10); "drink water" (v. 23); "superabounded" (i. 14); "suspicious" (vi. 4); "to-be-high-minded" (vi. 17); "love-of-money" (vi. 10); "tattlers" (v. 13); "speakers-of-lies" (iv. 2); "falsely-named" (vi. 20).

This Epistle is wonderfully rich in word-studies. It and the two companion Letters include a little group of medical terms, which may reasonably be accounted for by the Apostle's constant inter-course with "the beloved physician." Among such words are:

"Healthful" (i. 10); "bring-to-birth-alive" (vi. 13; cf. Luke xvii. 33; Acts vii. 19); "cancer" (2 Tim. ii. 17); "patient-of-ill" (2 Tim. ii. 24). "Healthful" is a key-thought in these Letters, occurring nine times. "Teaching" is another keyword, occurring eight times in 1 Timothy, three times in 2 Timothy, and four times in Titus. "Deposit-committed," a banker's term, is another interesting word, and recurs three times (1 Tim. vi. 20; 2 Tim. i. 12, 14).

Other arresting words are,

"Godly," "godliness," "fables," "genealogies," "faithful," "Saviour," "the faith," or "faith," occurring nineteen times in 1 Timothy, eight times in 2 Timothy, and five times in Titus ; "neophyte" (iii. 6).

Mark the addition of "mercy" to "grace" and "peace," in all three Epistles, but never in a Church Epistle.

The occurrence five times of the expression "a faithful saying" (1 Tim. i. 15 ; iii. 1 ; iv. 9 ; 2 Tim. ii. 11 ; Titus iii. 8), is of special interest, as it seems to point to certain Logia current in the early Churches, or the use of liturgical forms. The five together constitute a singularly full doctrine : Christ's *coming*—the way of sins' forgiveness (1 Tim. i. 15). Christ's *ministry*—the way of noble service (1 Tim. iii. 1). Christ's *life*—the way of spiritual progress (1 Tim. iv. 9). Christ's *world*—the way of honourable work (Titus iii. 8). Christ's *strength*—the way of successful suffering (2 Tim. ii. 11).

In the same connection may be considered such passages as iii. 16, and vi. 15, 16 ; which are hymn-forms, and, presumably, were two of a number of hymns sung by the early Church (Eph. v. 19). Dr. David Smith has suggested that there was extant a Teacher's Manual, composed, probably, by Luke. Such a Manual, it is suggested, would furnish an "outline" of the Evangelic Tradition ; directions for the Christian use of the Old Testament Scriptures ; a variety of evangelical truths and practical maxims, and a collection of Christian hymns. The "Faithful Sayings," and the "Mystery of Godliness," are supposed to be quotations from this Manual.

There are several weighty doctrinal passages in this Epistle. Notably chapter iii. 16, just referred to, which is a description of the work of Christ from His Incarnation to His final Glory. Six truths are set forth in as many lines.

Christ was :

"Manifest in the flesh," at His birth, and during His life ;
"Justified in spirit," when He died ;
"Seen of angels," between His death and Pentecost ;
"Preached among nations," at Pentecost and since ;
"Believed on in the world," during His Kingdom, which is to come ; and
"Received up in glory," His place at the Throne of God.

Other great doctrinal statements are, chapter vi. 15, 16, from which Handel drew inspiration for his great Oratorio, and from which the name Athanasius is derived (athanasia), chapter i. 17 ; where note "King of the ages" (cf. Rev. xv. 3).

Chapter i. 1. "Saviour" occurs only twenty-four times in the New Testament, and of these, ten are in the Pastoral Epistles. Of the twenty-four occurrences, eight refer to the Father, and of these eight, six are in these Epistles (i. 1; ii. 3; iv. 10; Tit. i. 3 ; ii. 10 ; iii. 4). Worthy also of special attention is chapter ii. 5.

NOTE 88

"The Christian Pastor" in 1 Timothy.

1. **His Office.**   i. 1, 11, 12, 18; ii. 7; iii. 1; i. 11; vi. 13.

2. **His Qualifications.**   i. 16, 18; iii. 2; iii. 4, 5, 6; iv. 6, 12, 15, 16; v. 21, 22; vi. 13, 14.

3. **His Duties as Preacher.**   i. 4; iv. 7; vi. 4; ii. 7, 8; iv. 6, 7, 11; vi. 17-19; iii. 8-15; iv. 13-16; v. 4-16, 20, 21; vi. 1, 2, 4, 17-19, 20, 21.

4. **His Duties as Pastor.**   ii. 1, 2; iii. 15; i. 3, 4; i. 18, 19; vi. 12; iii. 2, 3; vi. 10; iii. 4-7, 8-13; v. 1, 2, 4-16, 20-22; vi. 11, 12, 20.

5. **His Personal Life.**   i. 5, 16, 18; iii. 2, 4, 7, 8, 10, 15, 16; v. 22, 23; vi. 6-8, 9, 20.

Analysis of 1 Timothy

INTRODUCTION (i. 1, 2).

I. THE CHURCH OF GOD (i. 3-iii. 13).

1. **Its Doctrine** (i. 3-20).
   (i.) The Character and Content of the Truth,   3-11.
   (ii.) The Commission of Paul, and Charge to
       Timothy, ...   12-20.

2. **Its Worship** (ii. 1-15).
   (i.) The Matter of Prayer in Public Worship,   1-10.
   (ii.) The Manner of Women in Public Worship,   11-15.

3. **Its Oversight** (iii. 1-13).
   (i.) Bishops, their Qualifications and Func-
       tions, ...   1-7.
   (ii.) Deacons, their Qualifications and Functions,   8-13.

II. THE MINISTRY OF TIMOTHY (iii. 14-vi. 19).

1. **His Walk.** PERSONAL (iii. 14-iv. 16).
   (i.) His Relation to Truth in the Church,   ...   iii. 14-16.
   (ii.) His Relation to Error in the Church,   ...   iv. 1-11.
   (iii.) His Relation to All in the Church, ...   iv. 12-16.

2. **His Work.** OFFICIAL (v. 1-vi. 19).
   (i.) His Duty towards the Flock, ...   v. 1-vi. 2.
   (ii.) His Duty towards the Evil, ...   vi. 3-16.
   (iii.) His Duty towards the Rich, ...   vi. 17-19.

CONCLUSION (iv. 20, 21).

TITUS

GROUP 4.

Keyword : RESPONSIBILITY.   ECCLESIOLOGICAL.

Place of Writing : MACEDONIA (?)   DATE : 67 A.D.

THE TWELFTH LETTER IN POINT OF ORDER.

TITUS.

IT is evidence of the foresight and wisdom of the Apostle Paul that he selected two young men such as Timothy and Titus to assist him in his strenuous ministry, and to carry on the work when he would no longer be able to do so. They are a study in comparisons and contrasts. As to comparisons, both were young ; both were gifted ; both were most intimate with and appreciated by Paul ; both were sent on delicate and difficult missions— Timothy to Ephesus, and Titus to Corinth and Crete ; both were written to by Paul, and both survived him. As to contrasts, Timothy was half Jew, half Gentile ; Titus was a pure Gentile. Timothy was circumcised ; Titus was not. In several of his letters Paul associates Timothy with himself in the address, but never Titus. Timothy is prominent in the ACTS, but Titus is never named. Timothy was nervous and retiring in disposition, but Titus was of stronger and sterner quality. Their gifts were diverse, and, in consequence, so were their operations.

The home of Titus seems to have been in the Syrian Antioch, and he was one of Paul's converts. At the Jerusalem Conference, in A.D. 51, he was made a test case (Acts xv ; Gal. ii. 3) ; but he did not accompany Paul on his Second Missionary Journey.

On the Third Journey Titus was despatched from Ephesus to Corinth to discover and report to Paul what was the effect upon the Achaian Church of the Letter he had written to them (2 Cor. ii. 12, 13 ; viii.; ix). Titus met the Apostle in Macedonia with comforting news (Acts xx. 2 ; 2 Cor. vii. 5). From the Epistle before us we learn that this young man was left in Crete (i. 5), to attend to disorders which had arisen there, a work for which his experience at Corinth had eminently fitted him. From the comparatively few references to him, we judge that he was a man of strong affection, of devout enthusiasm, of practical capability, and of sound wisdom and discretion.

Paul had the eye and the intellect of a great general, and he appointed his helpers to tasks for which he judged them to be suitable by nature and endowment. He judged that Titus and not Timothy was the man for the crisis at Corinth and

Crete, and that Timothy and not Titus was the man for the task at Ephesus. Temperament and training must always determine our task.

THE CHURCH IN CRETE.

Crete was a large island in the Mediterranean, 270 miles in length, 50 at the broadest, and 589 in circumference, due south of the Ægean Sea. That the Cretans had an unenviable reputation is witnessed to not only by Paul, but also by Plutarch, Leonides, Livy, Polybius and others. A prophet of their own, Epimenides, said, "the Cretians are alway liars, evil beasts, slow bellies"; and Paul says, "This witness is true" (i. 12, 13). Leonides wrote, "The Cretans are always brigands and piratical, and unjust. Whoever knew justice among Cretans?" "Cretizing" was synonymous with "lying," and "playing the Cretan with a Cretan" meant "out-tricking a trickster." Yet, in such a place there were Christians. We have no definite knowledge of how Christianity was introduced into the Island, but we know that Cretes were among those who witnessed the wonder of Pentecost, and, no doubt, heard Peter's Pentecostal sermon (Acts ii. 11). It is most likely that some of these would believe, and would carry the Gospel back to their people. After Paul was released from

prison in Rome he visited Crete (i. 5). He was
there long enough to discern the character of the
inhabitants, and, no doubt, to make converts;
but feeling the necessity of wintering in some more
peaceful retreat (iii. 12), he was not able to organise
the Cretan Assemblies, nor to deal with errors
which threatened the Church. These things he
left to Titus to do (i. 5).

The Date.

This Letter must have been written shortly after
I TIMOTHY, probably in 67 A.D.

The Purpose.

The immediate occasion was to tell Titus that the
Apostle meant to send Artemas or Tychicus to
replace him in Crete, and to bid him "come unto
him at Nicopolis." But Paul always made an
immediate occasion one for the imparting of
instruction and exhortation. The lines followed
here follow those in I TIMOTHY. After a pregnant
introduction (i. 1-4), the topics are, the appointment
of elders (i. 5-9); warning against Judaic Gnosticism
(i. 10-ii.1); directions for the conduct of various
classes of the community (ii. 2-10), supplying a
doctrinal motive (ii. 11-15); a passage on Christian
conduct in relation to civil and social life (iii. 1-8);
warning against heretical persons (iii. 9-11), and a

conclusion dealing with some personal matters (iii. 12-15). Thus, the Epistle is occupied with Church order, ordination, and organisation.

NOTES.

Some of the notes in 1 TIMOTHY apply to this Epistle also. In Westcott and Hort's Text there are not more than 700 words in TITUS, yet, what words! It has been said that the Epistle is colourless and monotonous, but this estimate reflects rather upon the judgment of those who make it. Farrar has spoken of the Letter as "a priceless and unrivalled manual of pastoral advice;" and Luther said: "This is a short Epistle, but yet such a quintessence of Christian doctrine, and composed in such a masterly manner, that it contains all that is needful for Christian knowledge and life."

The basis of Paul's instruction is always doctrinal. As religion is the foundation of morality, so is creed of conduct. As in 1 TIMOTHY, so here, there are several great doctrinal statements. The first is in chapter i. 1-4, which is an amazingly pregnant utterance, reminding one of the introduction to ROMANS. What great notes make this music— God, Lord Jesus, Christ, Saviour, Elect, Faith, Truth, Hope, Eternal Life, Preaching, Full-Knowledge, Manifestation, Grace, Mercy, Peace!

A second statement is in chapter iii. 4-7, which has been spoken of as "unparalleled for beauty and perfectness."

But the *locus classicus* of the Epistle is chapter ii. 11-14. What a sweep of truth lies between Christ's advent of grace in verse 11, and His advent in glory in verse 13. We look *back* on the salvation grace has brought us ; we look *round* on our present duty ; and we look *forward* to the coming glory. There are two sides to the Christian life, a negative and a positive (12), and on the positive side we are to live "soberly" selfward, "righteously" manward, and "godly" Godward. There is the Kingdom within, the Kingdom around, and the Kingdom to come. Note also the teaching concerning the Lord's Second Advent in two stages (13) ; "the blessed hope," that is, of the Church, the hope of meeting Christ "in the air" (cf. 1 Thess. iv. 15-17); and "the glorious appearing," that is, Christ's appearing with the Church when He comes to the earth (2 Thess. ii.). Mark also, in verse 14, the three truths of salvation, sanctification, and service.

Here, then, is a summary of the New Testament. The Epiphany of Grace well describes the Gospels and Acts ; the instructions in holy living, the Epistles ; and the expectation of the Lord's Return, the Apocalypse.

Short as this Epistle is, there are no less than 44 words used which do not occur in any other of Paul's Letters, and of these, 29 do not occur again in the New Testament. The following are the latter :

"Heretic" (iii. 10); "not to be condemned" (ii. 8); "self-condemned" (iii. 11); "incorruptness" (ii. 7); "cannot lie" (i. 2); "abominable" (i. 16); "temperate" (i. 8); "perverted" (iii. 11); "mightest-go-on-to-set-right" (i. 5); "stop the mouths of" (i. 11); "as becomes sacred ones" (ii. 3); "Jewish" (i. 14); "teachers of what is right" (ii. 3); "deportment" (ii. 3); "vaintalkers" (i. 10); "keepers at home" (ii. 5); "passionate" (i. 7); "peculiar" (ii. 14); "let despise" (ii. 15); "aged" (ii. 3); "hateful" (iii. 3); "brings salvation" (ii. 11); "may school" (ii. 4); "discreetly" (ii. 12); "a lover of good" (i. 8); "lovers of husbands" (ii. 4); "lovers of children" (ii. 4); "mind deceivers" (i. 10); "may take care" (iii. 8).

Dominating words in the Letter are "Saviour," "sound," or "healthy," applied to the doctrine ; "sober-minded," and "good works."

NOTE 89
A Modern Note on Crete.

TUESDAY, May 20th, 1941.—"The German attack on Crete began with air-raids and the dropping of some 1500 parachute troops. A further 3000 were dropped next day." Saturday, May 24th, 1941.—"The fighting in Crete grew steadily more desperate." Sunday, June 1st, 1941.—"The War Office announced that the Allied troops had evacuated Crete. Allied losses were very heavy, and the failure was due to lack of air support. This was the first conquest of an island from the air." Tuesday, June 10th, 1941.—"In the debate on the loss of Crete, Mr. Churchill said that 17,000 men had been evacuated, and our total losses were about 15,000. German losses were estimated at 17,000." *The Daily Telegraph's* "Story of the War."

The Germans surrendered to the British at Crete in May, 1945.

Analysis of Titus

INTRODUCTION (i. 1-4).

I. THE RULE OF THE CHURCH (i. 5 16).
1. The Nature of it, ... 5-9.
2. The Necessity for it, ... 10-16.

II. THE WALK OF THE CHURCH (ii. 1-15).
1. The Guiding Precepts, ... 1-10.
2. The Enabling Power, ... 11-15.

III. THE STATE AND THE CHURCH (iii. 1-11).
1. Her Outward Duty, ... 1-7.
2. Her Inward Discipline, ... 8-11.

CONCLUSION (iii. 12-15).

NOTE 90

A Comment on Titus ii. 11-14.

VERSE 11 refers to the First Advent, which is of grace, and verse 13, to the Second Advent, which is of glory. The instruction of God's grace is both negative (12a) and positive (12b). On the negative side it consists in denying ungodliness and worldly desires; and on the positive side it sets before us a threefold relation and obligation: *selfward*, we are to live "soberly"; *manward*, we are to live "righteously"; and *Godward*, we are to live "godly."

The two stages of the Second Advent are here distinguished (13): "the blessed hope" of the Church is that Christ will come to the air for His people (1 Thess. iv.), and "the glorious appearing" tells of His coming to the earth.

Observe that in verse 14 are the three truths of salvation, sanctification, and service.

2 TIMOTHY

GROUP 4.

Keyword : FIDELITY.   ECCLESIOLOGICAL.

Place of Writing : ROME.   DATE : 67-68. A.D.

THE THIRTEENTH LETTER IN POINT OF ORDER.

TIMOTHY.

SOME particulars regarding this loved companion of Paul will be found in the introduction to the First Epistle addressed to him, but there are other particulars which belong specially to this Epistle. A discerning reading of it will show that, underlying the obvious affection of the great Apostle for his son in the faith, there is a note of misgiving and anxiety. We cannot be surprised at this if we appreciate the situation.

Paul again a prisoner, was not now in a "hired house" (Acts xxviii. 30), but in the common dungeon, probably the dark, damp, fetid Tullianum, known as "the sepulchre," for many in it were slowly eaten alive by rats. After the great fire of Rome, in A.D. 64, which was attributed to the Christians, and for which hosts of them were put to most horrible death, it was a crime to confess to being a Christian, and such were savagely persecuted.

This, surely, must account for Paul being so forsaken at last (iv. 16), and also, for his great gratitude
to Onesiphorus for having risked his life to visit
him in prison (i. 16-18).

Timothy, as we have seen, was of a timid disposition, and was, perhaps, easily discouraged.
He had been given a difficult task at Ephesus
(1 Tim. i. 3, 4), and seems to have been disposed
to leave it (1 Tim. i. 18 ; iv. 12, 16). And now
that his beloved leader and best friend was again
a prisoner at Rome, it would appear that he was in
danger of yielding to his natural inclinations, and
of succumbing to his timidity and fear. Only
this danger can account for the repeated exhortations of this Letter. We cannot imagine anyone
exhorting Paul as he exhorted Timothy, for he
was never in sight of that particular danger. Paul
bids this young minister to "re-kindle" or "fan
into flame" (*anazōpurein*) the gift of God in him
(i. 6). And he says : "God has not given us a
timid spirit" (i. 7, Moffatt). And he expresses the
hope, yea, the confidence that in Timothy will be
found the faith that was in his mother and grandmother (i. 5). But Paul exhorts him "not to be
ashamed to testify" (i. 8), and urges "Whatever
happens, be self-possessed, flinch from no suffering,
do your work as an evangelist, and discharge all

your duties as a minister" (iv. 5, Moffatt). Other such like exhortations are, "Join me in bearing suffering for the Gospel ;" "Now, my son, be strong in the grace of Christ Jesus ;" "Join the ranks of those who bear suffering ;" "Do your utmost to let God see that you at least are a sound workman ;" "Keep the great securities of your faith intact, by the aid of the Holy Spirit ;" "Hold you to what you have been taught, hold to your convictions" (i. 8 ; ii. 1 ; ii. 3 ; ii. 15 ; i. 14 ; iii. 14 ; Moffatt). Why such repeated exhortations, if Timothy was in no danger of falling short of these standards ? Paul was fully conscious that his own end was near (iv. 6), and so he was the more anxious to give his young friend every encouragement to stand up to his job. For this reason also, he wanted to see him once again (iv. 9, 21). It is in this light that we shall best understand the inner significance of this remarkable Letter.

The Date.

Although reference has already been made to Paul's movements at this time, it may be well to summarize the particulars on a basis of probability. He was released from his first Roman imprisonment in 63 A.D. Visited Philippi for the fourth time (Phil. ii. 24). Went to Colossae (Philemon 22).

Then, perhaps, to Spain (Rom. xv. 28). Back again to Ephesus (1 Tim. i. 3), where he left Timothy in charge, and himself went on to Macedonia (1 Tim. i. 3). From Macedonia he wrote the first Letter to Timothy ; and while there, probably he visited Philippi and Corinth. From thence he went to Crete (Titus i. 5), where he left Titus in charge, when he himself went again into Asia, probably to Ephesus, and from thence he wrote the Letter to Titus. He then went to Miletus, and left Trophimus there, sick (2 Tim. iv. 20), when he himself went on to Troas (2 Tim. iv. 13), and on to Corinth (2 Tim. iv. 20), on his way to Nicopolis to winter (Titus iii. 12). But he was suddenly rearrested, perhaps at Corinth, and spent that winter at Rome (2 Tim. iv. 21), instead of at Nicopolis as he intended. From Rome he wrote this last Letter to Timothy (i. 8 ; iv. 6). By this it is assumed (a) that these Letters are Paul's ; and (b) that they were written after and not before his two years' imprisonment at Rome. If Paul was executed early in A.D. 68, 2 TIMOTHY must have been written at the beginning of the winter of A.D. 67.

THE PURPOSE.

Paul's object in writing was, firstly, to confirm and encourage Timothy in his ministry, who, upon hearing of his friend's rearrest, seems to have begun to fear and to falter (i. 6-8) ; and, secondly, to bid Timothy to come to him to Rome with the utmost speed (i. 4 ; iv. 9, 13, 21). Paul earnestly wanted to see his dear young friend once again, and wanted him to bring certain cherished possessions which, on account of his precipitate rearrest, he had been unable to collect (iv. 13) ; and so he urges him to come before the winter storms closed the Mediterranean, or else, he hints, Timothy may arrive too late.

Thoughts which had occupied the Apostle's mind when he wrote 1 TIMOTHY and TITUS are found here—false doctrine, the presence of opponents, coming evil days, the glory of the Gospel, and exhortations to holiness of life and boldness of testimony ; but there is a change of outlook. When Paul wrote the other two Epistles he was free, but now he is bound ; when he wrote them, his hopes of continued ministry (Phil. i. 24-26) had been realised, but now, all such hope has vanished (iv. 6). This Letter is less formal and more personal than the other two, and its power and charm are largely due to this fact. Its outstanding claim to our special attention is in the fact that it is the last Letter which the great Apostle wrote ; the last utterance of one of the greatest men that God ever made.

NOTES.

In these four short chapters (83 verses) there are 77 words used which do not occur in any other of Paul's Writings; and of these, 43 do not occur again in the New Testament.

The latter are as follows:

"Contend" (ii. 5); "out of season" (iv. 2); "incontinent" (iii. 3); "to kindle up" (i. 6); "release" (iv. 6); "awake up" (ii. 26); "refreshed" (i. 16); "forbearing" (ii. 24); "savage" (iii. 3); "oppose" (ii. 25); "undisciplined" (ii. 23); "turn away from" (iii. 5); "complete" (iii. 17); "implacable" (iii. 3); "not lovers of good" (iii. 3); "gangrene" (ii. 17); "imposters" (iii. 13); "silly women" (iii. 6); "cowardice" (i. 7); "fully manifest" (iii. 9); "conviction" (iii. 16); "are entering" (iii. 6); "correction" (iii. 16); "will heap up" (iv. 3); "God-inspired" (iii. 16); "utterly corrupted" (iii. 8); "having itching ears" (iv. 3); "dispute about words" (ii. 14); "grandmother" (i. 5); "parchments" (iv. 13); "youthful" (ii. 22); "straightly cutting" (ii. 15); "assured of" (iii. 14); "enrolled as a soldier" (ii. 4); "suffered evils along with" (i. 8; ii. 3); "wise discretion" (i. 7); "cloak" (iv. 13); "lovers of self" (iii. 2); "lovers of pleasure" (iii. 4); "lovers of God" (iii. 4); "smith" (iv. 14); "profitable" (ii. 14).

Many of these words are little pictures, and will repay careful study.

Notice the "lovers" in chapter iii. 2-4; "self-lovers," "money-lovers," "pleasure-lovers," "God-lovers," and "not-lovers-of-good."

No fewer than twenty-three names are mentioned in this Epistle. Mark carefully what is said about each. Surely these references constitute a Judgment-Seat!

In chapter iv. 13, is one of the most pathetic references in literature. Dr. Farrar is eloquent over the cloak, the papyrus-rolls, and the parchments. The cloak, he says, was a kind of "over-all," which Paul may have made for himself, and which had done good service for many a long day. It must have been an old friend, over land, on the sea, and in the sea. The papyrus-rolls may have been presents which he had received, or relics of his student days. The parchments may have been some of the Old Testament Books (iii. 15), so dear to the Apostle. At the end of life he had not lost interest in life, he still wanted to read, as he had bidden Timothy do (1 Tim. iv. 13). For nearly twenty years Paul had been travelling, and so had not opportunity nor need to accumulate belongings ; yet, is it not pathetic that at last all he claims is a "cloak," a few "books," and "parchments," and we do not know if ever he received them ! But Paul's riches were in the world for which he had lived, and not in this world. In this he was followed by the great Tyndale, whose letter from the damp cell of his prison at Vilvoorde may well be placed by the side of this bit of Paul's.

"I entreat your lordship, and that by the Lord Jesus, that if I must remain here for the winter, you would beg the Commissary to be so kind as to send me, from the things of mine which he has, a warmer cap—I feel the cold painfully in my head. Also a warmer cloak to patch my leggings. My overcoat is worn out, my shirts even are worn out. He has a woollen shirt of mine, if he will send it. But most of all I entreat and implore your kindness to do your best with the Commissary to be so good as to send me my Hebrew Bible, grammar, and vocabulary, that I may spend my time in that pursuit. WILLIAM TYNDALE."

Another wonderful passage is chapter iv. 6-8, in which the Apostle reviews all his life, here and hereafter ; the present in verse 6 ; the past in verse 7 ; and the future in verse 8. That is how a great Christian faces death.

Other passages to study are—the prophetic reference to the "last days" (iii. 1-9, 13 ; cf. 1. Tim. iv. 1-3) ; the reference to his First Missionary Journey (iii. 10, 11) : the reference to Timothy's godly upbringing (i. 5 ; iii. 14, 15) ; the reference to the power and purpose of Holy Scripture (iii. 16, 17) : the reference to Onesiphorus (i. 16-18) ; and the illustrative figures in chapter ii., son (1) ; soldier (3, 4) ; wrestler (5) ; husbandman (6) ; workman (15) ; vessel (20, 21) ; and servant (24).

One cannot but notice the seeming inconsistency of verses 6 and 9, 21, of chapter iv. A perfectly natural explanation of this would be, that at verse 8, Paul was interrupted by a summons to appear before Nero, and that, contrary to his expectation, sentence on him was suspended, and that he was put back into prison for an unknown period ; and that, in the light of what had happened, he continued the Letter from verse 9, inviting Timothy to come to him.

Chapter i. is occupied with the past ; chapter ii., with the present ; chapter iii., with the future ; and chapter iv., with all three.

NOTE 91
Paul's Last Five Years.

A.D.	PAUL.	CONTEMPORARY EVENTS.
63	Roman trial and acquittal. In Macedonia—Philippi (Phil. ii. 24). At Colossae (Phile. 22).	
64	To Spain (Rom. xv. 24, 28).	Great fire at Rome, and the persecution of Roman Christians under Nero.
65	. . . . .	Death of Seneca.
66	At Ephesus (1 Tim. i. 3). In Macedonia (1 Tim. i. 3). At Ephesus.	The Jewish War begins.
67	Writes 1 Timothy. At Miletus—Corinth (2 Tim. iv. 20). Writes to Titus. At Nicopolis (Tit. iii. 12).	
68	Re - arrested and taken to Rome. Writes 2 Timothy. Trial and execution at Rome.	Death of Nero.

Analysis of 2 Timothy

INTRODUCTION (i. 1-5).

I. THE PERSONAL EQUIPMENT FOR THE MINISTRY
(i. 6-ii. 26).

1. The Essential Qualities (i. 6-18).

2. The Necessary Discipline (ii. 1-26).

II. THE PUBLIC FULFILMENT OF THE MINISTRY.
(iii.-iv. 18).

1. The Coming Change (iii.).

2. The Closing Charge (iv. 1-8).

CONCLUSION (iv. 19-22).

HEBREWS

Keyword : BETTER.

WE are placing this Epistle between the Pauline and Catholic Epistles, but do not bracket it with either group. It is in a class by itself, and must be judged of from its own standpoint.

For introduction the relevant questions are : Who were the original readers of this Epistle ? What was the date of writing ? Where was it written ? Who was the author ? What are the characteristics of the Epistle ? What was the occasion of writing ? What was the author's design ? Each of these questions has been a subject of much controversy, and here we can only glance at them.

THE READERS.

Not a little is said in the Epistle about those for whom it was first written. They were Hebrews (i. 1). They were well acquainted with the Writings of the Old Testament (i. 1, 5, 7, 8, 10 ; ii. 6, 12 ; iii 2, 17 ; iv. 14, 15 ; v. 1-4, 7 ; vii. 11 ; ix. 1-10, They were Jewish Christians, who had received the Gospel from the Apostles themselves, and from those who had heard the Lord (ii. 1-3 ;

iii. 1, 14 ; iv. 1, 2, 14). They had been witnesses of miracles and of the wonderful gifts bestowed by the Holy Spirit (ii. 4). They had been Christians for a long time, for they were old enough in spiritual life to have become "teachers of others" (v. 12) ; they are bidden "call to remembrance the former days" (x. 32) ; and their original instructors had passed away (xiii. 7). They had in time past ministered to the saints, and still were doing so (vi. 10). They had passed through "a great conflict of suffering" (x. 32-34), but their sufferings had not extended to martyrdom (xii. 4). The readers of the Epistle were members of a Church at some definite place (xiii. 19, 23). The location of this Church has been surmised to have been at Jerusalem, or Alexandria, or Corinth, or Ephesus, or Rome. They were in danger of drifting from the faith, back into Judaism (ii. 1 ; iii. 6, 14 ; iv. 1, 11 ; v. 11, 12 ; vi. 1-8, 11, 12 ; ix. 9, 10 ; x. 23, 36-39 ; xiii. 9-12). For a right understanding of the Epistle these particulars should be carefully considered.

THE DATE.

By the allusion to Timothy in chapter xiii. 23, and the absence of any reference to the fall of Jerusalem in A.D. 70, it seems clear that this Epistle was written in the critical period between A.D.

64 and A.D. 67, at which latter date the Jewish War commenced, which seems to be anticipated in chapter x. 25. If this date be correct, and it almost certainly is, it has a distinct bearing upon the authorship of the Epistle. If it were written at the end of A.D. 67, or at the beginning of A.D. 68, it could not have been written by Paul, for then he was either in a dungeon in Rome, or already dead ; and obviously 2 TIMOTHY was the last letter he wrote. If it were written after A.D. 63, and before A.D. 67 Paul was then travelling, between his two Roman imprisonments, and his mind was occupied with the matters of 1 TIMOTHY and TITUS.

THE PLACE OF WRITING.

There is nothing to indicate where the Epistle was written. The reference in chapter xiii. 24, admits of two opposite renderings. It may describe Italian Christians in their own country, or Italian Christians in a foreign land. On this point Bishop Westcott says : "The place of writing must be left in complete uncertainty. Plausible conjectures unsupported by evidence cannot remove our ignorance even if they satisfy our curiosity."

THE AUTHOR.

Much ingenuity has been exhibited in the effort to discover who wrote this Epistle, but the one

thing that can be said with confidence is that we
do not know. The names which have been suggested are Paul, Silas, Titus, Mark, Clement,
Luke, Aquila, Priscilla, Barnabas, and Apollos.
Of these ten, the claims of Luke, Barnabas and
Apollos, have been strongly presented. About
the Pauline authorship there has always been
doubt, and to-day the all but unanimous verdict
is that Paul did not write this Epistle. Dean
Farrar, who argues eloquently for the authorship
of Apollos, has given his reasons for definitely
rejecting the Pauline authorship. He says : "The
differences between the Epistle to the Hebrews
and the Epistles of St. Paul are differences which
go down to the roots of the being. That the same
pen should have been engaged on both is a psychological impossibility. The Greek is far better than
the Greek of St. Paul. St. Paul is often stately and
often rhetorical, and sometimes writes more in
the style of a treatise than of a letter ; but the
stateliness and rhetoric and systematic treatment
of the Epistle to the Hebrews in no way resemble
his. The form and rhythm of its sentences are
wholly different. . . . The writer (of HEBREWS)
cites differently from St. Paul ; he writes differently ; he argues differently ; he thinks differently ;
he declaims differently ; he constructs and

connects his sentences differently ; he builds up his paragraphs on a wholly different model. " But let no one suppose that anything is lost if the idea is surrendered that Paul wrote HEBREWS. Well has Dr. Adolph Saphir said : "Whoever is the author of this Epistle, its value and authority remain the same ;" and he quotes from Thiersch to this effect : "We may compare it to a painting of perfect beauty, which had been regarded as a work of Raphael. If it should be proved that it was not painted by Raphael, we have thereby not lost a classical piece of art, but gained another master of first rank. " There we must leave it, for, as Origen said : "Who it was who wrote the Epistle, God only knows certainly. "

CHARACTERISTICS OF THE EPISTLE.

As to its language, Bishop Westcott has said that "the Epistle is both in vocabulary and style purer and more vigorous than that of any other book of the New Testament. " It has not fewer than 157 words which are peculiar to itself. While in this Writing there is no striving after effect, yet, as Dr. Wickham says, "In a sense beyond any other Epistle in the New Testament HEBREWS is an artistic whole. " In its superb introduction (i. 1-4) many of the characteristics of the Epistle are discernible, its originality, its stateliness, its artistic balance of the language, its rhythm, its play upon words, its sweep of thought, and its profoundness.

"God having of old time spoken to the fathers in the prophets, in many parts and in many modes, spake to us at the end of these days in a Son, Whom He appointed Heir of all things, through Whom He also made the world. Who, being the effulgence of His glory, and the expression of His essence, and so bearing all things by the word of His power, after He had Himself made purification of sins, sat down on the right hand of the Majesty on high ; having become so much better than the angels, as He hath inherited a more excellent name than they."

This is a passage which must be placed by the prologue to the Fourth Gospel (i. 1-18), and by Paul's great passage in COLOSSIANS (i. 14-20). The author's love for musical euphony is seen in his amplitude of expression. For example, instead of simply saying "reward," he says. "recompense of reward" ; and instead of simply saying "blood" he says "shedding of blood."

It is difficult, perhaps impossible, to reproduce in a translation the author's play upon words (*paronomasia*) in the original, but the sound may convey some idea of this. He begins with the words *polumeros* and *polutropos*, "many parts," and "many ways" (i. 1). In chapter ii. 5, 8, are *hupetaxen*, "did He subject," *anupotakton*, "unsubject," and *hupotetagmena*, "subjected." In chapter v. 8, are *emathen*, and *epathen*, "He learned," and "He suffered." In chapter v. 14, are *kalou*, and *kakou*, "good" and "evil." In chapter ix. 10, are *brōmasin*, and *pomasin*, "meats" and "drinks." In chapter vii. 13, are *meteschēken* and *proseschēken*, "has part in," and "has given attendance at." These are only a few examples of what is to be found throughout. Then, the Epistle is rich in imagery. The word of God is likened to a sword (iv. 12). Hope is likened to an anchor (vi. 19). The figure of an amphitheatre is used to great purpose (xii. 1). A whole picture often lies in a single word ; as, for example, in chapter iv. 2, to mix with, to mingle together, to blend : in chapter iv. 13, the verb translated "opened" is a word which means to grip the neck ; to bend the neck back, so as to make bare or expose the throat, as in slaughtering animals ; and in chapter x. 33, "made a gazing-stock," is exposed as in theatre.

It is noteworthy that, whereas in Paul's Writings we get such full divine titles as "Lord Jesus Christ," or "Christ Jesus our Lord," some 68 times, in HEBREWS we get simply "Jesus," and "Christ," and "Lord."

It should also be observed how the writer of this Epistle quotes the Old Testament. All his quotations, except in chapter x. 30 (Deut. xxxii.

35) are taken from the LXX, even when that Version differs from the original Hebrew; and these quotations are introduced in a peculiar way, by such expressions as "said He," "the Holy Spirit saith," "while it is said," "He spake," "He that said" (i. 5-14 ; iii. 7, 15 ; iv. 3, 4 ; v. 14 ; vii. 14, 21 ; vii. 5, 8, etc.) ; and only once is a human author named (iv. 7).

No one can miss the recurrence of certain words in this Epistle, which either are peculiar to it, or here are given a special emphasis. Of such, two may be named, "eternal," and "better." Here are, "eternal salvation" (v. 9), "eternal judgment" (vi. 2) ; "eternal redemption" (ix. 12) ; "eternal Spirit" (ix. 14) ; "eternal inheritance" (ix. 15) ; and "eternal covenant" (xiii. 20) ; and, in addition, the kindred idea "for ever" occurs twelve times. The word "better" occurs more often here than in all the rest of the New Testament, namely thirteen times.   We have "better than angels," "better things," "a better hope," "a better coven-ant," "better promises," "better sacrifices," "a better possession," "a better country," "a better resurrection," "some better time," and "the blood of sprinkling which speaketh better things than that of Abel."

The three stern passages should be carefully

pondered, chapters vi. 4-8 ; x. 26-31 ; xii. 16, 17 :
and, of course, the magnificent faith gallery in
chapter xi. The Epistle is characterised by contrasts which are profoundly striking and significant.
These contrasts are—between the Son and Angels
(i-ii) ; between the Son and Moses (iii. 1-11) ;
between the rest of Canaan and the rest of God
(iii. 12-iv. 13) ; between Christ and Aaron (iv. 14-
v. 10) ; between babyhood and maturity (v. 11-14) ;
between apostasy and faithfulness (vi) ; between
the Melchisedecan and Aaronic priesthoods (vii) ;
between the Old Covenant and the New (viii) ;
between the offerings of the Law and the Offering
of Christ (ix-x. 18) ; between punishment under
the Law and under the Gospel (x. 19-39) ; between
faith and sight (xi) ; between sons and bastards
(xii. 5-13); between the earthly and the heavenly
congregations and cities (xii. 18-29) and between
the old and new altars (xiii. 10-15).

THE OCCASION.

We should endeavour to appreciate the viewpoint
of these Jewish Christians. Speaking of Israel,
in his Letter to the Romans, Paul said : "To
whom pertaineth the adoption, and the glory,
and the covenants, and the giving of the Law, and
the service of God, and the promises ; whose

are the fathers" (ix. 4, 5). Truly these are great
and blessed privileges. The Hebrews were inheritors of a wonderful past, and of a divinely-
given revelation. They had the Law, the Covenants,
the Tabernacle, the Temple, and the Sacrifices.
And they had Abraham, and Moses, and Samuel,
and David, and a long line of prophets, priests,
and kings.

"Israel's magnificent history of more than twelve
centuries, starting with Abraham the father and
founder of the race, ' the friend of God ; ' Israel's
radiant galaxy of the very greatest men, lawgiver,
conqueror of Canaan, priests, judges, kings, prophets, poets, warriors, patriots, statesmen ; Israel's
covenant relation with Jehovah, and the mighty future
promised the chosen race ; Israel's exalted morality,
her unsurpassed system of laws, religious, civil,
criminal, and even sanitary and dietetic—is it any
wonder that the heart of a Hebrew throbbed with
exultation and hope when he thought of it all ?
Is it surprising that such a people and such a
history had for him a strange fascination, a supreme
attraction ?"

And now, those of them who had embraced
Christianity were being taunted by the Jews as
apostates from Jehovah ; as renegades from Moses,
as abandoning their Law, and as forfeiting all the

blessings and promises of the Old Covenant, to become the followers of a crucified malefactor. Under such influence and pressure they were in danger of turning back from Christianity to Judaism. Many passages in the Epistle reflect this danger, notably the seven solemn warnings (see Analysis).

We must not suppose that this danger of apostasy was present to all Christian Jews at the time that HEBREWS was written, but it certainly was present to those to whom the Letter was sent, though we cannot say where they were. The two solemn passages, chapters vi. 4-6 ; and x. 26-31, must surely be understood to refer, not to what these Hebrews were actually doing, but to what they were in danger of doing. The passages are not without difficulties. Calvinistic theologians maintain that those who "fall away" have never been truly regenerated at all ; and in this view, we must not forget the profession, gifts, and privileges of a Baalam and a Judas, nor the solemn words of Matt. vii. 15-23 ; 1 Cor. xiii. 1-3. Of Heb. vi. 4-6, Bishop Westcott says : "It is significant that in the enumeration of the divine gifts received by those who are conceived as afterwards falling away there is no one which passes out of the individual. All are gifts of power, of personal endowment. There is no gift of love." But it is the love

of these Hebrews which gives the writer hope
(verse 10). It would seem, then, that those referred
to in these two solemn passages are professors and
not possessors of eternal life, and the warnings
should lead us to "make (our) calling and election
sure."

THE DESIGN.

In view of what has just been said, the purpose
of the writer of this Epistle is threefold ; to warn
against apostasy ; to make evident the typical
character of the Mosaic Institutions ; and to affirm
and prove the finality of Christianity.

The warning against apostasy runs throughout
the Epistle, and it is sevenfold (see the preceding
page, and the Analysis).

The typical character of the Old Economy is in
the warp and woof of the Epistle's teaching.
"Levitism is but a sketch in outline, a rough
copy, a quivering shadow of the things in Heaven,
which are supersensuous, invisible, immaterial,
immovable, eternal." In pursuance of this, mark
the terms which the writer employs : "the representation and shadow of the heavenlies" (viii. 5);
"a simile for the time present" (ix. 9) ; "figures of the
true" (ix. 24) ; "the removing as having been made
of the things shaken" (xii. 27) ; and all this over
against the true "house of God" (x. 21) ; "the true

tabernacle" (viii. 2); "the city which has the foundations" (xi. 10); "the unshakeable things" (xii. 28); "the heavenly Jerusalem" (xii. 22). The writer of HEBREWS and Paul both treat of Mosaism in relation to Christianity, but in quite different ways. To Paul it is "neither Promise nor Fulfilment, but a stern though necessary discipline which had been interposed between the two." He sharply contrasts the Old and the New, the Law and the Gospel, the Command and the Promise, Sin and Mercy, Works and Faith, inevitable Death and the gift of Eternal Life. But the writer of HEBREWS sees the same truth from another standpoint; for him the contrast is between Type and Reality; he sees Christianity as the antitype and fulfilment of Judaism. "St. Paul looked on Mosaism as a broken fetter; " this writer "regarded it as a vanished shadow." The writer of this Epistle and Paul arrive at the same goal, but they travel by different routes.

The third object of HEBREWS is to declare the finality of Christianity, and this note is struck in the opening words (i. 1-4). The previous revelation was fragmentary, "in many parts;" the present one is single: the one was manifold, "in many manners," or "by many means," such as type, dream, Urim, etc.; the present one is comprehen-

sive, a single Voice : the previous one was by many
agents, "the prophets ;" the present one is "in a
Son."

And not by the abandonment of the previous
revelation is Christianity established, but by the
fulfilment of it. Angels, and Moses, and Joshua,
and Aaron, and Melchisedec, and the Offerings,
and the Covenants are all in Christ, and infinitely
more ; He is as much greater than they and them
as the substance is greater than the shadow. But
for substance there would be no shadow ; and but
for the final revelation there would have been no
former revelation. This is a great conception, and
it is worked out in HEBREWS as nowhere else in the
New Testament. Paul warns his readers in GALA-
TIANS against bondage to the external forms of
Mosaism. Paul's emphasis is on Christ the Offering ; this writer's emphasis is on Christ the Priest.
In the preparatory revelation the priest was never
the offering, but in the perfect revelation He is
both (i. 3 ; ix. 11, 12).

The three great offices in the previous dispensation were those of the prophet, the priest and the
king. Christ fulfils them all. He is greater than
the prophet Moses ; greater than the priest Aaron,
and greater than the priest-king Melchisedec.

Our Divine Priest, Who is also the Offering, is

infinitely superior to Aaron and his offerings. Aaron had to offer for his own sins (ix. 7), but Christ had not. Aaron served in the earthly sanctuary, but Christ has entered into heaven itself (ix. 1, 24). Aaron carried the "blood of others," but Christ offered "His own blood" (ix. 25 ; v. 12). Those sacrifices sanctified to the purifying of the flesh, but Christ's offering cleanses the conscience (ix. 13 ; v. 14). The Levitical Atonement availed for one year only, but Christ's is eternally efficacious (ix. 7, 25, 12), 24-26 ; x. 12). These offerings could not take away sin, but Christ's Offering does (x. 1-4, 11, 14, 18 ; ix. 26). Aaron stood daily ministering, but when Christ had offered He sat down (x. 11, 12).

In this elaborate, profound, yet simple and conclusive way the writer unfolds to these Hebrews the deepest meaning of their own religious past ; warns them against apostasy ; and exhorts them to "go on unto perfection." For an exposition of this Epistle which is at once scholarly and spiritual, theological and practical, I know of nothing better, or as good, as "The Holiest of All," by Dr. Andrew Murray.

Analysis of Hebrews

PROLOGUE (i. 1-4).

DIVISION I. (i.-x. 18).

THE DOCTRINAL DISSERTATION.

A. THE PERSONALITIES (i. 4-vii. 28).

1. **The Angels and Christ,** ... ... i. 5-ii. 18.
   - (i.) Higher, ... i. 4-14.
     First Warning (ii. 1-4).
   - (ii.) Lower, ... ii. 5-18.
2. **Moses and Christ,** ... ... iii. 1-6.
     Second Warning (iii. 7-19).
3. **Joshua and Christ,** ... ... iv. 1-10.
     Third Warning (iv. 11-13).
4. **Aaron and Christ,** ... ... iv. 14-v. 10.
     Fourth Warning (v. 11-vi. 20).
5. **Melchisedec and Christ,** ... ... vii.

B. THE INSTITUTIONS (viii.-x. 18).

1. **The Sanctuary and Christ,** ... ... viii. 1-6.
2. **The Covenant and Christ,** ... ... viii. 7-13.
3. **The Tabernacle and Christ,** ... ... ix. 1-10.
4. **The Day of Atonement and Christ,** ... ix. 11-28
5. **The Offerings and Christ,** ... ... x. 1-18.

DIVISION II. (x. 19-39).

THE CENTRAL EXHORTATION.

1. **Exhortation to Freedom and Fellowship,** x. 19-25.
     Fifth Warning (x. 26-31).
2. **Exhortation to Patience and Perseverance.** x. 32-39.

DIVISION III. (xi.-xiii. 21).

THE PRACTICAL APPLICATION.

1. The "Work of Faith," ... ... xi.
2. The "Patience of Hope," ... ... xii. 1-24.
    Sixth Warning (xii. 25-29).
3. The "Labour of Love," ... ... xiii. 1-21.
    Seventh Warning (xiii. 9-15).

EPILOGUE (xiii. 22-25).

NOTE 92

Key Words of the Hebrew Epistle.

1. **Perfect.** This word in one or other of its grammatical forms occurs fourteen times. Perfect, of full age (*teleios*: ix. 11, v. 14). Perfect, make perfect, consecrate (*teleioō*: x. 14; ii. 10, v. 9; vii. 19; ix. 9; x. 1; xi. 40; xii. 23; vii. 28). Perfection (*teleiotēs*: vi. 1). Perfection (*teleiōsis*: vii. 11). Finisher (*teleiōtēs*: xii. 2).

2. **Eternal: For ever.** These words occur not fewer than fifteen times. Eternal, everlasting (*aiōnios*: v. 9; vi. 2; ix. 12, 14, 15, xiii. 20). For ever (*aiōn*, with *eis*: v. 6; vi. 20; vii. 17, 21; xiii. 8; vii. 28, 24). For ever and ever (i. 8; xiii. 21).

3. **Better.** This word occurs thirteen times (i. 4; vii. 7, 19, 22; viii. 6; ix. 23; x. 34; xi. 35; xi. 16; vi. 9; xi. 40; xii. 24).

4. **Partakers.** This word occurs nine times, and is the translation of five Greek words (*metochos*: i. 9; iii. 1, 14; vi. 4; xii. 8; *koinōneō*: ii. 14; *koinōnia*: xiii. 16; *koinōnos*: x. 33; *metalambanō*: xii. 10).

5. **Heaven, Heavenly.** These words occur seventeen times (i. 10; iv. 14; vii. 26; viii. 1; ix. 23, 24; x. 34; xii. 23, 25, 26; xi. 12; iii. 1; vi. 4; xi. 16; xii. 22; viii. 5; ix. 23).

NOTE 93

The Old Testament in Hebrews.

THERE are not fewer than eighty-six direct references to the O.T. in Hebrews, and these are traceable to at least one hundred O.T. passages. These references are made from the Septuagint Version, and, it would seem, the author knew the Jewish Scriptures only in that Version. This fact militates against the Pauline author-ship.

A striking feature of the O.T. references in Hebrews is the absence of the usual introductory formulas, so common with Paul, such as, *as it is written, for it is written, the Scripture saith, David says, Moses says, Isaiah says,* etc. The Epistle refers its citations neither to the *Scripture,* nor to *persons* or *authors,* but to God, or the Holy Spirit, with two exceptions (ii. 6; xii. 21).

The allegorising and spiritualising of the O.T. by this author, as also by Paul, has been discounted by many critics, but this matter must be considered in the light of whether or not the author was inspired. Chapter i. may be made a test passage. Verse 3; Psa. cx. 1. Verse 5; Psa. ii. 7; 2 Sam. vii. 14. Verse 6; Deut. xxxii. 43; Psa. xcvii. 7. Verse 7; Psa. civ. 4. Verses 8, 9; Psa. xlv. 6, 7. Verses 10-12; Psa. cii. 25-27. Verse 13; Psa. cx. 1. Those who hold that the writers of Holy Scripture were guided by the Spirit of God, and, therefore, were not left to their opinions as to the deepest meaning of the Old Testament, will readily believe that the O.T. passages cited in Hebrews i. are not humanly allegorised, but divinely interpreted.

THE CATHOLIC EPISTLES

JACOBEAN

James
Jude

PETRINE

1 Peter
2 Peter

JOHANNINE

1 John
2 John
3 John
Revelation

NOTE 94

The Epistles Called "Catholic."

"IT was probably in the last half of the third century that the Epistles of Jude and James, the Second of Peter, with the Second and Third of John, were added to the other two, forming with them one collection called *catholic*, because they were publicly read in the Catholic Christian Church. Eusebius does not use *catholic* as synonymous with *canonical* or *apostolic*, any more than his predecessors.

"In the majority of ancient MSS. the Catholic Epistles follow the Acts of the Apostles, and precede those of Paul. Lachmann and Tischendorf arrange them so in their editions of the Greek Testament. The Sinaitic MS. has them immediately before the Revelation which is the usual position.

"The First Epistle of John and Peter obtained general recognition sooner than the rest. Papias had already received them. The Letters of James and Jude, which were considered unapostolic at first, and therefore uncanonical, were afterwards put with the others, while the Second and Third of John formed an appendix to the rest.

"When the Second of Peter was adopted, it could only be placed after the First, though its alleged authorship was doubted much longer than any of the seven, and has always raised suspicions."
—Dr. SAMUEL DAVIDSON. *An Introduction to the Study of the New Testament.*

THE CATHOLIC EPISTLES

Introduction

THE TERM.

THE term "Catholic," as applied to certain Epistles of the New Testament, has been variously interpreted. It has been taken to mean : (i.) Letters addressed to Christians in general, or groups of Churches, and not as the Pauline Epistles to certain individuals and particular Churches ; (ii.) The work of the Apostles generally ; (iii.) Universally recognised Letters; (iv.) Containing "Catholic," or orthodox doctrine ; (v.) Their general acceptance as Scripture. This term for these Epistles occurs from the time of Clement of Alexandria, in the beginning of the third century.

THE NUMBER AND ORDER.

Before the time of Eusebius, in the fourth century, seven Epistles were spoken of as being "Catholic," and these are recognised by the Greek and Latin Churches. They are JAMES, 1-2 PETER, 1-3 JOHN, and JUDE, and this is the order observed in the chief Manuscripts, Versions, and Scriptural Catalogues. In the oldest Manuscripts of the New

Testament the Catholic Epistles are placed between the ACTS and the Pauline Epistles.

THE WRITERS.

Of these Letters there are four writers, James, Peter, John, and Jude. Two of them write one Epistle each, one of them writes two, and another writes three.

Of these authors two are Apostles, the two chief Apostles of our Lord, Peter and John, and two of them are brothers of Jesus.

THE DATE.

It may be helpful to relate these Epistles to that momentous event in Jewish history, the Fall of Jerusalem in A.D. 70. Before that event must be placed JAMES, A.D. 44-49 ; I PETER, A.D. 63, 64 ; 2 PETER, A.D. 64-68, and JUDE, A.D. 67-68. And after that event come the three Epistles of John. These relations will help to explain not a few references in the Letters written before the disaster.

COMPARISONS.

In our Introduction to the Apostolical Writings we have related the Epistles in certain ways to one another, but comparing the Catholic Epistles it may be said that JAMES is ethical, PETER is experimental, JUDE is exhortatory, and JOHN is expository. The subjects of the first are prayer and practice ;

of the second, hope and knowledge ; of the third, faith and conflict ; and of the fourth, love and truth.

The terms Pauline, Jacobean, Petrine, and Johannine have a significance beyond mere authorship ; they stand for apprehensions and aspects of Christianity, aspects which do not contradict but supplement one another.

NOTE 95

New Testament Writers Compared.

"ST PAUL dwells, not of course exclusively, but pre dominantly, on Christian doctrine, St. James on Christian practice, St. Peter on Christian trials, and St. John on Christian experience.

"St. Paul insists mainly on faith, St. James on works, St. Peter on hope, and St. John on love.

"St. Paul represents Christian scholasticism, and St. John Christian mysticism. St. Paul represents the spirit of Protestantism, St. Peter that of Catholicism, while St. James speaks in the voice of the Church of the Past, and St. John in that of the Church of the Future. St. Peter is the founder, St. Paul the propagator, St. John the finisher.

"St. Peter represents to us the glory of power and action, St. Paul that of thought and wisdom, St. James of virtue and faithfulness, St. John of emotion and holiness."

—DEAN STANLEY and DEAN FARRAR.

NOTE 96

The Men Called James.

IN the Galilean group of early disciples there are not fewer than six persons called *James*: 1. the Son of Zebedee (Mark i. 19); 2. the Son of Alphaeus (Mark iii. 18); 3. mentioned as one of Jesus' brothers (Mark vi. 3); 4. "the Less" (Mark xv. 40); 5. "the Lord's brother" (Gal. i. 19); and 6. "the brother of Jude" (Jude 1). These six can be reduced to three by regarding 2 and 4 as the same person, and 3, 5, and 6 as the same person. There are, then, James, the son of Zebedee; James, the son of Alphaeus, and James, the Lord's brother.

The question has been raised as to which of these wrote the Epistle. No ancient authority ever attributed it to James, the son of Zebedee, who early was martyred. Lange, Bishop Wordsworth, and others, held that the son of Alphaeus was the author of the Epistle, by supporting an ancient theory that he was the Bishop of Jerusalem, but a heavy weight of evidence is against this. James, the Lord's brother, then, must be the writer of the Epistle, and the Bishop of Jerusalem, the President of the Jerusalem Conference of Acts xv. (13), and the person referred to in Gal. i. 19; ii. 9.

THE JACOBEAN EPISTLES

JAMES

JUDE

NOTE 97

The Mother of James the Writer.

IT is by no means generally agreed who was the mother of James, "the Lord's brother" (Gal. i. 19). Three theories are held, which take their names from the promoters of them: 1. The *Hieronymian*; 2. The *Epiphanian*; and 3. The *Helvidian*.

1. **The Hieronymian View,** the Theory of Jerome, and that which is held by the Roman Catholic Church, is that the so-called "brethren" of Jesus (John vii. 5, *et al.*) were His "cousins," being the sons of Alphaeus and Mary the sister of the Lord's mother. This view is in the interest of the doctrine of the Perpetual Virginity of Jesus' mother, and had its origin in two unscriptural tendencies: (*a*) to exalt the Virgin to superhuman dignity, and (*b*) to disparage the wedded state, and exalt celibacy.

2. **The Epiphanian View,** the theory of Epiphanius, is that these "brethren," including James, of course, were the sons of Joseph by a previous marriage, and, therefore, were Jesus' step-brothers. This, like the preceding view, though accounted for differently, safeguards the Perpetual Virginity of Mary. This theory rests upon sentiment and apocryphal fiction, for there is no trace of an original historical tradition to the effect that Joseph was a widower, and had sons.

3. **The Helvidian View,** the theory of Helvidius, is that the "brethren" of Jesus were literally such, the children of Joseph and Mary, and this is the view which Scripture supports, notably Matt. i. 24, 25, where "until" means, "not till then, but afterwards"; and Luke ii. 7, where "firstborn" implies that others were born afterwards. The word "firstborn" is never used of an only son. James and Jude, the writers of the Epistles which bear their names, were, therefore, the sons of Mary by Joseph, and the younger brothers of Jesus.

THE EPISTLE OF JAMES

Keyword : ETHICS.

Place of Writing : JERUSALEM.   DATE : 44-49 A.D.

THE AUTHOR.

THE early death of James, the son of Zebedee, and brother of John the Apostle, does not allow of his being the author of this Epistle. The only other James of any prominence in the New Testament is the brother of our Lord, and brother of Jude, and the contents of this Epistle are in agreement with all that we know of this James (Acts i. 14 ; xii. 17 ; xv. 4-29 ; xxi. 18 ; 1 Cor. xv. 7 ; Gal. i. 18, 19 ; ii. 9, 11 ; James i. 1 ; Jude 1).

THE READERS.

The expression, "To the twelve tribes which are of the dispersion" (i. 1), must refer to Jews residing outside of Palestine, and more especially, if not exclusively, to Christian Jews.

THE DATE.

All the evidence goes to show that this Writing belongs to the primitive stage in the history of the Christian Church.   Two weighty considerations point to an early date : the Judaic type of Christ-

ianity apparent in it ; and the absence of controversy on subjects which came into dispute
about the time of the Conference in Jerusalem,
or soon afterwards (Acts xv).

The substance of the Epistle seems to show that
at the time of the writing of it there were no
Judaizers to be attacked, because as yet Gentile
Christianity had not taken a recognised position
in the Church, and Judaism did not yet exist in
that hostile form which it afterwards assumed.
Nor as yet had such heresies crept in as were afterwards found at Colossae ; no false doctrine about
the resurrection, as at Corinth ; and no despondency
as to the delay in the Advent of Christ, and therefore
no need of such warnings and consolations as were
addressed to the Thessalonians, or to the Hebrews
a few years later.

From these and other facts it may be assumed
that this Epistle was written before the Council
in Jerusalem, A.D. 50-51, that is, between 44-50
A.D. so that it is the earliest of the New Testament
Writings. Also, without doubt, the place of
writing was Jerusalem.

THE DESIGN.

While bearing in mind that this Epistle was
written to Christian Jews, we must understand

that these Christians had not ceased to be Jews ; that they were still strictly observing the Law, and were attending the synagogue (ii. 2). The object of the Writing is to exhort those Jewish Christians to patience under the trials to which they were exposed, the persecution from unbelieving Jews (ii. 6) ; to warn them against various sins and evil tendencies of which they stood in danger ; (iv. 1 ; iv. 11), and to instruct them in various points of Christian morality (i. 26-27).

THE STYLE.

It is a marked feature of the writer's style to link together clauses and sentences by the repetition of the leading word or some of its cognates. In this way one subject is made to lead on to another. For example :

i. 2-8.	patience (3), patience (4) ; nothing lacking (4), if any of you lack (5) ; let him ask (5), but let him ask (6) ; nothing wavering (6), he that wavereth (6).
i. 12-15.	temptation (12, 13, 14), tempted (13, 14) ; lust (14), lust (15).
i. 19-20.	Wrath (19), wrath (20).
i. 21-25.	Engrafted word (21), word (22, 23) ; doers (22), doer (23, 25).
i. 26, 27.	Religious (26), religion (27).
iii. 2-4.	Offend (2), offend (2) ; whole body (2), whole body (3) ; turn about (3), turn about (4).

Another feature of this writer's style is his use of metaphor and simile. Mark the following examples :

17

i. 6, sea wave driven and tossed ; i. 10, fading flower, and burning sun ; i. 12, crown reward ; i. 15, conception, birth, growth, death ; i. 17, God and the sun ; ii. 2, 3, fine and shabby attire ; ii. 26, corpse ; iii. 3, horse and bridle ; iii. 4, ship and helm ; iii. 5, the spark which sets on fire a forest ; iii. 7, 8, an untamable creature ; iii. 11, 12, water spring, and fruit tree ; iv. 1, pleasures like a hostile army encamped in our body ; iv. 14, shifting mist ; v. 2, 3, decay and rust, and wages ; v. 7, fertilizing rains.

This poetic vein, we may believe, was derived from the author's poetic mother (cf. the Magnificat).

The style of James is characterised by energy, vivacity, and vividness of representation. He has no liking for mere abstractions, but throws everything into picturesque and dramatic forms ; abstract qualities are exhibited in concrete shape, as, for example, in ii. 2-4, and v. 1-6.

He wastes no words, and uses no circumlocution (cf. v. 13, 14). In its rugged abruptness, in the pregnant brevity of its phrases, in the austerity of its demand upon the reader, in concentrated irony and scorn (*e.g.*, ii. 15, 16) this Epistle stands alone among the Writings of the New Testament. Of its style it has been said : "It combines pure, and eloquent, and rhythmical Greek with Hebrew intensity of expression. It has all the fiery sternness and vehemence of the ancient prophets, while it is chiefly occupied with inculcating the truths of the 'Sapiential' literature, the wisdom of the gnomologists. It is at once fervid and picturesque. It abounds in passionate ejaculations, rapid questions and graphic similitudes. It is less a letter than a moral harangue, stamped with the lofty personality of the writer, and afire with his burning sincerity."

NOTES.

It must be manifest to every reader that this Epistle stands apart from all others of the New Testament in substance. It contains nothing of an Epistle except the Superscription; for the rest, both matter and form assimilate its contents to the Scriptural philosophy which is called Wisdom Literature.

In place of the connected thread of argument making the unity of a Pauline Epistle, we have in this work independent sections; and these are found to be in form, maxims and essays, such as are found in the Books of PROVERBS and ECCLESI-ASTICUS, of which latter work James is clearly a deep student.

The subject matter of this Book represents the old conception of Wisdom, leavened with the new spirit of Christianity.

A number of subjects are dealt with by this writer in a manner at once brief, fresh, and arresting, subjects which bear upon the Christian life on its practical rather than on its contemplative side, such as temptation, pride, greed, strife, works, wisdom, speech, poverty, wealth, religion, prayer, selfishness, patience, and faith ; but owing to the peculiar style of the author these are not so many unrelated fragments of wisdom, but, in an ingenious way, are related to one another. It may be said, indeed, that in the form of Essay or Discourse ten subjects are here treated, some of which include several distinct themes.

1.	i. 2-18,	...	The Test of Temptation,
2.	i. 19-27,	...	Hearing and Doing the Word of God.
3.	ii. 1-13,	...	Respect of Persons.
4.	ii. 14-26,	...	Faith and Works.
5.	iii. 1-12,	...	The Ethics of Speech.
6.	iii. 13-18,	...	Wisdom True and False.
7.	iv. 1-12,	...	Marks of Worldliness.
8.	iv. 13-17,	...	Dependence upon God.
9.	v. 1-11,	...	Oppression and Judgment.
10.	v. 12-20,	...	Miscellaneous Precepts.

It will be observed that under 7, and 10, several subjects are introduced.

In addition to all this, there are other features which are worthy of our attention.

(*a*) The Epistle furnishes an unusual number of references or parallels to other Writings.

(i.) The Old Testament.

The writer makes reference to Abram, Rahab, Job, and Elijah ; to the Law, and some of the Commandments ; and there are other references or allusions to passages in all the Books of the

Pentateuch, Joshua, 1 Kings, the Psalms, Proverbs, Ecclesiastes, Isaiah, Jeremiah, Ezekiel, Daniel, and to no less than seven of the twelve Minor Prophets.

(ii.) The Apocrypha.

But more remarkable is the evidence of James' intimate acquaintance with the Old Testament Apocrypha, especially the Book of ECCLESIASTICUS, to which there are not less than fifteen allusions, and even as many as thirty-two have been claimed.

He also makes use of the WISDOM OF SOLOMON, as many as twelve allusions having been traced.

(iii.) The New Testament.

More than any other Book of the New Testament it reflects the language of the Sermon on the Mount, as the following passages show :

JAMES.	MATTHEW.
i. 2.	v. 10-12.
i. 4.	v. 48.
i. 5 ; v. 15.	vii. 7-12.
i. 9.	v. 3.
i. 20.	v. 22.
ii. 13.	v. 7 ; vi. 14, 15.
ii. 14-16.	vii. 21-23.
iii. 17-18.	v. 9.
iv. 4.	vi. 24.
iv. 10.	v. 3, 4.
iv. 11.	vii. 1, 2.
v. 2.	vi. 19.
v. 10.	v. 12.
v. 12.	v. 33-37.

These references, Prof. Mayor has said, "never amount to actual quotation," but are "like the reminiscence of thoughts often uttered by the original speaker and sinking into the heart of the hearer, who reproduces them in his own manner;" and Dr. Mayor affirms that James has preserved more of the teaching of our Lord than is contained in all the other Epistles put together.

(b) This Epistle is more wanting than any other in distinctively Christian and spiritual elements.

The word "gospel" does not once occur. Christ is named only twice. There is no reference to the Incarnation, the work of Redemption, the Resurrection, or the Ascension; and the morality inculcated is not urged from Christian motives or sanctions.

The reasons for this are chiefly the shallow religious professions of his day; his own character and past training; the intention to produce, not a theological treatise, but a moral appeal; and the early date of the Writing. But this lack notwithstanding, there are a few passages of great theological significance, and with profound implications, as for example, i. 1, i. 18, and ii. 1.

(c) Striking Themes, Words, and Phrases:

There are several passages of outstanding importance in this short Book, the passages on the

Origin and End of Evil (i. 13-15) ; Faith and Works
(ii. 14-26) ; The Tongue (iii. 1-12) ; The Two
Wisdoms (iii. 13-18) ; Patience and Reward (v.
7-11) ; and on Prayer (v. 13-18).

There are also a number of striking words and
phrases, as, for example, "a two-souled man"
(i. 8); "the Father of the Lights" (i. 17); "religious,
religion" (i. 26, 27), "How great a matter," literally,
"how much wood" (iii. 5); "the wheel of being"
(iii. 6), and the seven qualities of heavenly wisdom
(iii. 17).

NOTE 98

The Old Testament in the Epistle of James.

JAMES	O. T.	JAMES	O. T.
i. 10	Isa. xl. 6	iv. 6	Prov. iii. 34
i. 19	Prov. xvii. 27 ; Ecc. v. 2	v. 4	Deut. xxiv. 15, 17; Mal. iii. 5
ii. 1	Lev. xix. 15 ; Prov. xxiv. 23	v. 5	Jer. xii. 3
ii. 8	Lev. xix. 18	v. 7	Deut. xi. 14; Jer. v. 24; Joel
ii. 11	Exod. xx. 13-15; Deut. v. 17		ii. 23; Zech. x. 1
ii. 21	Gen. xxii. 2, 9	v. 11	Job i. 21, 22; xlii. 1 - 17
ii. 23	Gen. xv. 6	v. 17, 18	1 Kings xvii. 1; xviii. 41
ii. 25	Josh. ii. 1 ; vi. 17, 23	v. 20	Prov. x. 12
iii. 9	Gen. i. 26		

Analysis of James

ADDRESS (i. 1).

THE EPISTLE OF JUDE

Keyword : KEPT.

Place of Writing : PALESTINE.   DATE : 67-68

THE AUTHOR.

IN the New Testament are two Judes, each related to one of the name of James (Luke vi. 16 ; Acts i. 13 ; and Matt. xiii. 55 ; Mark vi. 3 ; Acts i. 14).

The Author of this Epistle is the *latter*, the brother of Jesus the Christ.

We know that Jude the Lord's brother became a Christian (cf. John vii. 5 ; 1 Cor. xv. 7 ; Acts 14).

He does not in his Letter call himself an Apostle, and seems to show that he was not.

His reference to James (1) is easily understood if the latter is the well-known head of the Mother-Church of Jerusalem.

His silence as to his being the brother of Jesus is accounted for by the fact that the Ascension had altered all Christ's human relationships, and His brethren would shrink from claiming kinship after the flesh with His glorified Body.

Nothing further is known of him, unless we may

draw the inferences that he was married (1 Cor. ix. 5), and was an Evangelist.

THE READERS.

From the contents of the Epistle it is evident that Jewish Christians are in view, notwithstanding the general address of verse 1. The Epistle, having regard for its brevity, contains more allusions to Jewish history than any other in the New Testament, except 2 PETER, which so closely resembles it, and, perhaps, the Epistle to the HEBREWS. Furthermore, it would seem that the Letter was addressed to some particular Church, most probably in Palestine ; for the reference in verses 4, 16, localises the occasion of the Epistle.

THE DATE.

It may safely be assumed that the Epistle was written before A.D. 70, and for the following reasons :

(a) It seems implied that some of those addressed had heard Apostles (17) ; (b) the general view of the church here presented ; and (c) the absence of any reference to the destruction of Jerusalem, which, had it taken place, would surely have been mentioned in the paragraph 5-7. We may assume, therefore, that the Letter was written about 67-68 A.D.

THE DESIGN.

This is plainly stated in verses 3, 4, which show

that the object of writing was twofold, namely, to instruct his readers in the common salvation, and to warn them against certain persons who had found stealthy entrance into the Church, and were introducing doctrinal error which had a licentious tendency, whose denial of the Lord led them to antinomian practices (4, 10, 18, 19), whose libertinism in life had its root in perverted views of Divine grace and Christian liberty.

THE STYLE.

In style this Epistle is much like that of James, poetic and vivid. These brothers inherited this vein, no doubt, from their mother, and, maybe, the ascetic and severe aspect of their character from their father. The style of Jude is "broken and rugged, bold and picturesque, energetic, vehement, glowing with the fires of passion. In the build of its sentences it is more Aramaic than Greek, but it has at the same time a considerable command of strong, varied, and expressive terms." Illustration of Jude's graphic style is seen in his reference to "hidden rocks," "waterless clouds," "fruitless trees," "wild waves," and "wandering stars" (12).

NOTES.

A feature of this Writing is the author's fondness

for triplets, of which there are some twelve groups in these twenty-five verses. Mark:

"Jude, servant, brother" (1) ; "sanctified, kept, called" (1) ; "mercy, peace, love" (2) ; "defile, despise, speak evil of" (8) ; "gone, ran, perished" (11) ; and double triplets are found in "kept," three times with reference to the godly (1, 21, 24), and three times with reference to the ungodly (6, 6, 13) ; and in "ungodly" (4, 15, 18).

Another feature is the writer's references to three groups of Writings.

(i.) To the Old Testament, Moses, Cain, Balaam, Korah, Adam, Israelites, Sodomites. (ii.) To the New Testament, Jesus, James, Apostles. (iii.) To Apocryphal Writings : (*a*) the Book of Enoch (14), and (*b*) the Assumption of Moses (9).

Other recurring words than those already referred to should be noted :

"Beloved" (3, 17, 20) ; "once for all" (3, 5) ; "railing—rail" (9, 10) ; "remembrance," "remember" (5, 17) ; and "how" (5, R.V. 24). Mark also, references to God (1, 4, 5, 6, 9, 21, 24, 25) ; to Christ (1, 2, 4, 14, 15, 17, 21, 25) ; to Michael and angels (9, 6) ; and to the devil (9).

It has been said that "the New Testament nowhere else presents so many strange phenomena, or raises so many curious questions, within so narrow a space." One such phenomenon is Jude's references to Apocryphal Writings ; and another is the relation of this work to 2 PETER ; compare Jude 4-16 with 2 Peter ii. 1-18 ; and Jude 17, 18, with 2 Peter iii. 2, 3. That one of these uses the other. we may assume, and it is widely believed that PETER is the earlier of the two, and that Jude quotes from it.

Notwithstanding the brevity of this Epistle, its teaching and moral values are considerable, on such matters, for instance, as the connection between belief and practice, the spread of error in the early Church, the teaching of the past on the judgment of evil, the security of the saints against apostasy, on discrimination, prayer, and other subjects of abiding importance. Contemplate especially verses 24, 25.

NOTE 99
Extra-Biblical Allusions in Jude.

IN verse 9 Jude refers to a personal contention between the Archangel Michael, and the Devil, about the body of Moses; and in verse 14, he alludes to a prophecy attributed to Enoch. The first of these references appears to have been derived from an apocryphal work of about A.D. 50, called *The Assumption or Ascension of Moses*; and the second appears to have been derived from the apocryphal *Book of Enoch*, which, it is supposed, was a production of the second and first centuries B.C.

That Jude should make such references need cause no surprise, for James makes use of the *Wisdom of Solomon*, and *Ecclesiasticus* (for instances see *The Epistle of St. James*, by Dr. J. B. Mayor, pp. cxvi-cxviii), and Paul quotes from Epimenides, Aratus, and Menander (Acts xvii. 28; 1 Cor. xv. 33; 2 Tim. iii. 8; Titus i. 12). There is no need to suppose that what was obtainable from extant and current sources was specially revealed to Jude. Honour is not done to God by our creating a miracle where there is no need for one. Jude uses these references by way of passing illustration.

Analysis of Jude

THE PETRINE EPISTLES

NOTE 100

The Influence of James and Paul on Peter.

DEAN FARRAR says, referring to I Peter, "We see in it the simple, unsystematic, practical synthesis of the complementary —but not contradictory—truths insisted on alike by St. Paul and St. James. St. Peter dwells more exclusively than St. Paul on moral duties; he leans more immediately than St. James on Gospel truths."

In evidence of this are the following references:

(a) JAMES AND PETER.

JAMES.	I PETER.
i. 2 - 4	i. 6, 7
i. 10	i. 24
iv. 6, 7, 10	v. 5, 9
v. 20	iv. 8

(b) PAUL AND PETER.

ROMANS.	I PETER.	EPHESIANS.	I PETER.
ix. 25 - 32	ii. 6 - 10	i. 4 - 7	i. 1
vii. 23	ii. 11	i. 3	i. 3
xiii. 1 - 4	ii. 13	ii. 8	i. 14
xvi. 17	iii. 9	vi. 5	ii. 18
vi. 6	iv. 1	v. 22	iii. 1
xii. 6	iv. 10	i. 20	iii. 22
viii. 18	v. 1	v. 21	v. 5

1 PETER

Keyword : HOPE.

Place of Writing : BABYLON.   DATE : 64-67. A.D.

THE AUTHOR.

FARRAR says that : "Of all the Writings of the New Testament the First Epistle of Peter is perhaps the most anciently and most unanimously attested." The writer is one of the three greatest Apostles. Peter's life may be said to fall into two unequal parts ; first, up to Pentecost ; second, on from Pentecost ; and each of these parts falls into two ; in part one, first, to the time that Jesus called him to discipleship ; and second, from that time to Pentecost ; and in part two, first, from Pentecost until the Council at Jerusalem (Acts xv) ; and second, from then to the end of his life. There are, therefore, four distinct stages with Pentecost in the centre : (a) from the beginning to the call to discipleship ; (b) from the call until Pentecost ; (c) from Pentecost to the Jerusalem Council ; and (d) from the Council to his death.

Of part (a) we do not know much, except that his name was Simon ; that his early home was at Bethsaida, and later at Capernaum ; that he was a fisherman ; that he was married ; and that in temperament he was impulsive and devoted. Of part (b) we know more than of any other part. His brother Andrew introduced him to Jesus ; he was one of the first four of Christ's disciples ; Christ predicted for him a spiritual change by giving him a change of name, Peter, which means "rock" (John i. 40-42 ; Mark i. 16-18). Later he received a further call (Luke v. 1-11), and later again, was made one of the Twelve Apostles (Luke vi. 13-16), always being mentioned first. He must have been with Jesus for fully two years, hearing His words, seeing His deeds, and studying His character. He was the first of the Apostles to confess that Jesus was the Son of God (Matt. xvi. 16), and the first to deny Him (Matt. xxvi. 69-75). He fled when his Master was crucified, but was among the first to visit the tomb (Matt. xxvi. 56 ; John xx. 1-6). Christ risen sent a special message to him, and specially appeared to him (Mark xvi. 7 ; Luke xxiv. 34 ; 1 Cor. xv. 5). After the ascension Peter took the lead of the Apostles and disciples during the ten days before Pentecost (Acts i. 13-26).

Part (c) is full of thrilling interest. On the day of Pentecost the Church was born. On that day Christ's promise and commission to Peter were fulfilled (John i. 42 ; Luke xxii. 32). From then,

A.D. 30, until the Council at Jerusalem, A.D. 51, he was the Church's leader (Acts ii.-xv), and, as Christ had ordained, he opened the door of the Gospel to the Gentiles (Acts x).

Part (*d*). After the Jerusalem Council Peter is not mentioned again in the ACTS; but connect with this event Gal. ii. 11-21. After Acts xii, Paul becomes the Church's leader, though James dominated the Church at Jerusalem. The references to Peter are now few (1 Cor. i. 12; ix. 5; Gal. i. 18; ii. 9, 11). It has been slyly said that tradition acquires definiteness in proportion as it is removed from the period of which it speaks. The claim that Peter was Bishop of Rome is without historical foundation, but tradition is practically unanimous that towards the end of his life he visited Rome, wrote his First Epistle there, and was martyred and buried there (cf. John xxi. 19).

Without Peter an irreparable gap would be made in Apostolic history, in Church history, and in human history.

THE DATE AND PLACE OF WRITING.

If tradition be correct, and it almost certainly is, and from the evidence which Peter's Epistles supply, he was in Rome after A.D. 64, the year when the Neronean persecution broke out, and he was dead by 67 or 68 A.D. Obviously Peter was acquainted with Paul's Letter to the Ephesians, so that his First Epistle must have been written after A.D. 62-63 ; and as A.D. 67, is the traditional date of his martyrdom, his Epistles must have been written between 63 and 67 A.D. Again, if tradition be correct, "Babylon," in 1 Peter v. 13, must be a mystical name for Rome. The reference to Mark in this connection is confirmation of this view, as Mark in all probability was in Rome with Paul at that time (2 Tim. iv. 11).

THE READERS.

These were "the exiles of the Dispersion" over a wide area in Asia Minor (i. 1), mainly Jews (i. 16 ; ii. 6, 8 ; iii. 5, 6) ; but also Gentiles (i. 14, 18 ; ii. 10 ; iv. 3).

THE OCCASION AND OBJECT.

We have seen that the latter part of the seventh decade of our era was one of terrible persecution of the Christians, and this condition of things is amply reflected in this Epistle. Christians were everywhere spoken against as evil-doers (ii. 12 ; iii. 16), and were undergoing grievous trials (i. 7 ; iv. 12, 13). The object, then, which the Apostle had in writing was to comfort and encourage the oppressed ; to strengthen their faith, to brighten their hope, and to exhort them to obedience and patience.

He does this in a most impressive manner, by showing that the vocation of the Christian is salvation (i. 3-ii. 10); that the behaviour of the Christian, in all life's relations, is to be characterised by submission (ii. 11-iii. 12); and that the discipline of the Christian is by means of suffering (iii. 13-v. 11); and throughout, Christ is shown to be the mighty Saviour, and the victorious Sufferer. Few of the Epistles will be so comforting and encouraging in these days as this one.

PETER AND OTHER WRITING APOSTLES.

Though the matter can be, and has been exaggerated, it should, nevertheless, be recognised that, though not contradictory, the standpoints of James and Jude on the one hand, and of Paul on the other hand, are different. James, Bishop of Jerusalem, was strictly Judaic; by temperament and training he was "a Jew to the Jews," a rigid ascetic, and a scrupulous observer of the Mosaic Law. The legal complexion of his Epistle, and its want of distinctively evangelical truth, reflect his point of view and that of the Mother-Church of Jerusalem.

Paul, on the other hand, had a much wider outlook, who was the Apostle to the Gentiles, and the theologian of the Church. Paulinism and Judaism are distinct, albeit, let it be said again, not contradictory. Paul and James represent in sharp contrast two aspects of truth, but there was room for another presentation, one that would, without controversy, be the synthesis of the other two. This we have in I PETER. It has been said that Peter "dwells with all the energy of St. James on the glory of practical virtue, and with much of the fervour of St. Paul on the distinctively Christian motives and sanctions. But it is no part of his object to follow St. Paul in the logical development and formulation of Christian theology, nor yet to dwell with the exclusiveness of St. James on Christian practice. . . . St. Peter dwells more exclusively than St. Paul on moral duties ; he leans more immediately than St. James on Gospel truths." John represents yet another aspect of truth. Each of these writers has his special emphasis. In Paul, it is Christian doctrine ; in James, it is Christian practice ; in Peter, it is Christian trials ; and in John it is Christian experience. The notes of Faith, and Works, and Hope, and Love are all needed in the harmony of Truth. Together they give balance to thought and life. Theology is fivefold, Jacobean, Pauline, Petrine, Hebraic, and Johannine. What is said of nature may be said of Truth. "How manifold . . . in wisdom hast Thou made (it) all."

NOTES.

Peter presents Christian truth in Jewish mould. Like the writer of HEBREWS he shows how all the essentialities of Judaism are realised in Christianity, and so, in chapters i-ii. 10, the first main division, the Old Testament is reflected in references to election, inheritance, a chosen generation, a royal priesthood, a people for God's own possession, Temple, Altar, Sacrifice. "There are in this Epistle proportionately more quotations from the ancient Scriptures than in any other Book of the New Testament."

Leading words in the Letter are, *Hope, Submission, Well-doing, Salvation.* Other words or expressions specially noteworthy are :

"Sojourners of the dispersion" (i. 1) ; "sprinkling of blood" (i. 2) ; "begotten-again" (i. 3) ; "fadeth not away" (i. 4); "impartiality" (i. 17) ; "unadulterated milk" (ii. 2) ; "praises" (ii. 9) ; "example" (ii. 21) ; "revile" (iii. 16) ; "excess of riot" (iv. 4) ; "busybody" (iv. 15) ; "fiery trial" (iv. 12) ; "gird yourselves with humility" (v. 5) ; "your allotted charge" (v. 3) ; "as a Christian" (iv. 14) ; "Bishop of your souls"; "adorning" ; "plaiting" ; "guile" ; "sanctify in your heart Christ as Lord" ; "conscience" ; "prison"; "arm yourselves with the same mind" ; "exceeding joy" ; "gospel" ; "suffer" ; "glory" ; "flock of God" ; "roaring lion."

Chapter iii. 18-22, is one of the most difficult

passages in the Bible, as all its principal words are capable of more than one meaning.

What is meant by "prison"? If that part of Hades where are the souls of the ungodly, did Christ go there? (cf. Luke xxiii. 43). Who are the "spirits," angels or men? (cf. Gen. vi. 4). Were they in a "spirit" state when they were preached to, or is the reference to a subsequent state? What is meant by "preached"? The word is *kērusso*, to proclaim as a herald, and not *euaggelizō*, to preach the Gospel, though the former word may have the latter meaning (cf. Matt. iv. 17). Was it only Noah's generation that was preached to? (cf. iv. 6). Was the preaching an announcement to fallen angelic powers of Christ's victory on Calvary? (cf. verse 22). Is this passage a ground for belief in Eternal Hope? When one realises the many difficulties of the utterance, he will at least be preserved from the indiscretion of dogmatism.

The Epistle remarkably illustrates the LORD'S PRAYER.

"Our, i. 4; Father, i. 3, 17; in heaven, i. 4, 12; hallowed be Thy name, i. 15, 16; Thy kingdom come, ii. 9; Thy will be done, ii. 15, iii. 17, iv. 2, 19; daily bread, v. 7; forgive, iv. 1, 8; temptation, iv. 12; deliver, iv. 13; kingdom, v. 11; power, i. 5; iv. 11; glory, i. 11, 21, iv. 11, 14, v. 1, 10; for ever and ever, iv. 11, v. 11; Amen, iv. 11; 5. 11."

The Epistle gives unmistakable evidence of

the influence on Peter of ROMANS and EPHESIANS.

Chap. i. 14, and Rom. xii. 2 ; chap. ii. 6-10, and Rom. ix. 25-32 ; chap. ii. 11, and Rom. vii. 23 ; chap. ii. 13, and Rom. xiii. 1-4 ; chap. iii. 9, and Rom. xvi. 17 ; chap. iii. 22, and Rom. viii. 34 ; chap. iv. 1, and Rom. vi. 6 ; chap. iv. 10, and Rom. xii. 6 ; chap. v. 1, and Rom. viii. 18.

Chap. i. 1, and Eph. i. 4-7 ; chap. i. 3, and Eph. i. 3 ; chap. i. 14, and Eph. ii. 8 ; chap. ii. 18, and Eph. vi. 5 ; chap. iii. 1, and Eph. v. 22 ; chap. iii. 22, and Eph. i. 20 ; chap. v. 5, and Eph. v. 21.

The influence of James on Peter is also evident.

Chap. i. 6-7, and Jas. i. 2-4 ; chap. i. 24, and Jas. i. 10 ; chap. iv. 8, and Jas. v. 20 ; chap. v. 5, 9, and Jas. iv. 6, 7, 10.

In "The Early Days of Christianity," Farrar has traced the references in this Epistle to events which occurred during Peter's association with his Lord. This line of thought is evidentially and spiritually most profitable. Compare the reference to "rock" (ii. 8), with Matt. xvi. 18 : and "offence" (ii. 8), with Matt. xvi. 23 ; also, chapter ii. 13-16, with Matt. xvii. 24-27 : chapter iv. 8, with Matt. xviii. 22 : chapter i. 5 ; v. 4, with Matt. xix. 28 : chapter iii. 20, with Matt. xxiv. 37 : chapter v. 5, with John xiii. 1-6 : chapter v. 8, with Luke xxii. 31 : chapter v. 8, "adversary," with Matt. v. 25 ; Luke xii. 58 ; xviii. 3 : chapter i. 8, with John xx. 29 : chapter ii. 25 ; v. 2, with John xxi. 15-17 : chapter v. 12, with Luke xxii. 32.

While the design of this Epistle is eminently practical, it is of great theological value. In contrast to JAMES, the fundamentals of the Christian Faith are presented none the less emphatically because non-controversially.

NOTE 101

The Interpretation of 1 Peter iii. 18 - 22.

THE literature of this passage is a library in itself. The difficulties are chiefly in verses 18-20. Matters which arise are:

1. Does "spirit" (18) refer to the Holy Spirit, or to Christ's human spirit ?

2. What is meant by "quickened" ? (18).

3. In the expressions "in the flesh," and "in the spirit" (R.V.), both datives must be regarded as of the *sphere*, "in" ; not the first of the *sphere*, and the second of the *instrument*, "by" (A.V.).

4. "In which" (19), that is, "in the spirit," Christ's holy human spirit.

5. "He went," must mean a local transference, as in verse 22, and so cannot mean that Christ preached through Noah, or through the Apostles.

6. "And preached." There are two principal words for "to preach" : *kērussō*, which means to *proclaim* as a herald, and *euangelizō*, which means to proclaim *glad tidings*. The former word is used in verse 19, and while it *might* refer to preaching the Gospel, it need not necessarily have that meaning, but only that a proclamation was made, without revealing the nature of it.

[Continued on page 530

Analysis of 1 Peter

(Continued from page 528.)

7. Does verse 22 throw light on the nature of the preaching ?

8. Who are meant by "the spirits" (19), of angels, or of men ?

9. What is meant by "in prison" ?   Hades, called Hell ?

10. Were the spirits in prison when they were preached to, or afterwards ?

11. Are only the "disobedient" in Noah's time referred to ? Why should a proclamation be made to a limited number, and not to all "disobedient" spirits ?

12. What was the issue of the proclamation ? Did these "disobedient" have a chance to repent ? And did any of them repent ?

13. Does this passage teach that sinners will have a chance of salvation after death ?

14. Does it teach, as Dean Farrar advocated, Eternal Hope ?

2 PETER

Keyword: KNOWLEDGE.

Place of writing: ?)　　　　　DATE: 68 A.D.

OF this Writing it has been said: "It is an Epistle for which we can offer the smallest amount of external evidence, and which at the same time presents the greatest number of internal difficulties." This should arouse our curiosity and lead us to an intensive study of the Letter, and such a study will be greatly rewarding. Within the purpose of this book we can only indicate what are the matters of principal interest.

THE AUTHENTICITY OF THE EPISTLE.

This raises two questions which are vitally related to one another and can scarcely be considered apart; first, is this Writing Holy Scripture? and second, was the writer of it the Apostle Peter? Practically all other questions are dependent on the answers which are given to these. The consideration of them is entirely dependent upon evidence, for "it must be remembered that this is a purely historical question; the authenticity of the Second Epistle of Peter is to be judged by the ordinary canons of literary criticism" (Gloag).

531

The evidence is twofold, external and internal, and, briefly stated, the facts are that for the authenticity of this Epistle the external evidence is weak, and the internal evidence is strong.

THE EXTERNAL EVIDENCE.

Here, summarily, the facts are that 2 PETER was not much quoted, nor widely known, nor generally accepted in the early Church as a part of Canonical Scripture. Eusebius divides the books of Scripture into three classes, those undoubtedly accepted; those not canonical, but disputed; and those that are spurious; and he places 2 PETER among the disputed books. It was, however, declared to be canonical by the Council of Laodicea, in A.D. 363, and by the Council of Carthage, in A.D. 397, and, presumptively, the evidence adduced before these Councils was such as to make the external testimony bear out the claims made in the text of the Epistle.

THE INTERNAL EVIDENCE.

This may be traced along several lines. First of all, there is the direct claim of the Epistle. The author calls himself Simon Peter, and says that he is an Apostle of Jesus Christ (i. 1); he states that he has already written an Epistle to those whom he is now addressing (iii. 1); he says that he saw Christ on the Mount of Transfiguration

(i. 16-18) ; he knows of Letters written by Paul (iii. 15, 16) ; he was evidently a Jew (mark his references to the O.T.) ; was an old man, and was expecting death soon (i. 13-15).

In the second place, the references to the readers favour the authorship of Peter. He says he had written to them before (iii. 1), and this must refer to 1 PETER, where we learn to whom he wrote (i. 1). Evidently the readers were Jews and Gentiles (ii. 5-9, and ii. 18). The writer is well acquainted with the spiritual condition of his readers (i. 1-4, 12 ; iii. 14, 17), and is on intimate and affectionate terms with them (i. 12, 13 ; iii. 1, 8, 14, 17, "beloved.")

In the third place, the two Epistles which bear Peter's name breathe the same spirit, and convey the same teaching. This is evident by comparing the references to—the end of the age (1 Peter i. 5 ; iv. 7 ; and 2 Peter iii. 3, 10) ; prophecy (1 Peter i. 10-12, and 2 Peter i. 19, 20 ; iii. 2) ; the Flood (1 Peter iii. 20 ; and 2 Peter ii. 5 ; iii. 6) ; Christian liberty (1 Peter ii. 16 ; and 2 Peter ii. 19) ; virtue, attributing it to God which is done nowhere else (1 Peter ii. 9 ; and 2 Peter i. 3). Prof. Lumly has pointed out that the writer of each of these Epistles uses very graphic words, words that are pictures, and although these are not the same words in both Epistles, the quality is the same in each. Examples of this in 1 PETER are, "to look," to stoop down that a good view of anything may be obtained (i. 12); "to silence," properly "to muzzle" (ii. 15); "buffeted," slapped with the hand (ii. 20); "be clothed," a word which indicates the putting on of a tight robe well rolled up, such as a slave would wear for hard work, used to indicate the way in which humility is to be the everyday wear of the true Christian (v. 5).

This graphic quality is found also in 2 PETER; for example in—"blind," "short-sighted," from which we get our word myopia (i. 9); the body as the "tabernacle" of the soul (i. 13, 14); "feigned," plastic, well-turned, easily bent words (ii. 3); "slumbereth," nods in sleep (ii. 3); "vexed," tormented (ii. 8); "great noise," the word implies the hurtling of weapons, or the splash of many waters (iii. 10); "wrest," to put on the rack (iii. 16).

Also it has been pointed out that words are used by the writer of this Epistle which are used by Peter in the ACTS, as, for example, "obtained" (i. 1, and Acts i. 17); "holiness" (i. 7, and Acts iii. 12); "unlawful" (ii. 8, and Acts ii. 23); "day of the Lord" (iii. 10, and Acts ii. 20); "wages of iniquity" (ii. 13, 15, and Acts i. 18). These are but a few of many instances, and they add to the evidence that the speaker in the ACTS was the writer of this Letter.

Another line of evidence is in recollections in these two Epistles of incidents during the ministry of Christ with which Peter was familiar. For example, in 1 PETER, "be clothed with humility" (v. 5) almost certainly reflects the scene in John xiii. 4 ; "feed the flock of God" (v. 2), is an echo of John xxi. 15, 16. We find the same thing in the Second Epistle. For example, "alluring" (ii. 14, 18), is to catch with a bait, a thought which goes back to the fisherman's life on the Lake of Galilee. Chapter iii. 3, 4, 10, recalls Christ's Olivet Discourse ; and chapter i. 12, is a remembrance of Luke xxii. 32.

If to these evidences is added this further one, the great superiority of this Epistle to every one of the uncanonical writings of the first and second centuries, we may safely conclude, on critical grounds, that Peter the Apostle wrote this Epistle, and that, therefore, it is inspired Scripture.

THE DATE AND PLACE OF WRITING.

Obviously it was written after the First Epistle (iii. 1) ; when some of Paul's Letters were widely read (iii. 15, 16) ; and shortly before Peter's death

(i. 13-15). Assuming that "Babylon" (v. 13),
means Rome, we conclude that this Letter was
written from the Capital after A.D. 64, and before
A.D. 70, probably in A.D. 67-68.

THE OBJECT AND OUTLINE OF THE LETTER.

This was, and is, to encourage scattered Christians
in the cultivation of the spiritual life ; to warn
against false teachers and doctrines ; and to re-
emphasize that hope of the believer, the Lord's
Return. These subjects largely correspond to the
three chapters of the Epistle.

The keynote is FULL KNOWLEDGE (i. 2, 3, 5, 6,
8, 16, 20 ; ii. 20, 21 ; iii. 3, 17, 18) ; and this is
related to the Christian's Growth, and Peril, and
Hope.

THE KNOWLEDGE OF GOD AND THE
CHRISTIAN'S GROWTH

1. *Our Ample Provision* (i. 2-4). The Apostle's
desire is that, in that knowledge, grace and peace
might be multiplied unto us. The reason for this
is, that by means of that knowledge, we are fur-
nished with all things that pertain to life and godliness, chiefly in the great and exceeding precious
promises. And the object of the foregoing is both
negative and positive ; separation from this world,
and participation of the Divine nature.

Where the provision is so great, the obligations

will be great also, and these are set forth in the next section.

2. *Our Actual Progress* (i. 5-11). The word "add" (5) may signify structure, or, furnishing with a chorus ; in any case the line of our development (5-7) is to be from faith to love, by way of virtue, knowledge, self-control, patience, godliness, and brotherliness. With these should be compared the "fruit of the Spirit" in Gal. v. 22, 23. The promises can be fulfilled to us only as we fulfil the precepts (Mal. iii. 10). Next (8, 9), the results determined are according to whether we obey or not. In the one case, we shall be fruitful, and in the other, we shall be blind. Hence, the great need for diligence (10, 11), with a view, both to present security (10) and ultimate safety (11).

Having set forth our Provision, and having exhorted to Progress, the Apostle now shows what is the ground of our assurance, and how solid is the knowledge on which we rest.

3. *Our Abiding Pledge* (i. 12-21). This is twofold, covering the entire Scriptures. First, Apostolic Testimony (12-18). Peter is anxious that his testimony shall be perpetuated, and made permanent ; thus, in view of the nearness of his violent death, predicted by Jesus (John xxi) he is writing these two Epistles (12-14), and proposes

to leave a record of the life of Jesus also (15), which thing was done in Mark's Gospel. The Substance of his testimony is "the power and coming of the Lord Jesus Christ," facts revealed on the transfiguration Mount, and witnessed by Peter himself. This is the New Testament pledge, and leads the Apostle back to the Old Testament, to the testimony of Hebrew Prophecy (19-21). By the happenings on the Mount, together with all the facts of the earthly life and ministry of Jesus, "the word of O.T. prophecy, concerning the Messiah, is made more sure," and to that word we should take heed in our hearts, knowing that such is not the "invention" of men, but the work of the Holy Spirit through chosen men.

The mention of "prophets" leads the Apostle to say that there were false among the true prophets, that in these days the false would abound, and that these constituted a real danger, threatening the Christian's progress. Thus, chapter ii. treats of

THE KNOWLEDGE OF GOD AND THE
CHRISTIAN'S PERIL.

False teachers is the subject throughout, and first of all :

Their Doctrine is Defined (ii. 1-3a). They deny the Atonement, and perhaps, the Deity of the Lord Jesus (1) ; with the result that they have a large following of religious persons, who bring the truth into disrepute (2); and the motive of these false teachers is shown to be covetousness (3a).

Their Destruction is then Declared (ii. 3b-9). It is first asserted that Judgment would overtake all such (3b), and then, that destruction is argued from analogies in the past; (*a*) the doom of the Angels; (*b*) the Flood; (*c*) the overthrow of Sodom and Gomorrha (4-8); and finally, the foregoing is affirmed in its aspects both of deliverance to, and from (9).

The Apostle lastly, sets forth the character of these teachers, as exhibited in their conduct.

Their Doings are Described (ii. 10-22). The points to be marked here are, their presumption (10-13a), their sensuality (13b-16), their entice-ments (17-19), and their apostasy (20-22).

Nor have we done with the false prophets yet. Not only did they attack the foundation of the Christian's faith, but also the reality of his hope. Hence the next chapter.

THE KNOWLEDGE OF GOD AND THE CHRISTIAN'S HOPE.

First we see:

The Advent Truth Assailed (iii. 1-4). Scoffers would arise who would ridicule the idea that Christ was to return to this world, and they would appear to have the uniformity of history on their side. But the Apostle shows that this is not the case. So we have next :

The Advent Truth Attested (iii. 5-10). Peter begins by refuting what the false teachers were saying (5-7). He shows that the former world did perish, and that these scoffers were "willingly ignorant" of that fact. They were not lacking in capacity, neither was there a scarcity of evidence. And as surely as that world was destroyed by water, this world would be destroyed by fire.

After the refutation comes an explanation of the delay of which the scoffers had made so much (8-10). Firstly, the Lord's relation to Time is set forth (8) ; He does not reckon as we do. Secondly, His relation to Men (9). The delay is not an evidence of indifference on the Lord's part, but of His tender longsuffering, not willing that any should perish. Thirdly, His relation to Evil (10). The Lord being what He is, must visit all the works of the world with judgment, and as predicted throughout the Scriptures, that "day of the Lord" would come suddenly. The Apostle, finally, brings these truths home to the hearts of his readers.

The Advent Truth Applied (iii. 11-18a). Our conduct must take shape in the light of these facts ;

we must both "look for" and "hasten" the day of God, and give diligence to be found, when He comes, spotless and blameless ; for, in the new earth and heaven beyond the judgment, only righteousness dwells. On this subject there is perfect harmony between the teachings of the Apostles. Therefore, knowing these things, we must "beware" and "grow," beware of the evil, and grow in grace and knowledge. As the Epistle began, so it ends, with the affirmation that in the full knowledge of God are peace, power, and progress to be found.

This Epistle and that of Jude.

No one can have read these two Epistles with any care without having observed the similarity between Jude's Letter and the second chapter of Peter's. Compare, for instance, chapter ii. 1, and Jude 4 ; chapter ii. 4 and Jude 6 ; chapter ii. 6 and Jude 7 ; chapter ii. 10 and Jude 8 ; chapter ii. 11 and Jude 9 ; chapter ii. 12 and Jude 10 ; chapter ii. 13 and Jude 12 ; chapter ii. 15 and Jude 11 ; chapter ii. 17, and Jude 12, 13 ; chapter ii. 18, and Jude 16 ; chapter iii. 2 and Jude 17 ; chapter iii. 3 and Jude 18.

How are these parallels to be accounted for ? As we said when considering Jude, one of four theories must be true. Either that Peter and Jude wrote independently, both being guided in their thoughts and expressions by the Holy Spirit ; or that both paraphrased the same document, written in some other language than the Greek ; or that Jude made use of the Epistle of Peter ; or that Peter made use of the Epistle of Jude. For the first of these theories we have no parallel, and it is extremely unlikely. For the second, we have no evidence. Either of the other two is possible, and, on the whole, the balance is in favour of the priority of Peter's Epistle.

It would seem that what in PETER is approaching is in JUDE present ; and that Jude expands what Peter had written (cf. the references above) ; but the matter is of more interest than importance.

NOTES.

Among words peculiar to 2 PETER are :

"Like precious" (i. 1) ; "short-sighted" (i. 9) ; "eye-witnesses" (i. 16) ; "obscure" (i. 19) ; "dawn" (i. 19) ; "morning star" (i. 19) ; "interpretation" (i. 20) ; "speedily," "swift" (i. 14 ; ii. 1) ; "feigned" (ii. 3) ; "of old" (ii. 3 ; iii. 5) ; "Tartarus" (ii. 4) ; "chains" (ii. 4) ; "seeing" (ii. 8) ; "blemishes" (ii. 13) ; "sporting" (ii. 13) ; "cease not" (ii. 14) ; "madness" (ii. 16) ; "vomit" (ii. 22) ; "wallowing" (ii. 22) ; "rushing noise" (iii. 10) ; "burning heat" (iii. 10, 12) ; "hard to be understood" (iii. 16) ; "unestablished" (ii. 14 ; iii. 16) ; "steadfastness" (iii. 17).

In addition to these are many striking words

and phrases. Some of these, cited by Farrar, are :

"To acquire faith by lot" (i. 1) ; "to give things which tend
to life and piety" (i. 3) ; "to bring in all haste" (i. 5) ; "to
furnish an abundant supply of virtue" (i. 5) ; "to receive
oblivion" (i. 9) ; "to furnish an abundant entrance" (i. 11) ;
"the present truth" (i. 12) ; "to bring in factions of perdition"
(ii. 7) ; "the judgment is not idle, the destruction is not drow-
sily nodding" (ii. 3) ; "to walk in desire of pollution" (ii. 10) ;
"to walk behind the flesh" (ii. 10) ; "to esteem luxurious
wantonness in the daytime as a pleasure" (ii. 13) ; "eyes full
of an adulteress" (ii. 14) ; "insatiable of sin" (ii. 14) ; "a heart
trained in covetousness" (ii. 14) ; "the mists of the darkness"
(ii. 17) ; "treasured with fire" (iii. 7) ; "the heavens shall pass
away hurtlingly" (iii. 10) ; "denying even the Master that
bought them" (ii. 1. Peter's momentary denial, at a moment
of strong temptation, differs wholly from this persistent
negation and apostasy).

What wealth of truth is in chapter i. 5-7 ; which
Moffatt translates : "For this very reason, do you
continue to make it your whole concern to furnish
your faith with resolution, resolution with intelligence, intelligence with self-control, self-control
with steadfastness, steadfastness with godliness,
godliness with brotherliness, and brotherliness
with Christian love." Here is a spiritual octave,
beginning with faith, ending with love, and with
manly energy, discernment, self-control, patience,
godliness, and brotherliness between.

How solemn are the following alternatives (8-11),
on the one hand, "neither idle nor unfruitful,"
and on the other hand, "lacking—short-sighted—
forgetful" !

Analysis of 2 Peter

ADDRESS (i. 1).

I. THE KNOWLEDGE OF GOD, AND THE CHRISTIAN'S GROWTH (i. 2-21).

II. THE KNOWLEDGE OF GOD, AND THE CHRISTIAN'S PERIL (ii. 1-22).

III. THE KNOWLEDGE OF GOD, AND THE CHRISTIAN'S HOPE (iii. 1-18a).

DOXOLOGY (18b).

THE JOHANNINE EPISTLES

1 JOHN

2 JOHN

3 JOHN

THE REVELATION

NOTE 102

The Viewpoints of Paul and John Compared.

IN his learned and luminous work, *The Early Days of Christianity*,
Dean Farrar summarises this comparison. He says:

"St. Paul is like a painter who works out his results by the use of
many colours, and with an infinitude of touch; St. John produces
the effect which he desires by a few pure colours and a few sweeping
but consummate strokes. St. Paul is discursive, St. John intuitive,
St. Paul begins with man, St. John with God. St. Paul passes from
anthropology to theology, St. John moves chiefly in the purely
theologic sphere. . . . The aim of St. Paul is human and practical,
and he dwells incessantly on Faith, Hope, and Love. St. John's
Divine idealism is mainly occupied with the abstract conceptions of
Love and Life and Light. St. Paul is pleading with men as they are,
and building them up into what they should be. St. John assumes
that the Christians to whom he writes are resting with him in the full
knowledge of Christ."

Paul is essentially the theologian of the Apostles, and John is
essentially the mystic. Both are necessary, and both together.
Theology may be hard without mysticism, and mysticism senti-
mental without theology.

1 JOHN

Keyword : FELLOWSHIP.

Place of Writing : EPHESUS.   DATE : 95-98 A.D.

IN respect of number, and we may assume in respect of value also, the Apostle Paul has made the largest contribution to the New Testament library, with thirteen Writings. Next to him, in both respects, comes the Apostle John, with five Writings, a Gospel, three Epistles, and an Apocalypse. These five are called the Johannine Writings, and constitute a distinctive group with unmistakable characteristics.

THE APOSTLE JOHN.

The story of John is rich and full. Only a bare outline of it is necessary here, but it should be studied carefully at the sources.

I. *His Home and Occupation.* (1) The Family Circle. Place of their home, Bethsaida (Luke v. 10 ; John i. 44). A family of four : Zebedee, Salome, James and John (i. 19, 20 ; xv. 40 ; Matt. xxvii. 56). Occupation of the father and sons: fishermen (Matt. iv. 21). Character of Salome : ambitious (Luke viii. 3 ; Matt. xx. 20). (2) Material Prosperity. Evidence of it (Mark i. 20 ;

Matt. xxvii. 56 ; Luke viii. 3 ; John xix. 27 ; xviii. 16). Source of it : the fishing industry was lucrative.

II. *His Discipleship and Service-life.* (1) A follower of John the Baptist (John i. 35, 40). (2) A follower of the Christ. The three calls : (*a*) to attachment (John i. 40) ; (*b*) to discipleship (Matt. iv. 21, 22) ; (*c*) to apostleship (Luke vi. 12, 13, 14). His relation to Jesus was unique. He was his cousin ; the mothers were sisters. He was one of the first two disciples called (John i. 35-40). One of the first four Apostles named (Matt. iv. 18-22). One of the three privileged Apostles (Mark v. 37 ; Matt. xvii. 1 ; xxvi. 37). One of the four who drew forth our Lord's prophetic discourse (Mark xiii. 3). One of the two sent to prepare the Passover (Luke xxii. 8). "The disciple whom Jesus loved," and who lay on His breast at the Last Supper (John xiii. 23 ; xx. 2 ; xxi. 7, 20).

III. *References to him in the History of the Church.* He appears three times in the Acts (iii. 1 ; iv. 13 ; viii. 14), but after Acts xv (cf. Gal. ii) there is no more mention of him for over forty years, and these references are in his own Writings (John i. 40 ; Rev. i. 1, 4, 9). This is surprising.

IV. *The Character of the Apostle.* Two seemingly opposite characteristics unite in him, passion and contemplation. He and his brother were called *Boanerges*, "the sons of thunder." John was fiery in zeal and severe in temperament; incapable of half-enthusiasms (cf. Mark iii. 17; Luke ix. 54; 1 John ii. 22; iii. 8, 15; iv. 20). But that he was retiring and contemplative in disposition is equally evident. In the early Church it was Peter who took the lead (Acts ii. 14; iii. 4; iv. 8), and John's references to himself are generally indirect (John i. 40; xiii. 23; xx. 2; xxi. 7, 20; cf. Rev. i. 4, 9). John was the first to appear on the stage of apostolic story, and he was the last to leave it. In matter of years he spans the first century.

JOHN AND THE APOSTLES.

In Gal. ii. 9, Paul refers to three "pillar" Apostles. These were James, the Lord's brother, Peter, and John. Paul himself made the fourth, and on these four pillars the Temple of New Testament revelation rests.

The Temple stands foursquare. The Christian revelation is manifold. No one presentation of it could be adequate, any more than one of the Evangelic Records could be adequate as a presentation of Jesus, the Christ. God in His wisdom chose four men to set forth Christianity cubically. James (and Jude) represents Judaic

Christianity. Peter represents Catholic Christianity. Paul represents Evangelic Christianity (with HE-BREWS); and John represents Mystical Christianity. These distinctions are not rigid and exclusive; they overlap and interpenetrate, yet, they are distinctly discernible. Peter's contribution is transitional from James to Paul, and John's contribution crowns them all. The times and circumstances in which these men wrote help to explain the form of their respective presentations, and disclose how their temperament and training fitted them for their task, under the guidance of the Holy Spirit.

Godet says : "The hour for work had sounded in the first place for Peter. He had founded the Church in Israel, and planted the Standard of the new Covenant on the ruins of the theocracy. Paul had followed. His task had been to liberate the Church from the restrictions of expiring Judaism, and to open the door of the Kingdom of God to the Gentiles. John succeeded them, he who was the first to come, and whom his Master reserved to be the last. He completed the fusion of those heterogeneous elements of which the Church had been formed, and he raised Christendom to the relative perfection of which it was then capable. It may be said, then, that Peter founded the Primitive Church, Paul emancipated it, and John established it."

Paul and John, as to their teaching, present many comparisons and contrasts. They wrote at different times, in different circumstances, from different standpoints, in different forms, with different objects, and in conformity to their different equipments ; yet, their Writings are not contradictory but complementary. By moving in the sphere of a few ultimate verities John consummates what Paul so grandly commenced. One feels that on John's Writings is the stamp of finality. The teaching of Paul and James is stated in apparent opposition, but John restates it in intimate and inseparable harmony. They are but two sides of the same truth. And as with truth, so with error. Dr. Plummer says : "St. Paul constantly reminds us that the believer has to meet the hostility both of the Jew and of the Pagan." In this Epistle neither Jew nor Pagan is even named. The distinctive hostility of Jew and Pagan to the Church has, says Dean Farrar, "melted into the one dark background of ' the world.'"

THE WRITINGS OF JOHN.

These present an interesting variety ; a Gospel Record, an Apocalypse, and three Epistles ; one

of the latter differing considerably from the usual
epistolary form, and the other two being short
notes of a more or less personal character. Though
differing in class and form these Writings are
intimately related to one another, and together
constitute a wonderful whole. The Gospel shows
that the Man of Galilee is God. The Epistles
show that it is God Who became Man. And the
Apocalypse shows that ultimate victory is through
and for the God-Man (Theanthropos). The Gospel
has been called a summary of *Christian Theology*,
the first Epistle a summary of *Christian Ethics*,
and the Apocalypse a summary of *Christian
Politics*.

It would seem that the Epistle was written to be
a companion to the Gospel, and they should be
read together. The main object is the same in
both, but the approach and emphasis are different.
This fact has been helpfully summarised by Dr.
Plummer, who says : "The Gospel is objective,
the Epistle is subjective ; the one is historical, the
other moral ; the one gives us the theology of the
Christ, the other the ethics of the Christian ; the
one is didactic, the other polemical ; the one
states the truth as a thesis, the other as an antithesis ; the one starts from the human side, the
other from the divine ; the one proves that the

Man Jesus is the Son of God, the other insists that the Son of God is come in the flesh. But the connection between the two is intimate and organic throughout. The Gospel suggests principles of conduct which the Epistle lays down explicitly; the Epistle implies facts which the Gospel states as historically true."

THE READERS.

We are not told by an epistolary address to whom John wrote this Epistle, but we may conclude that it was designed first of all for the Church of Ephesus, then for the other Churches of Asia, and finally for the whole Church of God. Like EPHESIANS it is a Circular Letter ; and as there are no quotations in it from the Old Testament, but a warning against idolatry (v. 21), it may be that the writer had converts from heathenism specially in mind. In the absence of anything to the contrary we may assume that the Letter was written at Ephesus.

THE DATE.

The Neronian persecution ended in A.D. 68 ; the overthrow of Jerusalem, under Titus, was in A.D. 70, and after that there is a quarter of a century of silence, so far as inspired Writings are concerned. Then, in the last decade of the first century the last of the Apostles wrote his Gospel and three Epistles (see Introduction to the REVELATION for its date). The First Epistle is then the final treatise of New Testament Scripture, and of inspired revelation.

THE OBJECT.

We are not left in doubt as to why John wrote this Epistle, for in thirteen references he tells us (i. 4 ; ii. 1, 7, 8, 12, 13 tr., 14t, 21, 26 ; v. 13). The writer assumes on the part of his readers an advanced knowledge of God ; he would confirm and extend this ; warns them against present perils (ii) ; and, by promoting their fellowship with God and one another, would increase their joy (i. 1-4). This matter of knowledge, as the basis of knowledge, with a view to experience is of the utmost importance. Two words are used in the Epistle for "to know ;" one (*oida*) implies the knowledge which comes from without, *objective* knowledge, and this word occurs sixteen times ; the other (*ginōskō*) expresses the knowledge as existing in the mind, *subjective* knowledge, experimental knowledge, and this word occurs twenty-five times (the intensified form, *epiginōskō*, does not occur in the Epistle). The relation of the objective to the subjective knowledge is well brought out in two verses in John's Gospel : "If ye know (*oida*) these things, blessed are ye if ye do them" (xiii. 17); and "If anyone desire to practise His will, he shall know (*ginōskō*) concerning the teaching" (vii. 17). Both in the Gospel and the Epistle John's object is to get apprehension of spiritual truth deepened into the experience of it.

THE PLAN.

It has been thought that there is no plan in this Epistle, that it is "incoherent," "an unmethodised effusion of pious sentiments and reflections," a series of aphorisms, a congery of scattered remarks. No doubt this view has been arrived at because of the obvious difficulty of the writer's method. That the Epistle does not lend itself readily to analysis is granted; neither does the face of the sky, nor of the sea; yet in all there is order. Every commentator has his outline of the Epistle, and no one of them would claim that it is *the* outline, yet each presents the truth from one or other of its many angles (cf. Bp. Alexander, Alford, Pope, Sinclair, Westcott, Haupt, Plummer, Farrar, etc.), and for this reason all analyses are suggestive.

THE STYLE.

It is claimed that John's style is "absolutely unique, supremely original, and full of charm and sweetness." Paul is syllogistic, the writer to the

Hebrews is rhetorical, James is gnomic and sen-
tentious, Peter is conversational, but John is
contemplative, and antithetic. Simplicity of language and majesty of thought are here united.
The still waters run deep. In ROMANS Paul
builds up his argument bit by bit, with logical
precision, but here John does not argue ; he just
states the truth and leaves it. The antithetical
structure and rhythmical cadence of his sentences
are noteworthy. Thought is set over against
thought in sharp contrast. He thinks in terms of
ultimates. His colours are white and black ; there
is no grey. He treats of life and death, truth and
falsehood, love and hate, light and darkness,
righteousness and sin, the Father and the World,
children of God and children of the Devil.

John passes from one subject to another in a
subtle manner, and it is not always easy to follow
the transition, but closer study shows a vital
connection. It is observable that he takes a word
and plays upon it, then passes to another, and to
yet another. In illustration, mark :

"Fellowship," in i. 3, 6, 7 ; "if we," in i. 6, 7, 8, 9, 10 ;
"keep" and "commandment," in ii. 3, 4, 5, 7, 8 ; "darkness,"
in ii. 8, 9, 11 ; "I write," "have written," in ii. 12-14 , "world,"
in ii. 15-17 ; "abide" (same as "remain" and "continue"), in
ii. 24-28 ; "sin," "sins," in iii. 5-9 ; "love," in iii. 10-18 ; iv.
7-12, 16-21 ; v. 1-3 ; "we know," in v. 15, 18, 19, 20.

It will repay one to study carefully this method of
the Apostle.

What has been called "triplicity" characterizes
this Epistle. The writer naturally thinks and
expresses himself in this way, and the unstudied
method is observable both in verses and sections.

> "If we say we have no sin,
> We deceive ourselves,
> And the truth is not in us."

> "If we confess our sins,
> He is faithful and righteous to
> forgive us our sins,
> And to cleanse us from all un-
> righteousness."

> "If we say that we have not sinned,
> We make Him a liar,
> And His word is not in us."

THE THEOLOGY OF THE EPISTLE.

Here, as in the Gospel, God is revealed in
Christ as Light, and Love, and Life, and the
believer is related to the God thus revealed. These
thoughts supply us with what of divisions may be
found in the Letter. In chapters i. 5-ii. 29, God
is Light, and the advance of the Christian is prominent. In chapters iii. 1-iv. 21, God is Love, and
the attitude of the Christian is prominent. In
chapter v. 1-20, God is Life, and the affinity of
the Christian is prominent. This corresponds
with the prologue to the Gospel (i. 1-18), where

the Life is revealed (1-5), the Light is displayed
(6-13), and the Love is expressed (14-18). Then,
in chapters i. 19-xii. 50, God as Life is revealed to
the world ; in chapters xiii-xvii, God as Light is
revealed to the disciples ; and in chapters xviii-xx,
God as Love is revealed to all. These are the
ultimate realities, and it was given to "the beloved
disciple," to "the eagle," as Dante called him,
to make this final contribution to Holy Scripture,
and so to crown divine revelation.

NOTE 103

Interpretations of 1 John iii. 6.

He cannot commit mortal sin (Romanists).

He cannot sin deliberately and intentionally (Ebrard).

He cannot sin in the way of hating his brother (Bede).

It is alien from his nature to sin (Grotius).

His nature and habit resist sin (Paulus).

He does not *wish* to sin, and *ought* not to sin (various commentators).

He cannot be a sinner (Wordsworth).

He *does* not sin, he only *suffers* sin (Besser: cf. Rom. vii. 17).

So far as he remains true to himself, he does not sin (Augustine).

The statement cannot be understood literally, but must
mean that sin cannot be the *habit* of a true Christian (cf.
i. 8; ii. 1).

Analysis of 1 John

INTRODUCTION (i. 1-4).

CONCLUSION (v. 21).

2 JOHN

Keyword : TRUTH.

Place of Writing : EPHESUS.   DATE : 95-98 A.D.

THE AUTHOR.

ATTEMPTS have been made to show that
Second and Third JOHN were written by a
"Presbyter" or "Elder" of that name, but it is
practically certain that no such person ever existed,
other than John the Evangelist and Apostle. All
the internal evidence confirms the view that the
writer of these two Notes was the writer of the
First Epistle and of the Gospel. Of the thirteen
verses of 2 JOHN no less than eight are found in
substance in the First Epistle.

THE PLACE OF WRITING AND THE DATE.

We have no data which would enable us to
speak with certainty on either of these matters,
but it may safely be assumed that the Epistle was
written at Ephesus, and written between 95-98
A.D. These two Notes were probably the last
New Testament Scripture to be written.

THE ADDRESS.

Not a little ingenuity has been exhibited in the
effort to determine to whom this Letter was sent.

The address : "Unto the elect lady and her children," is capable of more than one interpretation. It may refer to a certain Church, or to the universal Church, or it may refer to an individual. Each view has been influentially held, but on the principle that, where there are several possible interpretations of a phrase, the simplest and most natural one is the best, we conclude that this Letter was addressed to a now unknown lady, possibly a widow, and her children. Only in this view can verse 13 be understood. If this assumption be correct, then "elect" (*eklektē*) and "lady" (*kuria*) are not proper names, but appellatives.

THE OBJECT.

Apparently children of this lady had been on a visit to some of their cousins (13), and John, on one of his pastoral visits had met them. Delighted to find them living faithful Christian lives he writes this note to their mother, and he takes the opportunity to add some words of Christian teaching.

THE SUBSTANCE.

The keynotes are "truth" and "love," the one word occurring five times, and the other, four times. These God has joined together, and they should never be put asunder. Certainly we should walk in truth, but not in truth only, for that would be hard ; and certainly we should walk in love, but not in love only, for that would be soft ; but we should walk in both. The reference in the Letter to error shows how necessary are both truth and love. Either alone would lead us to a wrong relation to the people referred to in verses 9-11. We are not to take into our fellowship those who are against the true doctrine in respect of the Person of Christ. We must be uncompromising on the matters of Christ's real humanity and proper Deity ; but we must be careful not to apply verse 10, to anyone who may differ from us in some other and less important matters of doctrine. We must walk in truth, and also in love. It is the same Apostle who says : "Grace and truth came by Jesus Christ." Let neither triumph at the expense of the other.

NOTES.

In this Letter we have a glimpse of the every-day life of the Christian home ; we are allowed to see how the beloved disciple at the close of his life could write to a Christian lady, and in the second Epistle, to a Christian gentleman, respecting their personal conduct.

These two Notes, with PHILEMON, are precious specimens of the private correspondence of two of the greatest Apostles. How much poorer the

Church of God would have been if these had not been preserved!

The Apostle John is here seen in the capacity, not of a Metropolitan, but as a Shepherd of individual souls. The atmosphere of this Letter is that of the home rather than of the Church. It shows "with what vigilant affection the ministers of the Gospel ought to cherish the piety of those whom they have gained, and it shows no less the importance in the sight of God, of the station of a Christian mother, and the earnestness with which she should interest herself in the religious welfare of her children" (Angus).

In these thirteen verses there are forty-five variations between the Authorised and the Revised Versions.

In addition to "truth," and "love," recurring words are "commandment," and "walking."

"Grace" (3) is rare in John's Writings; only here, and John i. 14, 16, 17; Rev. i. 4; xxii. 21.

"Mercy" (3) occurs only here in John's Writings.

"Peace," "grace," and "mercy" occur together only here and in 1 Tim. i. 1; Titus i. 4; 2 Tim. i. 2.

In verse 9, "transgresseth" should read "goeth onward," "taketh the lead," or "goeth forward." Dr. Plummer's note on this is excellent. The verse "may be interpreted in two ways : (1) Every one who sets himself up as a leader ; (2) Every one who goes on beyond the Gospel. The latter is perhaps better. These anti-Christian Gnostics were *advanced* thinkers ; the Gospel was all very well for the unenlightened; but they knew something higher. This agrees very well with what follows ; by *advancing* they did not abide. There is an advance which involves desertion of first principles ; and such an advance is not progress but apostasy. "

NOTE 104

False Teachers and Hospitality.

"IF anyone cometh unto you, and bringeth not this teaching, receive him not into your house, and give him no greeting, for he that giveth him greeting partaketh in his evil works" (2 John 10).

In the interpretation of this statement two mistakes must be avoided: (*a*) the mistake of making it the ground for the persecution of all who do not hold our religious beliefs: and (*b*) the mistake of helping forward the dissemination of fundamentally false teaching by, in the interests of charity, allowing those who "abide not in the teaching of Christ" (9) to pervert "the church in our house," or by sending such on their way to other churches with our recommendation of confidence and goodwill. Between those who believe and those who deny the full N.T. doctrine concerning Christ's Person and work, there is "a great gulf fixed," and charity here is treachery.

Analysis of 2 John

INTRODUCTION (1-3).

(*a*) Love.
(*b*) Truth.

I. THE PATH OF THE BELIEVER (4-6).

II. THE PERIL OF THE BELIEVER (7-11).

CONCLUSION (12, 13).

3 JOHN

Keyword : HOSPITALITY.

Place of Writing : EPHESUS.   DATE : 95-98 A.D.

WHAT has been said in the introduction to the
Second Epistle as to authorship, place of
writing, and date, is applicable here : John the
Apostle ; Ephesus ; A.D. 95-98.

THE ADDRESS.

While there is reasonable doubt as to what is
meant by the address of the Second Epistle, there
can be no doubt here. It is to a man named Gaius.
All that we may know for certain of him is what
is said in this brief note. Gaius was a very common
Roman name, and at least three persons bearing
it are introduced in the New Testament ; Gaius
of Corinth (Rom. xvi. 23 ; 1 Cor. i. 14) ; Gaius of
Macedonia (Acts xix. 29), and Gaius of Derbe
(Acts xx. 4, 5). It is not unlikely that the Gaius
to whom John now writes may be one of these.
From this note we learn that he was a believer,
beloved of the Apostle, setting a good example to
other believers, noted for his hospitality to travelling missionaries, well known, possibly a well-to-do
layman, whom the Apostle hopes shortly to visit.

THE OBJECT.

This was to encourage Gaius in his good work, and to contrast his conduct with that of a man named Diotrephes. When we appreciate the importance of hospitality in the service of the Early Church, we shall not think such a subject to be unworthy of Holy Scripture.

But for such hospitality Christian missionary ministry could hardly have been carried on. Many of the early missionaries, like Paul, would take nothing from the Gentiles (7), and had not the homes of Christian friends been freely opened to them, it would have been impossible for them to do their work at all. Gaius had helped such, in a manner "worthily of God" (6), by forwarding them on their journey. Perhaps he had extended hospitality to those to whom Diotrephes denied it (10). For other references to hospitality, showing the importance of it, see Rom. xii. 13 ; 1 Tim. iii. 2 ; Titus i. 8 ; Heb. xiii. 2 ; 1 Peter iv. 9.

THE SUBSTANCE.

Brief though this Note is, it contains three pen portraits which the Apostle "etches in a few words with the same masterly psychological skill which we see in the Gospel"—Gaius, Diotrephes, Demetrius.

19

We have already summarized what is said of
Gaius. The reference to Diotrephes is not less
interesting, though for a very different reason.
He seems to have been the Presbyter of an Asiatic
Church, and with such power, that he could
repudiate the authority of the oldest and last
surviving Apostle, could suppress a letter which
John had written to the Church, could refuse to
receive the travelling missionaries, tried to prevent
other members of the Church from doing so, and
ventured to excommunicate those who did so
(9, 10). If it be thought that such a state of things
was not possible, let us remember that the great
Paul had his opponents (1 Tim. i. 20 ; 2 Tim. ii.
17, 18), and those who forged his name on letters
of their own (2 Thess. ii. 2 ; iii. 7). Well has Dr.
Plummer said : "The ideal primitive Church,
bright in the unbroken possession of truth and
holiness, is unknown to the historian."

Not much is said about Demetrius, possibly the
bearer of the Letter, but what is said is worthy and
noteworthy. Diotrephes set an example to be
abhorred ; Demetrius set one to be imitated.

Dr. Plummer thinks that "the Truth" in verse
12, refers to the Holy Spirit, in which case the witness borne to this man was both human and Divine.
Is it possible that this is the Demetrius who once

made silver shrines for Artemis ? (Acts xix. 24).

Thus, here, we have two bright pictures, and one dark one ; two worthy, and one unworthy ; two to follow, and one to avoid.

NOTES.

How amazing are these three Letters of the Apostle John ! Amazing in their profoundness in view of their brevity. In the First are about 2350 words ; in the Second are 245 ; and in the Third are 219, a few more than 2,800 words, the length of a short article, yet, this is writing of infinite significance and exhaustless power.

The Second and Third Letters are "specimens of the free and unreserved religious correspondence which in all ages has been interchanged between Christians. . . . They begin that branch of literature which has been subsequently enriched by men like Basil, and Gregory of Nazianzus, and Gregory of Nyssa, and Jerome, and Augustine, and Gregory the Great, and Luther, and Rutherford, and Cowper, and Wesley, and Robertson, and Maurice" (Farrar).

It may be that this Third Epistle is the last letter that John wrote. His great age disinclined him to write (13 ; 2 John 12), but he was still able to get about (14 ; 2 John 12).

Observe the occurrence of the words, "walk," "Church," "beloved," "write," "testimony," and "truth," "love," "ink and pen" (cf. 2 John 12). Words peculiar to this Epistle are, "to welcome" (8); "Love to have the pre-eminence" (9); and "to prate against" (10). The word "friends" as applied to Christians, is peculiar to John (cf. John xi. 11 ; xv. 13-15).

The Second and Third Epistles both centre in Truth and Love ; both speak of hospitality, the one of that which is forbidden, and the other of that which is enjoined ; and both refer to a visit which the aged Apostle proposes to make to the homes of his friends.

Analysis of 3 John

THE BOOK OF THE
REVELATION

THE REVELATION

Keyword : CONSUMMATION.

Place of Writing : PATMOS.   DATE : 68-70 A.D.

THE AUTHOR.

IT may be well to say that the value of this Book
is not dependent on the idea that John the
Apostle wrote it. It nowhere says that he did.
The writer's name was John (i. 4, 9 ; xxii. 8), but
that was a common name then, as now. Whether
the writer was John the Apostle must be determined
by external and internal evidence. The external
attestation of the Apostle's authorship is strong.
The internal evidence is definitely against it.
The question is which of these evidences prevails.
The evidence against the writer being the Apostle
is based on the unlikeness of theological terms and
ideas between the REVELATION and the other Johannine Writings ; on the unlikeness of style and
grammar, and on the unlikeness between the moral
tone and temper of the two writers. The briefest
word about each of these in the inverse order.

As to tone and temper. If love characterises
the Johannine Writings, and severity the REVELATION,
let us remember that there was *thunder* as well as
tenderness in the Apostle's nature (Mark iii. 17) ;

that the thunder appears in the Gospel and Epistles (I John ii. 22 ; v. 16 ; 2 John 10 ; 3 John 9, 10) ; and that the tenderness appears in the REVELATION (i. 9 ; vii. 14-17 ; xxi. 3, 4).

As to the style and grammar. Those competent to judge are agreed that the Gospel and Epistles are written in good Greek, and that the Greek of the REVELATION is not good. This fact would be all the more astonishing if we could be sure that the REVELATION was written in the same decade of the first century, as were the Gospel and Epistles. But further on this point is discussed under Date.

As to theological terms and ideas. Dionysius enumerates some eighteen characteristic Johannine phrases compared with which he says : "The REVELATION is utterly different and strange, neither touching nor approaching any of these, nor having a syllable in common with them." But of this Simcox says (Camb. Gr. Test.) : "Of these phrases we certainly meet with few in the REVELATION in exactly the same form or with the same frequency ; but, in some form, we meet with nearly all." It is noteworthy that the Apostle John never mentions his name in his Gospel or Epistles ; indeed, he studiously avoids doing so (JOHN i. 40; xiii. 23; I JOHN i, 1 ; 2 JOHN i; 3 JOHN i), but the writer of this Book names himself three times.

But these and other difficulties notwithstanding, and in view of what follows under Date, we take the view which has been influentially held for so long, that John the Apostle wrote the REVELATION.

THE DATE.

What evidence is available assigns one or other of two dates for this Writing, either A.D. 68-70, or A.D. 95-98 ; that is, either early, before the destruction of Jerusalem, or long after that event ; either in the times of Nero, Galbo, Otho, Vitellius, or Vespasian, or in the time of Domitian, or Nerva, or Trajan. Each of these periods is advocated by a large number of scholars, so that the matter cannot be regarded as settled.

The early date, however, would help to explain the difference between the Greek of the Gospel and Epistles, on the one hand, and that of the REVELATION On this point Simcox (Cam. Gr. Test.), says : "If we suppose that the Revelation was written by St. John the Apostle between A.D. 68-70, and the Gospel and Epistles A.D. 80-100, we get a credible view of the history of the Apostle's mind, or at least of his style. A Jew of Palestine, habitually familiar with both the Biblical Hebrew and the Aramaic vernacular, he was perhaps altogether ignorant of Greek till the age of 50 or 60. Then, being called on to take the pastoral charge of Greek-speaking Churches, he addressed them in their own language, which he had learnt as far as he could : but he refused to let his imperfect knowledge of the language hamper or even modify his expression of the message entrusted to him ; he would say what he had to say *somehow*, even if he did not know how to say it in grammatical Greek. But when he had lived from ten to thirty years in the midst of these Greek-speaking Churches he learnt their language thoroughly, and became able to compose in it with vigour and correctness, if not with the mastery of a native. "

Furthermore, the reference to Jerusalem and the Temple in chapter xi seems clearly to imply their existence at the time the Book was written ; and this, together with the expectation of Christ's speedy second coming, accords well with the early date. If this view be correct the REVELATION was the first of John's Writings, not the last, though its subject-matter naturally gives it its place as the conclusion of the New Testament and of all revelation.

THE PLACE OF WRITING.

"The isle that is called Patmos " (i. 9), in the Ægean Sea, a sterile rock, about eighteen miles in circumference.

The Readers.

God's "servants," of that and every age (i. 1 ; xxii. 6).

The Literary Form.

The REVELATION belongs to the class of literature known as " Apocalyptic," and in the light of this fact must it be read and interpreted. The function of apocalypse was "to encourage and stimulate the people in times of national distress by the assurance of a glorious future in the triumph of Israel's long-wished-for Deliverer." Half of the book of DANIEL is Jewish Apocalypse, and the Book before us is Christian Apocalypse. We should be careful not to apply the canons of history or dogma to this class of writing. Prof. Moulton has said that "in interpreting symbolism the first critical requirement is restraint." An unimaginative literalism will never lead to an understanding of these Visions, and the attempt so to treat them has been barren of results.

The Contents.

By chapters the contents are as follows :

I. Christ in the midst of the Asian Churches.
II. Messages to the Churches at Ephesus, Smyrna, Pergamos, and Thyatira.   III. Messages to the Churches at Sardis, Philadelphia, and Laodicea.

IV. The Heavenly Throne, the Elders, and the Living Creatures. V. The Lion-Lamb and the Sealed Book. VI. The Opening of the Six Seals. VII. The Sealing of 144,000 Israelites, and the Redeemed Multitude of all Nations. VIII. The Sounding of Four Trumpets. IX. The Sounding of Two Trumpets. X. The Little Book which was Eaten. XI. The Two Witnesses, and the Seventh Trumpet. XII. The Woman, the Man-Child, and the Dragon. XIII. The Two Beasts. XIV. The Angels and their Messages. XV. The Seven Angels with the Seven Plagues. XVI. The Outpouring of the Seven Bowls of Wrath. XVII. The Mystery of the Woman and the Beast. XVIII. The Fall of Babylon. XIX. The Marriage Supper of the Lamb, and the Supper of the Great God. XX. The Millennium and the Great White Throne. XXI. The New Heaven and Earth, and the Holy City, the New Jerusalem. XXII. The Holy City, and the Final Voice.

INTERPRETATIONS.

Of these there are four. 1. The PRAETERIST, in the view of which the greater part of the prophecies of this Book had their fulfilment in the early history of the Christian Church. 2. The CONTINUOUS HISTORICAL, in the view of which the Book presents prophetically a narrative of continuous history from the Apostolic age to the end of time. 3. The FUTURIST, in the view of which the greater part of the Book is still unfulfilled, its predictions belonging strictly to "the last days." 4. The IDEALIST, in the view of which the Book is the pictorial unfolding of great principles in constant conflict through all the ages.

Having regard for the fact that equal scholarship and spirituality may be found among the advocates of all these interpretations, it is difficult to believe that one of them must be right, and three of them wrong. The Book is too big to be crushed into the mould of any one interpretation, and no one school of interpreters has a monopoly of insight and understanding. The studies of men like Tyconius, Grotius, De Wette, Ewald, Bleek, Farrar, Vitringa, Newton, Bengel, Elliott, B. Wordsworth, Alford, Guinness, Bullinger, Milligan, Boyd Carpenter, Lee, and many others, cannot be set aside in the interests of the view of anyone of them, but rather, we must look for the common elements of truth in their various systems of interpretation. In his "Advancement of Learning," quoted by Angus, Bacon has said that Divine prophecies "have springing and germinant accomplishment throughout many ages, though the height or fulness of them may refer to some one age ; " and Bishop Boyd Carpenter, to like purpose : "The Praeterist may be right in finding early fulfilments, and the Futurist in expecting un-developed ones, and the Historical interpreter is unquestionably right in looking for them along the whole line of history ; for the words of God mean more than one man, or one school of thought can compass. The visions of the Book do find counterparts in the occurrences of human history. They have had these, and they will yet have these fulfilments, and these fulfilments belong neither wholly to the past, nor wholly to the future. The prophecies of God are written in a language which can be read by more than one generation." In other words, no one of these interpretations is by itself adequate. It is by a synthesis of them that we approach to the truth. History is the fulfilment of prophecy throughout the length of it, and there is good ground for believing that at the end of this age there will be a crisis-period in which all the characteristics of the present dispensation will be gathered up, accentuated, and consummated.

STRUCTURE.

The architecture of this Work will vary as it is seen from different angles, and as it is interpreted

in different ways. As we study it certain questions
will arise, such as, are these Visions presented
in the order of fulfilment, or of narration ; that is,
are they chronological and consecutive ? or, are
they contemporary ? or, do they partake of the
character of both these structures, each successive
group of Judgments overlapping the previous one ?

To the whole Book there seems to be a clue in
chapter i. 19. Some have thought that the "things
seen" refer to John's Gospel, the "things which
are," to his Epistle, and the "things which
shall come to pass hereafter," to the REVEL-
ATION ; but, not to speak of the difficulty
of the date of writing, a more natural interpretation is that which relates all three statements to this Book ; the "things seen," to chapter
i. 9-20 ; the "things which are," to chapters
ii-iii ; and the "things which shall come to pass
hereafter," to chapters iv-xxii. 5. This seems to
derive confirmation from the fact that the third
of these ideas is repeated at the beginning of chapter
iv. (R.V.), "Things which must come to pass hereafter" (*meta tauta*).

The first three chapters are straightforward, but
the remainder of the Book, as to structure, is
variously regarded. What is clear is that there are
three series of Judgments, the Seals, the Trumpets,

and the Bowls. These, it seems to me, are neither contemporary nor entirely consecutive, but tele-scope out of one another ; that is, the Trumpet Judgments are the seventh Seal Judgment, and the Bowl Judgments are the seventh Trumpet Judgment ; the last of each series is the beginning of another.

It is noteworthy that after both the sixth Seal and the sixth Trumpet Judgments there is a break in the narrative, and a long section is inserted before the seventh of each is announced. These particulars seem to supply the clue to the structure of the Book, which is in five parts, a Prologue, Three Series of Visions, an Epilogue, with explana-tory matter interspersed, as shown in the accom-panying chart.

RELATIONS.

Perhaps no Book of the Bible has so many relations to other parts of Scripture as has the REVELATION.

1. It is related to the whole Bible.

In GENESIS is the foundation of truth, in EXODUS to JUDE, is the superstructure, and in the REVELA-TION is the completion.   Or, in other words, beginning, way, end ; origins, processes, issues ; commencement, course, consummation.

2. It is related to the Old Testament.

The symbolism of the Book is neither Greek nor Roman, but Hebrew. The originality of the Writing is, for the most part, not in the presentation of new ideas, but in a new combination of old ideas. Almost all of it is traceable in the Old Testament ; every figure in it is drawn from the Old Testament. Of its 404 verses, 265 contain Old Testament language, and there are about 550 references to Old Testament passages. But for the Old Testament this Book would remain an utter enigma.

3. It is related to the New Testament, structurally, chronologically, and spiritually. The subject matter of each Testament is in three groups of Writings, and in the same order, the Historical, GENESIS to ESTHER, and MATTHEW to ACTS : the Didactical, JOB to CANTICLES, and ROMANS to JUDE : and the Prophetical, ISAIAH to MALACHI, and the REVELATION. MATTHEW to JOHN treats of the past ; ACTS to JUDE of the present ; and the REVELATION, of the future. In the first group we have the Christ ; in the second, the Church, and in the REVELATION, the Consummation.

4. It is related to the Book of DANIEL.

DANIEL treats of four Empires, the Babylonian, Medo-Persian, Grecian, and Roman. REVELATION treats of the last of these only. DANIEL presents the whole course of the Roman Empire, but the REVELATION tells only of the latter end of it. In DANIEL are the Seventy Sevens (ix) ; in REVELATION, the Seventieth Seven. DANIEL speaks of Jews and Gentiles ; REVELATION of these and of the Church of God.

5. It is related to the Book of GENESIS, both by comparison and contrast. In these, by comparison, we have the first and the last heaven and earth ; the first and the final rest ; Paradise lost, and regained ; the tree and the rivers, the Tree and the River ; the husband and wife, the Lamb and the Bride.

And in these, GENESIS and REVELATION, we have by contrast, Satan victorious and defeated ; Judgment pronounced and executed ; the gates shut and the gates open ; death, and no more death ; tears, and no more tears ; night, and no more night ; exiles and inheritors. These are a few only of the many points of relation between the two Books.

VALUES.

Above and beneath all possible interpretations of the details of this Book it has certain values which are supreme.

First, *it is an unveiling of the Lord Jesus.*

That is declared in its opening words : "*Apoka-*

lupsis Iēsou Christou," and this unveiling touches
His nature, His activities, and His relations. As to
His nature, He is Lord, Word, Alpha, Omega,
Jesus, Christ, King, Master, Lamb, Lion, and
Morning Star.

As to His activities, He is chastening the Church,
restoring the Jews, and judging the World. As to
His relations, they are to the Father, the Spirit,
Angels, saints, and sinners : He is related to heaven,
and earth, and hell.

Second, *it is an inspiration to the faithful in the
present.*

Here it is revealed that Christ is central and
crucial, relative to the Church (i-iii) ; to the
Heavenly Order (iv-v) ; to the Apostate World
(vi-xix. 10) ; to the Millennial Age (xix. 11-xx) ;
and to the New Jerusalem (xxi-xxii). Christ is
the same in the "yesterday" of the past ; in the
"to-day" of the present ; and in the to-morrow of
"for ever." Prophet yesterday ; Priest to-day,
and King to-morrow.

Third, *it is a revelation of the issue of history.*

Throughout the ages the conflict has been
ceaseless and fierce between the forces of Right
and Wrong, of Light and Darkness, of Truth and
Error, of Righteousness and Iniquity, of Holiness
and Sin, of Heaven and Hell, of Christ and Satan ;

and this Book shows that Right, and Light, and Righteousness, and Holiness, and Heaven, and Christ will prevail. The head which on earth had no resting-place will be crowned with "many diadems." The kingdoms of this world are to become the Kingdom of God and of His Christ. The last vision is not of Athens and intellect, nor of Babylon and luxury, nor of Rome and power, nor of Paris and pleasure, nor of New York and commerce, nor of London and splendour, nor of Berlin and force, but of the New Jerusalem, which stands for character.

NOTE 105

"The Lamb" in Revelation.

THE dominating designation of Christ in the Apocalypse is "The Little Lamb" (*arnion*). It occurs twenty-eight times, and nowhere else of Christ in the N.T. (v. 6, 8, 12, 13; vi. 1, 16; vii. 9, 10, 14, 17; xii. 11; xiii. 8; xiv. 1, 4, 4, 10; xv. 3; xvii. 14, 14; xix. 7, 9; xxi. 9, 14, 22, 23, 27; xxii. 1, 3).

The word in John i. 29, 36; Acts viii. 32; 1 Peter i. 19, is *amnos*, not *arnion*.

The origin of this idea, however, is not in the N.T., but goes back to the beginning of human history. The first occurrence of the *word*, though not of the *idea*, is in Gen. xxii. 7, 8 (cf. iii. 21; iv. 4), and from Exod. xii. it becomes the outstanding description of the Redeemer. The "Bride of the Lamb" (Rev. xxi. 9), therefore, is neither Israel, nor the Church, but everyone from the creation who has a saving interest in the Lamb, that is, the redeemed of all the ages.

Analysis of the Revelation

PROLOGUE (i. 1-8).

I. THE VISION OF GRACE (i. 9-iii. 22).

II. THE VISION OF GOVERNMENT (iv. 1-xix. 10).

THE REVELATION: A PLAN OF THE BOOK

By W. GRAHAM SCROGGIE, D.D.

PLAN (A).

PROLOGUE. I. 1-8.

SUPERSCRIPTION 1-3.	SALUTATION 4-8.

PLAN (B).

A BOOK OF VISIONS. I. 9—XXII. 5.

I. OF GRACE. I. 9—III.	II. OF GOVERNMENT. IV.—XIX. 10.	III. OF GLORY. XIX. 11—XXII. 5.

PLAN (C).

I. A VISION OF GRACE. I. 9—III.

1. THE SOVEREIGN CHRIST. I. 9-20.	2. THE SEVEN CHURCHES. II.-III.					
	(i). Ephesus. ii. 1-7.	(ii). Smyrna. ii. 8-11.	(iii). Pergamum. ii. 12-17.	(iv). Thyatira. ii. 18-29.	(v). Sardis. iii. 1-6.	(vi). Philadelphia. iii. 7-13.	(vii). Laodicea. iii. 14-22.

PLAN (D).

II. A VISION OF GOVERNMENT. IV.—XIX. 10.

1. THE GOVERNORS. IV.-V.	2. THE GOVERNED AND THE GOVERNMENT. VI.—XIX. 10. MANIFOLD JUDGMENTS.

(i.) The Almighty. iv.	(ii.) The Lion-Lamb. v.

(i). THE SEALS. vi.—viii. 1.

(1) Conquest. vi. 1-2.	(2) War. vi. 3, 4.	(3) Famine. vi. 5, 6.	(4) Pestilence. vi. 7, 8.	(5) Martyrdom. vi. 9-11.	(6) Convulsion. vi. 12-vii.	(7)

(ii.) THE TRUMPETS. viii. 1—xi. 15.

(1) Fire and Blood. viii. 7.	(2) Burning Mountain. viii. 8, 9.	(3) The Star Wormwood. viii. 10, 11.	(4) Heavenly Bodies. viii. 12, 13.	(5) Locusts. ix. 1-12.	(6) Horsemen. ix. 13—xi. 14.	(7)

(iii). THE BOWLS. XI. 15—XIX. 10.

(1) Grievous Sores. xi. 15—xvi. 2.	(2) Blood Sea. xvi. 3.	(3) Blood Rivers. xvi. 4-7.	(4) Scorching Sun. xvi. 8, 9.	(5) Darkness. xvi. 10, 11.	(6) Euphrates. (Armageddon.) xvi. 12-16.	(7) Earthquake. (Babylon.) xvi. 17-xix. 10.

PLAN (E).

EXPLANATORY PASSAGES IN THE VISION OF GOVERNMENT.

(1)	(2)	(3)	(4)	(5)	(6)	(7)	(8)	(9)	(10)	(11)	(12)
The Sealed Jews.	The Gentile Multitude.	The Angel by the Altar.	The Little Book.	The Two Witnesses.	The Lamb Victorious.	The Woman The Dragon.	The Two Beasts.	The Six Angels.	The Songs of Overcomers.	The Lord's Return.	The Fall of Babylon.
vii. 1-8.	vii. 9-17.	viii. 3-5.	x.	xi. 1-13.	xi. 15-19.	xii.	xiii.	xiv.	xv. 2-4.	xvi. 15.	xvii.-xix. 10

PLAN (F).

III. A VISION OF GLORY. XIX. 11—XXII. 5.

1. THE MILLENNIAL AGE. XIX. 11—XX.			2. THE NEW JERUSALEM. XXI.—XXII. 5.		
(i). Before it. xix. 11—xx. 3.	(ii). During it. xx. 4-6.	(iii). After it. xx. 7-15.	(i). Descent of the City. xxi. 1-8.	(ii). Description of the City. xxi. 9-21.	(iii). Delights of the City. xxi. 22—xxii. 5.

PLAN (G).

EPILOGUE. XXII. 6-21.

(a) Words of Comfort. 6-17.	(b) Words of Caution. 18-21.